Children First

Children First

The Story of UNICEF, Past and Present

Maggie Black

PUBLISHED FOR UNICEF

OXFORD UNIVERSITY PRESS

1996

Oxford University Press, Walton Street, Oxford OX2 6DP
Oxford New York
Athens Auckland Bangkok Bombay
Calcutta Cape Town Dar es Salaam Delhi
Florence Hong Kong Istanbul Karachi
Kuala Lumpur Madras Madrid Melbourne
Mexico City Nairobi Paris Singapore
Taipei Tokyo Toronto
and associated companies in
Berlin Ibadan

Oxford is a trade mark of Oxford University Press

Published in the United States
by Oxford University Press Inc., New York

British Library Cataloguing in Publication Data
Data available

Library of Congress Cataloging-in-Publication Data
Data available

ISBN 0-19-828094-7
ISBN 0-19-828088-2 (Pbk.)

1 3 5 7 9 10 8 6 4 2

Cover photograph by Greg Martin
Typeset by Teresa Buerkle
Printed in Great Britain
on acid-free paper by
Bookcraft (Bath) Ltd.
Midsomer Norton, Avon

Contents

Foreword

A Personal Tribute to James P. Grant

The title of this book, *Children First*, is the idea that drove Jim Grant during his years at Unicef. It not only drove him. It consumed him. And it shone from him wherever he went.

Many years ago, I went on my first field trip with Jim. This was soon after he became Unicef's Executive Director and soon after the beginning of the main story in this book. I was new to Unicef too, and proud to be its first woman Goodwill Ambassador.

I could not believe Jim's energy. We flew and we talked and he was never tired. We would run between villages in Africa and Asia because he had much to see. Time for Jim was always limited because the days had only 24 hours.

Upon reaching each new village or community or hut, he would stop and ask questions and see what was going on and explain his own point of view. Then off we went to new destinations. I was much younger than Jim, but still I was the one to be tired. He would turn around to me and wave 'come on!' There was no rest.

His purpose was always to make the world a better place for children. With him, it was always 'children first'. There was another way he used to put it: 'first call for children'. I shall always connect that idea with Jim. I remember his joy the day in September 1990 when he gathered 71 leaders from countries all around the world for the World Summit for Children in New York. What was it for? 'Children first.' I remember his determination that all the nations in the world, especially the US, should ratify the Convention on the Rights of the Child. That, too, was all about 'children first'.

This book is not strictly about Jim, although Jim is hidden somewhere in most of its pages. This book is about what Unicef did over 50 years, especially in the past 15, to make the idea of 'children first' real for millions of people. Jim wouldn't have liked a book that made it sound as though everything Unicef did during his time was because of him. That kind of self-importance was not his style.

But those of us who knew Jim, who saw him at work, coming up with his ideas, coming out with his roar of approval, coming on at a pace we could barely keep up with—we know that an incredible number of things Unicef did could be traced straight to Jim. Not just things done by Unicef, either, but by many other important people and organizations too—all sorts of things in which Unicef took a back seat because, he said, getting others to join in was what counted. So he always gave *them* the credit. Jim was an almost supernatural force who made impossible hopes and dreams come true.

When I was a child, one of my favourite stories was about a little boy who, by magic, became full of power. He spent his life flying on the back of a wild goose all over the world. In the wonderment of the boy's eyes, the whole world became clear to him. He did not always know if the goose would fly with him high or low, or where they were going. But he always knew there was a purpose—to learn and to do.

And he listened to the dreams of the old people and the young people. The more he knew, the more he did, so that he could make hopes and dreams become reality. The longer he flew, more and more birds with passengers flew with him to help make the world a better place. When I think of Jim, I remember that story.

When Jim listened to a mother in a village in Africa or Asia and looked at her sick baby, and when he stood in front of a President, he used to put his hand in his pocket. And you always knew what he was about to do. He would pull out a packet of those oral rehydration salts (ORS). He would show the mother or the President how you mix the salts with water, and how you save the life of a child with diarrhoea. And then they would become new messengers for his way of solving the sad fact that so many children die quietly each day from preventable diseases.

And on those travels, when night came, he would still want to have new meetings—with health workers, teachers, officials, whomever. And again, from his pocket, he would take out his packet of ORS. And sometimes, I would be ashamed and think that, no, he must let these exhausted people eat their meal in peace. But each evening ended with another official, or health worker, or

Minister, or President promising to carry out his—Jim's—programme for 'children first'.

And then, coming back to the same country years later, I would see strangers stand like Jim and put their hands in their pockets, and take out the packet of ORS. And I would hear them talk with his enthusiasm of the lives they had saved.

Jim's work was a revolution for boys' and girls' survival and the dignity of life. This revolution saved more than 25 million children's lives in the years I knew him. And his revolution saved even greater numbers of children from growing up handicapped from diseases such as polio and from vitamin A deficiency.

Jim would go anywhere to promote his revolution. And he had great courage. Near the beginning of the war in the now former Yugoslavia, the fighting soldiers and their generals promised a week of no shooting. They made this promise in the name of 'children first'. Jim phoned me and asked if I would come with him on a peace march and drive through the most dangerous passage of all—Snipers' Alley—to show that peace and talk were possible. 'But,' I protested, 'what if the cease-fire is broken?' 'Well,' said Jim, 'we'll be there and find out.'

It was Jim's idea that this book should be written. And it was Jim who asked Maggie Black to write it. She wrote a book for Unicef's 40th anniversary in 1986, *The Children and the Nations.* Jim liked that book very much. He was always telling people to read it. I'm sure he would do the same with this one. And like the little boy in the fairy tale, he would still be flying high, hoping that those who read it will feel the power of his message and help to make 'children first' a reality for millions more.

Liv Ullmann
Goodwill Ambassador for Unicef

Minister or President promising to carry out this—Jim's—programme for children first.

And then, coming back to the same country years later, I would see strangers stand like Jim and put their hands in their pockets and take out the packet of ORS. And I would hear them talk with his enthusiasm of the lives they had saved.

Jim's work was a revolution for boys' and girls' survival and the dignity of life. His revolution saved more than 25 million children's lives in the years I knew him. And his revolution saved even greater numbers of children from growing up handicapped from diseases such as polio and from vitamin-A deficiency.

Jim would go anywhere to promote his revolution. And he had great courage. Near the beginning of the war in the now former Yugoslavia, the fighting soldiers and their generals promised a week of no shooting. They made this promise in the name of children now. Jim phoned me and asked if I would come with him on a peace march and drive through the most dangerous passage of all—Snipers Alley—to show that peace and talk were possible. 'But,' I protested, 'what if the cease-fire is broken?' 'Well,' said Jim, 'we'll be there and find out.'

It was Jim's idea that this book should be written. And it was Jim who asked Maggie Black to write it. She wrote a book for Unicef's 40th anniversary in 1986, *The Children and the Nations*. Jim liked that book very much. He was always telling people to read it. I'm sure he would do the same with this one. And like the little boy in the fairy tale he would still be flying high, hoping that those who read it will feel the power of his message and help to make 'children first' a reality for millions more.

Liv Ullmann
Goodwill Ambassador for Unicef

Preface

It is important to stress at the outset that this book does not provide a full history of Unicef and the fields of activity in which it has engaged over the past 50 years. Jim Grant, who asked me to write the book, envisaged a sequel to my earlier volume, *The Children and the Nations*. This was published by Unicef in 1986 (a shorter edition was published with Macmillan Australia in 1987) and covered Unicef's history until that time—its 40th anniversary. However, this second book is not a 'Volume II'. I did not want to impose upon the reader any need to refer back to information given elsewhere. I have, therefore, adjusted the original brief by enlarging the historical perspective.

The first chapter contains an encapsulation of the entire Unicef story; and subsequent chapters, covering the various themes—child health, nutrition, education and so on—all begin with a review of how ideas evolved over several decades. Therefore, although the main period covered by the book is the decade and a half between 1979 (the International Year of the Child) and 1995—a period that coincides with the leadership of Unicef by the late James P. Grant—there is sufficient 'what happened before' to enable what has happened recently to be viewed within the framework of evolving ideas and practice. Those who need more detail can refer to the earlier volume. On specific subjects, readers may also want to refer to the Unicef History Monograph series, many of whose titles are mentioned in the bibliographic references.

To some long-standing associates and ex-staff members of Unicef, the approach adopted may seem to overstress Jim Grant's Unicef, and overglorify its—and his—accomplishments in comparison with the past. A considerable effort has been made to avoid the trap of projecting Unicef as springing newly formed into existence at the advent of Grant. This is not a version of the organization he would himself at all have supported, although some of his most ardent admirers have been known to imply it on his behalf. One ex-Deputy Executive Director, Margaret Catley-Carlson (1981-83) asked me to be sure, even in a contemporary review, not to understate the contribution of

E.J.R. (Dick) Heyward (Senior Deputy Executive Director 1949-81). It was her view—a view not in any way intended to be critical of Jim Grant—that Heyward had created a Unicef strong enough to withstand the maelstrom that Grant unleashed upon it. I understood this to mean the careful shaping by an earlier generation of leaders of a decentralized and relatively flexible organization, whose strength is in the field and grounded in local realities; an organization that has always valued highly the contribution of local national staff; and an organization that also, from its inception, cultivated popular support among civil society through its National Committees in industrialized countries and its Greeting Card Operation. This organizational character is unique within the UN system.

In some ways Grant might have liked the Unicef culture to be more attuned to unquestioned acceptance of directives from the executive centre. But at the same time he fully appreciated that these strengths of Unicef, while they must occasionally have seemed more like rocks in his path than a rock on which he might build, ultimately worked in favour of his grand designs. Certainly he showed great skill in persuading and enthusing the organization in all its many corners—staff at headquarters and overseas, National Committees, partner NGOs, the Executive Board, Goodwill Ambassadors, volunteers and associates—to believe in his vision and lend their energies to his initiatives. But without the existing strengths of Unicef, those initiatives might never have led where they did.

All of this I have tried to convey, but the importance of earlier leaders and thinkers in shaping the mission and its organizational expression can do with some reinforcement here. And if Dick Heyward was the most remarkable and the main intellectual powerhouse over more than 30 years, some others must also be mentioned: Dr. Ludwik Rajchman, Unicef's chief founder and first Board Chairman; Maurice Pate and Henry Labouisse, Unicef's two previous distinguished Executive Directors, both of whom were crucial in helping to build the unique character and strength of the organization; and Nils Thedin, the elder statesman of Unicef's Executive Board for many years. All their names appear in these pages, but not with the length of credit to their outstanding contributions that would be their due in a book with a less contemporary focus.

Apart from the existence of a fairly thorough previous history, there are, I believe, two arguments in favour of a book about Unicef that primarily covers 1979-95. The first is to do with the extraordinary changes in the international environment, coupled with increasing consciousness concerning the many predicaments of children in contemporary society, that have taken place in the last decade. When I wrote *The Children and the Nations* in 1984-85, there was really only one framework within which to examine Unicef's record: the effort to bring about 'development' in the regions collectively known as the third world or the 'South'. Almost everything (other than emergency relief) in which Unicef had been involved since the 1950s, in either the context of programmes or advocacy, had been directed at improving the well-being and family life circumstances of children disadvantaged by gross poverty in Asia, Africa and Latin America. Ever since the 1960s—a defining period in the Unicef story—the energies of the organization had been devoted to claiming on behalf of children a special priority within activity that formed part of this great post-colonial crusade. Under Jim Grant, that sense of organizational mission did not change, but other trends have recently overlaid and even begun to supersede it.

One of these is the end of the cold war and the huge sea change in international affairs that it has brought about—a change which has major repercussions on the old East-West, North-South dichotomies that provided the context in which the 'development' idea so long retained its potency. The loss of old certainties has helped to reveal that this idea—of an imagined community of nations undergoing an identical process of transition from the pre-industrial to the modern state—has run its historical course. At the same time, the Unicef mission has been deeply affected by the rise of the international human rights agenda, in particular the rise of children's rights and their encapsulation in the 1989 Convention on the Rights of the Child; this is now the most ratified international human rights instrument in history.

Meanwhile, the negative impacts of some aspects of 'development'—such as rapid industrialization and urbanization—on the cohesion of family life and on childhood itself have moved much closer to the centre of social policy concern in developing and industrialized countries alike. The overall effect is of increased attention to children and childhood as an important issue in its own right, rather than as a subset of the 'development' agenda. There is a mounting awareness in the world at large of the need to identify policies that will protect children and young people from the fallout of economic and social distress, as well as from the disastrous effects of the 'new world disorder' of pervasive violence and conflict. The seeds of many of these changes may have been present in 1986, but in 1996 they have become dominant characteristics of the framework within which any international mission on behalf of children must be examined.

The second justification for a book on the period that more or less coincides with the tenure of Jim Grant's Executive Directorship is Jim Grant himself. At present, it is unfashionable among historians to describe the ebb and flow of human affairs as dominated by heroic exploits and personalities. I myself subscribe to the view that it is the conjoining of forces rather than of individually decisive actions that bring about major changes of direction in public affairs. Any apparently instrumental role that an organization such as Unicef (or its chief executive officer) may have is, according to this view, mainly a reflection of the fact that it represents an organized expression of a cause at a time when that cause is rising in public popularity. I have been careful to attribute the rise of children on the international agenda that has occurred in the past 15 years to a number of trends, some of which have been slowly maturing over at least five decades and longer.

However, I also believe that it would be almost wilfully incorrect to downplay the influence certain individuals can have and have had on events. In the context of the recent story of the children's cause, the late Jim Grant was in a class by himself. He was an example of that rare type of leader who not only anticipates how a wave in public and official perceptions is forming and positions organizational efforts to take advantage of it, but he actually managed to help create the international wave on behalf of children, and even the ground swell out of which it was formed. I do not believe any larger claim could be made on behalf of a particular individual in their chosen field of human endeavour.

The way in which, through Unicef, Grant engineered the partnerships and the political action that propelled forward the children's cause during the 1980s and early 1990s is really phenomenal. Every new announcement of the identification of a major political figure—Hillary Clinton, for example—with the children's cause is, in part, a product of a seed sown by Jim Grant. I find this evidence of his advocacy of the children's cause so striking that it has caused me to rethink my views on the nature of potential relationships between people and events.

Under Grant's leadership, Unicef became an instrument for making happen things that were much larger and more significant than its size or character would ever have given grounds to expect. Some of this may be fortuitous; some is certainly due to people all over the world who made Grant's cause their cause and laboured to fulfil his vision. He himself always wanted to share credit with as many people as possible—partly because of his generosity of spirit, partly out of commitment to a common rather than a personal quest, partly out of a strategic sense that this encouraged them further. But much of it is due to him—to his energy, his optimism, his acuity, his unconventionality, his lack of self-importance, his capacity to transcend and to circumvent so as to keep his and others' eyes on the prize, and his refusal to accept that the undoable could not be done.

Many tributes were paid to Jim Grant at the time of his death and memorial service in February 1995. There was a quote from George Bernard Shaw he liked a great deal, which was used in the 1995 *State of the World's Children* report and in many memorial tributes, about life being like a great blazing torch that he had managed to get hold of for a while. I also have a quotation from George Bernard Shaw that I find especially apt for Jim, and I would like to add it here: 'The reasonable man adapts himself to the world; the unreasonable one persists in trying to adapt the world to himself. Therefore all progress depends on the unreasonable man.' Both as a reasonable man and as an unreasonable man, Jim Grant's contribution to the cause of children was immense. And if the frequency with which his name appears in these pages in comparison with that of others sometimes makes it seem as if he stood like a metaphorical Colossus over Unicef during his regime, the fact is that he did.

When I accepted the assignment to do this book, he and I understood this would not be a hagiography, an unqualified paean of praise for a great man. His selection of me for the task is, in my view, a clear indication that that is not what he wanted. Life in Unicef under his leadership was not always comfortable and by no means excited only unqualified support from all sides and at all times. Some of the tensions and differences of view have been captured here, especially as far as the evolution of policy is concerned. However, I would very much have valued Grant's own views on the text, and I know he would have taken considerable time and trouble to give them to me. When I wrote *The Children and the Nations,* he and his then wife Ethel (who died in 1988) were among my most assiduous readers and commentators. It is a great sadness that he lived long enough to read only the first two chapters of this book. His death, however, has made no difference other than that I lost a valued critic. In all the outpouring of appreciation of his life and work in early 1995, it was my conviction not to change in any way what the book would contain, or to add any degree of praise or detraction because he is not still around. I am sure that is what he would have expected.

I have tried hard in this history, as in the last, to avoid writing a 'vanity book'. Most literature that Unicef puts out as public information—as in the case of any organization—is, essentially, propaganda. Even if it is not about Unicef but about its cause—children—the stance of the publication is: 'this is the world according to Unicef'. But in my books, the task has been to treat both Unicef and 'the world according to Unicef' objectively. So this book contains comment and it contains admission of mistakes and naïve assumptions; to the limit of what is possible in a book commissioned by the organization itself, the book contains some of the tension in Unicef's world of human affairs without which human affairs would not be what they are.

For Jim Grant, this was a difficult issue. He always wanted everything and everyone to be better than they are. And he was afraid that if people got caught up in the tensions and dissensions intrinsic to the normal course of human affairs, the pace of the great movement he wanted to be a part and a leader of would slacken. And when things slacken, the strategic element of surprise—the momentum gained simply by being out in front—is lost. If you reveal your hand and open up discussion, the forces that spread doubt and disagreement have time to build obstacles to your advance. I know that there are many passages in this book, as in the last, that he would have wanted to discuss with me and over which he might well have pleaded an alternative case: on selective primary health care, for example; on the tardiness with which Unicef took up children's rights and child protection issues; on the degree to which water and sanitation and urban basic services became overshadowed by his 'child survival revolution'; and especially on Unicef's poor performance on gender and on family planning. But I also know he would have put his point of view to me, but never forced it. This is partly to do with his innate sense of respect for others. But it is also because he understood that if an account that claims to be historically accurate fails to be open and honest about what has not worked, its plausibility and credibility are suspect. On the occasion of the previous book, he said that he would respect my independence of view and he stuck to it. I'm sure he would have done the same on this occasion.

One other point of explanation about the textual content is necessary. Some commentators have regretted very much the lack of a personal touch—the mentions of individuals and their contributions other than those of Grant and a handful of top advisers and colleagues inside and outside the organization. I, too, regret this. But I found that any mention of one individual elicited a chorus of requests to mention 20 others. In a contemporary study this is understandable, but it makes the task of distributing credit virtually impossible. There seemed only one sensible course of action, which was to remove all names other than those of the indisputably significant, especially among those who were extremely senior, certain non-staffers, and a few staffers who are mostly mentioned in the context of other parts of their careers. To those many who look in vain for their names and those of colleagues, and richly deserve credit for their personal contributions to the cause, I apologize in advance.

The only remaining task is to acknowledge the help of many individuals in the preparation of the book. Apart from Jim Grant, to whom I owe the assignment, I would like to express appreciation to many of those who read and commented on the text: Manzoor Ahmed, David Alnwick, Sheila Barry, Robert Cohen, France Donnay, John Donohue, Brendan Doyle, Leo Fonseka, Gourisankar Ghosh, Jim Himes, Mehr Khan, Peter McDermott, Richard Jolly, Stephen Lewis, Bertil Lindblad, Erma Manoncourt, Nyi Nyi, Marti Rajandran, Jon Rohde, Michel Saint-Lot, Karin Sham Poo, Monica Sharma, Jim Sherry, Frances Stewart and Philip van Haecke. I would also like to thank the staff of Unicef offices in Brazil, Bolivia, Mexico, Indonesia, Thailand, India and Viet Nam, which I visited in the course of the book's research, and the government officials, programme and project managers, and programme participants with whom I came in contact. As always, it is ultimately these people from whom the most telling information is derived, and by whom my viewpoint has been most influenced over the course of 23 years of research and writing in this field.

At New York headquarters, the staff of the Evaluation and Research Office have been unfailingly helpful and supportive, and in this context I must mention in particular Krishna Bose, John Donohue, Pierre Mandl, Ludette San Agustin and Philip van Haecke. Staff of the UK National Committee for Unicef also have helped with research, especially Harriet Goodman and Rachel Lavender. Finally, I would like to thank Shalini Dewan, Vicky Haeri, Mehr Khan and Stephen Lewis of Unicef's external relations staff for their support for the project and its successful publication.

Maggie Black
Oxford, January 1996

Chapter I

Children: A Cause Comes of Age

Not long ago, the idea of statesmen sitting at a conference table to discuss the well-being of children would have been greeted with amazement, if not with derision. Compared with the waging of wars, the strength of the dollar, the price of oil and the signing of NAFTAs and Maastrichts, the subject of children is trivial. Or so it was thought if not spoken. At elections, babies might be kissed and rhetoric about 'our children, the future' flow freely. But to expect a Prime Minister to take an interest in nursery education or a President to concern himself with infant diarrhoea was to imagine the absurd. Times have changed.

Over the past few years, children's emergence as a topic of public and political concern has been striking. At national and international levels, leaders in all parts of the world have begun to identify themselves with family and children's issues. In this process, the World Summit for Children, which took place in New York in September 1990, was a landmark. The Summit was a symbol of the way in which children had gained a new degree of prominence in public affairs, and it also served to consolidate their presence in political and social debate. At this meeting, 71 Heads of State and Government signed the World Declaration on the Survival, Development and Protection of Children and a Plan of Action for its implementation by the year 2000. No higher level of political commitment to children could be given.

The year 1990 was the year before the Gulf War, the year in which the end of the cold war appeared to usher in a new era of international cooperation. This was still a time in which many believed that a 'peace dividend' would release large-scale resources for investment in human development worldwide.

But if much of that spirit of regeneration in international affairs has since evaporated, and if the expectation of a revitalized initiative to end world poverty has been dashed, the new recognition of the importance of children is still with us. There are no doubt still leaders and national policy makers around who cavil at being asked to take the subject of children seriously—as seriously as peace talks, as seriously as turmoil in the financial markets. But they are fewer than they were.

It would be wrong to suggest that children have been ignored by policy makers in the past. But the frameworks within which their problems have traditionally been noticed have tended to be confined to humanitarianism and social welfare. In both these contexts, children's profile has risen over the course of the 20th century. In times of war and disaster, the situation of 'innocent' and helpless children is today an axiomatic target of humanitarian concern. This has by no means always been the way of things: in some settings, the non-fighting and weakest members of the population used to be regarded as the least valuable and most expendable[1]; in a few, this may still be the case. However, the principle of 'children first' as recipients of relief in emergencies—first proposed in the wake of the First World War—has gained so much moral and intellectual ground over the century that it is today almost universally accepted as a norm.

Within the social sectors—health, education, welfare—children's condition has naturally been at the centre of policy focus in modern times. In the 19th century, their removal from the mines and factories of the Industrial Revolution and their universal presence in school were targets of lengthy campaigns in Europe and North America. In this century, along with the growth of the State's involvement in the provision of social services, many professions and sub-professions have developed around the nurture and care of children. Some of the members of these professions occupy formalized versions of roles traditionally played by family members: baby-minders, nursery school attendants, mother's helpers. Others—educationalists, paediatricians and child psychologists—enjoy considerable status in the post-Freud, post-Piaget, post-Spock era. Children have always been important, too, as objects of charitable concern. The orphaned child, the abandoned child and the disabled child have been for centuries primary targets of religious and secular philanthropy.

However, efforts to project the condition of children as seriously significant in economic or political terms were not until the very recent past greeted with much success. Education might be counted an exception: that their children should have prospects of doing well in the world is an issue of immense importance to parents. A well-educated teenager is also a potential voter; a disaffected and underqualified youth, a potential rebel and miscreant. But in most contexts, children were politically neither seen nor heard. For many leaders' macho tastes, they conjured too soft an image to complement the battle fatigues or the executive suit. No politician or policy maker would be unwise enough to suggest that he or she was less than positive about children: the universal sympathy their cause evokes has been one of children's most potent weapons. But few figures in positions of authority were prepared to cast themselves in the nurturing and mothering light that caring for children implies. At best, children were regarded in the national and international policy-making arena as under-age adult subsidiaries, or—because of their frailty—as sensitive barometers of distress in the general population.

Today, children are the target of much more serious attention. And this is not simply because they play an important part in demographic statistics or constitute a significant charge on the social budget. This attention is accorded to children not as a subset of something else but as a category of humankind who deserve consideration in their own right. Children are still minors, still under age, still dependent on adult care, guidance and economic support. But what is happening to them—from their earliest moments of supreme vulnerability, through the long voyage from infant, to toddler, to youngster and adolescent—is today subject to intense public and professional scrutiny[2].

In every country, rich and poor, developed and developing, children are constantly in the news. Stories about them no longer consist of pretty or poignant distractions from the real issues of the day. Children are among the real issues of the day, *en masse* and as individuals. Child safety, child survival, child health; child victims of violence and warfare; child heroes, child criminals; schoolchildren, street children, marginalized children, girl children, abused and displaced children—the list goes on and on. Behind the scenes, a growing number of researchers are examining the drama of modern upbringing and childhood. The world, it seems, is looking at its offspring—at their tragedies, their promise, their expectations—in a new light and with a different order of commitment.

Subjects have a tendency to ebb and flow on national and international agendas. This year, the environment. Next year, population and human rights. The combination of forces pushing one or other topic out in front is not always easy to analyse—it may be as whimsical as fashion. A sudden rash of concern about the environment may be triggered by a global scare—the discovery of the hole in the ozone layer, for example. In another case—women's rights—the gradual evolution of an issue into a whole new perspective on human affairs may result from campaigning by the affected group. Cataclysmic events such as famine, mass emigration and the fall of the Berlin Wall play their part in thrusting issues forward. International bodies can play an instrumental role in promoting this topic or that; a United Nations Conference or a 'Year of ...' both rides and helps to build an existing wave of public preoccupation.

Of course, children are notionally part of all such subjects—because they are such a large subgroup of the general population. But counting children in is no longer enough, any more than counting in women, or the disabled, or the poor, or the ethnic minority, is enough. Why have children become so prominent? Are they just the latest cleverly marketed designer concern due for their moment in the sun, which will be swiftly followed by prolonged eclipse; or does their new-found visibility stem from some profound shift within human values and behaviours?

Long-term changes in the make-up of society must provide part of the answer[3]. Everywhere, fertility is in decline. And where families are deliberately planned, smaller and nuclear, each child is more precious and parental investment, and love, more focused. The threat of the loss of a child, or a child's failure to reach maximum potential, is more significant in family affairs. Childhood must no longer be left to chance. Services that promote healthy childhood development, not only for treasured sons but for less-treasured daughters, are everywhere gaining in demand. At the same time, the period of childhood dependency is lengthening. In the industrialized and industrializing State, life prospects are incumbent on education and training, so more children everywhere are spending more time in school. Where parents can afford it, their children enter the world of work and employment later, and they marry later and start their own child-bearing later as well[4].

Thus the increased importance of the individual child—which reverberates on the public policy agenda—stems from a number of converging factors. These include changed parental expectations and levels of investment in childhood and the impact on society of the modernization and industrialization process. These combine with the ongoing transformation in gender relations that has marked recent decades, and—of even longer duration—changing personal and state reactions to the vastly improved rates of child survival that have marked the 20th century.

Whatever the underlying trends that have altered social values and perceptions in what could be called 'the century of the child'[5], their encapsulation at the international level in certain events and documentary expressions has played its own role in the advancement of children as an issue. There has been in the period since the 1979 International Year of the Child—one of the more successful 'Years' dedicated by the United Nations system to a given subject—a sustained and concerted effort to promote children's concerns. If there has been an underlying ground swell of change, its expression has been actively generated by movers and shakers championing the child. Some of their efforts derive from an elevated consciousness of the 'child in distress': not since the 19th-century social and legislative actions that removed children from the sweatshops of Europe and North America has such reforming zeal been demonstrated on behalf of children. This effort connects with another: the determination by activists for children to articulate and codify their rights to match a vision of childhood acceptable in all cultures and across all ideological and religious divides. This was achieved by the passage in 1989 of the UN Convention on the Rights of the Child, which has subsequently been ratified by an extraordinary number of States—181 at the last count.

And then there has been the worldwide campaign for child survival. This campaign had its roots in the post-colonial humanitarian preoccupation with mass poverty and underdevelopment in the third world. Spearheaded by Unicef, the campaign has focused on the major threat to child survival and health still posed to millions of children every year by the most common or garden infectious diseases. In an age of technological sophistication in which the scientific frontier moves constantly forward, a huge slice of the world's population—upwards of one billion—still live according to pre-industrial norms, outside the modern social economy or marginalized or rejected at its edges. The children of these people, the 'absolute poor', still suffer sickness and death from conditions that in most parts of the industrialized world have long since ceased to pose the threat of significant loss of life or widespread impairment: measles, whooping cough, tetanus, diarrhoea, pneumonia, tuberculosis, iodine deficiency, vitamin A deficiency or plain malnutrition. Every year, around 12 million children under five die, almost all from causes that are easily preventable.

The campaign for child survival reversed conventional wisdom about infant and young child mortality. Previously seen as a measure of a country's state of economic and social development, Unicef proposed a direct attack on infant and child mortality as an instrument of development. Partly by instinct, partly by skill, Unicef picked a cause and a campaign strategy that found an extraordinary degree of worldwide resonance. The bandwagon whose momentum began to grow from 1983 onward carried the children's cause up the national and international agenda, bringing in its wake an increased awareness of children's issues other than those tightly connected to survival and health. In the years since 1990, this momentum has continued to carry forward the children's agenda in spite of the strains experienced in almost every area of international affairs.

If the resonance of 'children first'—with parents, with communities, with governments, with Presidents, with organizations, with donors and with great-hearted individuals—made the campaign take fire, Unicef has been responsible for stoking the furnace and kindling the flames. It is fair to suggest that without that catalytic and transforming effort, children would not today be as high on the political and public agenda—even in industrialized countries—as they currently are. The basis for that effort did not materialize overnight: the ground was laid over three and a half decades of solid experience and of a particular type of institutional growth unique within the United Nations system. But unquestionably, the arrival of a particular leader at the head of Unicef in 1980 was of fundamental importance. Without Jim Grant in the driver's seat—without his vision, energy, persistence and strategizing knack—the historical context, the idea for the campaign and the resources, both human and financial, would not have come together.

The 1990 World Summit for Children grew out of the child survival campaign and represents its apogee. It also represents one of the proudest moments in Unicef's history. This book, written to celebrate the organization's 50th anniversary, traces the story of what led up to that moment, and what has since grown out of it. The period on which it concentrates begins immediately after the 1979 International Year of the Child and at the moment when Jim Grant began his directorship[6]. In addressing the Unicef experience of these 15 years, the book draws upon and recapitulates its evolution in the past. It also engages with many of the trends in social thinking and international affairs connected with the rise of the children's cause.

At Unicef, the World Summit was seen as the moment when a solemn promise was made to children that they would be given 'first call' on human resources and attention, and that by the end of the millennium the basic survival, health and educational needs of all, or at least of the vast majority, would have been met. Since that moment, a great distance has been travelled. But this and other quests on behalf of children, nationally and internationally, are still far from over.

The image of the suffering child is one of the most potent images of the 20th century. The child in distress is often used as a visual symbol of far larger issues: war, famine, pestilence, catastrophe, poverty, economic crisis. The evolution of Unicef in the decades after World War II reflected the response of humanity to such issues, and to many of the new versions of such issues that now crowd the international agenda: environmental depletion, population growth, women's rights, urbanization, food security, health and education 'for all', structural adjustment and debt.

The creation of the United Nations in 1945 represented the coming of age of an ideal of international cooperation. Although the immediate inspiration was the carnage of the Second World War, behind this lay a longer-term desire to promote harmony between the nations on a range of issues and within a variety of different institutions. There was, however, no idea of setting up within this constellation a special organization for children. The creation by the UN General Assembly in December 1946 of a UN International Children's Emergency Fund—an 'ICEF'—came about as an accident of cold war politics.

The postwar emergency in Europe and the Far East was very protracted, and in the bitter winter of 1946-47, millions of people were still without proper shelter, fuel, clothing or food. Children in particular were suffering: in some famine-affected areas, half of all babies born alive died before their first birthday[7]. But the descent of the Iron Curtain doomed the continuation of relief and rehabilitation under the auspices of the UN. In 1944, when the 'United Nations' still constituted the Allied powers, they had set up the UN Relief and Rehabilitation Administration (UNRRA). UNRRA's aid went to all countries devastated by war on both sides of the growing East-West divide. In late 1946, the United States refused to go on bankrolling this kind of neutral relief operation, later substituting the Marshall Plan for Western Europe only.

However, at the final session of UNRRA in Geneva, voices—particularly those of the delegates of Poland and Norway—were raised in protest at the fate of Europe's children. For children, an exception had to be made. The proposal that UNRRA's residual resources should be handed over to a special fund for children was accepted. This idea went forward through the new UN machinery and on 11 December 1946, resolution number 57(I) of the UN General Assembly brought Unicef into being. There was no idea at the time that this 'ICEF' was anything other than a temporary expedient for the postwar emergency. Fortuitously therefore, Unicef became a part of that great experiment in international cooperation that has since constituted the structured anarchy of the United Nations system.

Exceptionally, there were to be no restrictions about where 'ICEF' aid might go on grounds of ex-enemy status or the deepening East-West confrontation. Coincidentally and almost unnoticed, a principle of postwar international relations had been agreed upon: children were above the political divide. This principle was quickly put to the test. Not only were some of the most important early programmes supported by Unicef based in Eastern European countries—Poland, Yugoslavia, Romania—but in the late 1940s, Unicef provided relief assistance on both sides of the civil wars in Greece and China, and in the Middle East to children uprooted by the creation of Israel.

The most important figure behind the creation of Unicef was Dr. Ludwik Rajchman, a pioneer in international public health. Maurice Pate, Unicef's first Executive Director, was a veteran of ex-President Herbert Hoover's many postwar European relief initiatives. Pate both leaned on the US administration in his efforts to build a solid financial base for 'ICEF' and managed to harness public and political compassion for children from sources all over the world. Rajchman—who had made sure that the founding resolution allowed the fund to support 'child health purposes generally'—was determined to develop a permanent niche for Unicef in the cause dearest to his heart: large-scale disease control and prevention. The opportunity came in 1948 when the Scandinavian Red Cross Societies requested support for a mass immunization campaign with BCG vaccine—the first campaign of its kind—against a widespread epidemic of tuberculosis in postwar Europe.

Although the impulse that brought Unicef into being was the desire to help countries mend the lives of children damaged by war, the organization stayed in existence to help improve the lives of children damaged by poverty. There had been no intention on the part of UN States to prolong Unicef's life beyond the postwar emergency. But when the time came in 1950 for the UN to close down its 'ICEF', a successful lobby was mounted to save it. This time, it was the voice of the new nations of the 'developing' world that spoke up. How, asked the delegate of Pakistan, could the task of international action for children be regarded as complete when so many millions of children in Asia, Africa and Latin America languished in sickness and hunger not because of war, but because of age-old poverty? Again, the plea did not go unheard. This was the crucial turning-point in establishing Unicef as a fixture in the UN firmament. Its permanent status was confirmed by the General Assembly in 1953, and the International ('I') and the Emergency ('E') were formally dropped from its title.

In the 1950s, campaigns to control or eradicate epidemic disease became the predominant motif in international health. And their thrust moved far beyond Europe, to Asia, Africa and Latin America. They were among the first, and were certainly the most spectacular, extensions of international assistance to beneficiaries other than those suffering the after-effects of war—not only World War II but the other wars that gradually erupted in its wake. The geographical extension of Unicef's programme to countries in the Middle East, the Indian subcontinent, the Far East, Latin America and eventually sub-Saharan Africa, and its conceptual shift from emergency first aid to long-term health promotion for children, were the decisive factors in its survival beyond the temporary purpose for which it was set up. New medical technology seemed to offer the prospect that age-old scourges could be swept away: penicillin conquered yaws in Asia; mass onslaughts were pursued against tuberculosis, leprosy and trachoma; and at least for a while, the malarial mosquito seemed to be succumbing to DDT.

In almost all these campaigns, Unicef's 'material assistance'—vehicles, vaccines, injectors—was decisive. It also served to fix Unicef's character as a field-based, hands-on organization: the selection, receipt and deployment of supplies and equipment had to be properly overseen in the countries of destination. Gradually, the country office became the locus of Unicef's main programme activity, and a vital influence on policy. This was not the case for most UN organizations, whose field operations were ambassadorial or existed to carry out the orders of governing bodies and headquarters. The principal architect behind the special characteristics of Unicef's development was E.J.R. (Dick) Heyward, Senior Deputy Executive Director from 1949-81, to whom the solidity and decentralized nature of Unicef's organizational foundations are owed. Heyward, a figure held in immense respect, was also the intellectual powerhouse behind much of Unicef's policy and programmatic thinking.

The fact that Unicef did not automatically receive assessed contributions to its budget from UN member states meant that fund-raising machinery had to be developed. This had the effect of keeping the organization sensitive to the public mood and made Unicef well known to a degree enjoyed by no other member organization of the UN family. Although part of the international bureaucracy, Unicef always emanated a driving sense of its humanitarian mission—one to which names in show business and the arts attached themselves and which they promoted: in the early days and enduringly, Danny Kaye, later joined by Peter Ustinov; much later on, Liv Ullmann, Harry Belafonte, Audrey Hepburn and many others. A network of autonomous National Committee affiliates was built up in Europe, North America, Japan and Australasia from the late 1940s on, as well as the Unicef Greeting Card Operation and a strong public information programme.

Early in the 1960s, Unicef's concentration on child health gave way to a wider set of childhood concerns. This evolution came about in response to the great crusade of the post-colonial era: the movement to end world poverty. At a strategic level, the new enthusiasm for 'aid' was a reaction to the arrival of many newly independent countries—especially in Africa—onto the world stage and fear in the West of their assimilation into the Soviet camp. But it was also a movement fuelled by moral and humanitarian purpose. The word 'development' began to accumulate extra layers of significance; it became an academic discipline, an offshoot of economics, as well as a political cause and a focus for popular philanthropy. Accordingly, Unicef began to adapt its mission for children to the needs of underprivileged people in what was now described as the 'developing' world.

The result was a decisive shift in the way Unicef defined its mission. A central orthodoxy of 'development' in the 1950s and 1960s was that it must be planned: an idea copied from the example of economic transformation in the Soviet Union and other socialist states. In 1960, Unicef commissioned a special survey into the needs of children, in which the specialized agencies of the United Nations participated: the World Health Organization (WHO) on the health needs of children; the Food and Agriculture Organization of the United Nations (FAO) on their nutritional needs; the United Nations Educational, Scientific and Cultural Organization (UNESCO) on their educational needs; the UN Bureau of Social Affairs on their welfare needs; and the International Labour Office (ILO) on work and livelihoods. The subsequent report on *Children of the Developing Countries* set out the case for considering the needs of children—not just the health and nutritional needs but the 'whole' child's physical and intellectual needs—within the context of national development plans[8].

Child victims of poverty, according to this view, should not be seen merely as objects of welfare; children were part of a nation's incipient human capital, they were its 'most precious resource', and an investment in them was an investment in a country's future. Hitherto, attention given to children within the allocation of national resources had confined itself to special cases and casualties. Now, Unicef suggested, national policies for children should embrace all children, and do so across sectoral lines—health, agriculture, education, water and sanitation.

Children's well-being should be a target of investment and a major concern of the whole development effort. Their situation should be discussed with Ministries of National Planning, no less; it should be contemplated by research institutes and within national surveying and planning exercises—activities which Unicef would henceforth be willing to support. This zest for planning made a major contribution to the development by Unicef of its 'country approach', whereby programmes to benefit children, which Unicef would support, would be integral to social sector planning as a whole. But the idea that children should be a target of broader economic and social policy did not spread far beyond a Unicef-led inner circle.

Also ahead of its time was the idea that investment in people—human development—was a quintessential component of the development planning mix. At this juncture, the trinity of capital investment, technological transfer and growth was still held up as the means of propelling pre-industrial societies into the modern world. Not for another decade did people-centred development strategies begin to command serious attention; and not for another generation did 'children first' in contexts other than war begin to reverberate widely. In the meantime, under Henry Labouisse, its second Executive Director, from 1965-79, Unicef succeeded in winning for itself a place at the table of development cooperation. Its growing expertise, and its emphasis on taking its cue from field-based realities rather than from some detached vision of technical excellence derived from Western norms, won it respect and greater autonomy within the UN system. The formal recognition that Unicef was a development rather than a welfare organization came in 1972, when for the first time its work was reviewed as part of the economic and social, rather than humanitarian, activity of the United Nations.

By the 1970s, faith in the power of technology and capital transfer to dispense with poverty had begun to wane. Development was not a technological puzzle with a formulaic answer, analogous to putting a man on the moon. Nor was it something that could be conjured into being by the equivalent of a Marshall Plan. Economic growth had propelled some countries and some people forward. But far from 'trickling down' to the substrata of the population, the benefits had largely circulated among the privileged few whose occupations and lifestyle were integrated with the Western economic system[9]. Traditional economies had become depressed, even as the numbers depending on them rapidly swelled. The growing body of development analysts in universities, government departments and aid organizations began busily to diagnose what had gone wrong, and a quest for alternatives began.

In 1972, Robert McNamara, then President of the World Bank, made what was seen as a landmark statement. Governments in developing countries, he said, should redesign their policies so as to relieve directly the poverty of the poorest 40 per cent of their people. An explicit attack on poverty—albeit one mounted in such a way as not to damage economic prospects—was emerging as the cornerstone of the new development strategy. 'Redistribution with growth' and 'meeting basic needs' were its economic slogans.

The search for ways to realize the new development mission focused on projects and programmes in which things had gone right for people, especially for poor people, irrespective of their country's wealth. 'People-centred development' became the new catch-phrase. This contained the idea that people, not economies, were the object of development and were, too, its principal agents even if they were poor. In 1976, Unicef produced its own alternative philosophy for meeting 'basic needs', the 'basic services approach'. Fundamental to the concept was the recognition that if the poverty-stricken people of the developing world had to wait until they were reached by conventional forms of social infrastructure—roads, schools, hospitals, waterworks, credit institutions—they would wait indefinitely. The fruits of economic growth were too thin to support such investment, and 'aid' could never fill the gap. The 'basic services approach' suggested instead that ordinary members of the slum or village community should be trained to become front-line workers in the spread of services.

Some of the inspiration for this approach came from the 'barefoot doctor' idea pioneered in the Republic of China; the rest from community-based non-governmental organizations (NGOs) and the spirit of voluntary effort their projects and programmes captured and depended upon. The facilities provided by 'barefoot sanitarians', 'barefoot midwives' or 'barefoot teachers' might be modest but they would at least address the community's essential needs. Basic services chimed well with other elements of the evolving new orthodoxy: 'appropriate technology', 'development from below', 'popular participation' and emphasis on the role of women. In time 'empowerment' and 'democratization' would be added.

The new thinking had a dramatic impact on the field of public health. In the late 1970s, WHO—with Unicef collaboration—began to elaborate a strategy of 'primary health care'. Dr. Halfdan Mahler, then the Director-General of WHO, was deeply identified with this revolutionary attempt to make a UN specialized agency match its expertise and clout to the challenge of underdevelopment. The approach was a reaction to the typical pattern whereby high-technology curative services absorbed up to 90 per cent of a developing country's health budget while serving a small, city-based élite. Fundamental to the 'primary health care' philosophy was the notion that health care in the form of a service whose outer arm everyone could reach was a basic human right that the State has an obligation to fulfil. As with 'basic services', ordinary people would be enlisted in their own preventive care. Primary health care (PHC)—the alternative order in health—gained international endorsement at a 1978 International Conference in Alma-Ata, USSR, sponsored jointly by WHO and Unicef. This meeting set an extremely ambitious goal: 'Health for All by the Year 2000'.

During the first two 'Development Decades', so engrossed was Unicef with the need to demonstrate that working for children was part of a much larger social and economic movement that there was some loss of child-centred focus within its activities. This was less the case in the emergency context: Henry Labouisse strove quietly and diplomatically to advance the principle that 'children are above the political divide' by providing relief on both sides in countries torn by civil war. He managed to uphold this principle during the Nigerian Civil War (1967-70), thereby providing a channel for multilateral aid into starving Biafra, an enclave technically ineligible for aid from UN member organizations since it was in revolt against a UN Member State. Even more ambitiously, given US disapproval, Labouisse managed to organize the provision of Unicef assistance into communist Indo-China while the Viet Nam imbroglio was still at its height, uniquely supplying aid to both North and South Viet Nam. But outside the emergency context, the emphasis on 'development' meant that the special needs of childhood, and the needs of certain disadvantaged child groups, suffered some eclipse. The turning-point in the rediscovery of children as a special group came in 1979 with the International Year of the Child (IYC).

The initiative for a children's 'Year' came not from Unicef but from international children's NGOs. Their starting point was not 'the child in development' but simply 'the child', whose cause—they felt—was being drowned out by the clamour surrounding more fashionable debates. Unicef was hesitant about a 'Year of the Child', disliking the language of rights and fearing a loss of focus on development. But eventually the UN General Assembly agreed to an 'IYC' on the basis that this would be a Year of practical action, not of cosmetic events, and that there would be no crowning international conference.

The degree of enthusiasm for children's issues was wholly unforeseen. This was the first indication that child-consciousness could be made a feature of the international agenda; to an extent, it followed in the footsteps of international consciousness concerning women. No fewer than 148 countries established national IYC commissions, under whose auspices research was commissioned into children's issues, celebratory events conducted and new programmes initiated. The volume of media attention to children was deafening. Some of it exposed problems—drugs, abuse, vandalism, children in prostitution—whose sensitivity normally kept them under wraps. After the IYC, these issues did not go away. New child-related NGOs came into being in both the North and the South, and existing ones were fired up in new directions. The IYC also paved the way for the 1959 Declaration of the Rights of the Child to be replaced, 30 years later, by the Convention on the Rights of the Child.

IYC was a watershed year: it both revealed and enhanced the growing importance of children in the public mind. It was also a watershed year for Unicef: in 1979, the organization's income rose from $211 million (1978) to $285 million—over 25 per cent in a year—and the upward trend continued[10]. Towards the Year's end, Unicef was appointed lead agency within the UN system for the emergency in Kampuchea following the destruction of the 1975-79 Khmer Rouge regime and its expulsion by the Vietnamese army. This assumption of the lead agency role was a mark of the organization's increasing international prestige, and served to enhance it further. At the end of 1979, Labouisse retired. At the beginning of the new decade, Unicef and the children's agenda were poised to achieve an extraordinary momentum.

More than a decade separates the IYC from the World Summit for Children—a meeting far more ambitious than the international conference that no one wanted in 1979. That decade in Unicef was stamped by the drive and personality of one man: Jim Grant. The journey Unicef undertook over the next decade was shaped by the strategic thinking and operational style Grant brought into an organization that he was determined to propel onto a new plane of activity.

James Pineo Grant had already dedicated not just a career, but a lifetime, to the service of an ideal: the harnessing of modern ideas and modern technology to the benefit of all members of the human race. A lifelong commitment to 'development' was rare in a person of his generation, born into a world still governed by empire and locked into a value system whereby the poor, the darker-skinned, the subject peoples were irretrievably fixed in their firmament, while the rulers and the better-off remained fixed in theirs[11]. The explanation for Grant's particular brand of internationalism lay in his background and upbringing.

Born in China in 1922, he was the son of Dr. John B. Grant, a leading figure in Asian public health. His father's close associates included Dr. Ludwik Rajchman, then chief of the League of Nations Health Section, later the founder of Unicef. Visitors to the Grant household in Peking were passionate politicians of disease warfare; the ideas his father promoted in China, and later at the All-India Institute of Hygiene and Public Health in Calcutta, anticipated by some decades the evolution of the primary health care strategy and the goal of 'Health for All'[12]. All this had a strong influence on the young Jim, who inherited his father's energy and sense of mission, but chose law in preference to medicine as his own gateway to a career in international public life.

Grant's career took shape in the 1950s when he worked for the International Co-operation Administration (ICA), the precursor organization of the United States Agency for International Development (USAID), first in Sri Lanka—then Ceylon—later in Washington[13]. Thus he was based in Washington in 1961 when President John F. Kennedy gave an inaugural address that signalled a new sense of moral purpose in international affairs: 'To those peoples in the huts and villages of half the globe struggling to break the bonds of mass misery, we pledge our best efforts to help them help themselves.... If a free society cannot help the many who are poor, it can never serve the few who are rich.' These words of enduring inspiration struck responsive chords all over a world shaking off the dust of the colonial past. Grant was a member of the up-and-coming generation already in a position from which to influence such a crusade. Through all the twists and turns of this and subsequent Development Decades, Grant never lost sight of the mission President Kennedy outlined.

In the mid-1960s, Grant went to Turkey as local Director of USAID. There he oversaw the introduction of 'Green Revolution' technologies—an experience that transformed food production output in Turkey and had a lasting influence on his own approach to fostering the developmental transition from old ways to new[14]. It was evident that the merits of a new technology—in this case, high-yielding crop strains—which could make a profound impact on the fortunes of people bound by the traditions of peasant life, would not be sufficient to recommend themselves on a large scale without an intensive programme of persuasion and social organization. These were provided by guaranteed credit, financial inducements, mass training and insistent propaganda. In an authoritarian setting, the new technology also needed strong backing at the highest political level. And conversely, the leader who showed his country's numerous farming families the way to double and treble their farming yields himself reaped a harvest of political popularity. Turgut Ozal, then Prime Minister of Turkey and later its President, became a friend of Grant's and a staunch ally.

In 1969, Jim Grant became President of the Overseas Development Council (ODC) in Washington, a private think-tank he helped found to foster US understanding of third world problems. During all the reappraisals of aid and development policies in the 1970s and the search for an alternative order, he was active in the professional and intellectual circles where conventional wisdom was being thrown aside.

In particular, he was among those who advocated the dethronement of economic growth, measured by gross national product (GNP) per capita, as the yardstick of a country's capacity to provide a decent life for its citizens.

History taught that wretchedness, squalor and ill health succumbed only to the material prosperity brought about by economic advance. But some countries—notably in Asia, but to some extent elsewhere—had flouted history and shown that much could be done without prosperity and before the advent of the economically 'developed' country. At the same time, other developing countries had experienced rapid rates of economic progress; yet their new prosperity had barely touched the poor.

Grant was an early proponent of the view that human progress was what mattered. Investment in health and education was not simply a social charge with no developmental implications. Equity—affirmative action for the poor—was not necessarily economically inefficient. Grant believed that a wide-ranging analysis of development experience in countries as politically and ideologically divergent as Cuba and Taiwan, Mexico and Sri Lanka, Egypt and Viet Nam, taught lessons about investment in people which could be widely applied in favour of the poor. In the years before his appointment at Unicef, he wrote and spoke widely on this theme. A main text was the 1976 Report to the Club of Rome, 'Reshaping the International Order', to which he contributed. This called for the setting of global targets in infant mortality, life expectancy, literacy and lowered birth rate to be reached by the end of the century. At this time, Grant became a great believer in these targets and goals both as measurements of reductions in poverty and as a way of popularizing issues and creating political will behind social and economic programmes.

Under Grant's leadership, the ODC became a respected and influential voice in US development assistance policy, and he became a natural candidate of the Carter administration for a top position at the United Nations. Henry Labouisse had made plain his wish to retire from Unicef. But from 1976 to 1979, UN Secretary-General Kurt Waldheim procrastinated about the Unicef succession: he did not wish to cause affront to the Nordic countries—now leading Unicef donors—who were fielding a Swedish candidate. So Grant, a member of the US delegation to the Unicef Executive Board, had ample time to contemplate what he would do should he inherit Labouisse's mantle. He finally did so when Sadako Ogata, the 1979 Chairman of the Board, forced the issue with Waldheim[15].

From the outset, Grant saw Unicef's mission for children as part of the larger development crusade in which he had so long been active. He believed that, against the demands of this crusade, the resources Unicef spent annually in the developing world were too tiny to be significant. Unicef's assistance should therefore be targeted in such a way as to contribute to larger global objectives. Unicef's cooperation in 'basic services' was fine as far as it went. But since it could not go very far, it must be used as a springboard. He wanted to employ a cadre of experts to analyse and synthesize the 'basic services' experience in an effort to persuade governments, research institutes and big donors to put their combined weight behind people-centred strategies in a revitalized development movement[16]. He also wanted to increase the prominence given to advocacy and social communications as key methods of invigorating this movement. To this end he wanted greater emphasis within Unicef on external relations, the importance of which was recognized by the creation of a top-rank post to promote it. He had already invited an old friend and associate to serve in this new Deputy Executive Director position: the distinguished Sri Lankan journalist, at that time Director of Information at the United Nations Population Fund (UNFPA), Varindra Tarzie Vittachi.

Grant's desire to deploy Unicef's skills and expertise to buoy up the world-wide development movement in no way meant that he ignored the need to build up its own resources. A very hopeful prospect of expanded income lay in the Middle East, where a strong local contact had been forged during the IYC between a brother of King Khaled of Saudi Arabia, Prince Talal Bin Abdul Al Saud, and Unicef's country office[17]. In April 1980, Prince Talal visited UN Headquarters in New York at Grant's invitation and met UN Secretary-General Waldheim. As a result of Talal's subsequent initiatives, seven Arab governments joined forces in an Arab Gulf Programme for the United Nations Development Organizations (AGFUND), set up in April 1981. Although a generous contribution of $40 million was initially pledged by AGFUND for Unicef with the promise of more to follow, this sum was nowhere near as large as had originally been hoped. Over-optimism concerning these financial prospects from the Arab world played a part in the set-back to his plans Grant then experienced.

In 1981, when he submitted his ideas for reshaping the organization he wished to lead to Unicef's Executive Board, together with an extremely ambitious financial plan, Grant was rebuffed. Even the creation of his new Deputy Directorship for External Relations was postponed. Whether or not the members of the Executive Board fully understood his wider purpose, the prospect of a cadre of headquarters experts was enough to put them off. Unicef had always been a practical, down-to-earth, field-based operation. The Board did not want it to turn into a headquarters-based repository of wisdom, the pattern of many—some would say too many—other UN organizations. Its programme—the bird in the hand—was what many members liked best about Unicef, and its own expansion was the limit of their ambition. The birds in the bush that might be won by advocacy among the wider development and donor community were decidedly suspect. Grant's proposals came at a time, too, when the effects of global recession were beginning to bite, and coupled with the air of apathy and disillusion that had greeted the Third Development Decade, the mood in the Board—and internationally—was not conducive to grand plans and dramatic revitalizations.

Jim Grant was a visionary. This temporary set-back did not deter him from seeking a way of making Unicef's experience and Unicef's programme do far more to eliminate poverty and improve child well-being than their simple quantification could ever suggest. In retrospect, his failure to convince Unicef's governing body to commit itself to his proposals can be seen as a litmus test of whether a worldwide campaign with 'basic services' as the spearhead would have achieved the regeneration of the development crusade he was seeking. It probably could not have done so. It caused him to narrow his focus, to go back to the 'child health purposes' at the core of Unicef's original mandate and deeply etched in his personal background.

Many elements of inadequate child health and the consequent high levels of child mortality were symptoms of gross poverty—what Grant called the 'silent emergency'. If a worldwide campaign could be mounted to tackle these problems, not only would the results be immensely worthwhile for children but they would provide a point from which to broaden the front into other social and economic areas at a later stage. The reversion to a concentrated focus on child survival can be seen as a strategic decision to '*reculer pour mieux sauter*': there was no serious change of direction, simply a postponement until the position from which to propel development forward had been adequately secured.

In the late summer of 1982, Grant spent time in Haiti with his friend and colleague, Dr. Jon Rohde, who was based there with USAID. Rohde started the process of persuasion and illustration at field level that led Grant to believe that the technologies to avoid a large number of child deaths existed, that in many settings the basic health infrastructure to spread them was in place and that only the political will was lacking to put them to work on a significant scale[18]. In September 1982, a meeting of leading international health and nutrition experts took place at Unicef headquarters. Grant challenged the group to come up with a short list of interventions that were suitable for widespread promotion at a time of severe recession. They had to be low-cost, practicable and important for child survival and well-being, and their spread had currently to be inhibited only by lack of consumer knowledge and political inertia.

The group produced four, which swiftly became known by the acronym 'GOBI': child growth monitoring to indicate tell-tale signs of undernutrition in the very small child; oral rehydration to treat childhood diarrhoea, the largest cause of childhood death; breastfeeding, a practice currently on the decline in the developing world; and immunization against six vaccine-preventable diseases: tuberculosis, poliomyelitis, diphtheria, tetanus, whooping cough and measles. To these were attached two 'F's—interventions that also had a major impact on child health, but did so indirectly: food supplements and family planning; a third 'F'—female education—was later added. Fantastically, as many believed, Grant saw in GOBI the child health equivalent of the hybrid seeds that, 20 years before, had been the centrepiece of the 'Green Revolution'[19].

In December 1982, he launched the 'child survival and development revolution'. This drive was intended to reduce by half, by means of the GOBI formulation, the estimated annual 15 million deaths of children under five. The vehicle he used was his annual report on *The State of the World's Children*, a publication that had already become his main advocacy platform. His collaborator, a British development writer called Peter Adamson, had an exceptional ability to present the Unicef vision within the framework of an authoritative *tour d'horizon* of social and economic trends in developing countries. *The State of the World's Children* reports deduced global policies from an analysis that was grounded in, but did not necessarily derive from, Unicef's assistance programme. By proxy, the reports assumed the role that would have fallen to the cadre of experts—if Grant had been allowed to take them on. But it did so in a far more accessible and widely publicizable format.

In the past, Unicef advocacy had largely been seen as a public relations task, something necessary for fund-raising and to inform donors and the public about what Unicef was doing. As far as the programme and policy makers were concerned, it was not a task held in much esteem. Now, under Tarzie Vittachi's guidance, advocacy was elevated to another realm altogether. Every part of the organization—from the national NGO support organizations known as National Committees for Unicef in the industrialized countries, to the Unicef country offices in the developing world—benefited from Unicef's enhanced profile, and there was widespread enthusiasm for *The State of the World's Children* reports. But there was also a sense of shock in December 1982 when such an important new initiative as the 'child survival and development revolution' was launched not in a closely argued policy paper put to the Executive Board, not as a distillation of Unicef programme experience, but as an advocacy statement addressed to the world. This was indeed a different way—and a highly unconventional one in the UN system—of doing things.

For the immediate future, the four elements of GOBI were to become areas of chief concentration as far as Unicef programmes and advocacy were concerned. This sudden reductionism from 'basic services', not just to 'primary health care' but to certain selected elements of child-related PHC, caused tension not only within Unicef, but in Unicef's relationship with WHO and with some leading members of the international public health community. On the plus side, a wide range of allies—national, international, bilateral, non-governmental—enthusiastically came on board. They found the call to support this 'child survival and development revolution' concise, unambiguous, affordable and appealing—although some dropped the word 'revolution'. A programme of worldwide social mobilization began. This was aimed at bridging the gap between the existence of these low-cost technologies and their widespread use by those—the poor—whose children's lives were being lost.

Of the four GOBI components, immunization was the one that eventually captured most public and political attention. By the second half of the decade, in spite of economic recession, spiralling debt, the advent of 'structural adjustment', a succession of crises in Africa, the onset of AIDS, declining health service expenditures and growing despair about development set-backs, the immunization story was shaping up to be a success on a par with the eradication of smallpox in the 1970s. By 1986, some 75 developing countries had embarked on accelerated immunization drives, and coverage levels—which in most had been less than 10 per cent at the beginning of the decade—now averaged nearly 50 per cent. The impact was showing up in marked declines in measles, tetanus and polio, and Unicef estimated that 1 million children's lives a year were being saved[20].

In 1985, an all-out effort backed at the topmost international level and led by the then UN Secretary-General, Javier Pérez de Cuéllar, was set in motion to reach the target of universal child immunization (UCI) by 1990. To push GOBI and UCI, Grant visited Presidents and Prime Ministers by the score and stood on podia at national events in every corner of the world. Somehow he never tired of the repetition—the similarity of the ceremonies, the mantra of the 'child survival' message—and he never missed an opportunity to consolidate relations with political leaders. A large number, especially in Africa and Latin America, were attracted to the idea that their personal identification with the children's cause was a political winner. It began to seem as if commitment to children was a stronger political 'goer' than anyone—including Grant—had actually imagined. And undoubtedly, offering cheap, populist and doable solutions that a leader could visibly endorse—for example, by dropping polio vaccine into the mouth of a baby in front of the television cameras—was a decisive ingredient.

In spite of what looked like an obsession with vaccination and child survival, Grant always thought in terms of reducing child mortality as a fillip to development: by tackling the worst manifestations of poverty, new energies would be released to combat poverty itself. After health, education: in 1988, plans for an International Conference on 'Education for All' backed by UNESCO, the United Nations Development Programme (UNDP), the World Bank and Unicef crystallized, and it seemed that the social development front was really beginning to broaden. 'Basic services' were not advancing as a phalanx, but they were advancing one by one and with a reasonable degree of synchronization. The conference on 'Education for All', intended to achieve for basic education what the 1978 conference on 'Health for All' had done for basic health, was held in Thailand in March 1990. It laid stress on female education: one of the 'F's identified alongside GOBI.

Amidst all the excitement generated by universal child immunization and the extra resources and visibility Unicef's involvement with 'child survival' generated during the 1980s, there was a strong sense in Unicef that a phoenix was rising. But alongside the new concentration on children at the frontier of social development, in the wider community a new concentration on children simply as children had also begun to emerge. This parallel development was a product of very different forces. It derived from the immense stress on the social fabric—and the consequent child distress—caused by economic setbacks and development failures, and from the burgeoning movement for children's rights.

The story of the international movement for children's rights begins in 1924 with the adoption by the League of Nations of the World Child Welfare Charter[21]. This document had been first drawn up as a Declaration of the Rights of the Child by the Save the Children International Union (SCIU), an organization founded in Geneva by a remarkable Englishwoman, Eglantyne Jebb. Jebb had set out to establish as an international principle that there was no such thing as an 'enemy child'[22]. The 1924 Declaration or Charter laid down five principles: the child's right to the means for material, moral and spiritual development; to special help when hungry, sick, disabled or orphaned; to first call on relief in distress; not to be economically exploited; and to an upbringing that instilled a sense of responsibility towards society.

In 1946, at the end of another World War, the International Union of Child Welfare (into which the SCIU had been merged) began to press the Economic and Social Council of the newly formed United Nations to endorse the Declaration of 1924. Approval in principle was given, but work on a modified draft was delayed until work on other human rights instruments was completed. In 1957, the Human Rights Commission took up the task of producing a new Declaration of the Rights of the Child, and in 1959, this was brought to the UN General Assembly and unanimously passed. The new Declaration included several new rights. One was a prohibition on discrimination 'on the grounds of race, colour, sex, language, religion, political or other opinion, national or social origin, property, birth or other status'. Another was the right to 'name and nationality'. A third change was a much fuller elaboration of the child's social needs, including the right of parents to support for children's upbringing; and children's right to education, health care and special protection.

From its inception, therefore, the international movement for children's rights derived its force and inspiration from the voluntary and non-governmental community, particularly from a hard core of international child-related organizations based in Geneva. In this movement Unicef played little part, or was at best passive. It did not wish to embroil itself in the controversial field of human rights in such a way as to antagonize its governmental partners and jeopardize what had become its main activity since the advent of the development era: cooperation in child-centred development programmes.

Accordingly, when the NGO children's lobby pressed the UN to declare 1979 an 'International Year of the Child', the proposal evoked a sense of unease at Unicef. It feared a diversion of energy and resources away from 'development via basic services'—as yet making only limited headway. The NGO community felt, by contrast, that much of what passed for 'development' was having a negative effect on childhood and it was time that a child-centred focus was resuscitated. An IYC might soften the focus on 'development', but it would sharpen it on 'child'. Eventually, the NGO lobby brought around to their point of view both UN Secretary-General Kurt Waldheim and the Unicef Executive Board.

As well as helping raise the profile of children nationally and internationally, the IYC sparked off a move to articulate a new international human rights instrument on behalf of children. In February 1978, the Polish Government had submitted to the UN Commission for Human Rights a suggested text for a Convention on the Rights of the Child for adoption during the IYC. The text was simply the 1959 Declaration of the Rights of the Child recouched in legal parlance. This proposal was deflected in the Commission on the grounds that it was premature. But the UN General Assembly agreed that a working group should be set up within the Human Rights Commission to embark on a drafting process for a Convention.

This body might easily have met occasionally and pursued a debate on the irreconcilability of various ideological and religious positions vis-à-vis abortion, birth control, childhood, parenthood and the difficulties involved in awarding human rights to minors. There were many obvious opportunities, too, for confrontation on questions associated with how far, and at what point, the machinery of state should intervene in family affairs on behalf of a child at risk. But the Poles, who were in the chair, took the task in earnest[23]. Defence for Children International (DCI), an umbrella NGO group, lobbied hard for the Convention and pushed the process forward. The Canadian and Swedish Governments began to express active interest. Unicef, caught up in the 'child survival and development revolution', helped facilitate NGO input to the drafting process but was otherwise not deeply involved during most of the decade.

Meanwhile the dynamics that had prompted heightened NGO concern on behalf of children before and during the IYC were more than ever conspicuous in the 1980s. Damaging things were happening to childhood as a product of rapid rates of industrialization and urbanization coupled with recession, debt and structural adjustment. Population growth and low agricultural commodity prices were forcing people off the land; lack of employment was undermining livelihoods and changing the terms of childhood and family life. An increasing number of households were headed by women alone, and these households were almost invariably poor. One obvious symptom of social stress and family breakdown was the increasing number of children working—and in some cases living—on the street. Some of these 'street' children became brutalized and descended into crime.

These were phenomena similar to those that had sorely exercised 19th-century social and labour reformers in Europe and North America and had prompted into existence a host of charitable children's societies to deal with human waifs and strays. The late 20th century rediscovered the child victims of these phenomena as 'street children'. The phenomenon was at its most acute in Latin America where, in the early 1980s, millions of children were reported to be eking out an existence on the streets with little or no support from their families, some living in the streets by day and by night[24]. Gradually, NGO activists and social reformers began to identify street children not only as a subject for humanitarian concern, but as a product of the havoc development was wreaking in towns and cities in Latin America and all over the developing world.

In 1981, Unicef took its first step towards examining the predicament of child casualties of the urbanization process. A Canadian activist on behalf of street children, Peter Taçon, was invited to travel throughout the Americas and examine existing programmes for children of the streets. Gradually, both the international development and human rights communities began to recognize street children as a category of children in distress demanding something more coherent in terms of policy and programmatic action than a simple welfare response.

Over the next few years, mainly at the promptings of child rights activists, other categories of children damaged by forces beyond those embraced by the general rubric of 'poverty and underdevelopment' began to gain similar recognition. Nils Thedin, Chairman of Radda Barnen and long revered as a Swedish elder statesman of Unicef, had for many years promoted the idea of 'children as a zone of peace'. This was taken forward by Unicef and others in various ways, including special attention for child victims of mass violence and warfare. Children with disabilities, who like the orphaned and abandoned had previously been seen as individual targets of welfare, also began to be embraced in the language both of rights and of primary health care. Children suffering from exploitation—as workers and labourers, as objects of commercial sexual gratification and private sexual abuse—were similarly gaining in visibility. By the mid-1980s, Unicef had coined a term to cover all categories of disadvantage extra to poverty itself: 'children in especially difficult circumstances' (CEDC).

Since 'children in especially difficult circumstances' was not a discrete group, it was difficult to advance public policy on their behalf in the same way as, for example, in health or education. However, the CEDC designation indicated a heightened perception of children and childhood being subject to special problems of deprivation beyond those of the natural physiological vulnerability of the very young. It also pointed in a different direction as far as responses were concerned. Relieving 'difficult circumstances' required not only rehabilitative care for the victims; it required preventive action to stop exploitation occurring, confirmed by legislative action to bring perpetrators to book. Unicef was initially more concerned with analysing CEDC situations and—*sotto voce* so as not to offend governments—developing public policy perspectives. The key international NGOs—Radda Barnen, DCI, Anti-Slavery International, the International Catholic Children's Bureau—were more concerned with advocacy and legislation. This was the force propelling forward the Child Rights Convention[25].

By 1987, Unicef had begun to recognize the potential convergence of the worldwide campaign for child survival with the thrust for children's rights. Grant, previously sceptical that governments would accept that children had independent rights of their own, came fully behind the Convention with the proviso that the rights to survival and development be given their due weight within the text. A timetable was set for completing the draft Convention and orchestrating its tour through the necessary international committees and machinery of the UN approval system. Although the Commission on Human Rights was administratively and technically responsible for this process, Unicef's role in mobilizing support for the Convention's adoption was extremely important.

The Convention on the Rights of the Child was adopted on 20 November 1989, the 30th anniversary to the day of the adoption of its precursor, the Declaration of the Rights of the Child. On 26 January 1990, it was opened for signature at UN Headquarters, and 61 countries signed on that day. No human rights treaty had ever gathered so much support so early in its career. By September 1990, some 20 countries had ratified, enough for the Convention to enter into international law. Partly by luck, partly by design, this moment—at which a binding treaty setting out an internationally agreed-upon vision of childhood came into force—took place almost coincidentally with that other international signal of how high the children's cause was flying: the children's World Summit.

The idea of the World Summit for Children when first mooted was regarded by many of those consulted both inside and outside of Unicef as ambitious, audacious and unrealistic—a typical Grant pipe-dream[26]. The fact that it not only took place, but was a notable success, has earned for it a central place in Unicef folklore that is unlikely ever to be surpassed. The Summit also set an agenda for Unicef's country-level activities over the forthcoming decade, and work on its follow-up dominated the final four years of Jim Grant's leadership—and of his life.

The idea was first publicly floated—very carefully—in December 1988 in the 1989 *State of the World's Children* report as a suggestion of which Unicef strongly approved, not as a definite proposition. Grant hoped that the idea would be picked up by those who could run with it, but the question of whether it would be thus picked up was not left to chance. Informal overtures had already been made to Swedish Prime Minister Ingvar Carlsson and to President Robert Mugabe in Zimbabwe. Personal statements of approval for the Summit idea from Carlsson and Mugabe were issued on the day the report was launched.

Grant had invested time and energy over the period of the 'child survival revolution' in developing close associations with the upper reaches of political establishments all over the world. These contacts now stood the idea of the

Summit in good stead. Early in 1989, he sounded out West African leaders and he also began to expound on the Summit idea in public speeches wherever he found an opportunity. The case he made was by now a Unicef stock-in-trade: the technological and financial means for making a dramatic improvement in children's lives were available if the world chose to apply them; what was needed was an injection of political will. The price-tag put on preventing 50 million unnecessary child deaths before the end of the century was no more than $2.5 billion[27].

Most leaders in developing countries welcomed the Summit idea. But it quickly became clear that there would be resistance among donor countries. Some feared a 'cheque-book conference'—an occasion leading merely to extra demands on their aid budgets; others had become very resistant to Unicef's involvement in public relations extravaganzas of which they regarded this as another example. There were even those who thought the idea preposterous. Summit meetings were normally reserved for major political and economic decisions, and confined to a handful of participants: Reagan-Gorbachev, Carter-Sadat-Begin, or at most the Group of Seven. There had never previously been a Summit to which every Head of State of every country in the world had been invited. If all leaders of North, South, East, West and every political persuasion were so invited, did the notion of 'Summit' become diluted? The idea that national leaders of the Bush and Thatcher calibre would be willing to sit together with scores of less newsworthy leaders to discuss issues relating to children seemed fanciful. And if they would not attend, then the Summit would not be a truly momentous occasion.

In April 1989, the Unicef Executive Board discussed a far-reaching policy document: 'Strategies for Children in the 1990s'[28]. This was the product of more than a year of intense consultations throughout Unicef, in its country and regional offices, with other allies in the UN system—especially WHO—and with other allies in the international public health community. It listed quantifiable goals the world should aim to reach by the end of the century: significant reductions in infant and child mortality, malnutrition and illiteracy; improvements in diarrhoeal disease control and immunization levels, and reductions in acute respiratory infections; increases in access to clean water and family planning services, and in protection for children in 'difficult circumstances'. These 'Goals' were the centrepiece not only of the document, but of an attempt to apply 'management by objective' ideas to the international agenda.

In most UN documents, goals and objectives are expressed in the most general terms: they are neither time-bound nor specific. Almost all these child-related 'Goals' were both, and their articulation coincided with a shift in Unicef's own operational philosophy to what amounted to a 'goal-led' approach. The approach, and the actual list of 'Goals for the year 2000', was developed only after a long process of widespread consultation with WHO and other members of the international health and educational communities. Most of the 'Goals' had already been set in other fora, such as the World Health Assembly, ensuring that they needed no further debate. The list in its earliest form had first emerged in 1988 in a consultation of the International Task Force for Child Survival, a top-rank multi-agency group[29].

The 1989 Unicef Executive Board discussion on 'Strategies for Children' was to prove a vital piece of the pre-Summit jigsaw. It provided a preliminary answer to the question of what the substantive part of the Summit agenda would consist of, showing that it was in no way conceived as a purely celebratory event.

In the early part of 1989 the omens for the Summit were still very mixed. Grant—taking soundings in Moscow and Washington—felt that he was heard with empathy, but there was not enough push for the Summit idea to take wing. Gradually, prospects brightened. By the summer of 1989, Unicef had begun to use its established presence at regional fora where Heads of Government congregated—the Organization of African Unity (OAU), the annual meetings of the Non-Aligned and Commonwealth Movements—to talk up the children's cause and encourage support for favourable resolutions. The first of these came at the Francophone Summit in Dakar in May 1989, when Presidents Traoré of Mali and Diouf of Senegal put their weight behind a resolution stating that Africa wanted a World Summit for Children. Similar statements emerged from the OAU in July and the Non-Aligned meeting in Belgrade in September.

By now not only Mali, but Egypt, Pakistan and Mexico had begun to express active enthusiasm. The most important convert, however, was Joe Clarke, the Canadian Foreign Minister, who offered both political and financial support for the Summit so long as the event was substantive, inexpensive and took place in New York. These five countries and Sweden came together as an 'initiators group', which included representation from both North and South and from all geographical regions. In November 1989, UN Secretary-General Javier Pérez de Cuéllar gave permission for the Summit to be held at UN Headquarters in New York.

As with so many of Jim Grant's initiatives, the procedures used to enable the Summit to reach this point of lift-off were highly unorthodox. Within that amalgam of entities known as the 'United' Nations, there is such a wide divergence of perspectives and interests that consensus building via established channels is extremely painstaking and time-consuming. Grant did not trust the conventional apparatus of international affairs to demonstrate sufficient forward thrust to conquer the scepticism and prevarication that he knew might mire the Summit. So his operational approach was to circumvent 'normal channels', inspiring the creation of ad hoc mechanisms by planting ideas in friendly places and using positive responses to overcome resistance in others. The 'initiators group' was a case in point: this mechanism set up to guide the Summit preparations was independent, outside regular UN diplomatic or bureaucratic mechanisms.

The problem with this approach—however justifiable—is that official mechanisms have a history, and that history is closely associated with matters such as representation, accountability and the consultative process. The World Summit for Children nearly failed to clear the obstacle of the special Unicef Executive Board meeting called to discuss it in December 1989. It was unthinkable that such an event could take place without the Unicef Board's imprimatur, but the failure to consult the Board more actively at an earlier stage provoked considerable antipathy. They refused to agree upon the Summit budget. After protracted negotiations, some limited agreements were achieved, thanks mainly to the lobbying of African delegations. But it was clear that some Europeans would not be returning to their capitals with the idea of impressing on their Heads of State the urgent necessity of attending.

In early 1990, planning began in earnest. There was no previous Summit example to copy: matters such as attendance, content and format all had to be invented. By the spring, a draft Declaration and Plan of Action based on 'Strategies for Children in the 1990s' were already in circulation[30]. Suggestions for Summit 'themes' had been sought from governments; the most widely requested was education and literacy, followed by protection of children 'in especially difficult circumstances', child survival interventions and the Convention on the Rights of the Child. The Convention—now awaiting ratification by a sufficient number of countries to enter into law—was a useful boost to Summit interest, and the process of its ratification gathered momentum as a result of the Summit preparations.

Invitations to the Summit were sent out by the UN Secretary-General in February. Pessimists did not believe that more than 20 acceptances would be forthcoming. Many recipients inevitably held back until they saw who else had accepted. By the spring, Unicef country offices, National Committees and a large number of NGOs had begun to mobilize allies around the Summit, using its prospect as a stimulus for activity on behalf of children. Some of this activity was designed to promote Summit attendance: seminars with parliamentarians, media, religious leaders and professional groups could put pressure on a country's leadership. As in the case of the IYC, Unicef's presence all over the world could be used to maximize the potential of the Summit, turning it into a high point in an overall effort. All this activity, which gradually built to a crescendo over the summer, helped swell a tide of interest and expectation.

Until the summer of 1990, the prospects of a successful meeting were still doubtful. Then, in June, at a meeting of the Group of Seven in Houston, Texas, Canadian Prime Minister Brian Mulroney managed to obtain promises of attendance from four key leaders: George Bush, Margaret Thatcher, François Mitterrand and Giulio Andreotti[31]. After this coup, acceptances suddenly soared to 60 and then 65. As the meeting grew in significance, the organizational dimensions—security, protocol, media arrangements—became correspondingly more complex. The Economic and Social Council (ECOSOC) chamber had to be remodelled and a special circular table built so that Presidents, Prime Ministers and monarchs could sit non-hierarchically. Plans were drawn up for the arrival at the UN building of legions of motorcades in an orderly sequence without causing gridlock in midtown Manhattan. Never before had the UN had to accommodate a meeting that included even half the number of Heads of State now proposing to attend.

For 24 hours, starting on the evening of Saturday, 29 September, through Sunday, 30 September 1990, the needs of children claimed the exclusive attention of 71 of the world's assembled leaders. At this time, this was the largest such gathering ever to have been convened. Altogether, representatives of over 150 countries were involved. Around the world, thousands of candlelight vigils, religious ceremonies and special events were held to swell the throng of wishes and prayers that the Summit would deliver positive results for children.

The day of the Summit delivered all that anyone dared anticipate. For Unicef, the occasion was both nerve-racking and euphoric. For Grant, it was the unachievable achieved, the undoable done.

The joint chairmen were Brian Mulroney and Mussa Traoré, President of Mali. Altogether, 64 Heads of Government made statements. Brian Mulroney spoke of a 'better world for children'. Ingvar Carlsson, of a 'new era . . . a new commitment'. President Carlos Salinas of Mexico talked of a 'new age' and invited leaders to 'put a new look on the faces of the world's children'. For Robert Mugabe, the Summit represented a 'new level of consciousness and a new dedication to the needs of the child'. Giulio Andreotti spoke of a 'new solidarity' giving 'life to a united and determined world coalition'. Several leaders from the South pointed out that some of the problems their children faced stemmed from factors beyond their control: the adverse global economic climate, heavy burdens of debt and structural adjustment, intractable wars and environmental stress.

One of the more striking statements came from Vaclav Havel of Czechoslovakia: 'A thousand times I have heard people defend their servitude to a hated regime by the argument that they were doing it only for the children—to be able to feed them, to make it possible for them to study. . . . How much evil has already been committed in the name of children?' Yoweri Museveni of Uganda also struck a political note, laying responsibility for much child suffering in Africa on the 'prevalence of authoritarian, top-down styles of government' and the 'oppression of man by man'[32].

The lofty and often poignant language not only captured the misery endured by many millions of children in poverty-stricken countries, but recorded the plight of those in broken families and brutalized urban communities in the richer, industrialized lands. In the end what was striking was not so much the individual statements—for rhetoric about children tends to sound hackneyed to some degree—but their sheer concentrated mass and the fact that they came from such participants. Many referred to the Convention on the Rights of the Child as the embodiment of a new set of principles on which national legislation and action should be based; some took the opportunity to append their signatures to the treaty.

All over the world, media interest in topics concerning children was heightened[33]. Many reports focused on the opportunities for saving lives, which Unicef had done so much to publicize. Others looked at special predicaments of childhood and youth—drugs, juvenile crime, marginalization, child exploitation. There was no doubt that the Summit achieved its purpose—at least temporarily—in claiming for children the high ground in public policy debate, which had been the original intention. Unicef articulated this claim as demanding for children 'first call' on society's capacities as a normative principle of human affairs—in good times and bad, in peace and in war, in prosperity and in recession.

Much was being made at the time of the great changes taking place in international affairs as a result of the end of the cold war and of an incipient 'peace dividend'. Although the Gulf crisis was brewing—and was the main subject to which the Heads of Government were due to turn their attention in the General Assembly the very next day—still there was an air of optimism that the end of superpower confrontation would enable the nations to spend more of their energies making the world a better place to live in. Because of its timing, the Summit captured and encapsulated this atmosphere of promise.

The high point of the Summit was the joint signing of the World Declaration on the Survival, Protection and Development of Children and the Plan of Action for implementing the Declaration over the next decade. Here was the substance demanded of the Summit. Taken together with the Convention, these documents constituted an ambitious agenda to achieve measurable and time-bound improvements in children's well-being by the year 2000. The Declaration included seven major goals—four related to health, two to education and one to child protection—and 27 supporting goals with specific disease control, service coverage and educational objectives. To fulfil these obligations would require major national programmes of action. As Prime Minister Brian Mulroney told the closing session: 'The real work starts now.'

The glow then emanating from the 'new world order' was soon to lose its brilliance. Certainly, some problems that had long seemed intractable were to yield in the face of diplomatic pressure uncluttered by the old superpower rivalries. But a rash of ethnic and nationalist conflicts were soon to erupt, or to emerge from hibernation, in Europe, Africa, the ex-USSR and in parts of Asia. Far from succumbing to a new climate of peace, 'loud emergencies' would once more intrude, edging out the 'silent' and derailing longer-term developmental plans.

In the international arena, the children's agenda would begin to recede as other issues took their turn: the environment and 'sustainable development' in 1992, human rights in 1993, population in 1994, social development and women in 1995, the human habitat in 1996. On the other hand, because it came first, the Declaration to which world leaders had given their agreement in New York in 1990 provided a means of ensuring that all these discussions embraced the children's cause as well. More important, it also provided a renewed inspiration for action at country level on behalf of children and on the kind of progress that elevated the condition of humanity to priority position.

To Jim Grant and to Unicef, the Summit seemed to represent a watershed moment. It was the high point of a campaign that, viewed historically, had begun not in the 1980s, but way back in the 1960s when Unicef first took up the challenge of world poverty and development from the perspective of the child. Many of the goals and strategies for which it had won endorsement were those that had begun to emerge in the 1970s 'era of alternatives', when primary health care, basic services and participatory approaches had won widespread endorsement. The course of this campaign in the period before and after the Children's Summit is at the heart of Unicef's story between 1980 and 1995.

Chapter 2

The Global Drive for Immunization

If the World Summit was the high point of a year in which children achieved greater international visibility than they ever had before, it was only the most prominent of many landmarks. The year 1990 had been set as the date at which universal child immunization (UCI) should be achieved. In all countries where Unicef provided health care assistance, it was a year of maximum effort to go the extra mile towards the immunization target.

By this time, the drive for UCI had been in operational top gear for five years. The outcome, particularly in 1989-90, was what Unicef described as 'one of the biggest collaborative peacetime efforts in history'[1]. And truly, the mobilization of communities, districts and nations, stretching from the Amazon to the Himalayas, from megacities to hamlets unknown even to the postal service, to vaccinate against communicable disease children whose very existence had previously been unregistered was an unparalleled phenomenon.

The campaign for UCI was significant in terms of vastly improved vaccination coverage—from around 20 per cent of children worldwide in 1981 to around 80 per cent in 1990[2]; and of lives saved—3 million in 1990 alone, according to WHO[3] and 15 million during the decade[4]. Much more important, it showed that it was possible to mobilize large sections of society in a large number of countries behind a specific public health goal and to achieve what by any reasonable standard of measurement was an outstanding success. The development process, perpetually confronted by set-backs and disillusionment, sorely needs the oxygen of success. The immunization campaigns of the 1980s provided it. This was especially noteworthy in a period often described as the 'lost development decade', particularly in countries deeply affected by recession and debt.

In addition, the drive towards UCI created the circumstances in which a World Summit for Children became a practicable proposition. The political mobilization surrounding UCI involved many Heads of State and Government. Their support for immunization made them more cognizant of the children's cause, more willing to view kindly the idea of a Summit, more inclined to attend and more predisposed towards signing its Declaration and Plan of Action.

In many ways, the blockbuster campaign was a throwback to the past: to the postwar campaigns against tuberculosis; the campaigns of the 1950s against yaws, leprosy and trachoma; and the super-campaign of the early 1960s that spectacularly failed to eradicate the malarial mosquito[5]. In the 1970s, there had been the victorious WHO-led campaign to eradicate smallpox. But this had been a last gasp of the disease campaign era. The case for doing it at all had been accepted at the time only because the particular behaviour of the smallpox virus—its immutability, its method of transmission—meant that a strategy that quarantined every case and vaccinated every contact could not fail to be effective. The failure of the malaria campaign was etched into the international health conscience; it had given military-style disease campaigns a thoroughly bad name. The new generation of public health practitioners had consistently rejected this kind of strategy. Indeed, the elaboration during the 1970s of the primary health care approach, with its emphasis on putting health into the hands of ordinary people and developing basic services to respond to community needs, had been, in part, a calculated dismissal of the centrally driven vertical campaign as the way to advance the public health frontier.

All of this disease campaign history was thoroughly familiar to Jim Grant and the group that, in 1982, had come up with the GOBI prescription for the 'child survival and development revolution'. Resurrecting the disease campaign approach at a time when the prophets of primary health care (PHC)—notably Dr. Halfdan Mahler, Director-General of WHO—were still struggling to persuade Ministries of Health to drop 'medical fixes' and undertake a radical restructuring of their health delivery systems was bound to provoke controversy. Grant was very aware, too, that the motivating effect of targets and goals and the commitment of resources behind them could be a double-edged sword: if all the action produced results that fell long short of the goal, sceptics would be triumphant. Even if some of the results were good, the scheme might carry the stigma of failure. On top of these difficulties lay another: that of wrenching an international bureaucracy as obstinate to command as a ship in full sail out of its prescribed and agreed-upon course and onto a different, and narrower, point of the compass.

At the personal level, the institutional level and the international level, Grant's technique was to build alliances and partnerships with those who were keen, active and committed, and work his way around the rest, temporarily sidelining those who showed a lack of initial enthusiasm or were resolutely opposed. He was masterful in building commitment behind a cause that had relatively few followers to start with. During the two years following the launch of the 'child survival and development revolution' in December 1982, he went about this task with a single-minded sense of purpose, inside and outside Unicef.

Grant saw as his main task the creation of political will behind the GOBI prescription. 'Political will'—a very overworked phrase—is commonly seen as the decisive factor in whether those in positions of political leadership will put their weight sufficiently behind a given policy to put it into effect. In democratic societies, leaders may be persuaded to do so by popular demand; but even in democratic societies direct influence on the leadership will be as important. The need for political will, and public lamentation that it is lacking, are repeated in the activist domain to the point of banality. Rarely is a comprehensive strategy developed and operationalized to create political will. This is what Grant set out to do, and he needed all of Unicef to focus its energies on the 'child survival and development revolution' to draw in allies at all levels of society and make it happen.

The strategy adopted was both more subtle and more comprehensive than the standard advocacy campaign on behalf of policy change. Its hallmark was to stress the possible and the doable, to build positive momentum behind a goal in such a way as to dissolve the obstacles in its path instead of adopting an adversarial stance towards the obstacles themselves. The only adversary was a chimera: the goal itself. Everyone else, from parents to teachers, community leaders, priests, sheikhs, policemen, business and professional people, journalists, government officials, the military, politicians, princes and presidents, was a potential ally.

In his first two years at Unicef, Grant narrowed his focus on the issue that Unicef would immediately address. No longer was this to consist of the 'child within human development' or the spread of health care and other basic services. It was to consist simply of 'child survival'. (Although the full title of the CSD campaign was 'child survival and development', the main emphasis was always 'survival'.) This had been selected not as an abandonment of the wider issues, but as a symptom of them all and because it was more doable, comprehensible and politically appealing.

With the articulation of GOBI, the same reductionism that had first defined the issue had now been applied to the response: the four GOBI components were also doable, comprehensible and politically appealing. All were well-tried and respected elements of primary health care; all were low-cost—vital at a time when aid and social service budgets were under political and economic pressure; all were highly marketable. What was lacking was knowledge about them, especially among their potential consumers—knowledge that could, in theory, easily be spread by modern communications; and commitment to them by policy makers at national and international levels, from which would follow the necessary supply of human and financial resources.

The creation of political will behind the 'child survival revolution' was to be brought about by a wide-ranging campaign of social mobilization. At the topmost level, efforts were made to mobilize world leaders and opinion formers, as well as the entire international machinery of cooperation, including other UN partner organizations and the international research community. During 1983-85, Grant used his prodigious energy to become a peripatetic salesman of child survival and GOBI to Presidents and Prime Ministers in countries with Unicef programmes and to key members of the donor community. Unlike a specialized agency of the UN system whose point of contact with recipient governments is the relevant sectoral ministry—health in the case of WHO, agriculture in the case of FAO, education in the case of UNESCO—Unicef with its mandate for children had a freedom of manoeuvre that Grant exploited to the full. Obtaining commitment to an all-out effort for child survival from a country's Head of State meant that the command to mobilize could be addressed to people and organizations in all walks of life, not just to the officials in one or two ministries.

By the end of 1985, Grant had personally visited 39 Heads of State or national government in countries as far apart geographically and ideologically as Colombia and South Yemen, Haiti and Sri Lanka, India and Burkina Faso, Nigeria and Cuba, the Dominican Republic and China[6]. All these visits raised the profile of Unicef in the country concerned and gave the country representative access to government at an elevated level. Since the expressed target was to reduce by half child mortality rates worldwide by the end of the century, Grant naturally made a priority of those countries that had very large populations, extensive poverty and high rates of child death, as well as those that had a strategic value because of their regional or political influence.

Grant and senior colleagues—notably Dr. Richard Jolly, Deputy Executive Director for Programmes, and Dr. Nyi Nyi, Director of Programmes—also sought the active collaboration of other international bodies and of donors. The

International Paediatrics Association and the League of Red Cross and Red Crescent Societies were among the earliest worldwide non-governmental networks to give child survival a ringing endorsement. In 1985, Rotary International joined in with a commitment of $120 million[7] (later rising to over $370 million) to polio eradication via immunization. Among donors, the bilateral aid agencies of Canada, Denmark, France, Italy, Norway, Sweden and the United States quickly became strongly committed; the Italian Government was outstandingly generous, providing over $150 million between 1986 and 1990 and making a critical contribution to the expansion of programmes in Africa[8].

However, not all early reactions to the 'child survival and development revolution' were favourable. In April 1983, Dr. Halfdan Mahler addressed the World Health Assembly in Geneva in terms that made clear that a strategy that selected out certain elements of the PHC approach and packaged them as a global prescription ran deeply against his own, and WHO's, ideological grain. Given that Unicef had, fairly suddenly, reverted to a highly focused child health agenda—its historical starting-point—from a much broader set of child-related preoccupations, it is hard to see how a row between the two organizations could have been avoided. As had been the case in the past, WHO felt that its scientific and policy-setting ascendancy in international public health was being ignored by a non-specialist UN partner claiming the moral high ground. This was particularly difficult to bear since Unicef had been its closest international collaborator in the elaboration of the PHC approach, and co-sponsor of the 1978 Alma-Ata Health for All conference. On Unicef's side, there was a feeling of both betrayal and misunderstanding at this unnecessarily public castigation.

Mahler's 1983 statement was the opening salvo of a battle in the international public health community that continued to rumble on for several years—much longer than it took for Mahler and Grant to reconcile their own differences of vision[9]. The battle—the kind of 'inner circle' confrontation that can arouse inexplicable passion among the parties professionally involved—was between the protagonists of 'selective PHC' and those of 'comprehensive PHC'[10]. The irony was that all shared the same values: a concern with poverty eradication, equity and the need to 'democratize' and 'demedicalize' health. All wanted to make the goal of Health for All a reality rather than a distant dream. Their differences were ones of means rather than ends.

The case in favour of selective PHC, or GOBI, was that very few countries—especially given the economic problems of the 1980s—were in a position to advance all PHC interventions simultaneously to any significant volume of population or geographical coverage[11]. Choices had to be made. And these choices had to be made primarily by health professionals, whatever the new recognition won during the 1970s for the need to respect communities' willingness to cooperate. It was naïve to think of basing service design solely on community demand, especially since poor communities were often ignorant about the causes of sickness and how their health could be improved. 'Health by the people' was a useful corrective slogan, but services still had to be designed, managed and operated according to professional norms by staff appropriately trained, with or without paramedical assistance. And services had to be funded—and funds everywhere were tight.

The debate had many ramifications, quite a number of them ideological. But Unicef was an essentially pragmatic organization: its primary purpose was the delivery of services to children—all children, not a few today and some more tomorrow. Selective PHC simply meant prioritizing, given a variety of cost and other constraints. It made sense to concentrate on problems known to cause a great deal of illness and death, especially among the poor, and for which cheap and easy remedies were available. The advantage of running health campaigns—against diarrhoea and undernutrition, for immunization and breastfeeding—was not that they were technically superior as a method of service delivery, but that they were motivating and it was possible to mobilize around them. Peripheral health staff could be more easily trained to deliver one or two interventions well than a whole gamut; managerial staff could get their teeth into the technical and logistical problems of developing a well-oiled delivery system for reaching a large population with—initially—one or two interventions only. GOBI was not meant to substitute for PHC, nor to replace new-style participatory approaches with old-style authoritarianism. It was meant to boost the whole PHC movement by delivering some tangible and measurable results. It was also meant to do so on a significant scale, with all the boost to morale that successful results would bring with them.

Those arguing on behalf of comprehensive PHC insisted that tangible and measurable results achieved by a campaigning strategy would not be lasting, and would in the meantime have diverted resources away from the effective delivery of other vital elements of PHC. Only if the health care infrastructure was developed in tandem would a revolution in child survival be sustainable[12]. As with many such debates, there were valid arguments on both sides and much unnecessary polarization. But ultimately, Unicef argued, it was more important to get on and do something than to waste energy beating on the 'straw men' of intellectual construct instead of on the problems of poverty, low access to health care and unnecessary infant and young child death. If the course of action turned out to be wrong, it could always be changed[13].

Not only within the international public health community, but within Unicef itself, the suddenness with which the GOBI initiative was launched caused doubts and hesitations. Unicef is a decentralized organization and its muscle is on the ground. Some country offices, working away at programmes that had been carefully designed to match national priorities concerning children, were horrified at the prospect of switching to a relatively narrow set of child health objectives established in far-away New York. Part of this attitude stemmed from loyalty to previous organizational policy, itself evolved over many years; part from bureaucratic resistance to change; part from the lack of understanding that the rhetoric of GOBI was meant to be a mobilizing dynamic, not a rigid prescription. Programmes in other areas—water supply and sanitation, education, women's well-being, early childhood development, urban basic services—might take a lower profile, but they were not to be abandoned.

In an organization whose centre of gravity was much closer to headquarters and whose country offices waited to be told what to do, it would have been easier to swing in a new direction. The character of Unicef—the strong field presence; the autonomy of the country office; its capacity to plan, programme and advocate independently—led to a widespread internal debate. Ironically, the same organizational power to resist GOBI and the child survival and development revolution was also the organizational characteristic that made feasible the prospect of widespread social mobilization behind the new initiative. Few other UN bodies—if any—had the potential to do what Grant wanted of its outposted legions. Once motivated and technically equipped, the Unicef country office could become the engine behind GOBI, building the necessary alliances on the ground without which any amount of international mobilization would essentially be meaningless. The Unicef organizational network, whose individualistic character and strength had been carefully built up by a previous generation of leaders, had somehow to be pushed and cajoled into energetic commitment.

There is nothing like conspicuous success to quell the reservations of sceptics. At an early stage, therefore, Grant looked around among his many allies and converts inside and outside the organization and sought ways of proving that the 'child survival revolution' was not just a war of words. He wanted to create on the ground some successful examples of ideas in action. He wanted to show that the rhetoric worked.

In the earliest phase of the child survival revolution, Grant believed that among the four GOBI techniques, it was the spread of oral rehydration therapy

(ORT), both in manufactured sachet form as oral rehydration salts (ORS) and as a recipe concocted at home, that held out the most immediate promise.

In the early 1980s, diarrhoeal disease was the leading killer of infants and young children in the developing world, claiming 5 million lives a year and sapping the strength of millions more in repeated bouts of sickness[14]. Many mothers watching the fluids of their child's body drain away made what to them was the logical assumption that the only way to stem the flow was to deny their child food and drink. The result—a loss of salts, fluids and minerals, which dehydrated the body and could send it into life-threatening shock—was usually a much more serious threat than the infection itself. Most doctors advocated intravenous rehydration by saline drip in the controlled circumstances of a clinic. But most families in the developing world could neither reach nor afford medical attention of this kind.

During the 1970s, experiments in Bangladesh proved that diarrhoeal dehydration could be treated orally if the saline solution contained a specific quantity of sugar. This transformed the prospects of effective home care. In a country suffering from endemic cholera with a minimal health service structure in place, this therapy could be carried out by village mothers once they had been taught how to brew the mix correctly from ingredients available in the home. This discovery was hailed by the British medical journal *The Lancet* as 'potentially the most important medical advance this century'[15]. But for many years, with the exception of programmes inspired by the work of the International Centre for Diarrhoeal Diseases Research in Bangladesh and some other pioneers, ORT and its manufactured form, ORS, suffered a classic fate at the hands of the medical consumer society: its very cheapness and simplicity led to its widespread neglect.

This neglect, in which the medical profession and the pharmaceutical companies conspired, Unicef now proposed to end. It set itself the target of putting into the hands of the majority of the world's citizens an extremely cheap and effective remedy, of which they currently knew nothing, for a life-threatening condition.

The control of diarrhoeal diseases is, of course, far more complex than the provision of a remedy for dehydration. The prevalence of such infections in poverty-stricken environments is associated with the presence of dirt and germs and the lack of knowledge—or means—to keep food, utensils, hands, clothes and the household clean. The small child is also more vulnerable to infection if undernourished or malnourished, or less than adequately fed—by diluting infant formula in an unsterilized bottle, for example. A good supply of safe water and sanitary waste disposal are also closely associated with the reduction of diarrhoeal disease. To reduce the case-load of diarrhoeal infection worldwide required progress on all these fronts. Much of this would take time. The joy of ORT was that it provided an immediate and simple cure, not for the diarrhoea itself but for the dehydration it so easily induced. Those infants and children currently contracting several bouts of diarrhoeal infection every year could be saved from the peril of death and from some of the debility—if only parents and health workers knew about the remedy and used it.

Unicef, together with WHO, was already supporting national programmes for control of diarrhoeal diseases (CDD). After the launch of the child survival revolution, it boosted its provision of ORS mix—a pre-mixed sachet to which only boiled water needed to be added—and its support for local production of the WHO-approved formula. It also embarked on a strenuous campaign of advocacy to promote both the theory of oral rehydration therapy and the use of ORS. At least 20 new national programmes for the control of diarrhoeal disease had been launched by 1985, causing a dramatic rise in ORS production: from under 60 million sachets in 1982 to over 200 million[16]. But from 1983 onward, an important ally—USAID—effectively took over the torch for ORT, obtaining extra resources from the US Congress to back national campaigns around the world.

An example of such a programme was that operated by the Egyptian Ministry of Health[17]. When the anti-diarrhoeal programme went nationwide in 1983, oral rehydration therapy had already been an officially recommended treatment for 10 years. But the sachets of salts were available only on prescription and were not promoted to the public. Fewer than 1 per cent of mothers were thought to use them. The strategy adopted in Egypt included extensive retraining of medical practitioners in 100 special ORT training units. Once this was completed, health clinics all over the country set up oral rehydration centres to teach mothers how to use the therapy.

On the supply side, pharmacists were encouraged to stock ORS sachets. One of the problems with ORS is that the product is so cheap that pharmacists make little profit on the sale. Unless they know better, mothers may instead be induced to buy patent anti-diarrhoeal drugs that look more exotic and cost more money, but are almost certainly an inferior treatment for diarrhoeal dehydration and can even be dangerous. In Egypt, pharmacists were offered a 30 per cent profit margin on each ORS sachet they sold. And to promote public demand, television commercials were aired nightly at peak viewing time. This ambitious five-year programme cost $50 million, of which USAID contributed over half; it was intended to reduce the child mortality rate by 25 per cent.

This was just one of many ORT initiatives heralded in *The State of the World's Children* report at the end of 1985, in which it was claimed that the spread of knowledge about oral rehydration had saved a million children's lives over the previous 12 months. But in spite of the encouraging signs, ORT's promise was only beginning to be fulfilled: the same report estimated that 'only about 20 per cent of the world's families knew enough about oral rehydration to be able to use it'. However good the technique, it was not proving to be a swift and easy task to mobilize whole countries and communities behind its use. Existing methods of treating diarrhoea and beliefs about them had to be worn down and replaced.

ORT did not arrive to fill a vacuum: mothers, healers and doctors had long had their ways of dealing with something so commonplace as diarrhoea. Pharmaceutical companies and private practitioners had vested interests in preserving the anti-diarrhoeal status quo. Mothers had to be sufficiently convinced and practised to apply the therapy when the crisis arose: this was not something for which a 'Day' could be declared and children neatly lined up to receive a dose. There were, also, inhibitions about the subject. As a topic of general conversation or for airing on T-shirts and television, diarrhoea lacked appeal. Most Presidents and senior political figures are not keen to address their subjects on the bowel movements of the under-fives—although 'Baby Doc' Duvalier in Haiti, who gave over the presidential palace to a grand public song and dance extravaganza on the theme of infant diarrhoea, proved an exception[18]. Many Presidents were, on the other hand, willing to identify themselves with the virtues of something so clean and wholesome as vaccination.

The 1986 *State of the World's Children* report declared: 'Immunization leads the way.' Of the four GOBI techniques, the 'O' had started out as champion. But in terms of its potential to mobilize all sectors of society, the 'I' turned out to lead the field. Where ORT showed gains, immunization leapt ahead. Accordingly, from this point on, centre stage in the campaign for child survival was to be occupied unequivocally by immunization.

The expanded programme on immunization (EPI) had been launched by WHO in 1974 to make routine protection against immunizable diseases—diphtheria, pertussis (whooping cough), measles, tetanus and polio—available to all children under the age of one. In 1977, in the wake of the smallpox eradication, the World Health Assembly adopted a target of universal child immunization by 1990. But in spite of major improvements in the 'cold chain' technology required to reach children with vaccines that worked, the take-up of EPI programmes was sluggish. The picture varied, but in 1980 the average level of immunization in most developing countries hovered between 10 and 20 per cent[19].

Of all the GOBI elements, immunization illustrated *par excellence* the 'chicken and egg' conundrum associated with 'selective' and 'comprehensive' primary health care. EPI programmes in some countries were run just like the old disease control campaigns, with special fleets of vehicles and inoculation staff, divorced from—for example—maternal and child health care programmes. Experience showed that without the involvement of the regular health infrastructure, significant gains in control of a given malady could easily evaporate.

On the other hand, creating a primary health care system that depended for outreach on the participation of trained volunteers did require a starting-point, and the tasks associated with vaccination were eminently suitable. The lay vaccinator was a well-established health cadre, familiar from the smallpox campaign, even from the BCG campaigns in postwar Europe[20]. And where countries' health establishments allowed vaccinations to be given only by a trained professional, there were plenty of other useful tasks for lay participants: gathering children at the vaccination post, filling in health cards, checking registers of names, conducting house-to-house visits. The protagonists of the 'child survival revolution' believed that the organization of efficient vaccination services could provide a vanguard for the full range of PHC.

Coincidentally, in early 1983, Dr. Jonas Salk, creator of the first successful vaccine against poliomyelitis, broached with Robert McNamara, ex-President of the World Bank, the idea of a campaign to eradicate polio worldwide[21]. Talks were initiated with other influential figures in international public health, and Jim Grant became involved. From polio alone, discussions broadened to include the whole range of communicable diseases embraced by EPI. The outstanding question was whether Halfdan Mahler at WHO—the staunch opponent of the single-track campaign—could be persuaded to accept the idea that EPI was well positioned to assume the role of PHC's leading edge. McNamara was persuasive and WHO's vital imprimatur was affixed. A conference was organized at Bellagio in Italy entitled 'To Protect the World's Children'. The roll-call included many of the most famous names in immunology and disease control.

The Bellagio meeting took place in March 1984. Out of it came the formation of the Task Force for Child Survival, a body that included representatives of five international organizations—the Rockefeller Foundation, Unicef, UNDP, WHO and the World Bank—and whose executive secretariat was provided by the Centers for Disease Control (CDC) in Atlanta. The initial mandate of this specially constituted, neutral body was to accelerate immunization activities in a number of countries, look at unresolved technical issues and mobilize financial resources.

Already, as a result of Grant's salesmanship of GOBI to political leaders and to Unicef country representatives, some countries—in 'pilot' localities or on an experimental basis—had undertaken special stepped-up immunization drives. These were valuable in several respects. They offered examples of what could be done and a challenge to others to match it; they provided a methodological training-ground for solving technical problems; and they provided an opportunity for mobilizing Unicef itself. Many of those within the organization who were doubtful about selective primary health care, particularly when spearheaded by this particular intervention, quickly became converted to the immunization cause when successful models existed for what they were now being asked to do.

The first successful example of a new-style EPI campaign on a major scale came from Colombia. Jim Grant somehow persuaded President Belisario Betancur to back a National Vaccination Crusade. Betancur was the very first Head of State to associate himself personally with a children's initiative of this kind, braving the prospect that his personal association with the cause of small children might invite unspoken ridicule[22].

The strategy developed in Colombia was one frequently drawn upon later as a model elsewhere. Three days, one month apart, in mid-1984 were declared national vaccination days. (Measles and BCG vaccine—against tuberculosis—require one dose each, but polio and DPT—against diphtheria, pertussis and tetanus—require three doses to build sufficient immunity.) A mass mobilization was organized of 120,000 volunteer helpers from the Catholic Church, the Red Cross, the police, the labour unions, the Boy Scouts and the entire school network. Even the Air Force was recruited to fly in vaccines to remote villages. The target group was 900,000 children. To boost attendance, a media blitz was conducted, and President Betancur was televised vaccinating a child on each of the 'days'. This idea, of taking vaccination out of the exclusive domain of the health service and transforming it into a society-wide activity in which everyone had a role to play, was highly effective. The Crusade reached 800,000 children and pushed coverage levels to around 75 per cent[23].

Following successes not only in Colombia, but in Burkina Faso, Senegal and in pilot districts of India and Nigeria, Grant wanted to prove that the national vaccination crusade could work not only in a small country or a corner of a large one, but in a very large country with a considerable number of relatively inaccessible unvaccinated children. The country he picked was Turkey, where the target child population was 5 million. Nowhere in the country was the immunization rate higher than 20 per cent, and in some areas it was less than 1 per cent. A good case for a stepped-up campaign could therefore be made. As important, one of the key people to whom Grant would make the case was his old ally from his days with USAID in Turkey, the then Prime Minister Turgut Ozal. In February 1985, Grant visited Ankara and obtained a commitment to an immunization crusade at the highest political level[24]. He thereupon posted to Turkey Richard Reid, previously Unicef country representative in Nigeria, scene of a recently successful pilot EPI upgrade, and a person of great energy and commitment.

Within a few months, Reid and an international colleague, Sarojini Abraham, had recruited a local Unicef team and worked with the Ministry of Health and the entire political and civil establishment to set up the campaign. They had also procured 41 million doses of vaccine—some days' worth of the entire global supply—and helped the Ministry position it in refrigerators and cold storage depots throughout the country. A huge feat of mobilization was required: 45,000 vaccination posts had to be set up; 12,000 health personnel and 65,000 helpers trained; and the mothers of 5 million children persuaded that they must bring their children three times to complete their immunization.

As with Colombia, a decisive feature of the Turkish campaign was the backing obtained from the political establishment. In July 1985, President Kenan Evren summoned all 67 provincial governors to Ankara to discuss how to mobilize the local population. They enlisted the country's 200,000 schoolteachers, 54,000 imams—who spoke to their congregations about vaccination at the Friday prayers—and 40,000 *muhtars* (village leaders)[25]. The country's meat and fishing industries put their cold storage facilities at the disposal of the campaign, and as publicity increased, other companies, organizations and individuals offered their support.

By inauguration day in September, constant radio and television announcements had reached 30 million homes, ensuring that there was barely anyone in Turkey even in remote rural areas who had not heard what to do and where to go. The launch ceremony, in which the President, the Prime Minister, the Minister of Health, the Chief Imam and Jim Grant each vaccinated a baby against polio, was televised as a national event. In each province the ceremony was repeated. From stores and corner shop refrigerators, the vaccines were moved out by car, truck, on horseback or on foot. The tally of figures was reported nightly on television and radio. By the end of the final round in November, with winter weather setting in, 84 per cent of the target group had been immunized[26].

The success of Turkey's immunization drive had an immediate impact in neighbouring countries in the Middle East and North Africa: enthusiastic ministers from Egypt, Pakistan, the Sudan and Syria attended the launch ceremony. It also provided a spur to the whole worldwide immunization effort. The Turkish experience showed that it was possible to mobilize a whole society behind a child survival goal. And it elevated 'social mobilization'—a phrase new to the development lexicon—onto the same plane of respect as technical and managerial mastery in achieving health programme success. Not only had access to a service been provided, but demand for that service had been created.

In subsequent years, coverage rates for immunization in Turkey did slip back and legitimate questions were asked about sustainability. But the achievement spoke for itself. No one involved in the Turkish immunization crusade, even with the benefit of hindsight, would describe that remarkable surge of human and national energy on behalf of children as strategically 'wrong'. The cost per immunized child was estimated to be $7.25: hardly an exorbitantly wasteful sum[27].

The year 1985 also witnessed the first occasion on which a war temporarily ceased in order to allow children to be vaccinated on 'days of tranquillity'[28]. In El Salvador, three perilous daylong pauses in the country's bitter civil war allowed 250,000 children to attend vaccination posts set up on both sides of the fighting. The truce, which was fragile but held, was negotiated with the help of prelates in the Roman Catholic Church. This experience, as did that of Turkey but in a different way, also illustrated the magic of childhood immunization as an inspirational force for merging common differences. It produced a concrete manifestation of the idea of 'children as a zone of peace'.

The idea that children are above the political divide has advanced historically more often as a result of de facto precedent than as a result of legislation or international agreement. Up until the 'Days of Tranquillity' in El Salvador, this principle had been advanced during the 20th century to obtain agreement to cross enemy lines or breach blockades to bring relief to children in time of war. But never before had a war actually been stopped in order to administer routine protective health care to the general child population. The 'Days of Tranquillity' idea was later repeated in the midst of civil wars in Uganda, Lebanon, the Sudan, and in former Yugoslavia[29].

By the end of 1985, worldwide demand for vaccine was running at three times the level of 1983[30]. The two most populous countries in the world—China and India—had both announced ambitious immunization targets. Rajiv Gandhi announced that the target of immunizing every child born in India by

1990 had been set as a 'living memorial' to his mother, Indira Gandhi, who had been assassinated the previous year. In Brazil, the ongoing campaign of yearly National Immunization Days had succeeded in all but banishing poliomyelitis, targeted by the Pan-American Health Organization (PAHO) for eradication from the Americas by 1990[31]. In Indonesia, the existing network of child weighing and nutrition posts—the village- and hamlet-based *posyandu*—were about to be galvanized into incorporating EPI into their monthly schedules. Other countries with very large child populations—Bangladesh, Nigeria, Pakistan—as well as more than 30 with smaller ones had conducted surveys and finalized plans and preparations for their own immunization push.

In November 1985, at a ceremony in the United Nations General Assembly held to commemorate the 40th anniversary of the United Nations, the world community recommitted itself to the achievement of universal child immunization by 1990. Over 70 governments and 400 voluntary organizations pledged their support[32]. No one examining the statistics a few years back would have imagined that the target was remotely realizable. Levels of 40 to 60 per cent coverage were now being reported by certain countries. Suddenly it began to seem as if 'UCI 1990' was within feasible range.

The concept of 'universal' child immunization did not actually mean 100 per cent of children immunized with all six antigens. No country has ever managed to achieve this vaccination level. What it meant was that the *availability* of immunization should be universal: every child born into the world had a right to be fully vaccinated by his or her first birthday and the means of becoming so should be within the parents' reach.

All the countries accelerating their EPI programmes, of which there were 80 by the end of the decade[33], intended not only to make immunization available but to see that as many parents as possible took their children for their shots. Targeted coverage varied from country to country; in Africa, where 1986 was declared 'immunization year', the UCI goal for 1990 was 75 per cent. In most other countries the target was 80 per cent, but in China it was 85 per cent—not only nationally but in each province and for each vaccine. The 80 per cent level was sometimes projected as a threshold at which the pool of a given infection in a given area would have been sufficiently reduced to make epidemic outbreaks less likely and the disease less threatening[34]. However, this was not a position sufficiently supported by medical evidence for WHO to be willing to endorse any claim on behalf of the epidemiological potency of 80 per cent. Nonetheless, this was the level jointly understood by WHO and

Unicef to constitute the 'universal' immunization sought by 1990. This position was jointly agreed because truly 'universal' immunization coverage was quite simply undoable.

One aspect of the doability of UCI to which sufficient attention was not given at an early stage was the capacity of existing manufacturers to supply vaccines on a dramatically enhanced scale. In the first half of the decade, the worldwide supply of vaccines to EPI programmes by Unicef increased almost fourfold, from 130 million doses in 1982 to 494 million in 1986[35]. By the end of the decade, a total of 4.4 billion doses had been procured altogether through Unicef[36]. Its supply operation, the Unicef Packing and Assembly Centre (UNIPAC), based in Copenhagen, had to smooth out problems with manufacturers faced with rising demand to ensure that low prices and high quality of vaccines were maintained. Turkey was not the only country to seek Unicef's assistance in procuring such large quantities of vaccines for a short-term campaign that the entire world supply was temporarily snapped up. The need to streamline and upgrade supply delivery and logistics—not only for vaccines, but for all types of cold storage and needle-sterilizing equipment—was an important aspect of the drive for UCI 1990. UNIPAC began to assume an important leadership role in this area.

In most countries of Latin America, the gap between existing coverage and 80 per cent was not enormous—some had already reached this level or exceeded it, notably in the Caribbean. Health service infrastructures were also more or less in place and with some gingering up—clever promotion, immunization 'days', mobilizing of allies in the church, the educational apparatus and NGO partner organizations—the target was not overwhelming where it had not yet been reached. The same went for most countries in the Middle East and in North Africa. The big challenges were in sub-Saharan Africa and in Asia. It was very clear that the target of 80 per cent for the world as a whole could not be attained unless it was met in the most populous countries. China, where basic health care provision had long commanded a high political priority, had already shown that it could effect major improvements in coverage levels in a relatively short space of time[37]. The greatest challenge of all lay in India, where 20 per cent of the children in the world as yet untouched by immunization services were to be found.

Every year, 23 million newborns entered the world in India[38], compared, for example, with 1.5 million in Turkey. Some 40 per cent of Indian families lived at or below subsistence level, and a considerable proportion of their newborn children were beyond the reach of even rudimentary health attention. In many parts of this vast country, vaccination coverage levels were abysmal—where they were accurately reported. The case-load of illness from the six immunizable diseases was calculated at 40 million annually with 1.5 million deaths in the absence of an immunization programme[39].

The Indian public health administration was a committed exponent of comprehensive PHC—in fact, India could well claim to have been a cradle of the comprehensive PHC philosophy. In the 1970s, the example of some pioneering Indian programmes had been taken up by international enthusiasts shaping the doctrine of 'Health by the People'[40]. Thus, during the stampede for national vaccination crusades in the mid-1980s, India's health decision makers were not willing takers. It took time for them to reach their own conclusions about the value of EPI as an invigorating force for PHC as a whole. India was typical of Asian—and most Latin American—countries in preferring, finally, to adopt a strategy of building up the capacity of the regular health service to carry out immunizations on a routine basis, and using campaigning tactics to 'top up'.

The accelerated nationwide programme began to take serious shape only in 1985, after Prime Minister Rajiv Gandhi committed India to UCI by 1990 as a 'living memorial' to his mother[41]. In 1987, this centrally directed push was enhanced when he appointed an 'immunization mission' as one of five National Technological Missions spearheading the assault on Indian poverty.

The first two years of India's accelerated Universal Immunization Programme (UIP) were a time of experimentation. Thirty districts were selected as pilots for a series of inputs—cold-chain equipment, needles and syringes, training, vehicles, vaccines. David Haxton, then Unicef's Regional Director in South Asia, based in Delhi, encouraged the Government to 'go universal' with EPI from this base. In 1985, plans were drawn up to cover the country's 452 districts in a phased manner by 1990[42]. Indigenous capacity to manufacture all vaccines except polio was enhanced, and trained managers were put in place to ensure coverage and accountability[43]. The extra costs of the UIP over the period were estimated at $360 million, of which Unicef pledged to provide $126 million[44]; other donors—the Canadian International Development Agency (CIDA), the Swedish International Development Authority (SIDA) and USAID among them—joined in.

The strategy was to train existing health and family welfare workers to conduct the immunization sessions while building up the cold chain and the vaccine production and supply system. The early districts covered in 1985-86 showed such wide discrepancies in performance that some drastic rethinking had to be done. At this stage, with the full agreement of the Ministry of Health and WHO, Unicef decided to appoint a number of public health doctors to its own staff and become much more closely involved operationally[45].

The critical innovation in the programme was the concept of the 'fixed day' strategy[46]. The outermost extremity of the primary health care system in India is the sub-centre or health post, manned by an female auxiliary health worker or ANM. These sub-centres—of which there are over 150,000 in the country—have a room or two, a cupboard with a few supplies, but no refrigeration unit. Each serves around 5,000 people—the village in which it is situated and some surrounding hamlets. To carry out the immunization programme, a cold box of vaccines had to be collected from the Primary Health Care Centre and used before their potency expired. This centre was typically around 20 kilometres from the health post[47].

The concept of the 'fixed day' meant that each ANM would collect her vaccines on a set day each month, and then follow a fixed routine for visiting local villages for their monthly immunization session. Whether it was the first Monday or the third Wednesday for a given location, it must always be the same day. This meant that village leaders always knew on which day to round up mothers and children. It also meant that everything—from posters to radio messages, from vaccine supplies to monthly records—could be routinized; once routinized, the monthly 'day' would actually happen. No longer would the health worker turn up in a village at will, and finding no mothers and children waiting to see her, go away again. Simple as it sounds, the 'fixed day' revolutionized the potential of health service implementation—not just for immunization, but for all preventive services.

The UIP not only galvanized India's army of family welfare workers—a group demoralized by their association with the hugely unpopular national drive for family planning. It also breathed new life into another social programme: the Integrated Child Development Services (ICDS) run by the Department of Women and Child Development, whose earliest operations had begun in 1975[48].

Although ICDS had been conceived as an integrated package of nutrition, health, immunization, and preschool education, in practice the health component had turned out the poor relation. The mainstay of the programme was the *anganwadi* worker, a local woman equipped with three months' training. At the *anganwadi*, she prepared a daily meal for the 20 or 30 toddlers in her charge, played games and sang songs with them. Health care and immunization were supposed to be provided by the ANM from the health post. In practice, the health workers rarely turned up. The 'integration' of services rarely happened on the ground.

Unlike some of India's other experiments with services based on village volunteers, ICDS had enjoyed great staying power. By the mid-1980s, it had expanded to 1,000 development blocks. Its performance might have been patchy, but it was a genuinely community-based programme reaching into very poor and backward areas. With the advent of UIP, its potential began to be better realized. The health worker in an ICDS 'block', planning her schedule of 'fixed immunization days', found a link-up with the *anganwadi* worker invaluable. No one else was as knowledgeable about which women in the village had recently delivered. No one else was as well equipped to prepare for the session and generally make the day's work run smoothly. As a result, immunization performance in ICDS areas was conspicuously higher than in others. And the new links between the health centres and *anganwadis* could be developed for the provision of other services: distribution of vitamin A tablets, promotion of ORS and antenatal care.

As the UIP proceeded, to 60 districts in 1987, and 90 more in 1988, constant adjustments were made to every aspect—from training modules, to surveying techniques, to communication strategies, to planning methodologies. Still, some states seemed quite unable to deliver. The worst was Bihar, notorious for its ability to absorb programmes and development finance in such a way that they left not a trace on its poverty-stricken inhabitants. In early 1989, Unicef—with full approval from the Ministry of Health and close cooperation from the state authorities—took an unprecedented step. It temporarily assigned members of the regular staff from its offices in Delhi and Patna to a special Bihar Immunization Task Force[49].

Each task force member was assigned three or four problem districts, which they toured with local officials in an effort to make the inert machinery of cold chain, vaccine and syringe splutter into life. The task force did not attempt to organize the immunization service themselves; rather, they identified the loose connections, the small but critical missing parts—a defunct refrigerator, a missing plug, a lame vehicle, absentee personnel, a non-existent schedule—and remedied them either on the spot or by immediate intercession with the authorities. More important than anything else was its role in triggering an attitudinal change towards UIP throughout the state apparatus.

The task force strategy was so successful in Bihar that, in 1990, Unicef repeated the approach in the four other major problem states: Uttar Pradesh, Rajasthan, Madya Pradesh and West Bengal. Altogether, 120 of Unicef's staff spent part of their time on special secondment to UIP task forces during the final months of 1990[50].

State by state, the 1990 push towards universal immunization was planned with the precision of a military operation. A massive communication campaign ran nationwide to create a sense of urgency among parents. The campaign tried to build parents' confidence in the health care infrastructure and its personnel. Some states, for example West Bengal, planned a series of special immunization sessions during the cool months of October, November and December. Areas that were very difficult to reach, or where health centres did not exist, were chosen for these 'mop-up' operations. The offices of the District Magistrate and Rural Development Departments lent staff and resources for the statewide effort. Private medical practitioners also became drawn in through the Indian Medical Association. In some cities, between 10 and 25 per cent of children vaccinated received their shots from private doctors[51]. In Calcutta, a special plan of action was developed by the Municipal Corporation, and thanks to teamwork and intensive publicity, coverage levels were raised within the space of months from below 20 per cent to 85 per cent[52].

At the end of 1990, India announced that immunization coverage of children under one year old had surpassed 80 per cent. This was an important achievement, not only for India, but also for the global immunization tally. Although many observers thought the figure inflated, no one could deny that for such a vast country with so many poor and illiterate people to have reached anywhere near the target was a major achievement.

Although there was inevitably some slippage in subsequent years, strenuous efforts were made throughout the country to continue to advance the immunization frontier. The 'fixed day' strategy stood India in good stead. Not only has expansion been possible as the network of health centres and posts spreads ever outward; so also has been consolidation. Other components—some directed at maternal health, others at child survival—have gradually been added: vitamin A supplements, iron folate against anaemia in pregnancy, control of acute respiratory infections (ARI), ORT for diarrhoeal treatment, and family planning. The service offered by the local health worker is becoming 'comprehensive' according to the original concept of primary health care, but is doing so incrementally.

India is huge and diverse and its tradition is one of lively debate in all areas of human affairs. The Indian public health care community is not immune to the differences of an ideological and practical nature that have coloured international PHC discussion; the course of UIP has been the subject of considerable debate within India. Not all observers believe that because the system is capable of delivering immunization, it is able to deliver the full range of maternal and child health (MCH) services effectively[53]. Immunization is an intervention of a particular kind, easier to deliver and monitor than most others. And centrally initiated schemes—such as family planning—do not have a good reputation.

Even within the immunization programme there are important questions about sustainability and the scale of those who remain unreached. In 1991-92, national coverage levels were reported by Unicef to be 85 per cent for measles and close to 90 per cent or above for the other antigens[54]. But even very high national averages in a country such as India can disguise the fact that, in underserved areas, the absolute numbers of the unimmunized may run into the millions. And the figures themselves have been called into question. This problem has derived from the fact that targets have been used heavily for political purposes, and where targets are unrealistic, this can lead to the manipulation of data[55]. Indian systems of data collection are far from perfect, and statistics are open to constant dispute. A National Family Health Survey conducted in 1994 suggested that in some of the largest Indian states, only 50 per cent of children were immunized[56]. Undoubtedly, the UIP won great gains for the lives and health of Indian children and helped give the whole primary health care service system a boost. In such a country, final judgements about the scale and potential of this achievement are bound to remain open.

Many other Asian countries adopted immunization strategies similar to India's. In Bangladesh, Indonesia and the Philippines, EPI was used as the 'leading edge' of an improved MCH service, with social mobilization and media publicity used to accelerate coverage. In both China and Viet Nam, where primary health infrastructures were more developed, planning managed to become so 'micro' that defaulters for second or third DPT and polio shots were even tracked by name[57]. In Asia as a whole, the proportion of children who had received their third DPT immunization dosage rose from 44 per cent in 1985 to 83 per cent in 1990. This was as fair an indication as any that, one way or another, countries had managed to 'go the extra mile'. In this effort, not only Unicef's country offices but its supply operation in Copenhagen—UNIPAC—made a vital contribution.

The challenge of the 1990s would be not only to sustain the immunization advance, but to use it to promote both universal PHC and comprehensive PHC. Given the extraordinary ambition of the UCI drive, it was not overstating the case to suggest that a genuine 'child survival and development revolution', in Asia at least, had been set in progress.

The problems facing EPI in Africa were, by definition, of an order different from anywhere else in the world. Few sub-Saharan countries, and those mostly very small and relatively better-off—Botswana, Gambia, Lesotho, Mauritius, Swaziland—had managed to set up and staff a service network that brought health care within close range of virtually everyone in the country. In a few others, such as Malawi and Tanzania, the PHC system was sufficiently developed to form the backbone of an expanded immunization programme, given political commitment, an injection of financial and managerial resources and a strong dose of social mobilization to build up popular demand. But in many settings, mobile teams were the only way to reach far-flung rural populations.

More problematic still was the fact that many countries had been disrupted by war and civil conflict. Roads were mined, infrastructures destroyed. Whatever unprepossessing buildings labelled 'health centre' once existed in the hinterlands beyond the main towns and cities of countries such as Angola, Chad, Ethiopia, Liberia and Mozambique, many now lay deserted or in ruins. In Africa as a whole, the 1980s had been a decade of economic set-back, falling export prices, debt and structural adjustment. In country after country, health care services—already skeletal in rural areas—had seen their budgets slashed. Health workers went unpaid, drugs became scarce for long periods, and the maintenance backlog of broken equipment and crippled vehicles steadily grew. In these circumstances, the difficulties facing the delivery of all child health and survival interventions, let alone 'universal' immunization (set at 75 per cent for Africa), were immense.

During the mid-1980s, Jim Grant's strategy of visiting Heads of State to solicit their endorsement for child survival had paid great dividends in Africa. The importance of family and kin is deeply embedded in all African cultures, and African leaders were quick to respond to the theme that Grant presented. The first African country to embark on a high-voltage immunization campaign was Burkina Faso in 1984: Operation Commando, launched by the President, succeeded in immunizing 1 million children within three weeks[58]. Shortly afterwards, African Ministers of Health declared 1986 'African Immunization Year'; and in 1987, the OAU summit in Addis Ababa declared that 1988 would be the 'Year for the Protection, Survival and Development of the African Child'. But political commitment to the cause, however essential as a precondition, could not of itself overcome the profound difficulties facing the average health care system.

In late 1987, Grant played an influential role in helping to launch a more practical African health initiative. Meeting under the auspices of WHO's Regional Committee for Africa, African Health Ministers discussed the crisis situation facing health care delivery in their countries and agreed upon a new approach towards the provision of 'universal' PHC. Called the 'Bamako Initiative', after the capital of Mali where the meeting took place, this approach had many radical, not to say risky, characteristics as well as a heavy initial price tag. It was bound to cause a new round of controversy among public health practitioners, and it did.

The centrepiece of the Bamako Initiative was the removal of responsibility for running and managing primary health services from the centre to the periphery—onto the shoulders of the communities the services were meant to serve. Thus far, Bamako was consistent with the 'Health by the People' thinking, which had been around since Alma-Ata in 1978. But its corollary was new: not only should the community run the services, but it should bear most of the burden of financing them[59].

This suggestion provoked considerable dismay. It ran right against the standard orthodoxy governing attitudes towards health care provision that held that a basic service is the right of every citizen and should be met from the public purse. Of all people for whom this principle might be relaxed, surely the villagers of Africa—whose disposable cash income was among the very lowest in the world—were the least suitable. To this, Bamako enthusiasts replied that what was actually happening at present was that these villagers were obliged to spend their precious resources on drugs and treatments because they had no alternative. Studies showed that, even in the poorest countries, between 5 and 10 per cent of family income was regularly spent on fees for doctors, clinics, traditional healers, mission hospitals and pharmacists[60].

Where public systems were starved of funds, health centres had no drugs to give their patients. In town, if they could afford to, people took their prescriptions to a pharmacy. In rural areas, they were usually forced to resort to local markets, quacks and unscrupulous drug peddlers. Often the remedies and brightly coloured capsules they purchased were overpriced and of dubious quality, and the patient could rarely afford a full course of treatment. Pragmatism suggested that if the household funds currently being wasted on inappropriate and ineffective cures could be better applied, patients' prospects of recovery would dramatically improve. On top of this, the revenue raised could—theoretically—subsidize preventive care, such as immunization, and curative care for the truly indigent. What equity demanded, however, was that if people were expected to pay for services, the income generated should remain under their control and not be sucked up the line to be spent on large city hospitals to which the rural poor had no access.

The ingredient that made Bamako appear viable was the existing international programme for 'essential drugs' operated under the auspices of WHO and Unicef. The start-up for the new type of programme in a given setting would involve external funding to pay for kits of generic drugs. These would be purchased and packaged internationally to reduce costs to a minimum. Many countries in Africa—Kenya, Mozambique, Tanzania, Ethiopia—were already taking advantage of this international effort to avoid dependency on expensive pharmaceutical branded products. Tanzania, for example, was receiving funding from the Danish International Development Agency (DANIDA) to pay for the regular distribution of sealed, pre-packaged kits purchased from Unicef containing items such as aspirin, anti-malarials, ORS sachets and broad-spectrum antibiotics[61]. The costs of these drugs came to less than $0.45 a head per year, and Tanzania was able to reduce its annual drug bill by half.

Bamako envisaged that similar kits could be supplied to rural health centres, for use by community health workers operating under the supervision of local health committees. More sophisticated packages of drugs and medicaments would be supplied to the next stratum of the health service—the district centre. Their sale would not only cover the cost of their replenishment, but also remunerate local health workers and pharmacists and meet other operational costs. Some experimental schemes in parts of West Africa were already being run along these lines. They had shown that it was possible to provide a service in which people had confidence, and which they were therefore prepared both to use and to pay for. One such scheme was the Pahou PHC project in Benin, which had been pioneering community part-financing of health since 1983. Within a few years, it had led to the creation of projects in many parts of Benin with locally managed pricing systems for drugs and user fees[62]. Another scheme in the Equateur province of Zaire was already covering 80 per cent of recurrent expenditures. Bamako banked on examples such as these, believing that decentralized, community-managed health care programmes could in time become mostly self-financing.

The Bamako Initiative got off to a much slower start than Jim Grant had hoped. To some extent, this was because insufficient time was allowed for it to be properly discussed and internalized within both WHO and Unicef. In 1988, the Unicef Executive Board proved very reluctant to agree to the setting up of a large global fund to finance Bamako Initiative projects, although both the Board and the World Health Assembly did endorse the Initiative and commit some funds. The brake that this necessarily exerted was a blessing in disguise, for it allowed time for both organizations to prepare the ground more thoroughly.

During 1988-90, Unicef's newly established Bamako Initiative Management Unit embarked on a careful process of building up experience and knowledge so as to ensure that this effort to revitalize Africa's PHC infrastructure would bear its promised fruit. A few countries were quick to adopt the principles of Bamako, with variations, and from these experiments much could be learned. A country to borrow from the experience in Benin and elsewhere and institute Bamako-style reforms was Guinea on the West African coast[63].

In 1986, an evaluation of the country's programmes for primary health care and immunization of children had revealed that the country's outlying health centres and clinics were extremely weak and understaffed, and that the immunization coverage rate was below 5 per cent. There were no vehicles, no petrol, no refrigeration units and no vaccines, and the health staff were demoralized and unpaid. A plan was drawn up to reactivate the entire system. The four areas needing immediate attention were transport and the distribution of drugs and medical supplies; training and counselling; follow-up and evaluation; and community participation and education. After an infusion of external funds, the hope was that the infrastructure would become self-sustaining as local communities took over much of the management and financing.

The architects of Bamako had taken as their starting-point the simple truth that no medical service, be it provided by a white-coated specialist in a fancy consulting room or a traditional herbalist behind a market stall, has any appeal to its potential customers unless it provides pills and potions, cures and remedies. This realization lay behind the emphasis on 'essential drugs'. In the event, reliable and affordable drugs proved to be very important in drawing people back to the health centres; but as important was the quality of the care and personal attention they received.

For this reason, the Guinean Ministry of Health, with Unicef's assistance, conducted a series of workshops to retrain their staff. Not only were they instructed in the management of new responsibilities, but they were encouraged to be much more responsive to their patients. Under the new system of community management, they would meet regularly with the local village health committee. Their joint decisions would cover matters such as planning the schedule for visits to outlying villages, when to hold immunization days and what prices to charge for drugs and treatments. No longer would isolated health workers, buried in the countryside, confront problems such as equipment failure or maternal indifference with helpless inertia. They could bring their problems to the management committee, and together they would solve them.

Guinea started to implement Bamako in one third of its 300 health centres in 1988. The monitoring of the first 30-odd centres in mid-1989 showed a strong increase in people's utilization of both curative and MCH services. The average drug cost was \$0.50 per treatment, with an average charge to the patient of $0.80. The proportion of local operating and drug costs recovered was 90 per cent on average[64]. By 1991, expansion had brought the number of centres under the Initiative to 192 covering a nominal 4 million people, although an independent evaluation suggested that only around one half of these were effectively reached as yet[65].

By 1990, four countries had made considerable progress in implementing Bamako Initiative programmes: Benin, Guinea, Nigeria and Sierra Leone. Their success helped to overcome some of the resistance to Bamako ideas that still lingered in certain quarters, and 24 other African countries began to develop similar programmes of health care reform. Throughout the continent, in response to economic crisis and the vicissitudes of structural adjustment, more and more countries were introducing user fees for health care. Where this was done without adequate planning and public education—as in Ghana and Swaziland—there had been a drop-off in the number of patients coming to government health centres to seek treatment[66]. The whole question of user charges was therefore still highly contentious.

However, where the quality of services had been improved along Bamako lines before the charges had been introduced, there had been no reduction in service usage. In Benin, on the contrary, patient visits to health centres had doubled in the year following the introduction of charges, and had increased by a further 25 per cent in the following year. Not only had more patients come for curative treatments, but there had also been more demand for antenatal services and other preventive services, and in many Bamako areas immunization coverage was as high as 70 and even 80 per cent for some antigens[67].

The adequacy of community financing for the long-term sustainability of Bamako-style services was still an open question. Although some preliminary results were encouraging and positive experiences of community health care management were accumulating, it was still difficult to say whether the central hypotheses of the Initiative—that health services would be better and cheaper if they were run and paid for by the community—were valid. In 1990, the Unicef Executive Board—whose members included several Bamako sceptics—agreed that an independent, external evaluation of the Initiative should be carried out. This evaluation was conducted by the London School of Tropical Hygiene and Medicine and paid for by the Overseas Development Administration of the United Kingdom (ODA), DANIDA, the Norwegian Agency for International Development (NORAID) and SIDA; its report, including case studies of five countries (Burundi, Guinea, Kenya, Nigeria and Uganda), was submitted to the 1992 session of the Executive Board[68]. By this stage, certain countries outside Africa—such as Honduras, Nepal, Peru and Viet Nam—had also started to utilize Bamako ingredients to revitalize or expand their health care systems.

The Bamako evaluation report was hesitantly positive. 'The overall conclusion is that much looks promising', it stated; but the wide range of forms the Initiative had taken in very different contexts made it impossible to generalize about overall success or failure, especially after such a short period. The implication was not that a perfect formula had been found for health care design in rural Africa, but that with careful adaptation to the local setting, the Bamako principles offered signposts to a new sense of health care direction. Although many critical issues were still in the exploratory and research phase, the general thrust was forward.

One positive development was that a 1992 World Bank report entitled *Better Health for Africa* seemed set to pave the way for a new alliance between the Bank, bilateral and multilateral agencies and NGOs to invest in Africa's health care systems; and that the Bamako experience would be used to help shape this new initiative to revitalize health care on the continent[69]. By this stage, over 20 million people in 26 African countries had theoretical access to more affordable health care because of Bamako-influenced restructuring. On the negative side, some African countries were becoming weighed down with a new health care disaster: AIDS. Only time would tell how far across the great landscapes of Africa the much-needed campaign for health care reform would travel.

When 1990, the year of UCI, was over, the moment had come to calculate what the 'biggest mobilization in peacetime history' had achieved for children.

At the beginning of the decade, around 5 million young child deaths were being caused annually by vaccine-preventable disease, and half a million children were being crippled by polio. The drive for 80 per cent vaccination coverage had approximately halved this toll[70]. Major efforts were still needed to pursue the goal of 80 per cent coverage not as an average but everywhere, as well as to eradicate polio and improve coverage for measles, still responsible for 1.5 million deaths a year. Nonetheless, immunization had been *the* public health success story of the decade. And the mobilization of national leaders around the campaign paved the way for their willingness to support the idea of a World Summit for Children and to agree to a much broader range of health, welfare and education goals.

However splendid the achievement, there was no room for complacency. Not only between regions but within regions, and even within countries, there were very wide coverage discrepancies—as, for example, in India. There had always been some risk attached to a drive that declared its aim as 'universal' childhood immunization: not only was the 80 per cent target far from universal, but the sense of accomplishment—should it be reached—might easily be followed by a relaxation of effort. Immunization had absorbed large quantities of national and international resources for health care; other demands were equally pressing; yet the job was far from done. The snare of unsustainability lay in wait, as did the prognostications of those who had never believed that anything resembling a vertical campaign could pave the way for effective delivery of integrated PHC.

Against its detractors, UCI 1990 had proved very resilient. This global disease campaign had turned out quite differently from any of its predecessors. The onslaught against the six 'killer diseases' added up to much more than immunization per se. Success or failure could not be judged on the narrow basis of how many antigens had been injected into how many tiny bodies. In trying to reach 80 per cent of all infants, health workers all over the world in their many different settings—on mountainsides, in jungles, on dusty plains, in urban slums—had begun to think of the population they served not as patients who walked through their clinic doors and whose appearance they should passively await. They had begun to think of their charges as the entire population of women and children in a given area. The concepts of enumeration and accountability, of reaching out to the unreached, of working in a complex and interdependent system to achieve a common end—all of these had begun to take root as a consequence of the immunization effort. In many places, a genuine transformation of the primary health care services from the perspective of both caregivers and care-receivers had begun.

Every district and subdistrict where immunization programmes had been mounted had experienced a strengthening of their health logistics system, which could now be used to add on other interventions. Similarly, almost every small health post and sub-centre now had an information collection and reporting system, which they could use to monitor and manage other types of maternal and child health care. For the first time, thousands of community health care workers in country after country existed who had a clear idea of exactly what they were trying to achieve and how to go about it. UCI 1990 had had so many multiplier and ripple effects in strengthening the primary health care delivery system in a large number of countries that most of the critics of a supposedly 'vertical' programme found themselves—at least temporarily—silenced.

In the post-UCI 1990s, Unicef's health brief for children broadened to give equal focus to other elements of the primary health care package. For a time, the immunization imperative had somewhat eclipsed organizational attention to even the other elements of GOBI, let alone to other important causes of child death, sickness and disability. In 1991, Unicef co-sponsored with WHO and UNDP the first International Consultation on the Control of Acute Respiratory Infections, the most acute of which—pneumonia—was regarded as responsible for 4 million child deaths a year[71]. Many countries began to introduce or upgrade acute respiratory infections (ARI) control programmes during the early 1990s, in some cases integrating the training of local health care workers and supply of antibiotics with Bamako Initiative or essential drugs programmes[72].

'Safe motherhood' also began to receive more Unicef attention: antenatal care to detect at-risk pregnancies began to be emphasized in 'EPI plus' PHC. Specific reductions in both ARI and maternal mortality were targeted by World Summit for Children goals. From the late 1980s onward, Unicef also began to be concerned with the impact of AIDS on children, less in the context of paediatric and medical care than in the social and economic context of orphanhood and parental destitution[73]. In the 1990s, the spectrum of Unicef health-related concerns broadened further to include more emphasis on the promotion of healthy adolescence and womanhood, especially in relation to sexual and reproductive health[74] (see also Chapter 7).

But immunization could by no means be abandoned. Besides the moral obligation of Unicef to stick with what it had begun, the Summit had set a goal of 90 per cent global immunization coverage by the year 2000, with measles and polio specifically targeted. One step already under way was the Children's Vaccine Initiative. Announced a few months before the Summit, this Initiative was backed by Unicef, the Rockefeller Foundation, UNDP, the World Bank and WHO, and involved governments, NGOs, industry and research groups. It was intended to apply modern science to the development of new vaccines—cheaper vaccines, simpler-to-administer vaccines, non-perishable vaccines. During its first two years, the Initiative examined such issues as vaccine quality control in countries that had just developed local production and explored the prospects for vaccines that would combine extra antigens with DPT, and ones that could deliver several doses in one shot by slow release[75].

The more important question as far as Unicef's country programmes were concerned was that of sustainability. Many of the 'extra mile' activities of 1990 had depended on conspicuously non-sustainable strategies: high levels of external funding, Unicef's temporary diversion of its own staff to problem locations, even short-term pay incentives for health workers and communities[76]. For many Unicef country representatives and health programme officers, there was much holding of breath over the next two or three years to see what would happen to immunization tallies now that the big thrust was over. In 1994, Unicef commissioned a group of independent experts to conduct a major inquiry into how immunization had fared post-1990: was coverage advancing or was it retreating?

There was no doubt that in Africa as a whole, and in countries with weak health networks or where there had been war or major economic problems, coverage had dropped[77]. This was particularly marked in West Africa. However, in the large majority of countries—70 per cent—coverage had been maintained[78]. Although only a few countries that had achieved UCI in 1990 had made further advances by 1993, 38 per cent of those that had not achieved it had done so. These results were reassuring; however, they did not indicate that the year 2000 target of 90 per cent would be easy to reach. There was no recipe for 'sustainability'; much depended on circumstances that varied widely from setting to setting, delivery system to delivery system, and many other factors. The evaluation brought out the wide fluctuations between countries and implied that meeting a global target was ultimately less important than making solid, sustainable and measurable gains against realistic targets set at the country level.

In one sense the report brought the immunization story full circle. It backed the view that the disease campaign—the old 'vertical' approach—was not the way forward. 'Over the long run, sustainability of immunization services and the expansion of primary care [will] best occur in the setting of fixed health centres with outreach activities.'[79] This conclusion underlined the built-in ambiguity of the 1980s immunization achievement. Almost all members of the professional public health community distrusted vertical approaches and disliked the military language of disease control 'attack'—just as they had before GOBI was ever invented. Yet the process that had brought a health care intervention within the reach of virtually every child on earth for the first time in history would never have occurred without the disease warrior éclat with which Jim Grant conjured worldwide political support for the UCI 1990 campaign. The tension between campaigners and consolidators will never finally depart the primary health care arena. Meanwhile, the quest for the spread and sustainability of basic health services for all women and children goes on.

Chapter 3

Unravelling the Nutrition Complex

During this century, the impact of war and famine on the innocent and helpless child has been a mainspring of international compassion. At times of natural and man-made disaster, the plight of the hungry child epitomizes human suffering and conjures extraordinary flows of public generosity. In the post-colonial era, the same image has been used to symbolize acute disadvantage in the countries of the developing world. But outside the provision of basic relief for emergency victims or in cases of extreme deprivation, what to do about hunger and malnutrition has been one of the most difficult of all human development problems to analyse and address. More mistakes, and more crass mistakes, have been made in this field than perhaps in any other. The reason is that hunger and malnutrition are symptoms not only of casualty and disaster-induced stress, but of a phenomenon far more fundamental, more complex, more varied in both its nature and its settings, and less temporary in its manifestations: poverty.

When Unicef came into existence, there was one central idea in its institutional mind: to provide extra rations—mostly milk, but some vitamins and cod-liver oil—for feeding hungry children in countries torn apart by war[1]. Its earliest form of programme assistance was cargoes of skim milk dispatched to Europe, and later further afield to Asia, Africa and Latin America, for use in schools, clinics and refugee camps as dietary supplements. This was a time when the particular alchemy of milk—its blend of animal fat and protein, vitamins and minerals—was believed to eclipse all other potential solutions for responding to the problem of the undernourished child. Unicef not only became a major recipient and exporter of US surplus dried skim milk to parts of the world where milk was in short supply, but also provided pasteurization and milk-drying plants to countries whose dairy industry was primitive. Unicef's early approach to child nutrition was encapsulated by the observation expressed in a 1951 report by a technical mission to Central America: 'Civilization follows the cow.'[2]

As the 1950s progressed, Unicef's attention became more focused on the needs of children in poor and backward parts of the world where neither cows nor dairy industries were much in evidence. For these environments, the perception of malnutrition in children became dominated by the results of a nutritional exploration of the African continent by leading WHO/FAO authorities[3]. The resulting study, published in 1952[4], concentrated on kwashiorkor, a condition in young children first described in West Africa in 1933 by a British physician, Dr. Cicely Williams. The cause of kwashiorkor was ascribed to lack of protein rather than to some more generalized cocktail of food and nutrient deficiency. 'Protein malnutrition' was now identified as the number one malnutrition 'disease' the international community ought to address, not only in Africa but elsewhere. It was talked of as an epidemic, like measles or diarrhoea. This implied that it could be treated by the consumption of a dietary medicine: protein. From this point on, the need to fill the 'protein gap' became the predominant thrust of WHO- and FAO-led nutritional policy.

In many tropical settings, this 'gap' could not be filled by milk—or not, at least, by locally produced milk. Accordingly, from the mid-1950s until the mid-1970s, a great deal of international resources and energy were expended on trying to develop cheap, locally manufactured protein-rich equivalents[5]. This was the heyday of belief in technology as a means of solving such world problems as hunger and this new slant on it: the 'protein crisis'. Unicef was deeply involved in the scientific quest centring on pulping and grinding oilseeds, peanuts, soya beans and fishes, conducted under the auspices of the UN Protein Advisory Group. But the experiments failed to produce foodstuffs that were viable. Most were either unpalatable or far too expensive; a few were even poisonous. Only in the late 1960s did Unicef, which had subsidized food plants in Indonesia, Algeria, Chile and Guatemala, finally reach the conclusion that to put a factory between the poor and their food supply simply put the food in question out of reach[6].

In the 1970s what was dubbed the 'Great Protein Fiasco' was finally exposed[7]. Nutritionists had reconsidered whether protein deficiency was really the demon of malnutrition, and most now concluded that calorie deficiency was at least as much to blame. Some eminent practitioners were now singing a very different song about the deficiencies of local diets. In most areas of the world some combination of familiar cereals and legumes, beans and pulses constituted a perfectly adequate diet for children as long as it was palatable and they ate frequently and were able to absorb enough of it. Only where the basic staple was a starchy root with almost no nutritional merit, such as cassava, was there a need for fundamental change in what went onto the young child's plate[8]. In this scenario, malnutrition was less a disease than a condition induced by inadequate feeding of the young child, partly out of ignorance, partly because of the household food shortages associated with seasonal change and with poverty.

If energy, not protein, deficiency was the main feature of childhood malnutrition, it followed that the problem must be addressed as one not only of public health, but also of outright lack of nutritious food. A new approach adopted by Unicef in the 1960s and 1970s—'applied nutrition'—was based on small-scale agriculture, livestock-raising and horticulture. It used appropriate technology—improved versions of traditional techniques—to increase poultry output and vegetable crops, store and preserve food better and cook it in fuel-efficient ways[9]. All of this was to be taught to mothers. In the more enlightened programmes, these measures were meant not only to help women improve their children's diets, but also to increase their incomes from expanded food production, processing and sale[10].

The early 1970s was a time of severe food shortage and famine in parts of Africa, notably in the Sahelian countries and the Horn in 1973-74. The fall of Emperor Haile Selassie, whose regime was destabilized by famine in the northern provinces of Ethiopia, drew attention to the role of political economy in hunger and malnutrition. The presence or absence of food on the child's metaphorical plate depended on a multiplicity of factors. At the UN, as the Protein Advisory Group was disbanded and a Subcommittee on Nutrition took its place, the place of nutritionists as key policy advisers was for a time assumed by economists and planners[11]. The connections between poor diet, gross poverty and underdevelopment were thrown into sharp relief by the 'world food crisis'—a temporary hiatus in supplies induced by the disastrous world harvest of 1972 (followed by another in 1974). This re-concentrated the global mind on the problem of world hunger and led to the 1974 World Food Conference.

From this point onward, hunger and malnutrition attracted considerable attention as the outcome of skewed political and economic power relations, and—as time went on—of environmental stress. Poor nutrition was seen as a disease of the international body politic, not of the small human frame. The emphasis was on the national food supply, on agricultural policies that ignored food production, especially by the smallholder and especially by women, in favour of exportable cash crops. In due course, analysts were to distinguish between *national* food security and *household* food security, and between the different factors that affected the distribution of food within different social units. In the meantime, Unicef continued to try to find ways to tackle poor child nutrition via interventions of various complementary kinds—public health, small-scale agriculture, appropriate technology, the organization of women's groups—which did not require waiting until the whole problem of poverty was solved.

In the late 1970s, the development of the primary health care approach and its absorption of the latest thinking on the diagnosis and treatment of childhood malnutrition brought nutrition back into the public health arena. The compounding biological relationship between poor nutrition and childhood disease became the outstanding theme: reducing the degree to which children suffered from common infections would reduce malnutrition, and vice versa. The impact of rapid urbanization and the advent of the 'consumer society' on child nutrition in some environments also were causing increasing alarm[12]. Slums and squalid shanty towns were rapidly springing up in all parts of the developing world, especially in Latin America. This was leading to a new phenomenon of childhood malnutrition: a significant decline of breastfeeding in favour of the bottle in environments where mothers had neither the wherewithal nor the knowledge to prepare adequate and safe solutions of infant formula[13].

By the 1980s, questions relating to feeding for the weanling and the toddler had become overshadowed in Unicef by other preventive activities, such as immunization, good hygiene and prompt attention to diarrhoeal infection, with which they were interconnected. Crude estimates doubled the risk of dying from a given disease for a mildly malnourished child, and multiplied it by 11 times for a severely malnourished child[14]. Micronutrient deficiencies were also now regarded as complicit: the risk of fatality from measles or diarrhoea rose by one third to one half in a child whose diet was short of vitamin A. Primary health care had hijacked primary nutritional care and suggested that they were one and the same thing.

The new emphasis on the 'nutrition-infection complex' had the effect of re-emphasizing malnutrition as a condition susceptible to preventive medical approaches: in some cases by micronutrient supplements such as vitamin A or by the reduction of the young child's burden of infection. Those related to other aspects of the food and nutrition conundrum, most of which were related to poverty, were not ignored by Unicef but were downgraded and tended to be addressed in contexts other than 'nutrition': within urban basic services or women's programmes, for example[15]. These other interventions included the reduction of women's working burden, the improvement of household incomes, the planting of fuel-wood, day-care services, appropriate technology for food conservation and processing, and the attempt to curb the inappropriate promotion and use of infant formula. In 1982, the new WHO-Unicef Joint Nutrition Support Programme (JNSP) was launched with $85 million from the Italian Government. Initiatives under this scheme fell mainly under the broad heading of PHC, but all types of nutrition-related programmes were eligible[16].

Within the GOBI strategy for Unicef's 'child survival revolution', also launched in 1982, the dual importance of nutritional support and disease control were recognized. Of the four ingredients, two—'B' for breastfeeding and 'G' for growth monitoring—were primarily about nutrition, even if by this time it was well established that nutrition was about a much broader range of issues than those encompassed by primary health care. Moreover, since impaired growth in the small child could be the outcome either of poor nutrition or of a bout of sickness, 'G' had some claim to be the linchpin of them all. Nutrition, in the form of advocating the widespread use of growth charts, was about to be given the full Unicef and Jim Grant campaigning treatment.

There was nothing novel about the concept of weight as a standard indicator of the small child's physical health and well-being. Unicef had been providing weighing scales to maternal and child health (MCH) clinics all over the developing world as a basic item of equipment for decades.

However, weighing began to take on a new dimension in the 1960s when Dr. David Morley, a leading tropical paediatrician, developed the idea of providing each child with a chart on which his or her weight-for-age could be systematically plotted month by month[17]. The chart was an aid to the health worker, for it made instantly visible a child's current growth status and showed that special care and feeding were needed long before the child became visibly malnourished. The 'monitoring' in 'growth monitoring' was, therefore, more than simple measurement: the chart was an early warning system of deteriorating child well-being. In the 1970s, Morley set up the Tropical Child Health Unit at the Institute of Child Health in London and preached the gospel of child growth monitoring far and wide[18].

In the era of primary health care—'Health by the People'—a new step was proposed. Every woman who sold or purchased food in the market was familiar with the use of weighing scales. So why not take the equipment and the organization needed for weighing children out of the clinic and place them in the community instead? Not only would proximity mean that the monthly weighing session was much easier for mothers to attend, but the community's operation of the programme would make the faltering growth of any infant a problem for them and the mother herself, not for some distant clinician, to address. Weighing would become a community activity in which mothers took part, not just a diagnostic tool for health care or nutritional surveillance services. Mothers and the community would themselves undertake corrective action, providing extra meals for preschool children, setting up income-generating projects, and putting into practice cookery and horticultural instruction.

One of the pioneering countries to develop a model for the mass growth monitoring of children at community level was Indonesia. In 1973, a national nutrition survey was undertaken to evaluate the previous decade's activities in applied nutrition[19]. The survey exposed an extent and severity of malnutrition entirely unexpected: half the country's children under five were undernourished to some degree. Over the next few years, an intersectoral board established by President Suharto explored ways of addressing the problem. Out of their efforts grew the Village Family Improvement Programme—its Indonesian acronym was UPGK—run almost entirely by nutrition volunteers, or 'cadres'. Traditional social gatherings of neighbourhood women evolved into occasions on which they weighed their children and shared information about child care. The 'weighing post'—a room borrowed for the purpose or a shelter erected from village funds—gradually became an established community fixture.

The moving force behind the UPGK programme was the PKK, the National Women's Welfare Association, to which all the wives of civil servants right down to village level belonged. The local PKK leaders selected around 20 young women volunteers from the village to undertake a five-day training course. Each weighing post was supplied with a robust beam-balance typically used in the market, from which the child was suspended in a trouser bag or village basket. The weight would be plotted on his or her KMS or 'Towards Good Health' card. Then a trained volunteer would discuss with the mother the child's growth pattern. She would stress the need for an upward curve. Where the curve flattened or dipped, advice would be offered about appropriate feeding and protective health care. The whole emphasis of the programme was on promoting behaviour among mothers that would ensure regular weight gain for every child in every month. The mother's ability to see on the KMS when her child's growth was faltering, and the motivation this would give her to take corrective action, were central to the programme's conceptualization[20].

Between 1979 and 1984, the programme's rate of expansion was nothing short of phenomenal. The Religious Affairs Ministry became involved, issuing injunctions to all village imams to encourage their congregations to have their children weighed; so did Indonesia's aggressive family planning movement. To growth monitoring was added contraceptive promotion and a nutritional first-aid package: iron-folate tablets to prevent maternal anaemia, high-dosage vitamin A against blindness and sachets of ORS to treat diarrhoeal dehydration. By 1984, monthly weighing and nutrition education activities had expanded to 80,000 posts located in 34,000 villages. Around 10 million children were being reached. In the same year Indonesia embraced the goal of UCI 1990. The power of village-based activities to reach such a large proportion of the population was now to be harnessed to the immunization target.

The UPGK weighing post was now upgraded into the *posyandu*, or village-based integrated service post. Here was a case in which the initial stimulation for community-based health care was provided by the desire to end child hunger and malnutrition, and other PHC actions were later added. For the first time, the Department of Health assumed responsibility for the *posyandus* and provided health workers to run them. At the same time, the programme was scheduled for a further massive expansion, to all 65,000 villages in all provinces. By 1988, 200,000 posts were serving 18 million children, over 80 per cent of the under-five child population in the country.

Although Indonesia's *posyandu* programme is regarded as a model of primary health care, its medicalization and the speed of expansion had some unfortunate consequences. In the past, the monthly sessions had been entirely run by volunteers—the ladies of the PKK and the nutrition cadres. The presence of a health worker at the *posyandu* downgraded the sense of community ownership and involvement—although it rapidly enhanced immunization progress. Children whose growth was faltering were referred to the health worker, sidelining the nutritional cadres. The *posyandu* sessions became mini-clinics conducted in the village. Nutritional advice became medical advice dispensed with tablets or even injections[21]. When this happened, the loss of the intimate chat between peers about the growth curve and what it meant reduced the KMS to a clinical measurement tool. Only if it was used properly, as a way of warning mothers where their children's well-being was headed, was its potential fully realized[22]. Sometimes the card was marked without any explanation to the mother, and the nutritional component of the *posyandu* session was no more than a ritualized talk about body-building foods.[23]

The experience of a Unicef-assisted programme in the Iringa Region of Tanzania with growth monitoring as a tool for growth promotion was much more reassuring. This programme, launched in 1982, was one of the very first to be funded by the Italian Government under the WHO-Unicef Joint Nutrition Support Programme.

Tanzania's political ideology, formulated by President Julius Nyerere in the Arusha Declaration of 1967, placed people at the centre of all development activity. The guiding philosophy of the Iringa Nutrition Programme (INP) echoed this fundamental principle, taking as its starting-point the notion that the agents of nutritional change must be the people themselves[24]. The INP assumed that rural families were unlikely to make a wholehearted commitment to any change in farming and nurturing practice unless they had first analysed their own problems and decided what action to take. The philosophy underlying the programme came straight from the 1970s era of alternatives with all its accompanying jargon: 'The nutritional status of an individual is the outcome of a complicated process embedded in the fabric of society and, therefore, sustained change in the nutritional status of a population can be brought about only by changing that process.'[25] In other words, this process—of how food was procured and what children ate—would only be lastingly changed by the people themselves on the basis of information about themselves that they found persuasive. In the villages of Iringa, growth monitoring was to become their key analytic tool.

The first year of programme implementation—1984—was the 'Year of Mobilization' in the 168 villages in the first programme area. MCH clinics were already conducting child-weighing sessions, but these did not reach more than one quarter of the villages. No discussion took place between health workers and the children's mothers about the implications of weighing for their health. So a film entitled *The Hidden Hunger* was made, explaining the nature of 'invisible' malnutrition and its causes. The film was taken around each of the villages as part of an orientation process. The revelation of hidden hunger was so persuasive that communities began to demand to see what was hidden—through growth monitoring. Volunteers were sent for training and Village Health Committees set up. A regular 'Village Health Day' was inaugurated, to be held once every three months, when children were weighed, immunizations given and other health activities undertaken. By the end of the year, around 80 per cent of all children under five out of a total of 50,000 had been enrolled. Already, levels of both severe and moderate malnutrition had begun to decline.

The centrality of growth monitoring in the Iringa programme went beyond its capacity to reveal hidden hunger and motivate action to prevent it. The information collected from the 'Village Health Day' formed the basis of a local data-gathering system on child well-being, which itself provided a basis for programme decision-making. Village leaders and health committees gave their full cooperation, and village members—schoolteachers, health workers, party secretaries—were trained to undertake the work of enumeration and analysis. After assessing the situation and analysing the growth data, they would decide what kind of action to take. This cyclical process became known as 'Triple A': assessment, analysis, action.

Proponents of the Iringa approach emphasized from the outset that good nutrition could never be the outcome of a pre-packaged set of interventions. Instead, a variety of options should be made available from which the village health workers and programme managers could choose. These included health care campaigns, water and sanitation provision, household food security initiatives and income generation. Certain households might need extra contact with village health workers; others—especially those headed by widows—might be suffering from a shortage of food; yet others might be guilty of poor domestic management of their food stocks or poor food hygiene. What was to be done and how it should be done, with and by whom, were subjects to address and resolve at village level, drawing on external advice and resources where appropriate. On the next round of assessment and analysis, the chosen course of action could be adjusted.

In 1986 an internal review of the programme concluded that the problem of malnutrition in Iringa seemed to be primarily one of inadequate child care[26]. Because of their heavy workload and need to be away in the fields, busy farming mothers were allowing long intervals to elapse between their children's meals. The low number of feedings and the bulkiness of the diet made it impossible for children to absorb enough nutrients. Once they realized that this was pushing their youngsters off the 'road to health', the villages responded by setting up their own day-care services to look after children and feed them while their mothers were out working. Communities committed their own resources, managing to pay a stipend to 70 per cent of their day-care attendants.

This change of direction illustrated the degree to which the thrust to improve their children's well-being had been taken into community ownership. Under the combined influence of mobilization, orientation and training, local people had been empowered to take action on their own behalf. The fact that they were prepared to spend their own money on stipends for voluntary workers, food for feeding programmes, kerosene, utensils and other programme ingredients was an indication that the strategy had worked. In 1987, the Iringa approach was extended throughout the Iringa region, and adopted for use in Unicef-supported basic services programmes in three other regions of the country. By the end of 1990, all other regions in Tanzania had begun to prepare similar programmes, and a number of external agencies besides Unicef—including the World Bank, the European Community and the Nordic bilateral agencies—had expressed their willingness to provide funds for programme replication.

In the meantime, an evaluation in 1988 showed conclusively that the impact on malnutrition in the original programme areas had been substantial[27]. Over a period of four years, severe malnutrition had dropped from 6 per cent to 2 per cent, and moderate—'hidden'—malnutrition from 50 per cent to 37 per cent. Elsewhere in Iringa the prevalence of severely malnourished children was still nearly 6 per cent. Only the programme could explain this marked difference. Over 85 per cent of mothers and children in the target area had been reached; four fifths of mothers questioned fully understood how the growth chart worked, and this understanding correlated with better growth among their children. This vindication of the Iringa approach was already having a profound impact on nutritional policy in Tanzania. It was to have a similar impact on nutritional thinking in Unicef itself.

By the mid-1980s, around 80 countries had introduced growth monitoring and growth charts as key ingredients of MCH programmes[28]. Increasingly, the chart was being used not only to record weight, but to keep track of immunizations and other aspects of the child's health progress and to convey to mothers health-promotive messages. In some areas, especially in drought-prone parts of Africa and other emergency zones, it had become a stock in trade of 'nutritional surveillance'. So widespread had growth monitoring become that the image of the child dangling in a trouser-bag from a scale tied to a roof beam or the branch of a tree had come to represent good primary health care in action.

However, the efficacy of growth monitoring as the linchpin of PHC was beginning to come under fire by child health specialists in India and elsewhere[29]. The key question concerned its impact. The time and energy expended on weighing was of questionable value if growth charts did not have the motivating power earlier attributed to them of changing mothers' child-feeding practices. Millions of mothers had become well used to the routine of weighing. However, studies showed that the capacity of illiterate women, and even of trained health workers, to understand a graph composed of a horizontal age and a vertical weight measurement, and to read and act upon the growth curve, had been overestimated[30]. A review in India complained that growth monitoring was cumbersome and expensive—$21 million for the scales alone in India—and that there was widespread error in filling in the cards[31]. Even where weighing had been done regularly and accurately, it appeared that health workers often saw growth charts as a method of selecting out the already malnourished for clinical treatment, not for facilitating the promotion of child growth maintenance at home.

The evidence that growth monitoring had little impact on nutritional knowledge or feeding behaviour was not by any means conclusive. Unicef's 1985 *State of the World's Children* report cited a study in Ghana that indicated that 66 per cent of near-illiterate mothers could interpret charts correctly. And contrary to the evidence that women did not understand the importance of the growth chart, in one health centre in the Philippines only 1 per cent of over 2,000 regularly attending mothers forgot to bring their cards—a success attributed to the education conducted at the clinic[32]. When used in tandem with education about feeding and diet, experiences in Jamaica and Narangwal in India showed that mothers managed their children's nutritional care far better with the aid of the chart[33], and within their existing resources, as they did in Iringa. This was not an issue over which it was possible to reach a cut-and-dried judgement. The most that could be said was that growth charts were not a quick-fix 'technology'; like many other public health interventions, growth monitoring needed careful adaptation to local circumstances and much depended on how it was done.

In 1987, a Unicef workshop on nutrition policy took place in Kenya. Many topics were discussed—including the nature of nutrition programmes and how nutrition related to the GOBI package for the 'child survival revolution', as well as the impact of macroeconomic policies on child nutrition[34]. Dissatisfaction was expressed with the way in which many Unicef programmes were addressing nutrition: in some countries growth monitoring within the GOBI formula had become a surrogate for a rounded approach[35]. Some Unicef programmes went so far as to address the problem of child malnutrition merely by purchasing scales and growth charts and giving them to the Ministry of Health with the wherewithal to train health workers in their use.

In the end the Kenyan meeting made no definitive judgement on growth monitoring, although it recognized the failings with which growth monitoring had often been introduced. However, the meeting did something much more important. It paved the way for an entirely new organizational approach to nutrition. This would begin with proper analysis of the causes of malnutrition in a given environment and be less constrained by the current child survival and GOBI agenda.

The enthusiasm for GOBI technologies had led to some overstatement by its advocates of the intrinsic value of weighing children and plotting charts. Once a more sober assessment had been made, there remained some ambiguity in Unicef's approach. On the one hand, substantial sums of money have been invested—so far unsuccessfully—in developing a new electronic scale in an attempt to bring the benefits of the micro-electronics revolution to bear on the problems of poor growth. On the other, Unicef has ceased to advocate growth charts and child weighing with the unhesitating enthusiasm of the early days of GOBI advocacy. This more restrained attitude reflected the reality that mass weighing and charting of babies is no nutritional panacea. It has to be accompanied by the absorption and use by mothers of the information thus gleaned, which cannot be guaranteed without the kind of comprehensive community-based effort invested in Iringa, Tanzania.

In the early 1990s, Unicef undertook a thorough evaluation of its growth monitoring experience and found the results very mixed. On the whole, support for growth monitoring was thought warranted where people understood the activity and wanted to know their children's nutritional status. Where this was not yet the case, it was suggested that scarce resources might be better spent on helping parents to understand the causes of malnutrition and take elementary protective steps relating to diet, feeding patterns or nurture[36].

The debate about how best to undertake growth monitoring will continue, but child weighing and the growth chart are here to stay. The system of issuing mothers with such a card is also now extensively used in some industrialized countries. As a stimulus to maternal involvement in preventive child health, growth monitoring has many distinguished followers. It also has an important role to play in data collection for the purposes of nutritional surveillance of the young child population. Like any technology, its capacity to fulfil its potential depends ultimately on its use and its users—both professional and lay.

'G' was one of the key nutritional components of GOBI; 'B' for breastfeeding was the other. As with growth monitoring, Unicef's endorsement of nature's perfect infant food as part of the child survival prescription had the merit of training a spotlight on it. However, not for some years was a device found for popularizing the promotion of breastfeeding in the same way that growth charts and ORS sachets were used to popularize 'G' and 'O'.

From their earliest support to child health care in the developing world, WHO and Unicef had stressed the supreme desirability of breastfeeding for newborn health. By the late 1960s, breastfeeding had begun to show a precipitous decline, especially in Latin America and parts of Asia. This was closely associated with the rapid growth of cities and the social and economic pressures of the urban lifestyle—particularly the need of many poor urban women to go out to earn. The maternal stampede towards the bottle not only attracted the attention of WHO, Unicef and concerned nutritional experts; during the 1970s, NGO activists around the world began loudly to accuse the leading infant formula companies of rating the sales promotion of their products above the well-being of infants in the developing world. For a poor mother in an urban slum, the cost of formula was prohibitive and the likelihood that her infant would receive the correct dilution with boiled water in a sterile bottle was negligible. Even if the feed was perfectly prepared, the squalor of the living environment put the child at constant risk of infection, a risk increased by the lack of health protection associated with bottlefeeding as compared with breastfeeding. The case against the infant food companies was that they were not taking the realities of bottlefeeding in these circumstances into account.

For some years, activist campaigning against food manufacturing corporations dominated the public perception of the breastfeeding debate. The companies formed their own producers' association and devised a code of marketing ethics, but this did little to abate the hue and cry against them. In 1979, WHO and Unicef held an international meeting on infant feeding in Geneva attended by representatives of governments, UN agencies and the infant food industry, as well as nutritional experts and NGO and consumer activists. The meeting adopted a wide-ranging set of recommendations on ways to promote breastfeeding, including the development of an International Code of Marketing of Breastmilk Substitutes. Such a Code was passed by the World Health Assembly in 1981.

Among the Code's provisions was a ban on all advertising and distribution of free supplies of breastmilk substitutes to health centres and hospitals. Except where used for medically approved purposes in the hands of health personnel, infant formula would no longer have a place in maternity wards and no company employees in nursing uniform would be permitted to darken their doors. At the same time, governments should actively promote sound infant feeding. The Code provided a policy check-list for countries trying to halt the growing ascendancy of bottle over breast. A government that tried sincerely to put it into effect would have to undertake legislation and commit itself to the promotion of breastfeeding as a public policy.

One of the first countries to adopt the Code was Brazil. Between 1940 and 1974, breastfeeding in the first month of life had declined from 96 per cent of mothers to 39 per cent, the results of which were showing up in malnutrition wards in many urban hospitals as well as in infant mortality statistics. A study in Recife showed that over half the deaths among infants aged between one and five months occurred among those who had been weaned before one month of age[37].

The Brazilian Ministry of Health believed that certain aspects of breastfeeding's decline were susceptible to programme intervention. These included the widespread ignorance about breastfeeding, its neglect in medical and nursing training and the lack of nursing facilities for working mothers. In 1981, a programme primarily inspired by the WHO/Unicef Geneva meeting of 1979, and keenly supported by Unicef, was launched. Its purpose was to reinstate exclusive breastfeeding in the first four to six months of life as the optimal route to infant health.

The campaign took a leaf out of the formula manufacturers' book by deploying the latest in modern marketing techniques[38]. The use of advertising and mass media to support a social programme in this way—particularly one featuring an intimate part of the human body—was relatively uncharted territory. Careful research went into developing its messages. Findings showed that low-income urban mothers often abandoned breastfeeding out of a sense of personal inadequacy. So what a mother needed was not an admonition to breastfeed, but reassurance. She had to be encouraged to believe: 'You *can* breastfeed.'

In March 1981 the programme was launched with a national campaign on television, on the radio and in the press using space and air time paid for by the Government. The messages—in spots, films, women's shows, variety acts, soap operas—were carried by nearly 100 TV stations reaching 13.5 million households and by 600 radio stations. Messages carried on lottery tickets, electricity bills and bank statements all over the country helped to sensitize the public. Following the launch, some 30,000 health workers were exposed to breastfeeding training. For six subsequent months in three high-priority cities, free air time was provided by TV Globo, Brazil's leading broadcasting network. The involvement of the media moguls of the private sector in this campaign set a precedent that has been greatly to the benefit of subsequent child survival activities in Brazil.

By 1983 a Brazilian version of the Marketing Code for Breastmilk Substitutes had passed into law, the medical profession had lost its previous indifference as to whether a mother breastfed her infant or not and the cultural environment had ceased to be formula-permissive. These positive signs notwithstanding, the results of the campaign were not as decisive as its enthusiasts had wished. There were local increases in both prevalence and duration of breastfeeding in the big cities. But the underlying social and economic trends that were prompting its decline—rapid urbanization, changes in family structure, industrialization, female employment—were all pulling in the wrong direction.

However, the Brazilian programme was very important internationally in pioneering social marketing techniques and illustrating that an extensive range of actions could be taken to dispel ignorance about breastfeeding and to motivate mothers. By 1988, over 130 countries had taken some action—albeit often not very effective action—to control the marketing of infant formula; a few had passed the Code into law[39]. But there was little sign that the war against the bottle was being won. Gradually, the battleground began to shift away from the advertising hoardings into maternity and infant wards.

In many parts of the developing world it was no longer the case that the majority of births were taking place at home, outside formal health care institutions. In Latin America and much of Asia, and even in some parts of Africa, the majority of urban women were now choosing to give birth in a modern medicalized setting[40]. In most maternity hospitals, routine practices surrounding birthing and post-partum care imitated their counterparts in the West. Most of these practices were designed to make life easier for the nursing staff rather than the nursing mother. Some—such as the separation of mother and infant immediately after delivery—actually interfered with the successful initiation of lactation and breastfeeding. Others, such as the routine provision of bottles for supplementary feeds, endorsed and opened up the formula route. By the time a mother discovered the costs and hazards of hygienic bottle-feeding, she was irredeemably hooked.

A pioneer in modifying the hospital environment was Dr. Natividad Relucio-Clavano of Baguio General Hospital in the Philippines[41]. Until she took charge, Baguio's maternity facility had been run along the lines of a Western teaching hospital. Newborn babies were taken from their mothers at birth, kept in the nursery and routinely given bottle feeds. Under Dr. Clavano's regime, nursing began in the delivery room, babies 'roomed-in' around the clock with their mothers and artificial feeds were banished. Within two years the newborn mortality rate dropped by 95 per cent and infant infection in the nursery by 88 per cent. Dr. Clavano's success with 'baby-friendly' maternity care became widely known among international child health specialists during the 1980s.

In July 1990, a new meeting on the promotion of breastfeeding was convened by WHO and Unicef (with USAID and SIDA) at the International Child Development Centre (ICDC) in Florence, Italy. During the previous decade, new scientific interest in breastfeeding had prompted a flurry of research into all its aspects, including its immunizing and fertility regulation capacities. WHO now maintained that a bottle-fed baby in a poor community was 15 times more likely to die from diarrhoeal disease and 4 times more likely to die from pneumonia than an exclusively breastfed baby[42]. Although the benefits of breastfeeding became every day more apparent, bottlefeeding was not yet seriously relaxing its hold, and a new effort was needed.

The ICDC meeting issued the 'Innocenti Declaration'[43]. This called for the creation of an environment 'enabling all women to practice exclusive breastfeeding, and all infants to feed exclusively on breastmilk from birth to four to six months of age'. From this point onward, the breastfeeding lobby began to gain a new lease of life. In 1991, a new international NGO consortium was formed: the World Alliance for Breastfeeding Action (WABA)[44]. A few months later the International Association of Infant Food Manufacturers was persuaded to stop the distribution by its 29 members of free and low-cost breastmilk substitutes to hospitals and maternity centres throughout the developing world by the end of 1992. Although this goal was not entirely achieved, and violations of the Code of Marketing of Breastmilk Substitutes continued to be reported in 1994, the process of tightening up on infant formula marketing gained new momentum from this time onward[45].

In association with this development, the idea also emerged of a campaign directed at hospitals to encourage them to become 'baby-friendly'—a term coined by Unicef's Jim Grant. Special recognition would be given to hospitals that followed joint guidelines on maternity practice developed by WHO and Unicef and popularized as the 'Ten Steps to Successful Breastfeeding'. This amounted to a second 'Code' relating to breastfeeding. It required that every maternity facility have a written breastfeeding policy in which all health staff were trained. Everything possible should be done to inform mothers of the advantage of breast over bottle and to help them to establish and maintain lactation. Babies must not be separated from their mothers after birth, and newborn infants must receive no food other than breastmilk unless medically indicated. Rooming-in should be the rule, as should breastfeeding on demand, and hospitals should foster breastfeeding support groups and refer mothers to them upon discharge.

During 1991, the anniversary year of the passage of the original Code, the ground was prepared for the launching of the Baby-Friendly Hospital Initiative (BFHI). This was also the year following the World Summit for Children, whose Declaration had included a provision supporting breastfeeding. As a part of Summit follow-up activities, 12 countries distributed between Africa, Asia and Latin America—including both Brazil and the Philippines—were approached by Unicef and agreed to take the baby-friendly lead[46]. All received intensive support during the next few months to ensure that, by February 1992, a number of hospitals would put the 'Ten Steps' into effect and could be classified 'baby-friendly' by an independent expert panel. Unicef paid for health staff training in lactation management and helped persuade infant food manufacturers operating in the countries concerned to stem the flow of free supplies into hospitals and clinics.

One of the countries to take up the baby-friendly gauntlet was Mexico. A national health survey carried out in 1988 had found that 81 per cent of mothers started out breastfeeding, but that three months after the birth of their children only 10 per cent were feeding by the breast alone. In May 1991, a National Commission for the Promotion of Breastfeeding was created by the Minister of Health. The following month, during a meeting called by President Salinas to evaluate Mexico's progress in achieving the World Summit for Children goals, Jim Grant proposed that Mexico now develop a baby-friendly initiative[47].

With the support of Unicef, the Ministry of Health set up a working group whose first decision was to broaden the concept to include mother-friendly actions as well. To the 'Ten Steps' another 15 were added, focusing on maternal and child health in general. Thus was launched '*hospitales amigos del niño y de la madre*'—hospitals that were friendly not only to babies, but to mothers, communities and society as a whole. The commitment of the Mexican Maternal and Child Health teams at national level was wholehearted. The programme moved into action in September 1991 and went ahead rapidly. By the end of the year, 46 hospitals had enrolled and several had been designated *amigos* in time for the global launch of the BFHI, which took place in March 1992 in Washington, DC.

From the start the Mexican Ministry of Health wanted all hospitals to join the Initiative, not merely those under its own supervision. It therefore set up a mechanism to coordinate the actions of all nine Mexican institutions that administer hospitals. The Ministry also wanted the Initiative to be country-wide, so one hospital in the capital city of each of Mexico's 31 states was selected to become a *hospital amigo*. By September 1992, 214 hospitals and maternity centres out of a total of 700 in the country had joined in. In addition, the 'Twenty-five Steps' had been widely disseminated throughout the primary health care network: in Mexico, hospitals and maternity wards were only the initial target of the campaign.

In Zacatecas, the capital of one of the northern states, all public hospitals have been certified mother- and baby-friendly. The hospital run by the IMSS, the Mexican Institute of Social Security, was certified *amigo* in December 1993. In its maternity unit, visual reminders constantly endorse breastfeeding: posters, red no-entry signs for bottles and teats, a video in the waiting-room. Mothers recovering from childbirth recount without embarrassment the means by which they established lactation and proudly show off their skill. Local medical directors state that the hardest challenge was to bring hospital staff fully on board. The 'culture of the *biberón*' was so well established in professional mentality that there was initially a lot of resistance. Now that attitudes have changed, hospitals are running outreach programmes to extend success through the rural health care network.

By the end of 1994, some 748 hospitals and maternity centres were participating in the Mexican BFHI Initiative and 224 had received their *amigo* plaque. By this time, the number of countries to have joined the Initiative had risen to 171, and the number of hospitals to have received a baby-friendly plaque to over 3,000[48]. Some 10,000 maternity facilities had made a public commitment to achieve baby-friendly status by the end of 1995. These included 230 hospitals in industrialized countries, for the BFHI goals apply equally in rich as well as poor countries. Although the last two decades have seen a wider appreciation worldwide of the properties of breastmilk as a perfect infant food, a very large number of hospitals in Europe and North America as well as in the less industrialized regions have still to accord lactation and its management the priority they deserve.

If the technological fix as a method of solving the mythical 'protein gap' became discredited in the 1970s, it gained credibility during the 1980s and 1990s to address a different set of age-old nutritional problems: micronutrient deficiencies. The main dietary culprits of a range of debilitating and disabling conditions threatening up to one third of the world's population were a vitamin and two minerals: vitamin A, iron and iodine.

Of the 'big three' micronutrient deficiencies, lack of iron—responsible for around half the world's 1.5 billion cases of anaemia—was the most prevalent[49]. Of these cases, 50 per cent occurred in pregnant women and preschool children. Not only did the condition induce tiredness and lassitude, making it harder to fulfil the daily work burden and to be alert, but anaemia in an expectant mother was a principal cause of low-birth-weight babies, of which 23 million were born annually. In the mother, severe anaemia was thought to be responsible for 20 per cent of deaths in childbirth and pregnancy. In the infant and child, iron deficiency weakened the body and reduced cognitive development. The simplest remedy for most of this unnecessary death and impairment was the distribution of iron-folate tablets to mothers as a stock ingredient of basic antenatal care. This was an important strand of the WHO-led 'Safe Motherhood' initiative, launched in the late 1980s[50].

Shortage of vitamin A has long been associated with an eye affliction—xerophthalmia—which affects around 14 million children under the age of five[51] and causes blindness in around 250,000 every year[52]. Although in the postwar period, the distribution of cod-liver oil—rich in vitamin A—had been widely promoted to protect the young child's health, the full significance of vitamin A deficiency in the small and growing body were not appreciated until the early 1980s. It transpired that even relatively mild deficiency in vitamin A impaired a child's immune system, increasing vulnerability to sickness and death. This was revealed almost haphazardly during the analysis of data from a large-scale study in Indonesia in 1982[53]. Evidence suggested that the prevention of vitamin A deficiency would not only reduce blindness from xerophthalmia, but could reduce the overall death rate among young children by between one fifth and one third. This discovery, when reported in the professional medical journals, was greeted with disbelief. It seemed too good to be true that up to 3 million children's lives could be saved every year by something so cheap and simple as a course of vitamin A tablets costing only a few cents. But further studies bore out the finding: deaths among Tanzanian children hospitalized with measles fell by half when vitamin A capsules were administered[54].

For many years, nutrition educators had been encouraging mothers to feed their children items rich in vitamin A, especially carrots and green leafy vegetables. Not only was this a slow and uncertain remedy, especially for children in families deeply stressed by poverty, but nutritional scientists also began to question whether it was possible to make up sufficient lost ground by this method[55]. In the industrialized world, the problem was partially solved by the fortification of common foods, such as margarine, with vitamin A. In Guatemala, one of the earliest countries in the developing world to attempt a similar strategy, sugar has now been similarly fortified. Unlike the fanciful experiments with protein-rich foodstuffs in the 1960s in which the food industry was unwilling to invest, there seems a very good prospect that their cooperation in eradicating vitamin A deficiency can be successfully solicited. One company in the Philippines has recently increased by 10 times the vitamin A content of its low-cost margarine, and another major multinational is considering the same step in a number of African countries[56].

The third major micronutrient deficiency was lack of iodine. Around 1.5 billion people lived in areas where their dietary intake of iodine was inadequate, according to WHO[57]. As a result, between 200 and 300 million people suffered from goitre: an enlargement of the thyroid gland which caused an ugly swelling in the neck[58]. Worldwide, iodine deficiency caused mental retardation in 20 million people, of whom 6 million suffered the acute mental disability of cretinism[59]. A child born to a mother with goitre had a considerable chance of suffering from physical or mental disability, including speech and hearing defects. Grouped together, these conditions were known as iodine deficiency disorders (IDD).

A cheap and effective solution to IDD lay ready to hand: another food fortification 'fix', this time of table salt with iodine. Salt is an item of diet purchased even by the poorest family. The iodization process was relatively cheap and so—theoretically—a kilo of iodized salt should cost only a few extra cents. If countries' entire salt supplies could be 'spiked', the world's leading cause of mental retardation could be removed at a stroke. However, this was not as straightforward as it sounded. Many of the areas whose people suffered from iodine deficiency were mountainous or flood prone: the iodine supply had leached from the soil over generations. These areas, almost by definition, also tended to be remote. Their inhabitants did not buy their salt from the kind of retail outlet supplied by food marketing and distribution systems. Nor were their health problems of heartfelt concern to city-dwelling leadership elites.

When Unicef began to support IDD control in the 1960s, the full ramifications of these problems were not widely understood. This was the heyday of high-tech nutritional fixes via food processing, and salt iodization plants were provided to several countries in Asia and Latin America[60]. These efforts were mostly ineffective in putting paid to IDD. Salt manufacture was a cottage industry employing thousands of people in countries such as India and Indonesia. A farmer tended a salt 'mine' (a shallow pond dug out when the water evaporated) by the edge of the sea or a salt-water lake; this salt harvesting was often undertaken in the same way that a pasture-dwelling counterpart would tend a few sheep as a sideline. Salt raked up and sold in sacks by small producers was outside the reach of government control and far from any processing technology. Even in the early 1990s, with salt harvesting as a cottage industry everywhere declining and the quantities produced occupying a relatively small place in the market, over 70 per cent of all salt producers in the IDD-vulnerable parts of the world were classified as 'small'. Not all could be made to iodize salt, nor would it be just or desirable to force them all out of business[61].

In the early 1980s, Bolivia was a textbook example of a country with very serious IDD that simultaneously enjoyed all the topographical, social and salt-manufacturing problems that typically confront IDD control. One of the poorest countries in South America, all of its territory—from the high Altiplano to the sparsely populated Amazonian jungle—had soil deficient in iodine. The majority of the population lived in rural areas where there were few roads and no regular transportation. The most inaccessible mountain-top communities were the very ones hardest hit by IDD.

Reports of an unusually high incidence of goitre and cretinism in Bolivia dated from colonial times[62]. In the 1960s, the Ministry of Health had taken a few tentative steps to address what had previously been regarded as an insignificant natural phenomenon. Various laws were passed declaring that all salt should contain iodine and that everyone should consume iodized salt; but efforts to enforce these laws—or to create the circumstances in which they could be enforced—were desultory. In 1983, the Ministry of Health created a new entity in the National Office of Food and Nutrition to revive the fight against IDD: PRONALCOBO. The country's difficult terrain, underdeveloped infrastructure and a history of poorly planned programmes all had to be confronted. PRONALCOBO was strongly supported by WHO and Unicef and funded by the Italian Government under the Joint Nutrition Support Programme.

One of the programme's immediate actions was to distribute iodine capsules to 2 million people in the most affected areas. This short-term measure of protection against goitre would last for up to three years, so it was seen as a temporary measure to be superseded by salt iodization. But in 1983, there were only two salt iodization plants in Bolivia, and the salt they produced met less than 10 per cent of national consumption. Its price was high; at $.75 per kilo it cost five times more than common salt. The rest of the salt industry in Bolivia was extremely dispersed since there were salt deposits in all parts of the country, and manufacture was mostly conducted by *campesinos* using traditional evaporation techniques.

PRONALCOBO's first priority was to increase the production of iodized salt and reduce its price, without forcing the *campesino* producers out of business. As it was impracticable to iodize the salt of every individual *campesino*, PRONALCOBO encouraged them to form cooperatives. This was not easy: members had to learn how to run their enlarged businesses. Yet some not only became viable, but managed to introduce a number of improvements: piped-water supplies and preschools. Their range of products also expanded, with PRONALCOBO's help, to include iodized block salt—salt in its traditional unpackaged variety. Towards larger salt manufacturers PRONALCOBO took a different approach, offering loans and subsidies to underpin the economics of iodization. By the end of 1986, 14 iodization plants were producing enough salt to cover nearly half the estimated human consumption in the country. After this, the participation of private industry grew rapidly.

Production, however, was only one side of the picture. As important was the need to smooth the path of cheap iodized salt into the commercial market. As a result of two marketing studies, PRONALCOBO decided to take its most radical step: it would itself enter the salt marketing business directly, in order to exert a stabilizing influence on prices and to bring the new salt to those who purchased their supplies in remote *campesino* markets. So a National Salt Commercialization Company (EMOCOSOL) was set up as a private limited corporation within the Ministry of Health, with participation from both WHO and Unicef. This marriage between 'social' and 'commercial' objectives was surprisingly effective.

EMOCOSOL set out to work closely with the salt cooperatives, providing them with technical support and guaranteeing the sale of their salt on the market. It also purchased—sometimes confiscated—quantities of common salt and iodized it at its own manufacturing plant in La Paz. In rural areas where the normal system of *campesino* trade was by barter, EMOCOSOL accepted goods and resold them in payment for salt. It set up its stalls at religious and cultural festivals, and developed sales strategies for different segments of the consumer market. In the process, it became the largest salt marketing company in Bolivia. It was able to set quality standards, and intervene to push prices up or down to ensure the salt market's smooth transition into 'iodized only' for all human and livestock consumption.

The impact of PRONALCOBO's operations was dramatic. A 1989 survey showed that the prevalence of goitre among schoolchildren had dropped from 65 per cent in 1983 to around 20 per cent, and that the incidence of new cases of cretinism was near zero[63]. By early 1994 the production of iodized salt was sufficient to cover 90 per cent of human consumption in the country, at prices nearly equal to those of common salt. All elements of subsidy previously provided via Unicef had ceased. The market had become 'pure' and self-sustaining. Only the most remote bastions of iodine deficiency in the high Bolivian mountains had yet to tumble.

In 1986, the international drive to bring IDD under control entered a new phase: the International Council for Control of Iodine Deficiency Disorders (ICCIDD) was established. Its purpose was to develop a network of expertise to support the growing number of national IDD control programmes and undertake other international activities to bring IDD to an early end. In 1989, Unicef approved a major programme of support to the ICCIDD. A number of other international programmes and bodies now entered the IDD fray, including the

Centers for Disease Control in Atlanta and the Task Force for Child Survival. Political leaders also were beginning to attach themselves to the IDD cause: the profound implications of iodine deficiency for the national IQ were found to be remarkably persuasive. A much bigger IDD ball was finally rolling.

The World Summit for Children in September 1990 set three goals for the reduction of micronutrient deficiency by the year 2000. These were the virtual elimination of IDD; the virtual elimination of vitamin A deficiency and its consequences, including blindness; and the reduction by one third of the 1990 levels of iron deficiency anaemia in women. Almost exactly 12 months later, an international conference was held in Montreal, Canada, entitled 'Ending Hidden Hunger'. Convened by WHO and Unicef, and co-sponsored with CIDA, USAID, FAO, UNDP and the World Bank, the conference attracted 300 senior officials and technical specialists from 50 countries[64]. Out of it came a new 'Micronutrient Initiative' and the establishment of a new international body to tackle micronutrient malnutrition, based at the International Development Research Council (IDRC) in Ottawa and supported by CIDA, UNDP, IDRC and Unicef[65].

Just a few days before, Jim Grant and WHO Director-General Hiroshi Nakajima had certified the achievement of 80 per cent immunization coverage of children worldwide. The triumph of UCI 1990 was fresh in many minds. The degree of energy and political will now accumulating behind the micronutrient bandwagon was considerable. In 1993, a mid-decade goal associated with IDD was set: not elimination of the disorders but universal salt iodization—USI. So popular was this goal that it soon began to seem like the UCI of the 1990s.

In 1990, as a result of the process originally triggered at the nutrition workshop convened in Kenya in 1987, the Unicef Executive Board was invited to endorse a new Unicef nutrition strategy[66]. Between 1975 and 1990, the prevalence of protein-energy malnutrition among children in the developing world had dropped in every region except sub-Saharan Africa. But the hungry and malnourished child was far from being relegated to the pages of history. Around 190 million children worldwide aged less than five were underweight and 20 million suffered from severe protein-energy malnutrition[67]. Child malnutrition, therefore, remained a problem of huge dimensions, and some re-thinking and re-energizing on this front were felt to be due.

For some years Jim Grant had been hoping for a low-cost technological breakthrough in the nutrition field—something equivalent to ORS in public health, based on improved crop strains and simpler cultivation. This would enable the attack on malnutrition to be mounted from an agricultural, as well as a disease reduction, direction and the latest scientific research breakthroughs to be put to popular use. Grant himself had been closely involved with the introduction of Green Revolution technology into Turkey in the 1960s and was very aware of what such advances could bring[68]. In pursuit of this goal, Unicef embarked in the late 1980s on a collaboration with the International Institute of Tropical Agriculture in Ibadan, Nigeria, to disseminate in various African countries a better-yielding, quicker-growing and more resistant strain of cassava.

But this venture was controversial within Unicef. Its social goal—better child nutrition, improved household food security, increased incomes for women cassava farmers and processors—was never clearly established[69]. And its starting point—an increased yield of one of Africa's least nutritious staples—attracted some derision. Unicef's senior nutrition adviser—Urban Jonsson—was currently engaged in an effort to re-establish the problem of malnutrition as one of great complexity, not as a subset of agriculture and public health that could be remedied by the equivalent of GOBI-type interventions associated with the plant and animal kingdom. Coming from Tanzania where he had been Unicef's country representative during the experiments with nutritional improvement in Iringa, Jonsson was determined to re-establish the view that people's food intake had to be examined from a layered perspective that included the distribution of power and resources both within society and within the household, between haves and have-nots, males and females, young and old.

This was the central theme of the new strategy for nutrition submitted to the Unicef Executive Board in 1990. The policy paper traced the history of the 'nutrition problem' and the consecutive preoccupations of its protagonists—from vitamin deficiencies, to protein deficiency, to multisectoral nutrition planning, to the 'nutrition-infection complex' within the 1978 doctrine of primary health care[70]. It suggested that the location of nutrition within the PHC hearth had produced a number of successful 'nutrition-oriented' programmes—many of which had been supported under the Italian-funded WHO/Unicef Joint Nutrition Support Programme; but it also asserted the need to remove nutrition from under the shadow of the health sector in which it had become somewhat marginalized. The reason for the success of these 'nutrition-oriented' programmes was attributed to non-health service factors: to their emphasis on the community, on monitoring nutritional status at community level, on enabling the community to decide what to do, on providing services wanted and appreciated by the community[71]. Although unacknowledged, the thinking in the paper was strongly influenced by the experience of the JNSP-supported programme in Iringa, Tanzania. The conceptual framework developed at Iringa for analysing the causes of malnutrition in the community, and the Triple A approach as the way to resolve it—assessment, analysis, action, to be undertaken in and by the community—were presented as the centrepiece of the new strategy.

Although care was taken to give due respect to disease control as a means of reducing malnutrition and associated child deaths, the strategy was in other ways the antithesis of GOBI-style prescriptions. Its philosophical thrust was a specific rejection of pre-ordained packages of technical interventions. Instead, it proposed that households, communities and officials at district and national levels be taught how to assess and analyse the problem of malnutrition in their midst, and thereby identify the most appropriate actions to undertake. In this scenario, the *context* in which action to improve nutrition would be taken was all-important. By implication, improvement in the whole quality of family life—including the reduction of poverty, or 'development'—was not something that could be done to people or for them or merely with their duly mobilized cooperation; it had to be done via their empowerment. Unless they were central to its achievement, development was not sustainable.

The conceptual framework at the heart of the new nutrition strategy, independently of its utility in the practical task of programme development, served an important function. It synchronized all past and present strands of nutritional thinking and described their relationships to one another. It did this by disaggregating the causes of malnutrition into three tiers: 'immediate', 'underlying' and 'basic'. Immediate causes were illness and inadequate food; underlying causes included family and food supply circumstances, and the presence or absence of services such as health care and environmental sanitation; basic causes were the structural and societal causes, such as pricing policies, agricultural investment policies and trends that marginalized the poor, the landless, the female and other disadvantaged groups. While basic causes would need to be tackled at the national and political levels, there was a great deal that communities—with the right kind of facilitating inputs—could do about the immediate and underlying causes of malnutrition.

Underlying causes were grouped into three main clusters: the absence of services that would permit the control of infection in children; shortage of food in the household; and insufficient care. At one step removed from the actual manifestations in the body, therefore, the dyad of infection and lack of dietary energy was transformed into a trinity of causal agents for childhood malnutrition, including care prominently for the first time. In this context, care meant exclusive breastfeeding in the early months of life, regular and frequent feeding, knowledge and facilities to prepare suitable food, washing and keeping the child's environment clean, as well as time spent with the child on play and other forms of stimulation and cognitive learning.

This was the first time for some years that a major Unicef policy had been couched in terms of 'people's participation' and 'bottom-up' approaches popularized during the 1970s. The language of 'participation' and, more recently, of 'women's empowerment' had been co-opted by the exponents of the 'child survival revolution'; but its use was synthetic, as in the 'empowerment of women to breastfeed'[72]. The nutrition paper was much more radical in intent; it expected decision-making power to be vested in the community. It even took as its starting-point the notion that freedom from hunger was a basic human right and cited the newly passed Convention on the Rights of the Child—the first Unicef programme policy to do so. Despite its rejection of universalist and prescriptive approaches, it set out nutritional goals for the 1990s: measurable reductions in protein-calorie malnutrition and micronutrient deficiencies. It proposed that the ways in which goals and targets should be reached would require local adaptation and local participation in the planning process.

Because it was so unconventional by the current standards of Unicef policy statements, this document was a landmark. Its emphasis on situation analysis based on community self-assessment as the springboard for action, and on the need for constant measurement and reappraisal, was an attribute of the programming process with far wider implications than for nutrition interventions alone.

Within a few months of the Board's agreement to the policy, the World Summit for Children had taken place. The acceptance by world leaders of a set of goals for children and development in the 1990s, which included targets not only for reductions in protein-energy malnutrition and micronutrient deficiency but for many other areas involving 'food, health and care', was to be the dominant influence on the Unicef policy agenda for the next several years. The need to reconcile what appeared to be opposite approaches—a goals-led strategy established at the international level and a strategy driven by community assessment, analysis and empowerment—was therefore first identified within the context of nutrition policy. Whether or not there was an inherent tension that needed to be resolved, nutrition-related activities advanced on a variety of fronts in the pragmatic style typical of Unicef. Undoubtedly, the policy paper of 1990 had given the issue of child hunger and malnutrition a higher profile than it had enjoyed for a considerable time. However, the proportion of Unicef resources allocated to nutrition remained constant over the next few years, at just over 30 per cent[73].

During 1991, preparations began for an International Conference on Nutrition (ICN) to be organized by FAO and WHO in Rome in December 1992. This was to be the most important international gathering to discuss nutrition since the World Food Conference in 1974. To its understandable chagrin, Unicef was not invited to be a full sponsoring partner[74]. Nor—initially—were positions already established in the UN Subcommittee on Nutrition, in which Unicef played a significant part, taken fully into account.

However, after some negotiation, Unicef did become involved in the preparatory activity for the ICN at country and regional levels. Its key concern was to ensure that what happened in the lead-up to, and as an outcome of, the Conference did not set governments off along some other track than that already agreed at the World Summit for Children. The Declaration emanating from that meeting had led to the development of follow-up national programmes of action in 135 countries in just over two years[75]. The goals already agreed upon—for reduction of malnutrition and of low-birth-weight babies, for universal iodization of salt and control of IDD, for support to breastfeeding and for the spread of baby-friendly hospitals—had to be echoed by the Conference if future confusion about nutrition-oriented support provided to governments was to be avoided. Unicef's insistence that there should be unanimity within the international community on nutritional policy and targets was ultimately rewarded by the inclusion in the Conference's World Declaration on Nutrition of a commitment to the previously agreed-upon goals.

Addressing the Conference, Jim Grant represented the articulation of the nutrition goals for the 1990s as a moment of historical convergence between what morality had long demanded and what science with its empirical knowledge was now able to deliver. There was no longer any justifiable reason why 200 million children around the world went to bed hungry at night or suffered physical or mental deformity because their dietary needs could not be met[76]. 'What can be done,' Grant asked, 'to ensure the nutritional security to which each and every child has a right? Unicef's experience tells us that lasting solutions require the mobilization of the very fabric of societies in pursuit of shared goals, and the empowerment of the disenfranchised to change and improve their own lives.' In Grant's conception, 'bottom-up' advance was not an alternative to 'top-down' advocacy and policy development. There was no inconsistency between setting national and international goals and targets, and at the same time working to empower the partners in a process whose ultimate aim was human development and social justice. From this point onward, the elimination of childhood hunger and malnutrition was to be projected by Unicef as a fundamental issue of human rights.

Over the past few decades, the perspectives from which the problem of the persistently hungry and malnourished child had been addressed had grown and multiplied. Some themes remained constant: the need for effective programmes of relief feeding for child victims of war, famine and disaster and for the nutritional rehabilitation of cases of extreme debility and starvation. Other themes changed as a result of new nutritional and scientific knowledge: the focus on certain nutrients—conspicuously protein—had given way to a broader focus on energy, and had then again embraced specific nutrients, particularly micronutrients such as iodine and vitamin A. Advances in nutrition-oriented agricultural science had shifted from concern with food quantity to quality, from conservation to production, from leaves, to pulses, to animal products. Breakthroughs in biotechnology and the food-processing industry had been first greeted with overenthusiasm, then reassessed and later brought back into the picture with a new emphasis on community involvement. Yet other themes had ebbed and flowed on the nutritional agenda: direct and indirect links with public health and the control of infectious diseases; the interactions between nutritional well-being and the general state of political, environmental and economic affairs.

Interwoven with all these changing perspectives was the story of changing livelihoods and lifestyles in the industrializing or 'developing' setting; the story of breastfeeding's decline and efforts to arrest it; and increased awareness of the need for care and of the impact on children's nutritional status of gender discrimination. A great deal of progress had been made in the resolution of how to help the hungry child—the quintessential problem of poverty and human development. But of all the human and child development goals set for the millennium, a major reduction in protein-energy malnutrition will be the hardest to accomplish. On the other hand, if it is accomplished, this will indicate that much more has happened in terms of poverty eradication and improvements in the quality of life than the achievement of any other single goal would imply. In the closing years of the 20th century, the many intricacies of the child hunger and malnutrition complex are finally being unravelled.

Chapter 4

Water, Environment, Sanitation: The Changing Agenda

Since the hygienization of daily life that followed the Industrial Revolution, no major decline in human mortality has been thought possible without a large dose of public health engineering. Even in the heyday of the disease control campaigns of the 1950s and 1960s, it was not forgotten that dirt, especially in drinking water, was the most efficient spreader of disease. As well as cholera, typhoid and the diarrhoeas, many infections were connected to poor hygiene: scabies, trachoma, intestinal parasites; others such as guinea worm disease and schistosomiasis entered the body via a water-dwelling vector; and yet others—malaria and yellow fever—were carried by insects that bred in and around water. Inevitably, given the unsanitary character of the developing world, both WHO and Unicef began in the 1960s to become increasingly involved in disease prevention via the science of public health engineering as well as that of medicine[1].

For Unicef, the water supply programme that emerged in the 1970s was arguably its most significant and influential in the years before the 'child survival revolution'. The reason was that—anomalously for an organization helping children—Unicef found itself more operationally involved in public health engineering than in virtually any other programme area, hiring hydrogeologists and master drillers and investing in 'hands-on' technical research. This was because when it became involved in providing water supplies for poor and remote rural communities, it confronted a glaring operational and technological gap. The gap was between grand, heavily engineered public works schemes and simple, low-cost installations that required neither expensive supplies of fuel nor elaborate skills to operate. The pioneers of 19th-century public health had cleaned up the urban environment with pipes, sewers and treatment plants. But this solution was entirely inappropriate for almost all the rural, and many urban, inhabitants of the developing world.

Much of the early work to identify 'intermediate' water-well technology was undertaken by mechanically minded missionaries as part of their humanitarian work among the poor. But these actors had neither the resources nor the attitudinal reach to address the water supply problems of rural populations *en masse*. The size and organizational character of Unicef, together with its commitment to basic services and the poor, fitted it to play a bridging role. It drew on technologically simple, low-cost options and promoted them as the basis of a nationwide approach.

However, there were also important external influences on the development of the Unicef programme. One was the worldwide consciousness of environmental issues that began in the late 1960s. Another, not unconnected, was the increasing number of drought and famine emergencies in whose wake many water supply programmes were launched[2]. The setting for these was often an accumulating upset in the fragile balance between human pressure and the natural environment, which finally tipped over the edge into disaster. Such was frequently the pattern in Africa, where a continental swathe from the Sahelian zone in the west to the Horn in the east was beset by frequent drought from the early 1970s onward.

The two programmes that established Unicef's role in low-cost rural water supplies were both precipitated by emergencies; both were also on the Indian subcontinent. The first was the 1966 famine in Bihar, during which hard-rock percussion drilling was introduced into India. When the emergency was over, the Indian Government decided that since the water table was dropping all over India's central and southern hard-rock peninsula, the old, painfully slow, water-well blasting and boring methods should now be superseded. In 1970, Unicef agreed to provide 125 'down-the-hole' air hammer rigs at a cost of $5.9 million for a nationwide rural drinking water programme for 575,000 'problem villages'—one of the largest grants the organization had ever made up to that time[3].

This investment led to another important technological evolution. In 1974, surveys in the states of Tamil Nadu and Maharashtra revealed that 80 per cent of the handpumps installed on the new boreholes were out of action. The very high breakdown rate was explained by the fact that the handpump used could not withstand continuous use by a whole community. In addition, the assumption that the *panchayat* (village council) would organize maintenance and repairs had proved misguided. This disaster led to the development by Unicef, in partnership with government and private industry, of the India Mark II deep-well handpump. This sturdy, durable and cheap pump, designed for heavy use in areas where the static water table was far below the surface, was the only one of its kind then available. Within a decade Unicef advocacy had turned it into a subcontinental best seller, the standard deep-well pump for rural and shanty-town areas not only in India but in other countries around the world. The development of the India Mark II, its institutionalization in India's national rural drinking water programme and the transfer of its technology worldwide have been some of the most important successes in Unicef's history.

The Indian rural water supply programme, especially in its early phase, focused heavily on technology, its management, installation and repair. This stemmed naturally from the complex hydrogeological problems the programme confronted. The programme that was initiated in Bangladesh, also in the 1970s, had those features in common with the Indian programme. But the geological setting, and therefore the technological complexity and expense, were entirely different. Where India's main problems centred on hard-rock areas and water shortage, Bangladesh had barely a rock at its disposal from one end of the country to the other and was water-abundant. A fertile and overcrowded country, Bangladesh is situated in the world's largest delta area. Here, too, the balance between humankind and nature had been upset by the pressure of rising numbers, but the outcome was not soil erosion and drought. The annual inundation of between one third and one half of the country's land surface swept all dirt and detritus before it, transforming the countryside into an open sewer. Endemic cholera and diarrhoeal disease were spread by the pollution of the open ponds in which people bathed, swam and fished, and from which they drank[4].

In Bangladesh as in India, Unicef supported a national rural drinking water supply scheme that aimed to place a communal handpump within reach of every village household. But here, given the soft soils and the high level of the water table, the technology needed was rudimentary. Tube-wells could be sunk to a depth of around 50 metres by a traditional method requiring only a bamboo scaffold and a few lengths of galvanized iron pipe. A simple suction pump on top brought water to the surface. Initially, Unicef provided the means to construct or re-sink 160,000 shallow tube-wells and cap them with pumps. Existing technology was improved, and later a cheap and durable pump for use in water tables just below the suction level was developed. As the programme progressed, its purpose became to install enough tube-wells across the countryside to implant in the rural Bangladeshi mind the notion that, for drinking especially, but also for cooking, washing and laundry, pond water should be abandoned in favour of tube-well water.

In the cases of both India and Bangladesh, therefore, Unicef was a partner of government public health engineering departments helping develop what amounted to a new concept: a service operating right down to village level, overseeing a system based not on underground pipeline and household connections, but on a network of detached handpump tube-wells. This required not only new technological approaches, but managerial ones that took into account the wishes and capacities of local communities. Before this time, no one had attempted to build an institutionalized water supply delivery system using low-cost, appropriate technology and applying the principles of standardization and economies of scale. Suddenly, estimated costs of providing facilities for the world's unwatered could be cut from a minimum of $300 per head to $30 per head or less[5].

In 1977 the UN World Water Conference in Mar del Plata, Argentina, called for the declaration of an International Drinking Water Supply and Sanitation Decade (IDWSSD). The Decade's primary goal would be to achieve 'universal access' to water and sanitation by 1990. By the time it was launched in 1981, the modest handpump, the lowly latrine, the capped spring and the gravity-fed cistern were starting to attract attention and resources from the World Bank, UNDP, major donors such as DANIDA and SIDA, and other members of the international development community. By this time, Unicef had already become involved in water supply and sanitation programmes in a number of countries in Africa and Central America as well as in India, Pakistan and Bangladesh. Internationally, it saw its role as advocating and popularizing the low-cost, low-technology approaches it was helping to develop within its own programmes of cooperation, together with appropriate systems for their management.

In the field, Unicef was already beginning to address the next generation of problems associated with these pioneering public health engineering activities. All manufactured installations—even the sturdiest and the most modest—need maintenance and repair. Where water and waste disposal systems are in the hands of a central body that controls faucets and flows at a distance, management is a specialized affair. Services based on handpumps are different. They have to be managed on a day-to-day basis by the users, and if the users are not equipped technically and organizationally to do so, management and maintenance will falter. In India, the first strategy had been to depend on the *panchayats*—the village councils; when this failed, professional engineering teams were assigned to the task. But it soon became obvious that the communities the handpumps served would have to be involved. The authorities could not watch over hundreds of thousands of separate installations day in and day out.

This led to the idea of the 'village handpump caretaker'. In the era of 'basic services', which sought outreach and community ownership of services by enlisting local volunteers, it was a small step from the 'barefoot doctor' to the 'barefoot mechanic'. At an early stage it was also proposed that some 'handpump caretakers' be women. This was the first deliberate attempt to ensure the involvement of women in decisions about a service that, because they were both the haulers of the household water supply and its managers and main users, affected them deeply.

The idea of community, and female, involvement in handpump maintenance, later synthesized by World Bank technicians as 'village-level operation and maintenance', or VLOM, was another major contribution to the evolving pattern of water supply programmes. In due course, ease and simplicity of parts replacement with a minimum of tools became an important design criteria for new or improved versions of handpumps—including a later version of the India Mark II. Some VLOM enthusiasts even believed that sturdiness was a less important handpump design criterion than VLOM potential—especially VLOM by women caretakers. In the 1980s, the unlikely image of the village woman with a spanner in her hand became the latest water and sanitation trademark; the twin themes of women's involvement and VLOM as essential components of new-style rural water supplies management dominated the second half of the Water Decade. In a number of programmes, for example in Kordofan, the Sudan, in Imo state, Nigeria, and in Bangladesh, community levies for pump maintenance—spare parts, tools and occasionally labour—were introduced so as to ensure a sense of community ownership for the water supply system[6].

When the Water Decade had been launched, much emphasis had been placed by WHO and others on the public health advantages of safe water and sanitation. Between 10 million and 25 million deaths each year, and 80 per cent of all bouts of sickness, were attributed in some degree to inadequate water or waste disposal[7]. Five million of the 14 million annual deaths among children under five were attributed to diarrhoea, in which impure water and poor hygiene were undoubtedly complicit[8]. This was the underpinning rationale for a drive to provide facilities for that half of the developing world's population without a water supply, and the three out of four people with no method of sanitation other than a bucket or a walk in the fields[9]. But the reason why water supply—less so sanitation—schemes had proved so popular with rural communities had little to do with health considerations obscure to those who knew nothing of the germ theory of disease. To its customers—especially women, who had to haul the water—the new water supply was a convenience, and a wonderful relief from hours of drudgery[10]. But extra water use as a sanitary aid did not necessarily follow the installation of handpump or standpipe, especially where collection was still a burdensome affair requiring heavy pots and lengthy porterage.

Gradually it became clear that low-tech public health engineering could not in itself eliminate dirt- and water-related disease. Here was a familiar lesson: technology, however appropriate, was not a 'fix', especially if what it was supposed to fix was a different problem from that experienced by the community. Handpumps and standpipes only provided the environmental preconditions for improving health; such improvements might be non-existent unless other things happened as well. That they did drastically improve quality of life, reducing time spent by women on water collection and easing their domestic and child-rearing burden, was sometimes overlooked in the obsession with water as the bedrock of public health.

One of the other things that had to happen was an improvement in sanitation—comparatively much neglected[11]. Sewerage was unaffordable for most of the citizens of the rural and poor urban developing world. Meanwhile, excreta is not a popular subject in any culture, and the practitioners of 'appropriate' public health found that there were few places in the world whose inhabitants could be easily persuaded to attach social cachet to a latrine. In the early 1980s, efforts began—and again, Unicef was a keen supporter—to improve latrine technology. For water-short areas, the odourless 'ventilated improved pit' or VIP latrine was developed; for water-abundant areas, the 'pour-flush' latrine with a water-sealed pan[12].

In the end, however, the only sure way that major advances in public health could accompany technologically cheap and simple engineering systems was by a transformation in human behaviour. If villagers used the new borehole supply only in the dry season; if they failed to clean their water pots; if they never washed their hands before meals; if they bathed in polluted ponds and their children went barefoot, then the best intentions of the engineers could not reduce the diarrhoeal infections and parasites that invaded their well-being. By the 1980s, research was showing that it helped to supply water in quantity to every household, thus encouraging much greater use for washing and bathing[13]. By definition, a handpump for 200, 300 or 500 people several hundred yards away did not achieve this. The focus on quality—on *safe* water—had obscured the need for easily accessible volume. And quality was unappreciated by users: no one had convincingly explained its health-related virtues and the need to protect them all the way from pump head to mouth.

The Water Decade was barely under way before Unicef had shifted its attention away from the 'basic services' strategy in which water supplies, and increasingly sanitation, were central components, towards GOBI and the 'child survival revolution'. With its strong emphasis on the immediate saving of child lives, the message to the engineers was that they—for the moment—had become sidelined. Water and sanitation might be important over the longer term; but in terms of dramatic and demonstrable reductions in infant deaths, they had no primacy. Although both were necessary, more could be done, much faster, and much more cheaply to save diarrhoeal deaths with cure—oral rehydration therapy—than by the preventive strategy of installing handpumps and latrines. Over the next few years, the financial assistance provided by Unicef to water and sanitation as compared with child health was significantly reduced: in 1982, Unicef spent $60 million on 'Watsan' compared with $51 million on 'basic health'; in 1987, the corresponding figures were $64 million and $152 million[14].

But the engineers were not deterred. If their technology did not 'fix' health, they would reset their sights. They would produce the missing link between handpumps and standpipes and the health benefits they were supposed to confer. Unicef's water and sanitation team would set about establishing themselves firmly on the side of child survival and health, as well as on the side of women's and community convenience. The time of exclusive concentration on 'hardware'—drilling rigs, handpump design and coverage targets—had ended. The time for 'software'—for health education and behavioural change—had begun.

For much of the 1980s, Unicef's primary attention to the millions of cases of diarrhoea threatening young children's lives continued to take the form of promoting oral rehydration therapy.

The campaign on behalf of ORT was coordinated by WHO's programme for the control of diarrhoeal diseases, which set an ambitious target of 50 per cent ORT use in diarrhoeal treatment by 1989[15]. The achievements of the campaign paled into insignificance beside the drive for UCI; nonetheless, there were some considerable gains. By 1990, 350 million packets of ORS were being manufactured annually compared with 40 million in 1980[16]. Unicef had helped establish local manufacture in a number of countries, 62 of which now produced their own supplies. With improved availability came improved access: 61 per cent of the world's people could now obtain ORS to treat diarrhoeal dehydration from their local health centre or pharmacy. In fact, only 32 per cent did so; but this compared with the 1980 figure of less than 1 per cent[17]. WHO estimated that the increased use of ORT was saving around 1 million child lives annually—an impressive statistic but for the fact that 3 million more were there for the saving[18].

These achievements were mainly due to the push provided by the 'O' in GOBI and the 'child survival revolution'. In particular they were due to Jim Grant's unflinching promotion of a remedy to a condition not normally discussed in polite society. Grant was prepared to take out the sachet of ORS he always carried in his breast pocket in almost any setting, however prestigious. Whether he was on a podium, at a state banquet or in the receiving room at Government House, he promoted diarrhoeal rehydration with a lack of self-consciousness that frequently left his entourage blushing. His salesman's techniques worked. As important, the enlistment of USAID and the Task Force for Child Survival under the ORT banner created professional and technical momentum[19].

By the late 1980s, from the growing number of national programmes for the control of diarrhoeal disease (90 by 1988[20]) had emerged a wide variety of strategies for overcoming obstacles to the spread of ORT. Both in the clinic and in the household these were more numerous than anticipated. ORT's simplicity and effectiveness as a remedy for diarrhoeal dehydration had led its protagonists to expect that the operational ramifications of getting ORS onto every pharmacist's shelf and into every home medicine chest would be less complex than turned out to be the case. The obstacles ranged from professional resistance in the medical establishment, to the contrariness of human nature in preferring fancy drugs, to technical disagreements about the correct mix, to the lack of training and familiarity with ORT among health workers, as well as a host of other issues[21]. As a consumer product ORS did not win converts in the same way as aspirin or cough mixture because, while it solved the problem of dehydration, it did not stop the diarrhoea itself.

In some minds, OR'T' was a product: sachets of ORS. The challenge was to ensure their distribution to the consuming public. Typical issues in this context were pricing—keeping the price low enough for the purchasers, yet high enough not to drive commercial interests away; standardization of mixes and messages on the packet; marketing and communications to create demand. Others saw the spread of ORT primarily as a behavioural matter: maternal knowledge, motivation and the skills to mix the ingredients from household items confidently and correctly were the key issues in this context. Some medical practitioners saw ORS as a medicine to be applied strictly to cases of diarrhoeal dehydration that were presented at the clinic; others saw it as the equivalent of a typical home remedy. The basic difference was between those who wanted to keep the treatment of childhood diarrhoea mainly in the hands of the professionals—medical and pharmaceutical—and those who saw ORT as a technique that could be demedicalized and taken over entirely by well-informed mothers, with support from the local community-based health volunteer. On such differences of view hinged important questions of strategy for ORT promotion.

The much-lauded Egyptian programme (see Chapter 2) was heavily based on ORS in packets, gaining the cooperation of manufacturers and pharmacists and saturating television and radio with clever marketing messages. This led to a rapid increase in the use of ORS, covering around 50 per cent of diarrhoea episodes throughout the country[22]. This approach was well suited to countries where family incomes were reasonable—or at least not at the very edge of survival—as was the case in much of the Middle East and Latin America. In such settings most people live urbanized lives and are within reach of health centres and pharmacies, and purchasing a commercial medical remedy is a standard response to illness.

However, in settings where poverty and squalor were a greater problem, as in South Asia, where 40 per cent of the world's under-five mortality occurred, the product approach could run into problems. In Pakistan, the Government began its anti-diarrhoeal push with a massive free distribution of millions of ORS sachets. The EPI programme vaccinators (many programmes piggybacked ORT on the back of immunization) gave two packets to each mother and taught her how to mix and use the solution. But when it came to their replacement, the Ministry of Health could not afford such high recurrent costs. The programme had to restart using home-mixed solutions.

The first country in which a mass outreach ORT programme was based on a home-mixed solution was Bangladesh, the original home of ORS and of much of the most important clinical and field-based research into diarrhoeal treatment. In 1980, a prominent NGO, the Bangladesh Rural Advancement Committee (BRAC), launched an ORT campaign intended to reach all 13 million homes in the country within a decade. ORS was seen as too expensive for the typical Bangladeshi family. So teams of trained women workers—900 were recruited in the first phase—went from house to house, showing mothers how to mix a solution known as *lobon-gur*: a handful of molasses and a pinch of salt in half a litre of tube-well water. Using flip charts, the workers put across the seven messages that every mother needed to know about how to handle a case of childhood diarrhoea. An incentive system of payment meant that workers were remunerated according to their results: a monitoring team would follow in their wake and test mothers' knowledge and mixing skills[23].

Early surveys revealed that while 80 per cent of mothers had retained the messages and mixed *lobon-gur* correctly, the solution was being used in only 10 per cent of diarrhoeal bouts[24]. Then the programme managers discovered that even the trainers were not using the solution, but preferred pills and tablets. Part of the problem was that the programme had targeted only women. Men were important decision makers in the home, and women would not take a major action concerning the illness of a child without their menfolk's concurrence. Accordingly, the programme revised its strategy, training a number of male teachers whose job was to talk to the village men in market-places and in mosques. Gradually the ORT usage rate rose to 20 per cent and by 1988, to 40 per cent[25]. In 1987, the worst floods that Bangladesh had endured for 25 years led to an outbreak of diarrhoeal disease and cholera. In the past, a death rate of 10 per cent would have been expected. But because ORT and ORS were used, the death rate was held to less than 1 per cent[26].

The experience in Bangladesh, and increasingly elsewhere, illustrated how important it was for programme design to take into account entrenched patterns of human behaviour and belief. The idea that food and liquids should be withheld from infants with diarrhoea had been very difficult to dispel; the most important message for the prevention of dehydration—that children should be given more to drink—did not seem to have penetrated maternal consciousness on a sufficiently wide scale. Many parents still thought that an anti-diarrhoeal drug that they purchased in the market or obtained from the doctor was a superior treatment. As the 1980s gave way to the 1990s, the battle to have ORT recognized throughout the world—in the US as much as in Bangladesh—as the first-class scientific remedy that it is, both by the medical profession and by parents, was still far from won. There was still a pronounced tendency to see it as a second-class remedy for the poor, or to ignore its use altogether.

By the early 1990s, according to WHO, 3 million children under the age of five were still dying from diarrhoea annually as an outcome of 1.3 billion diarrhoeal episodes[27]. Despite the progress in spreading both information about and sachets of ORS, ORT was still being used in only 38 per cent of diarrhoeal episodes[28]. In the hope of renewing the momentum of the global anti-diarrhoeal campaign, the World Summit for Children set a goal of reduction by half of diarrhoeal deaths during the forthcoming decade, and a further goal of reduction by a quarter of diarrhoeal incidence. Meeting these goals would require a new push for ORT and vigorous commitment to all aspects of diarrhoeal disease control strategies.

A country that took up the challenge with alacrity was Mexico. The Mexican Ministry of Health had launched a national CDD programme in 1983-84[29]. In its early years the programme concentrated on training physicians in oral rehydration, both so that they would set up oral rehydration units in hospitals for clinical case management and so that they would instruct outpatients correctly in the use of ORT. The programme managers also reassessed their marketing strategy for ORS, then known as oral electrolytes. It turned out that mothers thought the name had something to do with electricity. The metaphor of the child returning to life as rain revivifies a tree was adopted instead, with a new packet and name: *viva suero oral*. The revamped programme led to a speedy decline in the number of cases of diarrhoea hospitalized. But somehow, by 1987, still only 17 per cent of mothers knew how to administer ORT at home. Efforts were made to increase ORS distribution and to step up the training of medical personnel in correct diarrhoeal case management including the use of ORT: doctors were still perceived as the vital interface with mothers.

The Mexican CDD programme would have continued along these lines but for the intrusion of the World Summit for Children. President Carlos Salinas de Gortari, one of its six co-sponsors, decided to identify himself with the children's cause and make a major attempt to reduce infant mortality before his term of office ended in 1994. Given Mexico's existing infrastructure and level of development, its diarrhoeal disease rates were disproportionately—even shamefully—high. With a larger CDD programme it ought to be possible to make major inroads on diarrhoeal deaths, thereby helping to achieve the main task—reduction of young child mortality—by the quickest route.

A new and expanded strategy for CDD was drawn up, among whose targets was an increase in ORT use to 80 per cent. Partly at Unicef's suggestion, the new strategy was designed along radical, demedicalizing lines to shift the programme's centre of gravity away from total dependence on health personnel and involve mothers themselves. The Ministry of Health was reviewing this proposal at a time in 1992 when Jim Grant was visiting Mexico to attend a post-Summit national programme of action (NPA) review. Grant was therefore able to intercede with President Salinas on the proposal's behalf. The mobilization of political will behind the strategy was central to the acceleration of the CDD programme that then took place. This was exactly the sort of situation in which Grant's cultivation of contacts with Heads of State paid spectacular dividends for children.

The main organizational change in the strategy was that for the first time a range of other institutions and sectors—educational, water and sanitation, indigenous peoples, as well as the entire health system—was brought into the programme. A National Council for CDD was set up, and counterpart councils in all 32 states. One of the key programmes with which it was linked was the *la salud empieza en casa* ('health starts at home') programme run by the Maternal and Child Health directorate. This set out to train health *agentes* in every community; they in turn trained and supported groups of health *procuradoras*—pregnant women, mothers of young children—in elementary health and child nurture. Prominent among these simple actions was the case management of diarrhoea and the use of ORT; household cleanliness and personal hygiene was another. By 1993, the 'health starts at home' programme had trained 82,000 *agentes* and 760,000 *procuradoras*.

One of the most important CDD programme innovations was a system of epidemiological surveillance[30]. Every death of a young child in Mexico from this point onward had to be described and registered. Since 70 per cent of deaths took place at home, a responsible member of the community would have to interview the parents and ascertain by verbal autopsy the course of events leading to the child's decease. The death certification process had to be swift and efficient, even in remote rural areas. It was the basis of a health information system that made it possible for the national CDD programme to know within a month of any death from diarrhoeal disease; when the programme had begun in 1983-84, all its information on diarrhoeal deaths was eight years old. The analysis of death registers made it possible to identify places where child populations were at high risk from diarrhoea and concentrate efforts accordingly.

Further evidence emerged of the inadequacies of doctors. In three quarters of all deaths at home, the mother had consulted a physician about her ailing child. He either had not taught her to use ORT or had not made a good diagnosis; since almost all the deaths were avoidable, the physicians had let their clients down. A new strategy was initiated. In areas where health facilities were few, the programme set up 'ORS houses': a local woman was trained in oral rehydration, given a supply of sachets, and was on stand-by for any local mother who needed her assistance.

The intensive CDD strategy in Mexico involved many other elements—television and radio campaigns, monitoring and coordination with many programmes that target children or target ill health, or both. National Health Weeks, with quantified outputs not only for ORT promotion but also for immunization and distribution of vitamin A, gave the programme an important boost. Under another programme known as the 'White Flag', villages where all mothers were able to recite the correct use of ORT and other child survival activities were entitled to raise a white flag. By 1994, five million mothers had been trained in the use of ORT. The target of reducing diarrhoeal deaths by 50 per cent was met two years early—in 1992. The programme was so successful that it attracted visits from health officials from all over Central America, Asia and Africa, and its approach was widely copied.

During 1992, a major effort was made to give CDD programmes a new impetus; Jim Grant impressed a number of intergovernmental Head of State regional meetings—those of the South Asian Association for Regional Cooperation (SAARC), OAU and the Arab League, for example—to adopt 80 per cent usage of ORT as a mid-decade goal[31]. At the same time, emphasis was given to other parts of diarrhoeal disease control strategy. Since the number of diarrhoeal deaths caused by dehydration had dropped to one half of the total, or 1.5 million, an increasing proportion of the remaining deaths could be attributed to infections requiring antibiotic treatment[32]. New evidence showed that there was a strong link between persistent diarrhoea in the small child and malnutrition. Loss of appetite, the impact of fever on the body's energy store and the draining away of nutrients could be a lethal combination, especially if one bout followed closely on another. Thus the new CDD strategy emphasized the three Fs: 'fluids', 'feeding' and 'further help'; this strategy incorporated the need for a mother to seek further help if the diarrhoea was persistent, bloody or accompanied by fever, or if signs of dehydration were present. Included in the strategy was the provision that every child seeking care outside the home would receive ORS and that every health facility would offer correct case management for diarrhoea[33].

Also emphasized was the need for increased public investment in safe water supplies and sanitation. After all the miracles of modern campaigns against disease have been performed, the sanitarians and engineers must also have their day.

Soon after the International Drinking Water Supply and Sanitation Decade of 1981-90 began, Unicef launched its 'child survival revolution'. The hot pursuit of a reduction in deaths from diarrhoeal disease by curative means thereafter pushed long-term preventive action and quality of life improvements somewhat into the background. Water and sanitation programmes had a much reduced organizational profile over the next few years, and when some came up for review—the Pakistan programme in 1986, for example—they might find themselves unfavourably compared to CDD control via ORT and fighting to remain in existence[34].

Water and sanitation programmes were not only popular with governments and communities, however, they were well-established elements of the Unicef country programme portfolio. Even during the fundamentalist phase of GOBI, they did not all languish; in some cases, the opposite was the case. However, there was no escaping that a challenge had been posed to the water supply and sanitation engineers: to bring their work within the sight-lines of child survival, and make 'water mean health'—as measurably and affordably as possible. This meant that much more effort needed to be invested in the 'software' elements of education and community participation, particularly of women, as compared with the hardware elements of borehole drilling and handpump development.

A programme that from its drawing-board stage was designed to forge the link between safe water supplies and improved health for women and children was the Unicef-assisted programme in Nigeria. This was launched as a Water Decade programme in 1981, initially in Imo state. This was a state with a high incidence of guinea worm disease, of which Nigeria was an acute sufferer with 2.5 million victims annually. Although expenditure on drilling rigs and support vehicles constituted a large slice of the Unicef capital contribution to the scheme, much more management effort, personnel and time went into the software components. The linchpin was health education, to be conducted by 'village-based workers' (VBWs) from the participating communities. Their training ran the gamut of maternal and infant care as well as pump care-taking, safe waste disposal, breastfeeding and nutrition[35].

The programme had another unusual feature. One of its teams focused exclusively on sanitation—on promoting the construction and use of the VIP (ventilated improved pit) latrine. Such an item had never previously been seen in the rural hinterland of Nigeria and—initially at least—little demand could be anticipated. So the Imo state project was planned on the basis that communities would have first to build a certain number of VIP latrines before they would be entitled to the installation of a borehole. Demand for water was to be used as leverage for the introduction of hygienic excreta disposal. Although this idea was to be widely copied elsewhere, the Nigerian programme was one of the first to start out with an interdependent water, health education and sanitation strategy.

In its very early days, the Imo State Watsan Project could almost be said to have overcompensated for previous water supply programmes' lack of attention to 'software', with teams of community organizers to set up water and sanitation committees in the community, VBW training, maintenance schemes and the establishment of centres for VIP latrine production. As the model developed and was replicated in four other Nigerian states, the balance between the various activities shifted and some of the emphases changed according to experience. Also influential was a major study carried out in Imo state in conjunction with the London School of Tropical Health and Hygiene. This set a trend of closer evaluation of water and sanitation programmes worldwide to understand more about the connection with health and whether it was truly measurable.

The study found that guinea worm infestation had significantly dropped among people living within 500 metres of a handpump. More significantly, the project was responsible for a reduction in malnutrition from 7 per cent to 3 per cent in three-year-old children in participating villages[36]. It seemed that quality of life improvements could produce health benefits other than the cause-and-effect associations of impure water with specific water-related infections. The study also found that new knowledge was having an impact on health behaviours—household water was being more carefully kept, for example—but that this was more often learned from the project personnel than from the VBWs. From 1986 onward, the programme began to depend less heavily on the VBWs to provide the missing link between water and health and instead adopted social mobilization techniques. Schools were enlisted as well as mothers' clubs, television and radio; T-shirts and posters were produced and project notice boards were erected in the communities. The numbers of VBWs were reduced and their training confined to water use (including guinea worm prevention), drainage and human waste disposal, mobilization for immunization and diarrhoeal case management including ORT.

One of the original goals of the International Water Decade was eradication of guinea worm disease, or dracunculiasis. This extremely unpleasant condition is unique among water-related diseases in that it has no connection to sanitation, and can only be contracted by imbibing water containing the specific agent—a tiny cyclops that produces a worm. This gestates in the body over several months and gradually emerges through a painful ulcer in the skin. If the victim exposes the emerging worm in a water source—perhaps to soothe the pain—that water source becomes reinfected. By the mid-1980s, the condition was already highly localized—confined to several West African countries and to parts of India and Pakistan. Not only in Nigeria, but elsewhere, a determined international effort was mounted to reduce the case-load of infection and bring total eradication within possibility for the 1990s. Ex-US President Jimmy Carter undertook a leadership role in this context, especially for West Africa.

In 1986, a Unicef-assisted integrated programme for guinea worm control, water supply, sanitation, hygiene education and community health care began implementation in the Indian state of Rajasthan. Funds were provided by the Swedish Government for what became known as the SWACH programme—a word meaning 'clean' in Hindi. The two SWACH districts contained 11 per cent of the total guinea worm case-load in the entire country[37]. A priority was to break the cycle of transmission by preventing victims—those with worms emerging through the skin—from wading in drinking water sources. This meant altering the traditional 'step-wells'—wells with a flight of steps down into the water—so that the water could be drawn only by bucket and pulley. By mid-1988, nearly 3,000 step-wells had been converted. To supplement local supplies, over 2,000 of a projected 4,000 handpump tube-wells had also been installed[38].

From the outset SWACH set out to do far more than reduce dracunculiasis cases. The underlying assumption of the programme was that people's desire to rid themselves of a painful and debilitating complaint, once they understood how it was caused, could be parlayed into a more wide-ranging transformation of their water use and cleanliness behaviour. This was to be achieved by an innovative strategy of health education and the mobilization of the community, especially of women. One technique was the 'Village Contact Drive'—a 15-day peregrination of the countryside by teams of young men and women. They visited villages to discuss guinea worm, give out filter cloths to use over water pots, and generally start the ball rolling in a lively and entertaining fashion[39]. Local girls, specially selected and trained as animators and 'guinea worm scouts', would then follow up.

A 1988 study carried out in SWACH areas found that not only had guinea worm incidence dropped by 55 per cent, but that there had been significant change in practices concerning the collection, storage and consumption of drinking water[40]. Over the next few years, the programme consolidated its gains both in water supply protection and in hygiene promotion. By 1993, the number of patients reporting with guinea worm had gone down to 47, all of whom had their worms surgically extracted before they began to emerge from the skin and become infective[41]. Eradication of guinea worm from its strongest redoubt in India was within sight. In the country as a whole, the number of reported cases had dropped from nearly 38,000 in 1984 to just over 1,000 in 1992, and the number of endemic villages from 13,000 to 250[42].

By the end of the Water Decade, a growing number of country programmes—in Bangladesh, the Sudan, Uganda, Burma and elsewhere—were beginning to find a successful balance between 'hardware' and 'software' components. One advance was a dramatic reduction in the costs of installing deep wells by borehole drilling, partly by the use of more modest and appropriate equipment; partly by improved borehole location using hydrogeological mapping techniques; partly by better logistical management of expensive drilling equipment[43]. Another important gain was the use of social communications and message marketing in 'Watsan' as was also taking place in nutrition and health.

A new set of operational principles based on the use of appropriate technology, community management, the integration of water with sanitation and hygiene education and the increasing involvement of women, especially for health promotion, was gradually emerging; this was reflected in a Unicef policy review submitted to the Executive Board in 1988[44]. Meanwhile the 'health' benefits from water and sanitation were reinterpreted to include many things other than disease control: a higher standard of household and personal cleanliness, lower case-loads of malnutrition, savings in women's time and convenience. At the same time, new evidence from WHO showed unequivocally that improvements in both water quality and availability had the effect of considerably reducing diarrhoeal sickness and death[45]—a finding that helped restore the sector's confidence in its contribution to child health and survival.

The International Drinking Water Supply and Sanitation Decade, in spite of the fact that it did not manage to reach the ambitious goal of 'Water and Sanitation for All', was widely regarded in the international community as a success[46]. Many countries that had previously refused to contemplate handpump and latrine technology as the way to bring extremely basic services to underprivileged and underserved populations had been won over. Very important, the Decade had seen an unprecedented degree of inter-agency collaboration between the World Bank, the UN Department of Technical Cooperation for Development (UNDTCD), UNDP, WHO and Unicef; and an unusual degree of common vision, as exemplified in statements issued at international review meetings at Abidjan (1986) and Interlaken (1987)[47]. Although Unicef was a very small donor in comparative financial terms, providing approximately 1 per cent of investment in the sector ($70 million annually)[48], it had successfully played a pioneering and catalytic role. Because of its low-cost, low-technology approach, the programmes it supported had managed to serve 14 per cent of the population provided with water, and 4 per cent of those provided with sanitation[49].

Although the task of service provision was still daunting—in 1990, 1,330 million (37 per cent) people in developing countries were still without safe water and 1,900 million (61 per cent) were without sanitation[50]—the gap between the rhetoric of 'Water and Sanitation for All' and practical reality was beginning to close. Only 20 per cent of the annual $10 billion a year invested in public health engineering had gone into low-cost technology during the Decade; but the increased credibility of such approaches had dramatically reduced prospective costs of universal coverage spread. It was therefore agreed that the goal of 'Water and Sanitation for All' could be realistically rescheduled for the year 2000. There was now a chance that this target represented something more than an aspiration.

At the World Summit for Children, universal access to water and to a sanitary means of excreta disposal by 2000 was adopted as one of the seven main goals. Elimination of dracunculiasis by 2000 was adopted as a subsidiary goal; this was later adopted by Unicef and WHO as one of the 10 priority mid-decade goals for children targeted for achievement by 1995[51]. Its complementarity to health and nutrition goals—which would otherwise not be achieved—was fully recognized. At the same time, a new consciousness was developing around water and sanitation as not only a health asset, but environmental and socio-economic assets as well. The new perspective could be summed up in a word that had made its international policy debut only at the end of the 1980s but had already been widely adopted into development thinking. That word was 'sustainability'.

During the 1980s, the acute pressure of modern technology, population growth and consumer demand on the planetary fabric, an issue that had been smouldering away unobtrusively since the early 1970s, re-erupted on the global agenda. A new generation of international environmental worries—species loss, ozone depletion, global warming, deforestation, toxic wastes—had begun to capture not only scientific but popular attention. The world's environmental resources were being rapidly squandered, often in the name of 'development'; yet, at the same time, the poverty that development was supposed to correct was still widespread.

In 1983 the UN Secretary-General invited Prime Minister Gro Harlem Brundtland of Norway to chair the World Commission on Environment and Development and explore these twin dimensions of global stress. In 1987, the Commission published its report: *Our Common Future*. From this point on, environmental issues played a dominant role on the international agenda. This continued up to, and beyond, the UN Conference on Environment and Development, which took place in Rio de Janeiro in June 1992. The Earth Summit was the crowning event of the Brundtland process, and it was intended to usher in a new world order of planetary resource conservation.

Ever since the state of the environment first became a matter of international concern in the late 1960s, committed publicists for development such as the economist Barbara Ward had linked its plunder with world poverty. Waste and overconsumption of the earth's natural wealth were counterpoised with humankind's unwillingness to do much for the poor. Others laid responsibility for incipient disaster on the poor, whose extraordinary fertility was precipitating a global population crisis. Brundtland linked the twin concerns in a different way.

Our Common Future stated that poverty in the developing world was both a cause and effect of current environmental degradation. The insensitive kind of technological transfer that pauperized land, people and natural systems would lead to no common future at all. For the first time, a body commanding widespread respect convincingly argued that what passed for progress was not an inevitable fast-forward towards a more comfortable world, at least for the majority, but a reckless adventure full of global self-destruction. Only 'sustainable' forms of development could blend the fulfilment of human needs with the protection of soils, waters, air and all forms of life—from which, in the longer term, planetary stability was inseparable.

Thus was launched the idea of 'sustainable development': development based on the equal right of all humanity to a healthy and productive life, but one that did not jeopardize the right of coming generations to their own slice of the earth's pie.

During the early 1980s, Unicef did not engage with the rising environmental storm. Preoccupied by the 'child survival revolution', issues such as climate change and industrial pollution seemed remote from the organization's main agenda. But after the publication of *Our Common Future* and the call for an Earth Summit, it became clear that a huge energy flow was moving in the environmental direction and that, philosophically and practically, children's concerns must be placed within it. In 1989, the Unicef Executive Board discussed a review on 'Children and the Environment' and agreed that all Unicef programming should be placed within a 'sustainable development' framework[52]. The following year, Unicef teamed up with the United Nations Environment Programme (UNEP) to co-publish a report entitled *Children and the Environment*, which explored the specific ways in which, as the most vulnerable members of the human race, children suffered from an overstressed and polluted environment[53].

Since Unicef's efforts were spent on extending basic services to those outside their reach because of poverty, the style of programme it supported already matched in most essentials the criteria of 'sustainable development'. Basic services programmes were low on capital resources, strong on appropriate technology, minimal in their environmental implications, keen on soliciting people's active participation and aimed to build capacity within communities to underpin service delivery on their own behalf.

Where people's traditional economic activity—farming, fishing, herding—had previously been in ecological balance but was now contributing to environmental degradation, as on the eroded hillsides of Nepal or in the dry-land scrub of the African Sahel, basic services programmes were grounded in this reality. Household food security and village-level food processing; groundwater and surface water development schemes; fuel-efficient stoves and community wood-lots; loans for small livestock and gardening plots, were all intended to help families re-establish control over their economic lives in environments where the subsistence resource base was steadily shrinking. All these were, in fact, programmes that attempted to cut into the downward spiral resulting from the simultaneous and compounding experience of poverty, population growth and environmental degradation.

In more general terms, the accumulating conquest of disease, malnutrition and illiteracy was in itself a contribution to a better and more sustainable environment. These interactions between environmental care and child-centred development were underlined in a special chapter of the 1990 World Summit for Children Plan of Action, which began: 'Children have the greatest stake in the preservation of the environment and its judicious management for sustainable development, as their survival and development depend on it.'

The commitments of world leaders at the Children's Summit to survival, protection and development goals with a strong bearing on the environmental crisis of gross poverty and underdevelopment were initially overlooked in the preparations for the Earth Summit. At the Third Preparatory Conference in Geneva in August 1991, Richard Jolly, Deputy Executive Director for Programmes, spoke on 'A Human-centred Strategy for Environmental Improvement: The Children's Dimension.' In a statement that began the process of incorporating children's issues more distinctly into *Agenda 21*, the Summit's follow-up action plan, Jolly placed meeting human needs at the centre of any strategy for environmental conservation. He used the phrase 'Primary Environmental Care', originally coined by Oxfam and other NGOs, to describe the sensitivity to the environment that should be built into all development programming so that communities could protect the health of their soils, trees, water, plants and animals—their livelihood base[54].

At the Earth Summit itself, Jim Grant and a strong Unicef team did a great deal to advocate the children's cause. The Viking ship *Gaia* sailed into Rio harbour carrying aloft the legend: '*De um mondo melhor para todas las criancas*'—'A better world for every child'; this was just one of many events and spectacles in which children played a leading part. In his address to this second UN 'Summit', Grant called attention to the 'older face of the environmental crisis: ... I am talking about malnutrition and disease, early death and life-long disability, paucity of choices, discrimination against women and children, and structural violence—all the consequence of, or closely associated with, poverty and underdevelopment.'[55] He made a strong plea that the follow-up programme to the Earth Summit should incorporate 'the list of "doables" already embraced by the world's leaders in September 1990', and that children should be seen not only as victims of environmental degradation, but also as protagonists for a more environmentally stable world.

Unicef had reason to feel satisfaction that the children's message was coming across. Children's visibility in events linked to the conference—Rio de Janeiro is the world capital of street child culture—was itself an illustration of the heightened consciousness worldwide of children's issues. In addressing Unicef's areas of concern, *Agenda 21* exceeded Grant's expectations. It included a special chapter on 'Children and youth in sustainable development', which called governments' attention to the World Summit for Children Goals and demanded a place for the voices of children and youth in the 'participatory process for sustainable development and environmental improvement'.

Many other chapters of *Agenda 21* covered topics of importance to Unicef: health, poverty, women, demographics, education and training, finance. And there was one chapter in the all-important section of 'Conservation and management of resources for development': the protection of the quality and supply of fresh water. When all the Earth Summit rhetoric was over, water supply and sanitation was the most important programmatic context in which the interests of Unicef and those of planetary and human subsistence met.

At the end of the Water and Sanitation Decade, a Global Consultation on 'Safe Water and Sanitation for the 1990s' was held in New Delhi, at which the leading international experts in the sector established a principle for the next decade: 'Some for all, rather than more for some'. Implicitly, this reiterated the pronounced shift in international thinking towards the low-cost approach. The New Delhi Statement also emphasized the need for a transformation of attitudes and structures in water boards and public service utilities if the goal of 'Water and Sanitation for All' was to have any hope of being met; and the need to devolve management of services away from their centralized control into the hands of communities themselves. The scene was set for a more widespread application in the 1990s of the operating principles developed during the Decade, within the framework of international collaboration so carefully built up.

In the run-up to Rio, an International Conference on Water and Environment was held in Dublin early in 1992; this meeting produced the key recommendations on water resource development and management on which the relevant chapters of *Agenda 21* were based. Of direct concern to Unicef were two chapters: one on protecting and promoting human health, by ensuring universal access to safe drinking water and sanitary means of excreta disposal, and one on the protection of fresh water resources[56]. In the latter, emphasis was placed on the vulnerability of fresh water as a finite resource, on water as an economic and social good with a corresponding price tag and on the management of water by a participatory approach involving users, planners and policy makers at all levels—especially women. The thrust of current international thinking in the sector now tended to stress not only the public health benefits of water supplies and environmental sanitation, but their sustainability and their important role in enabling communities to improve their members' quality of life and socio-economic status. This was to have a profound effect on Unicef's evolving policy in the sector.

The immediate task for the 1990s was, however, to help develop strategies to reach the water and sanitation goals established by the World Summit for Children, and to try to ensure that behavioural change to promote good health would go hand in hand with increased service coverage. During the Water Decade, the most significant advance had been in village water supply coverage: there had been a jump from 30 per cent to 50 per cent of rural inhabitants[57]. But there had been very little change in the proportion of people with sanitation, either in rural or urban areas, and a number of Unicef programmes now set out to improve the coverage of latrines. A few pioneering projects in poor urban areas had had some success in the 1980s: a soak-pit project in Baldia township, Karachi, had proved very popular, for example, as a way of replacing bucket latrines with a more hygienic method of waste disposal. But while crowdedness and lack of natural facilities created some demand for sanitation in the towns, there remained a major challenge of creating demand for sanitation in rural areas, especially in the countries of South Asia where poverty and squalor were rife in large parts of the countryside.

Bangladesh, where cholera was still endemic, was an example of a country where improved sanitation was a critical need. By the late 1980s, tube-well water had become a popular consumer item—similar to a refrigerator elsewhere. But only 4 per cent of people used a sanitary latrine[58]. The same popularization process was now needed for latrines if lasting benefits were to be made for public health. An intensive sanitation push orchestrated by Unicef began in 1989. Extensive social mobilization was conducted through the media and many social institutions, including the Islamic clergy and village defence corps. Political backing was cultivated at the highest level behind the concept that Bangladesh was suffering from 'pathogen overload'. By 1992, sanitary waste disposal had gained sufficient respectability for Prime Minister Begum Khaleda Zia to address a national rally on the subject, exhorting women to change their families' habits. By 1994, pit latrine coverage had risen to 35 per cent[59].

During the early 1990s, the role of sanitary promoter in poor rural and urban areas was increasingly assumed by NGOs. 'Software' development and application, especially the nuanced negotiations surrounding personal hygiene and health education, were not within the expertise of the typical sanitary engineering department. Nor were the social mobilization and message-marketing techniques necessary for fundamental behaviour change. Accordingly, public utilities were increasingly seen as having a service design, facilitation, large-scale construction and technical role; NGOs, community leaders and committees and the 'private' or artisanal sector were seen as the key movers and shakers in small-scale construction, maintenance and local management and the promotion of hygienic behaviour.

A strikingly successful programme modelled along these lines was the Intensive Sanitation Project in Medinipur district in West Bengal, India. Set up with state government approval and Unicef support, this project was an attempt to prove that rural dwellers could be persuaded to pay for, build and use pit latrines. The subject of excreta is especially loaded in India, to whose 'untouchable' caste the task of removing night-soil—'sweeping'—was traditionally assigned. Sanitation, especially in rural areas, had always lagged pitifully behind water supplies in India, having reached a coverage of 3 per cent as compared with 78 per cent by the early 1990s[60]. The lacklustre performance was the result of the authorities' lack of commitment to rural sanitation, largely based on the conviction that it was almost impossible to persuade people to use latrines. The Medinipur project set out to develop a provable, replicable model that could transform both official attitudes and the squalor of the rural environment.

In 1987, Unicef identified an organization well suited to break down ingrained attitudes: the Ramakrishna Mission Lokasiksha Parishad, a leading NGO with an extensive network of youth clubs throughout Medinipur district[61]. Although somewhat daunted by the scale of Unicef's sanitary intentions—to reach 80 per cent of the 8.3 million population of the district with messages about hygiene and to see latrines installed and used in 50 per cent of households—the Ramakrishna Mission took up the challenge. The project was formally launched in March 1990 and by 1994 had reached more than 2,600 villages[62]. Although in its first two years relatively few latrines were constructed, thereafter attitudes began rapidly to shift. By late 1994, over 52,000 latrines had been built, more than two thirds of them by poor families. Around 40 villages had been declared 'sanitation villages', meaning that 80 per cent of households had installed latrines and taken other measures to improve the environment[63].

The project achieved this breakthrough by putting first priority on awareness-building and mobilization, and second priority on technology and construction. The Ramakrishna Mission conducted motivational camps and instructional sessions for all kinds of personnel: door-to-door motivators in the village, women handpump caretakers, village masons, local drillers and *mistris* (handymen), singing squads, wall painters and leaders of the *panchayati* or local councils. This intensive effort proved that age-old habits thought to be intractable could be dislodged. Many people—especially women who valued the privacy of a latrine and its round-the-clock availability—were prepared not only to abandon 'open defecation' but to push the idea to reluctant neighbours. The cleanliness of the village—its fitness to receive visitors—became a status symbol.

The members of the youth clubs constituted the 'motivator' group, each visiting 200 families. The club would provide an interest-free loan for a latrine if the customer put down half the price, but no subsidies were permitted. Production centres for latrine-ware at a wide range of prices were set up so that families could select their facility according to their pocket. Many motivators—female as well as male—found paid work as sanitary masons. Gradually, a whole new local employment, manufacturing and sales sector developed around a previously unwanted consumer item—the latrine. Its fullest expression came with the creation of the 'sanitary mart'. This was a retail shop with construction materials such as pans, traps and foot-rests, as well as other items: soap, nail cutters, toothpaste, water filters, ORS packets, bleaching powder and iodized salt.

The Medinipur strategy interlocked directly with water supply provision and with control of diarrhoeal disease. After 40 families had built latrines, they were entitled to the installation of a handpump. The villagers made a contribution to maintenance and women caretakers were trained. So effective has cost recovery been that each village will be able to afford a new pump when the old one wears out. To deal with diarrhoeal disease, an intensive community-level drive backed by the health authorities has set up ORS depots in villages, similar to Mexico's

CDD programme. Designated village women keep a stock of sachets and are trained in helping mothers to administer rehydration correctly.

The intensive sanitation project in Medinipur has galvanized the authorities not only in West Bengal but in a number of other Indian states and the central government. The social mobilization and 'sanitary mart' model is now being tried in districts all over the country. Central government has rewritten its national policy and guidelines on sanitation, and the policy of heavy subsidization—especially for those who can easily afford to construct facilities—has been dismissed as non-sustainable.

In Indonesia, an extraordinary effort on behalf of sanitation in the district of West Lombok has similarly had provincial and national repercussions. In this case, the moving force was the *bupati* (district head). Before he launched his latrine campaign, West Lombok's infant mortality rate was 120, the highest in Indonesia, and its sanitation coverage rate 8 per cent—the lowest[64]. In discussions with Unicef, the *bupati* became convinced that given the district's good immunization and growth monitoring record, the main culprit of child death was the unsanitary environment. In June 1993 at a public meeting, he challenged the assembled representatives of the district to construct 20,000 family latrines. Unicef backed the subsequent campaign, offering financial subsidies of $12 per latrine to help get communities interested.

As in the case of the child health and nutrition programme, the involvement of the Indonesian women's organization—PKK—was essential to the programme's success. The local PKK chapter drew up lists of candidate beneficiaries for latrines and set up a village production centre where local boys learned how to make squatting slabs, latrine pans and cement rings. Unicef subsidies paid for the materials. In spite of the fact that previous efforts to promote latrines in the island of Lombok had been very discouraging, not only were 20,000 latrines built within months, but by the end of 1994, sanitation coverage in West Lombok was nearly universal[65]. This success is credited to the pressure women exert on their menfolk and on the emphasis on hygiene as part of religious duty. People with no latrine are refused permission to marry or to travel to Mecca for the *haj*. The man who has become known as the 'latrine *bupati*' of West Lombok subsequently launched a movement called 'Clean Friday'—an idea taken up elsewhere in Indonesia and launched nationally by President Suharto in November 1994[66]. Islamic leaders in Indonesia are now promoting an association of the day of prayer with activities to promote healthy and hygienic living.

Although most of Unicef's cooperation in the water and sanitation sector still went to underserved rural areas, by the early 1990s increasing attention was being paid to the expanding populations of slums and shanty towns in the developing world. In many metropolitan environments, services to those in the better-off suburbs were heavily subsidized, with people paying on average only 35 per cent of their costs[67]. Meanwhile, people in slums and squatter settlements had no services at all and were obliged to buy water from vendors. This might absorb as much as 20 or 30 per cent of their income, while still providing only a small quantity of water of very dubious quality[68]. In a number of countries—Bangladesh, Haiti, the Sudan, India—Unicef began to feel that the public health situation of poor urban residents demanded more attention. Since coverage rates in towns and cities are higher on average than those in the countryside, there had been some tendency in the international water and sanitation community as a whole to neglect the very high disease and death rates related to squalor and filth among children of the urban poor[69].

One pioneering programme was in Tegucigalpa, capital of Honduras. Residents of the *barrios marginales*—shanty towns—were obliged to pay a vendor 10 times as much for a litre of water as people with a piped supply. In 1987, the Honduran water and sanitation agency, with Unicef support, began installing wells and communal tanks and trucking in water for 50,000 people in 26 *barrios*. The cornerstone of the strategy was that each *barrio* elected its own water board to take on the responsibility of recruiting labour, organizing the system's management and maintenance and ultimately repaying the investment made by the Government and Unicef. Here was a case in which the communities created their own organizations and the official body adopted a facilitating role. Within five years, household expenditure on water in the participating *barrios* had been cut from 40 to 4 per cent of annual income[70].

In 1993, along with other mid-decade goals, water and sanitation sector goals were set for the year 1995: to reduce the water coverage gap by 25 per cent and the sanitation gap by 10 per cent[71]. At the same time, moves went ahead to articulate a new Unicef strategy for water supply and sanitation that would identify its particular contribution within the consensus about sector policy reached by the international water and sanitation community. This consensus had been informed not only by the Earth Summit's call in *Agenda 21* for water resource management within the framework of development for sustainable livelihoods, but by the various international consultations that had taken place and were continuing to take place in the Water Decade's and Earth Summit's wake[72]. In due course, Unicef's environment unit merged with its water and environmental sanitation section.

Unicef was concerned that its strategy should reflect the new thinking and experiences of the recent past—taking advantage of the lessons learned in many programmes around the world. The dictum agreed upon in New Delhi: 'Some for all, rather than more for some' was to be the main theme of Unicef's work—as it had been in the past. But beyond the coverage targets laid down for the new decade, services must also be provided and managed in such a way as to maximize their potential health benefits and—an equally important target from the perspective of the communities they served—they should also have the capacity to reduce women's drudgery and improve families' socio-economic situation[73]. These and other principles of the new strategy were established at various consultations at which international partners and experts in the sector participated.

The starting-point of the new strategy agreed upon by Unicef's Executive Board in 1995 was that access to clean water and sanitation at an affordable price was a basic human right. And the way to ensure that services were not only provided to the most modest community but were used, maintained and brought the necessary benefits was to involve that community—especially its womenfolk—to the maximum extent possible. Official and public health engineering management structures should be geared not to shouldering the entire burden themselves but to helping communities to shoulder most of the load: the emphasis should shift from service delivery by the authorities to employment and capacity-building in the community. Only if services were fully 'owned' by the community and responded to their own internally generated consumer demand would health and socio-economic benefits be maximized and a hygienic lifestyle permanently take root. The community had to be in charge of organizational and technological management, as well as paying for repairs and—where practicable—some of the installation costs. It, too, had to be responsible for mobilizing its members around the programmes' health, environmental and economic goals. The importance of communications to bring about behavioural change, especially through education in schools, was also stressed, and a conceptual model for programme development was proposed, similar to that developed for the nutrition sector[74].

By the mid-decade, 1.3 billion people in the developing world (40 per cent) were still without a safe water supply and 1.9 billion were without sanitation[75]. There was still a great way to go to reach close to the end-decade targets. However, there was a genuine feeling within the sector that—despite all the difficulties and resource constraints—a revolution in sanitary thinking almost equivalent to that which had taken place in the 19th century in the industrialized world had now taken place vis-à-vis the rural and poor urban dwellers of the developing world. This new thinking had in its way reversed the process of earlier sanitary reform, which had so elevated the role of engineering in the hygienization of daily life as to move issues of public health from the province of individual action into the realm of public administration[76]. What was now proposed for the hygienization of life in the developing world was the de-thronement of officialdom and engineers and the reintroduction of individual and community action as the key to sustainable service provision.

On the successful advocacy of such ideas, the survival and healthy development of millions of underserved children still depend.

Chapter 5

City Streets and Children's Rights

During the early part of the development era, organizations concerned with poverty in the developing world as it affected people rather than as it affected nations concentrated their efforts in the countryside. Convention held that poverty in its most grinding form was to be found in the lined face and prematurely ageing bodies of the peasant farmer and his wife, working in the fields from sun-up to sundown in everlasting backwardness and ignorance. Rural life was regarded as invariably harder than town life since all work demanded unremitting toil, prospects were severely limited, services were fewer and disease rates and illiteracy noticeably higher. Some of these assumptions have been increasingly challenged in recent times by those championing the urban poor[1]. But two decades ago it was received wisdom that children born into poverty-stricken rural families were automatically much worse off in terms of exposure to disease and malnutrition, as well as educationally, than their counterparts in town.

This view was substantiated by the historical reality that cities had always been both the products and the engines of wealth. The laws of productive enterprise demanded that resources for development investment were skewed in favour of metropolitan centres, the sites of industry, government and intellectual life. That cities had poor neighbourhoods was an inevitable part of the process of wealth creation, which beckoned the go-getting and the disenfranchised from the countryside, offering paid jobs, casual work or petty entrepreneurship in the 'informal sector'. Slums had been a feature of everyone's industrial revolution and while they presented public health and security hazards, the expansion of the city would in time act as an absorbative, devouring its problems in a continuing process of more wealth creation. That at least had been the experience of the Western world.

In the early 1970s, it became apparent that cities in the developing world were growing far too fast for the usual assumptions about patterns of urbanization to apply. It took London over a century—1800-1910—to multiply its population by seven to 7.3 million, a growth rate now being achieved by many third world cities within a generation[2]. It was in Africa especially, and in Asia, that growth rates were highest: the process had begun earlier in Latin America, where the urban presence of two thirds of the population was causing increasing social and economic strain[3]. Urbanization was taking place at a speed out of any synchronization with the rate of expansion in employment, housing or services. The result was a proliferation of barrios, *favelas*, *bustis*, *bidonvilles*—squatters' settlements of flimsy shacks in disused nooks of the city centre or wastelands on its edge. These blots on the municipal escutcheon were growing at a pace far faster than that of the cities themselves, in which half the population might typically live in slums[4].

The widespread alarm felt by demographers and planners about the phenomenon of 'exploding cities' led to the first international conference on human settlements, HABITAT, held in Vancouver in 1976. Some of the leading cities in the developing world were growing at rates of between 7 and 10 per cent a year[5]. Although 60 per cent of the city 'explosion' was attributable to high birth rates among existing urban residents[6], the phenomenon was mainly associated with the exodus from countryside to town. This was universally frowned upon, as if urban newcomers consisted mainly of ne'er-do-wells drawn by bright city lights. The reality was that the average pioneer opting for urban migration was typically driven by poor agricultural prices, landlessness, lack of employment, debt, drought or flood disaster—forces far outside his or her control.

The typical municipal reaction was to regard squatters and shanty-town inhabitants as transients who had strayed temporarily from home. The migrants constructed 'temporary' shelters out of waste materials and occupied—illegally—vacant land that was usually low-lying, precipitous or hazardous in some way. Treated as marginal to the city's economic life, slum-dwellers endured an imposed culture of impermanence. Tenure, security and amenities were withheld on the basis that service availability would attract more rural indigents into town. The only welfare available—food hand-outs, medicines, second-hand clothes—came from religious orders and charitable institutions. Extreme measures—bulldozers and mass evictions—were often used against the urban poor, and still occasionally are.

These policies proved futile. As fast as slum-dwellers were trucked away to new settlements on the outskirts of cities such as Nairobi, Metro Manila and Delhi, their places along the railway tracks, beside the river bed and around the municipal garbage dump were reoccupied. For all the indications that they were not wanted, those exchanging agricultural life for the mud and garbage of the slum were not prepared to go away. Work, cash and amenities beckoned the new city-dwellers. The squalor, the high cost of city life, the loss of traditional community ties and the resultant changes in family life were a price that they were willing to pay for a foothold on the ladder to the modern world.

By the late 1970s, the proportion of slum and shanty-town residents in many cities was between 30 and 60 per cent, and in some was spectacular: in Addis Ababa, 79 per cent; in Calcutta, 67 per cent; in Bogota, 60 per cent[7]. Poverty was well on its way to becoming as much an urban as a rural phenomenon. Between two thirds and three quarters of this rapidly expanding group—the 'urban poor'—were women and children[8]. The poorest households were those headed by women, which in some cities constituted a third of the total[9]. Encumbered with child-rearing responsibilities and without skills or access to salaried employment, such families were totally dependent on cash for items that, in the countryside, were supplied from the fruits of stream, field and furrow. Childhood malnutrition, infection and general ill-health were the rule rather than the exception.

Striking as the evidence of urban misery was becoming, many observers remained locked into the perspective that poverty as a development rather than a welfare issue was a rural phenomenon, and that where it intruded into town the best policy was to leave well alone. Unicef, however, took the line as early as 1961 that if need was its principal criterion of assistance, there was no justification for excluding urban children from its assistance[10]. Although it was more than another decade before urban activity began in earnest, Unicef never allowed itself to be deflected from the problems of childhood in the slum by the false assumption that all those who live in cities are better off than those in the countryside simply because almost all the better-off people live in town, thereby skewing comparative statistical analysis.

In 1971, the Executive Board gave its approval to the social policy recommendations of a special study into problems of urban poverty[11]. Gradually a portfolio of projects for deprived urban areas—in Egypt, Ecuador, India, Indonesia and Zambia—was assembled. In 1978, a second report—'Basic Services for Children of the Urban Poor'—was prepared[12]. This report came at a time when enthusiasm for new, people-centred doctrines was at its height and reflected the 'alternative' thinking of the time. Thus the development of a coherent Unicef approach towards children in slum neighbourhoods and the creation of a worldwide programme with a shared perspective was very much a part of the emerging 'basic services' approach then dominating Unicef's perspective.

One of the landmark programmes in the formative years of 'urban basic services' was to be found in the *bustis*—pocket slums—of Hyderabad, India's fifth largest city. First supported by Unicef in 1976, the project was run by Hyderabad's municipal staff, which included veterans of India's community development experience[13].

The Hyderabad team concentrated on building a spirit of *busti* cooperation before trying to upgrade housing and other physical amenities. They fostered human development: welfare committees, youth clubs, women's self-help groups. Their resources were extremely slim—a factor to which much of their success was later attributed: they could not afford to do things *for* people, only *with* them, but they did not stint on time and energy, especially in the early stages. Whatever activities they undertook had to be sounded out with the community via a representative and democratic mechanism in which not only men but women participated. The role in slum development played by the Hyderabad municipal team was that of 'facilitator', then a relatively novel role for project managers.

No activity proceeded without there first being a clear statement of neighbourhood need and commitment. Welfare and economic activities took the lead: preschools (*balwadis*), women's mutual aid, cooperatives for rickshaw drivers and *papad* makers, loans to informal sector workers such as washerwomen. *Busti* committees were formed and training provided. In time the project was expanded to cover all Hyderabad's 450 slums (500,000 inhabitants) and housing improvement was added. Those 'squatting' on government land were given deeds to their plots and low-interest loans from the banks. By 1984, around 13,000 new houses had been built, all but 10 per cent of the cost being provided by the householders[14]. This could never have happened unless a spirit of self-help and community endeavour had not first been created.

The Hyderabad project was one of those linchpin projects that help to fashion an entirely new approach to a major social problem. Within India, this strategy for slum improvement was rapidly taken up as a model, and over a brief period of years became a blueprint for nationwide urban renewal. Unicef played an important facilitating role in developing the Indian urban basic services strategy. Between 1981 and 1984, it was extended to 42 towns and cities; then to 168 towns during the seventh Five-Year Plan period (1985-89); and finally, during the eighth Plan (1990-94), to 500 new towns and cities[15].

Over 15 years, Unicef's role in funding has been progressively reduced and taken over by central and state governments. The community-based methodology has been consistently refined, and new interventions—immunization services, for example—introduced[16]. What is now known as the Urban Basic Services for the Poor (UBSP) programme is a remarkable example of Unicef's involvement in a pioneering approach sensitive to the needs of women and children that is later adopted and absorbed into the public policy mainstream. Today, Unicef continues to provide support to UBSP, but in more of a 'back room' way: funds for training and monitoring cells at the state and national levels, and the preparation of information and educational materials.

The Hyderabad project not only had future ramifications within India; it provided a forceful illustration of the fact that slums and squatter settlements were not parasitic growths on the city fit only for condemnation, but a response, often a very adequate response, to their inhabitants' situation. Many slum residents were determined and upwardly mobile. Far from getting in the city's economic way, they were anxious to work hard in petty trading, manufacturing or service ventures—as drivers, domestic servants, fast-food vendors, stall-holders. That they met their own needs for jobs, housing and utilities against official hostility was an indication of resourcefulness, not a black mark against them. What was needed was to channel their energies and resources, to build on an existing community base, however fragile, and to remove obstacles—insecurity, lack of tenure, underemployment—standing in people's way.

Up until this time, typical programmes of slum improvement had mainly consisted of tearing down flimsy dwellings and resettling their inhabitants in 'low-cost' (actually quite expensive) high-density mass housing or 'sites and services' schemes for self-help house construction. No attempt was normally made to take into account the views of slum inhabitants. Like standard water and sanitation programmes, slum clearance and urban renewal were dominated by the physical planners and engineers. Their responsibility was to boards of public works rather than to any representative body of those whose habitat was being altered. The results were predictable. Not only did the installations they provided suffer from lack of maintenance and quickly become as dilapidated as their original setting, but in some places—the squatter compounds of Lusaka and slum communities in Madras, for instance—the inhabitants actually organized against them[17].

Unlike most municipal authorities, and donors such as the World Bank and bilateral agencies, Unicef did not see the 'software' of urban basic services as an extra, and somewhat inferior, component compared to the glories of buildings, roads and drains. Community consultation and organization were the foundation on which multisectoral service delivery could be built. Physical improvements should be introduced only when the community was ready. This kind of reversal was very difficult to put across to local engineers and those used to centralized planning and pre-established schedules. To them, community involvement was simply a means of ensuring local people's cooperation in construction and maintenance, a source of cost recovery and free labour for installations pre-planned on their behalf. They did not see it as the precondition of a successful transformation of the squalid, cramped and unhealthy urban scene.

Unicef's commitment to 'planning from below' demanded that priorities be established by the community and that the 'facilitating partners'—from different sectors and administrative levels—respond on a flexible basis. Such ideas epitomized the ideological correctness of the late 1970s that elevated people to the centre of development. But their application in schemes rather larger than the NGO micro-project had still to be worked out. Unicef and its implementing partners—usually government and statutory bodies—were obliged for reasons of budgetary planning, forward purchasing and fiscal transparency to work out expenditures ahead. Unicef's urban programmers had to find ways of resolving the tension between this requirement and 'planning from below'. One innovation was the introduction of the 'block grants' concept—originally in the Kampung Improvement Programme in Indonesia[18]—whereby money was allocated ahead of time to 'block grants' and called upon when suitable proposals emerged from community organizations. Another move was to develop links with NGOs working in slum neighbourhoods which were more able or willing than the municipality to run services such as credit schemes and preschools.

These approaches were an extension of Unicef's commitment to flexible and decentralized programming—and they worked. One example was a scheme for Environmental Health and Community Development in what were known as 'the gardens'—slums—of Colombo, Sri Lanka[19]. The Ministry of Housing had become convinced that community motivation was an essential ingredient of any significant, and permanent, upgrading of 'garden' life, so the new scheme was heavily biased towards health education. 'Health wardens', motivated young men and women, were recruited from 'the gardens' and given a two-month training course. Once they had gained the confidence of their local communities, the wardens persuaded them to set up Community Development Councils. These Councils provided the bottom layer of a three-tier consultative and management system: 'garden', district and city. Within three years, 291 Community Councils had been set up, and many hundreds of local men and women were responsible at the community level for the maintenance of taps and toilets and other preventive health activities. From these beginnings they could in time move on to other issues: women's income-generating activities and reducing the high level of school drop-out.

The fundamental goal of setting up this network of Councils was to wean the slum communities from an attitude of passivity. Their meetings were a forum to which any local resident could bring topics of common concern. The Councils also reinforced the activities of the health wardens, backing their immunization drives, nutrition demonstrations and 'little mothers' classes' for unmarried teenaged girls. Members were elected to sit on the District Development Councils and on the City Development Council. On many occasions, their feedback convinced city officials to change the course of a project to accommodate the views of the garden residents. Not only did the scheme manage to raise immunization coverage to 80 per cent in 23 council wards and bring about the mass legalization of unregistered marriages; it also helped promote participatory democratic institutions.

In 1982, a further report—'Urban Basic Services: Reaching Children and Women of the Urban Poor'—was submitted to the Executive Board[20]. This report contained a thorough and definitive statement of 'UBS' strategy, and was accompanied by case-studies of Unicef-assisted UBS programmes. In some countries, the Unicef strategy and its special emphases on flexibility and on multi-level coordination were actually beginning to have an impact on overall urban policy for low-income areas. Urban basic services had earned recognition in terms of cost, effectiveness and all-around social and economic benefit.

As the 1980s progressed, experimentation in urban basic services continued. The ingredients of programmes were similar, but the 'entry point' varied according to diversities of setting, as did priorities. In several Latin American schemes, the provision of day-care services or nutritious breakfasts for the children of working mothers predominated; a project in Baldia township, Karachi, selected soak-pit latrines as the starting-point, and later established home-based schools for girls[21]; in slums in Dhaka and other major towns of Bangladesh, a squalid and dirty environment was usually seen by slum inhabitants as their number-one problem, and initial action centred on path-laying, washing and laundry facilities, and handpump tube-wells[22]. In many schemes, the predicament of women without sufficient money and time to care for their children was high on the list.

The declaration of the 'child survival and development revolution' at the end of 1982 was a mixed blessing from the urban basic services perspective. In one sense, there was a great potential for the conjugation of forces: the existence of a basic services network in an urban area meant that an immunization campaign or any other preventive health intervention could be organized on a house-to-house basis relatively easily. The density of shanty-town populations, their accessibility and their proximity to electricity and water supplies eased logistical problems. Mass communications made it possible to put across information and 'messages'. The city of Addis Ababa was just one of many examples where an existing involvement in community development in slum *kebeles* (neighbourhoods) could be used as the launch pad for a full-scale metropolitan immunization effort[23]. Urban primary health care was integral to UBS; child survival interventions could ride on the back of urban basic services programmes, and this was the strategy that many Unicef country programmes adopted.

However, there was a fundamental difference in the underlying philosophies of the basic services and child survival approaches, a difference that had already emerged in the debate over 'selective' versus 'comprehensive' primary health care (see Chapter 2). This difference had to do with whether programmes should ultimately be led by universalist analysis and prescription, making few accommodations as to 'what' should be done—GOBI, in the case of the 'child survival revolution'—but adjusting the 'how' according to local circumstances; or whether both the 'what' and the 'how' of programmes should depend on a local situation analysis, preferably one that reflected both the subjective and objective reality of the target population. Both approaches recognized the need for services to be demand-led, but in the first case, demand would be created by social marketing techniques aimed at bringing about attitudinal change to support GOBI interventions; in the second, demand was primarily expressed by the community's articulation of its existing felt needs. In this scenario, meeting these needs provided an 'entry point' for a range of interventions mutually agreed upon between providers and recipients, in which child health and survival measures would tend, but could not be guaranteed, to rank high in the list.

At the zenith of ideological 'alternative' thinking, so discredited had doing things *for* people become that the pendulum had swung to an extreme antithesis: the only things, or the priority things, that should be done were those that the people themselves were able to articulate—in consumer parlance, those for which there was already demand. To many for whom 'basic services' and 'primary health care' had represented an important ideological shift, the CSD approach, because it was prescriptive, appeared a regression to the old, discarded way of imposing solutions on people rather than doing things with them. They found it difficult to perceive that a push for preselected activities could be interpreted not as an opposite and outworn strategy, but as a useful corrective to the shortcomings of the new approach. In this interpretation, the overriding purpose of CSD was to put the benefits of modern science and technology at the service of the poor. Since these were by definition people who, because they knew nothing about the benefits of modern science, did not feel an existing 'demand' for its products, it was necessary to provide them with the information both to sense and to articulate one.

Without doubt, Unicef's UBS strategy as expressed in 1982 was very much in tune with the 'alternative' thinking to which GOBI and CSD were counterposed. Until the early 1980s, Unicef had supported a policy of identifying particular groups of children especially affected by poverty—in backward areas, in urban slums, among ethnic minorities—and focusing services on them. The 'child survival revolution' signalled a decline for this kind of selectivity, as well as for the 'let the community decide' approach to service delivery. But whatever the prominence given to GOBI interventions throughout the 1980s, most country programmes represented a mix of inspirations and strategies. Although in some countries UBS and 'area-based' services found themselves eclipsed, in others they were adapted to become vehicles for CSD without losing their integrity. Certain UBS programmes—those in India, the Philippines, Bangladesh, Ethiopia, Sri Lanka, Central America and Kenya, for example—flourished. UBS programmes helped to keep alive within Unicef the concepts of community participation and 'basic services' that were such an important inheritance of the 1970s[24].

The quality of these programmes and their effectiveness gained Unicef credibility with Ministries of Local Government and Municipal Authorities—partners with clout and resources. These relationships were to prove fruitful for child survival advocacy. In 1990, an initiative of the Italian Committee for Unicef with 300 mayors of Italian cities set in motion the idea of creating a worldwide movement of 'Mayors as Defenders of Children'[25]. At the global level, this initiative was launched jointly by Unicef and the Mayor of Dakar in Senegal in January 1992, at a ceremony that included 20 mayors and municipal leaders from 16 different countries. They pledged to take up the challenge of preparing municipal Plans of Action in line with the national programmes of action currently under development as an outcome of the World Summit for Children. A second colloquium of Mayors was held in July 1993 in Mexico City, and a third in

Paris in December 1994 at the invitation of Mayor Jacques Chirac, in collaboration with the French Committee for Unicef[26].

In the final decades of the 20th century, whatever the position of the urban child on Unicef's organizational agenda and however muted the enthusiasm at headquarters level for strong promotion of the urban basic services strategy, every day a higher proportion of the world's people were becoming city-dwellers. Urban children had to be included as a Unicef programming target, whether as part of a universalist strategy or as a specific group. And among urban children, one group was becoming daily more visible: those who had taken to working and living on the streets.

During the 1980s, the structural problems of poverty prevailing in most cities of the developing world were exacerbated by economic crisis and recession. Here was a new strain to add to the existing configuration of rapid population growth and rapid urbanization[27].

In an attempt to plug the economic dike, many countries adopted drastic measures as part of International Monetary Fund (IMF) rescue packages. Subsidies and price controls on food and other essentials were removed; employment in government and municipal establishments was reduced; public investment programmes and social expenditures were cut. The brunt of 'adjustment' was borne disproportionately by the urban poor. One result was a mushrooming growth in the number of people seeking work in the informal sector—as market porters, street vendors, stall-holders, street-walkers, car-washers, rickshaw drivers, scavengers, fast-food suppliers—and an increase in the number of people forced to seek work in servile and unprotected occupations. A conspicuous feature of this volatile, disorganized and statistically elusive workforce was that it contained a high proportion of women and youth. Some of its participants were no older than five or six, and many were in their early teens[28].

The growth of cities in the developing world and the increasing hardship experienced by many of their inhabitants were altering the terms of family life. In the traditional rural setting, children participated in the daily working round on the land or in the household as an integral part of their upbringing. As soon as she could walk, the small girl in rural Asia or Africa collected twigs for fuel or carried a tiny water jar. The young boy herded goats or assisted his father in the workshop. Few occupations in the modern city lent themselves to a parallel process of learning and working under family tutelage. But the need for all members of the family to contribute to the household economy was as severe, if not more so, because cash was needed for all basic necessities: food, shelter, water, fuel. So as soon as the child accompanying her or his mother to the market stall in Lagos or Lima, Bombay or Brazzaville, could carry a tray, run errands or mind the stall, earning became part of daily routine.

Even if the youngster's working life began at a parent's side, it rarely stayed that way. In most cities a hierarchy of informal occupations developed, some of which were dominated by the young—usually by boys but occasionally by girls as well: flower girls, parking boys, vendors of newspapers or chewing-gum through car windows, scavenging on city garbage heaps, collecting fares on taxis, selling artefacts to tourists. Many such occupations exposed youngsters to hazardous influences, especially accidents[29]. As the children became caught up in the street world, their peers often began to exert more affective influence than parents. As the bonds of family life weakened, children might gravitate to a lifestyle centred on the street, the railway station, the promenade or the dazzling shopping complex. Some became separated from their families altogether, taking up an open-air or doorway abode, sleeping rough, living rough and sometimes descending into drugs, alcohol and crime.

During their own period of rapid urbanization in the 19th century, the cities of Europe and North America had similarly nurtured their populations of barrow-boys, waifs and strays, and their gangs of miniature hooligans. Until a relatively advanced stage of the urbanization and industrialization process in the developing world, the presence of children on the street and in the marketplace was so familiar a feature of the urban landscape that it had barely attracted notice. But as their numbers rose, and as in some cities their presence began to feel not only ubiquitous but threatening, the late 20th century rediscovered these child victims of poverty-stricken urban sprawl as 'street children'. This label principally described the venue in which they were noticed and their dirty and unkempt appearance; it implied a mix of abandonment, vagrancy and youthful criminality.

The phenomenon was most evident in Latin America, where by the end of the 1970s two thirds of the population was urbanized. Some estimates—much of the early information about street children was speculative—put the number of children living wholly or partially without parental support in Latin America and the Caribbean in the many millions. Of these, between 5 and 10 per cent were children whose living, eating, working and sleeping place was the street, the rubbish dump, the car park and the deserted building[30]. Whatever the true dimensions of the problem, the numbers implied that the city was becoming increasingly antithetical to childhood and that the scale of family dislocation within the urbanization process demanded a public policy response. Most efforts to respond to the urban child in distress were still limited to religious and charitable social welfare, or outdated systems of institutional incarceration that amounted to an even worse abuse of childhood than street life itself.

During the International Year of the Child in 1979, many problems relating to children—exploitation, abuse, child prostitution, children on the streets—that had previously been denied or ignored by city authorities projecting a travel poster image were given an international airing. One of those imperceptible changes in the moral climate began to occur. The exposure of child maltreatment—which happened in industrialized as well as developing countries—might cause national embarrassment and offend national pride, but even quite touchy governments were beginning to acknowledge that such practices were wrong and that steps should be taken to stop them. Reluctantly at first because it had feared antagonizing governmental partners, Unicef began to assist in the exposure of these child protection issues by providing fora—publications, meetings—in which they could be discussed[31]. Fuelled by European NGOs, the debate moved rapidly forward and Unicef found itself under pressure to get programmatically involved. Street children were the obvious starting-point.

In 1981, Peter Taçon, a Canadian who had been working with street children in Latin America for several years, was appointed by Unicef to conduct a situation analysis on street children in the Americas region and recommend a course of action. Taçon was instrumental in gaining recognition for street children's perception of their own reality: that they were workers, not vagabonds, and not out of choice but of necessity; that their values were the values of survival, not of conscient criminals and thugs. Taçon did more than any other single person to speak out sympathetically for street children and put their cause on the international map. He was an advocate, and exemplar, of the thesis that such children needed, above all, support in their working and personal lives, not adult rejection and condemnation. Street children needed to stay with their families or be offered alternative family settings, not to be thrust into corrective institutions whose likely outcome was to harden their resistance to the rules of society, completing their marginalization and making their delinquency a foregone conclusion. Taçon left Unicef in 1986 to set up Childhope International, an organization dedicated to the street child's cause.

The problem was at its most prolific and its scariest in the cities of Brazil. In 1981, Peter Taçon accompanied Brazilian officials from the Ministry of Social Assistance and Welfare and FUNABEM, the national body responsible for abandoned children, on a visit to NGOs around the country working with street children in unconventional ways[32]. The result was a project funded by

CIDA and the Canadian Committee for Unicef, initially for two years: the 'Alternative Programme for Street Children'. This was the first Unicef-assisted, government-backed effort to offer technical support to NGOs working with street-based children and their families. The project team saw themselves as facilitators of community responses to a social problem, not as a new street children's organization. They held meetings and workshops for NGO personnel, offered training, brought isolated groups into communication with one another and enabled the members of a growing network to build a strong organizational base[33].

To counter the official inclination to view the street child problem from a delinquency perspective, the project managed to create a 'policy dissonance, instituting within the public sector a counterweight to its own existing policies and programmes in order to challenge and change them'[34]. It also helped build up an attitude of public ownership of the street child issue. By 1986, voluntary bodies made up of individuals and organizations acting on behalf of street children had been set up in many Brazilian cities to defend them from abuse, maltreatment, even murder. These bodies were able to mobilize resources for all kinds of activities—street education, soup kitchens, sports and recreation, preschools—as well as mount vigorous campaigns on behalf of children's rights.

An increasing number of Unicef country offices—in India, Kenya, Ecuador, Guatemala, the Philippines and elsewhere—were becoming exercised about urban children in distress. Although the 'child survival revolution' was just getting into its stride and the Unicef upper echelon was anxious that organizational energy and resources not be swept hither and yon, some contemporary issues concerning children could not be ignored. In the aftermath of the International Year of the Child, certain Unicef Executive Board members were not prepared to let issues it had brought into the open fade away, nor did the international political and economic climate give any cause for complacency. One of those who persistently championed the protection of children from the fallout of man's inhumanity to man in all contexts in which children's vulnerability laid them open to special deprivation was Nils Thedin, the leading delegate of Sweden and a senior statesman of Unicef.

In 1984, on the fifth anniversary of the IYC, an NGO forum was held alongside the Unicef Executive Board annual session, meeting in Rome[35]. This created pressure on behalf of street children and other categories 'in especially difficult circumstances'. The Board therefore asked that a special policy review be undertaken on programmes relating to children suffering from disadvantages typically associated with poverty, but extra to poverty itself. A two-year process of study and collective review began. After discussion, it was decided that the catch-all phrase 'children in especially difficult circumstances' (CEDC) should cover street and working children, abused and neglected children and child victims of armed conflict[36]. Among these categories, street children were the most prominent as a new target of Unicef programming. This was not because they were necessarily the worst off, but because they were highly visible, there was growing public and philanthropic interest in their plight and they had become a symbol worldwide of the rediscovery of children outside the health and survival framework as an international *cause célèbre*.

Economic stress and the necessity of children working to help support their families were now increasingly seen as the dynamics behind the street child phenomenon. As a result, the Unicef policy review was prepared with the cooperation of the International Labour Office (ILO). This partner organization within the UN system had long been concerned with the abolition and regulation of child work, primarily via advocacy and international labour conventions. The policy review also provided an opportunity for multi-organizational discussions on child protection in different parts of the world. Increasingly, NGOs were being seen as the front-line organizations for CEDC, with Unicef helping to bring government and municipalities into a technically supportive role—the pattern pioneered in Brazil.

Unicef could also play a role alongside ILO at the international level in advocacy and research, helping to act as an instigator and facilitator of local child-centred NGO associations and occasionally to act as moderator between campaigning NGOs and the officialdom they challenged. Unicef's engagement in programming and advocacy on behalf of street children presaged a deepening of the relationship with the NGO community commenced under UBS—a relationship that was less paternal and ceremonial, more equitable and respectful of NGOs' comparative advantages than had often been the case in the past.

The 1986 report to the Board on 'Children in Especially Difficult Circumstances' took the line that child work per se was not the problem; that work was a natural part of growing up. It stated: 'It is largely through work, usually in a family context, that children become socialized and learn adult skills and responsibilities. But child work becomes *exploitative* if it threatens his physical, mental, emotional or social development.'[37] Research showed that most street children were neither abandoned nor runaway; they turned out to be living at home, even if 'home' was not the safe and protected haven that childhood deserved. A distinction was drawn between 'children *on* the street'—children working in the open-air economy and still integrated with their families; and 'children *of* the street'—the 5 to 10 per cent who had run away from home or been rejected. Families stressed by poverty to the point of sending a 12-year-old son off to shine shoes or scavenge trash needed an approach different from children reduced to begging and petty theft as a means of independent survival.

In countries where programmes for urban basic services existed, the candidate families in the slums were the same families whose children had a tendency to drop out of school and ended up roaming shopping malls looking for ways to earn money. In such settings, urban basic services and efforts on behalf of street and working children naturally converged. This was the case in the Philippines, where a UBS programme had been taking shape in experimental form since 1983[38].

During the early 1980s, as economic recession bit deep into Filipino urban pockets, the phenomenon of children adopting public spaces as their regular haunts began to grow more conspicuous. To begin with, the civic authorities greeted the increasing presence of children on the streets with old-style punitive responses, flinging these young transgressors into jail. Gradually, the Department of Social Welfare began to realize that—as with the eviction of squatter populations from illegally occupied land—the forces propelling children onto the streets were not susceptible to the coercive removal of the victims. In 1984, senior child welfare officials visited Brazil at Unicef's invitation to see what happened when a programme was sensitive to the street child's world view and repudiated institutionalization in favour of family and community reintegration. This marked the beginning of an attitudinal and policy transformation.

In 1986, sweeping political change came to the Philippines with the election of President Corazon Aquino. The new administration pledged to do much more for the poor—and much more for children. With some behind-the-scenes prompting from Unicef, a 'Year for the Protection of Filipino Exploited Children' was declared for 1986-87. The Council for the Welfare of Children was revitalized and given the task of reforming Philippine policies towards street and working children. In a society with a deeply ingrained view of poverty as antisocial and reprobate, such changes could not take place overnight. Police who overzestfully rounded up 'truants' needed re-education; antiquated laws that imprisoned children alongside adult offenders needed replacement; and city halls had to be persuaded that policies towards the urban child in distress would be more effective if they were more humane.

Just as the cause of street children gained ground in the new political environment, so did urban basic services. A Presidential Commission on the Urban Poor was set up to coordinate programmes for slum improvement. Between 1988 and 1992, the Unicef-assisted urban basic services programme targeted over 1 million children under six years old, over 200 mothers and

35,000 street children in the poorest *barangays* (neighbourhoods) in 10 cities. As well as each city hall, the Presidential Commission for the Urban Poor and hundreds of NGOs and urban poor associations were involved[39].

The participatory process at the heart of UBS in the Philippines was centred—as in the case of all successful Unicef-backed initiatives—on the fabric of people's lives. Instead of officialdom making an assessment of what the community needed and then delivering improved roads, drains and buildings, the community itself was responsible for assessing needs and drawing up appropriate plans. The hallmark of the process in a neighbourhood or sub-neighbourhood (*barangay* or *purok*) was evidence of community self-monitoring: the presence in a prominent place of a large board on which were displayed the demographic and social indicators of the locality. These included the number of families and children, immunization coverage, the number of mothers receiving livelihood loans and the number of children enrolled in the scholarship programme that kept them away from the lure of the streets. Community assessment, service delivery and monitoring were matters fully in the public domain.

Based on its initial survey and analysis, the Barangay Development Committee drew up an improvement plan. Once completed, the plan was forwarded to the city authorities, and after the necessary consultations with health, education and other departments, it entered the overall city plan for urban basic services. When the necessary resources had been allocated from various budgets and from Unicef, the plan could go into implementation. With guidance and material inputs from the appropriate departments, the Barangay Development Committee and its subcommittees for health, sanitation and so on carried it out. Technical guidance—training, advising, capacity-building—was often provided by an NGO.

In Olongapo, a city notorious for a 'hospitality industry' set up to cater to the off-duty needs of American servicemen at Subic Bay, twin programmes for UBS and street children emerged in the late 1980s. Among the *barangay* subcommittees set up in the communities was one to deal with street children. Within UBS, families with street children were among those identified for special loans and scholarships. At the same time, street educators from a project known as 'Reach-up' worked directly with the 400 or so children who had lost contact with their families. They provided basic education and a cheap daily meal, and helped child workers form occupational associations: plastic bag vendors, pushcart boys, scavengers and bus-washers 'unions'. The entry point for preventive and protective work directed at children under stress was both the street and the family; the combination meant that the epidemic of children lured into street life could be checked.

For many NGOs around the world working with street children, the immediate concern was loss of education. The Undugu Society of Kenya, one of the earliest organizations to work with Africa's street children, in this case with Nairobi's parking boys, regarded children on the street primarily as out-of-schoolers and set up community schools at which they could make good their loss of educational opportunity[40]. The Underprivileged Children's Educational Project (UCEP) in Bangladesh similarly focused on basic education, leading on to vocational training in carpentry, electronics, tailoring and secretarial skills[41].

Shelter was a concern of many NGOs. A great number of small, local philanthropic organizations all over Asia and Latin America ran drop-in centres for street children where they could wash, cook themselves a meal, play board games and attend literacy classes if they wished. Another priority was health: Project Alternatives (*Projecto Alternativos*) in Tegucigalpa, Honduras, took as its entry point 'street PHC', alongside basic education, psychosocial counselling, and community kitchens. Many NGOs also worked with the families of street children, trying to support parent-child relationships and help cash-starved mothers create a better domestic base. In the Philippines, Brazil, Kenya and India, national and city fora of street children's organizations began to work with police training institutions to reduce police violence against street children. In Syria, the police themselves initiated programmes of street child activity[42].

An increasing number of Unicef offices began to develop working relationships with the growing number of NGOs—both new ones brought into existence by the problem and old ones newly taking it up—providing services for children on the streets. In most cases, the approach adopted was similar: elastic, unstructured, aimed at building networks and capacity among NGOs, welding their existing efforts into the equivalent of a rather anarchic programme, guiding technically and topping-up financially but not superimposing an unwanted managerial direction. Sometimes this worked well as an enabling and motivating process; sometimes it did not. Bringing diverse NGOs together—Moslems with Christians, soft-spoken nuns with activist firebrands, highly professional executives with untrained amateurs—to develop a joint action plan was difficult enough, let alone persuading them to work with officialdom and vice versa. Sometimes differences were irreconcilable and the role of the coordinating body—arbiter? manager? clearing-house?—never crystallized.

In India, Unicef felt its way slowly into a strategy, fostering the establishment of NGO fora on street children in the large cities. These were open and democratic grass-roots networks of organizations involved with street children.

In Calcutta, it took until 1992 to make the city NGO Forum on Street Children fully operational[43]. At a workshop convened by Unicef, 45 assorted NGOs pooled information about their activities and capacities. Out of this a citywide picture of what was being done for street children emerged, as well as a plan of how different groups could supplement each other's services. The NGOs were gradually able to expand their total reach among the many thousands of street children in Calcutta geographically, demographically and by type of intervention, at very little extra cost. Unicef's role in all of this was to underpin, facilitate, pay some joint costs, mediate and make sure that city hall and its departments duly shared responsibility.

By the early 1990s, Unicef had developed methodologies for researching the situation of children in the streets (leading to studies in Dhaka, Mexico City, Quito, Bombay, Madras and elsewhere) and had accumulated a large body of programmatic knowledge. What had evolved was a loose-leaf approach, not a tight policy with systematic guidelines. NGOs small and large, some of which had previously kept aloof from government and Unicef, had discovered the usefulness of enrolling an intergovernmental organization in their cause[44]. On its side, Unicef had entered into a new kind of partnership with the NGO community, initially via UBS but more thoroughly and pervasively through the street child issue.

Although at headquarters level Unicef was still reserving its most powerful guns for child survival and was therefore a rather muted champion of children in especially difficult circumstances, this was an issue whose star had risen independently, developing an international momentum of its own. Urban poverty was one part of the picture. The other was the fact that CEDC were, above all, children in need of protection. Their cause was therefore right at the heart of the effort to articulate, and carry onto the international statute book, the UN Convention on the Rights of the Child.

During the period in which Unicef began to recognize that the pervasiveness of children working on city streets required coherent policy and programmatic action, the child-related NGO community was becoming increasingly vocal. The IYC had prompted research into the plight of many disadvantaged groups, and these predicaments the NGOs now sought to bring further into the international and media spotlight. The two most prominent categories of children attracting their attention were street children, whose multiple predicaments ran the gamut of child protection problems: abandonment, homelessness, exploitation, hazardous work, risk of sexual enticement, drugs, vagrancy, crime, trouble with the law; and child victims of warfare and other types of emergency[45]. The language of child-related protest was changing in tone. To the traditional emotionalism of appeals on behalf of children was being added the vocabulary of social justice and human rights.

Not surprisingly, therefore, the NGO community saw an international convention on children's rights as a key instrument and campaigning basis for the protection of childhood from the stresses of the contemporary world. During the 1980s, the NGOs maintained strong pressure on the post-IYC intergovernmental drafting group set up under UN auspices to develop a text for such a convention[46]. As more governments—notably the Swedish and Canadian—began to give their backing, by the mid-1980s the realization of a convention appeared a distinct possibility.

Through Defence for Children International, the NGOs' umbrella body on child rights, human rights organizations and specialists in international law became involved. The NGOs also asked Unicef to take a more active part in the process: it had, after all, been designated by the General Assembly as lead agency in the UN system for IYC follow-up. Nevertheless, Unicef's position throughout the first half of the 1980s remained that of passive observer. It helped the NGOs by convening meetings and offering facilities in Geneva, which allowed them to hammer out their positions. But the idea of a convention was not one to which Unicef was itself—initially at least—institutionally seriously committed[47].

Under Jim Grant's leadership, Unicef had become much more involved in—and professional at—advocacy, especially in support of the 'child survival revolution'. However, this was not the same kind of campaigning advocacy in which many activist NGOs engaged. To Unicef, delivery of concrete benefits to children was the most important task; the advocacy it engaged in was normally an attempt to leverage certain principles and practice—those exemplified in its own programme—into broader public policy. Advocacy to Unicef was not a matter of exposure, critique and campaigns for political or legislative reform.

The campaigning NGOs operated in a very different culture. In the case of many rights issues—sexual exploitation, abuse and neglect, servitude, economic exploitation—their standard response was to undertake advocacy on behalf of civil liberties, or on versions of civil liberties not yet universally absorbed into cultural and legal systems. Unicef was inhibited by its intergovernmental character from engaging, or wishing to engage, in this kind of confrontational campaign. Its emphasis was on programming, and in the case of CEDC, its programming approach was still embryonic. It had yet to view an incipient convention on children's rights as an instrument that could support existing programmatic activity or open up new programme opportunities.

What perhaps was not understood in Unicef's New York headquarters was the degree to which, within the European perspective, the language of human rights had already begun to be co-opted into the development discourse. Campaigns on what in the US were traditionally seen as two quite separate sets of issues—the one political, the other social and economic—had on the other side of the Atlantic begun to converge. A structural analysis of poverty in the South had, by the early 1980s, come to dominate development thinking in intellectual circles and leading NGOs, not only in Europe but in Latin America and elsewhere[48]. This suggested that without the kind of democratic changes that would unsettle the domination of power in much of the South by élites—class élites, racial or ethnic élites, élites fashioned economically by the workings of the Western capitalist system, or politically by the machinations of both Eastern and Western blocs—the development process would continue to discriminate against the poor. This was the era of heightened international opposition to South African apartheid and US intervention in Central America, and the establishment of safeguards for human rights was seen in such settings as a *sine qua non* of equitable human development. But these settings were only the most conspicuous instances of the natural convergence of the rights and development agendas; the principle was general.

If the development debate was moving on, so was the debate about childhood. The terms of family life and upbringing were undergoing seismic change, especially, but not exclusively, in the developing world[49]. One of the fundamental influences was the 20th-century decline in infant mortality, made possible by rising prosperity and the spread of life-saving medical and public health technologies. This decline had already made the brunt of its impact felt in the industrialized world. In the poorer parts of the world, as Unicef's call for a 'child survival revolution' had underlined, this transition with all its potential impacts on family structure and reproductive behaviour was far from complete. Increased child survival led to a preference for small families; this in turn led to a much larger parental investment in each individual child.

At the same time had come a corresponding demand from parents that the State should fulfil its share of the raising of the new generation by investing in maternal and infant care, education, child care, family planning and family support. In the past 50 to 100 years, childhood had undergone an expansion in every direction. It had lengthened in years and become more protected; it had become in the eyes of society a vitally important passage in which investment could not be skimped; children's upbringing had become a major target of social policy, scientific inquiry and popular debate. A revolution had occurred in which the child had become the quality product of the industrialized and industrializing society[50].

At the same time, many pressures on family life were ambiguous at best in terms of their outcome for children—especially since children had now become the repository of high levels of parental hope and expectation. The growth of commercialism and material expectations that accompanied rapid urbanization and the drive for educational qualifications exacerbated individualism and pressures on the family purse. Evolution in labour and employment markets was everywhere making the future for young people potentially more exciting, but also much more uncertain and insecure. Women's demand for equality with men was helping to reduce male oppression within the family and society; but there were repercussions on the stability of homes and married life. The number of women raising children on their own was rising all over the world, as were divorce rates; there were increases in reported domestic violence, drug use, alcoholism and juvenile crime. There was also an effect on family structure of the new preoccupation with the individual's rights over his or her sexuality: precocious sex, postponement of marriage, and more frequent, or more frequent exposure of, child sexual abuse. Since the advent of the middle-class industrial society in the late 19th century, childhood had been mythologized as an idyll of pre-adult bliss, governed by the postponement of maturity in a cocoon of discipline, innocence and love. Now childhood was in turmoil. It was increasingly apparent that a large number of children, even in well-heeled societies with their growing 'underclass', experienced childhood as a time of deprivation, psychosocial distress and broken promise.

The pursuit of rights as a rallying cry helped redefine the children's cause. It provided a framework in which to view childhood universally, across cultures and societies, across the North-South, rich-poor divides. It stripped away the welfarist connotations that had clung to the children debate in spite of the efforts of Unicef and some others to centralize it in a world poverty and development perspective. In most intellectual settings, such an idea had never been truly persuasive. In spite of the common use of the suffering African or Asian child in charitable appeals, children were mostly seen by development analysts and campaigners for solidarity with the South as too sentimental an object for serious attention. The rights dimension gave a much sharper edge to the children's cause and the inherent value system associated with championing the child. The chord it struck brought on board a new and wider constituency.

The pressure from the European NGOs and some of the National Committees for Unicef to be more active on behalf of child rights and the incipient

Convention was communicated strongly to the 1984 Executive Board meeting by the parallel NGO Forum[51]. This thrust to widen the Unicef agenda was not altogether welcomed by the Unicef secretariat at a relatively early stage in the promulgation of GOBI and the 'child survival and development revolution', which was after all a purposeful attempt to narrow the focus in a very different direction. Grant was personally sceptical at this stage of events that governments—especially the US Government—would really, when faced with it, be willing to back an international instrument that entitled children—by definition minors who do not vote—to claim rights, independently of parents and adults[52]. However, the mood of the Board itself was more positive. It was this same Board meeting that set in motion the study into 'children in especially difficult circumstances'.

The turning point in Unicef's willingness to throw its weight behind the Convention came during 1985-86. The handful of those in Unicef who passionately believed that the passage of a Convention deserved Unicef's wholehearted support finally convinced Jim Grant that the time had come to get more actively involved. An important ally was Philip Alston, a lawyer who had been on the staff of the UN Centre for Human Rights and made a specialization of the application of international human rights legislation to children; he now became an influential Unicef adviser. Grant sent his Deputy Executive Director for External Relations, Tarzie Vittachi, to the 1986 drafting group session to indicate a different level of Unicef intent. And the debate on the CEDC review at the 1986 Executive Board meeting gave an important boost to organizational involvement: the Board Chairman, Anwarul Chowdhury of Bangladesh, an advocate of the Convention, managed to obtain the passage of a resolution committing Unicef to greater involvement in the drafting process[53].

The critical point of persuasion as far as Grant was concerned was that a Convention could be used to underpin the 'child survival and development revolution'. He had perceived the Convention as heavily emphasizing the protection of exploited and abused children, and believed that many governments would be antagonized by an international legal instrument that confronted them with their failures. Once he was persuaded that rights on behalf of child survival and development could be included, he became attracted by the idea that signatory countries could be obliged to shoulder mandatory obligations to undertake immunization campaigns and other child survival actions. However, for this potential to be realized, the draft Convention needed considerable amendment.

Up until 1987 the draft contained no mention of 'the child's right to survival', and less than adequate mention of rights to health care, food and nutrition, education and minimum standards of social provision. If these rights could be fully articulated, the Convention would become an enduring mechanism for gathering political will behind GOBI, CSD and subsequent child-related human development campaigns. During 1987, suitable amendments were introduced into the draft text, and a target date of 1989—the 30th anniversary of the Declaration of the Rights of the Child and the 10th anniversary of the IYC—was set for the Convention's passage[54].

Over the next two years, Unicef threw the formidable powers of advocacy it had originally developed to promote the 'child survival revolution' behind the movement to pass the Convention into law. Grant pushed the Convention at ECOSOC, at other intergovernmental fora, within the UN system, and by personal initiative among Ambassadors at the UN of the more reluctant member states. He also began to bring it into his speeches at meetings of all kinds and on every continent, enlisting the support of First Ladies, professional associations, parliamentarians, NGOs, the press and television media. It was at this time that the Unicef *State of the World's Children* reports began to talk of a 'new ethos for children, a new worldwide awareness and concern, a powerful "sea-change" in what world opinion considers to be morally acceptable and what it does not'[55]. Both the gains of the 'child survival revolution' and the forthcoming Convention were attributed to the 'onward march of ethics with awareness, morality with capacity'. This was a theme that Grant was to develop in the period leading up to the Children's Summit and far beyond.

Within Unicef, a Convention Task Force developed contacts with government delegations, set up an information service for country offices and National Committees, and generally saw that the Convention was internally perceived as having a high priority for advocacy. Unicef Goodwill Ambassadors were encouraged to mention the Convention in their Unicef public appearances. A combined Unicef/DCI Information Kit was produced and widely distributed. Some National Committees were important movers and shakers for the Convention from a relatively early stage. One of these was the Italian Committee led by the energetic Aldo Farina. With the NGO Committee for Unicef, the Italian Committee hosted a meeting in Lignano in September 1987 that attracted the participation of 120 representatives of NGOs and National Committees. This meeting helped to recruit to the cause a wide NGO constituency and bring on board some of the Unicef National Committees that were still hesitant about engaging in such a potentially controversial area as children's rights[56].

One of the most important tasks perceived by Unicef was to mobilize support for the Convention in the developing world. Unicef representatives all over Africa, Asia and Latin America made approaches at senior levels in government and simultaneously developed programmes of events to sensitize the general public. As a result of these approaches, a number of new national bodies were created to examine the text of the Convention from a technical, legal and cultural perspective, and conferences, workshops and symposia were held. Examples included a meeting on Children in Armed Conflict in Kenya in July 1987 under the auspices of the African Network on Prevention and Protection against Child Abuse and Neglect (ANPPCAN), followed by another on Child Rights the following year; 1988 saw the formation of an intersectoral group on the Convention in Mozambique and of an Asian Task Force on the Convention in Bangkok. In Buenos Aires, NGOs from all over Latin America met to review the proposed Convention and drafted a Latin American Charter on the Rights of the Child. In Egypt, a National Council for Childhood and Motherhood was set up with First Lady Suzanne Mubarak at its head, and a national conference on the Convention was held in Alexandria in November 1988. All of these activities brought in new partners on behalf of children, especially lawyers and academics for whom the championship of childhood was a novel concern.

They also helped build support within government, which was translated into diplomatic backing for resolutions at international meetings. Special fora on children's rights were held among established regional groups of countries such as the OAU (Organization of African Unity), ASEAN (Association of South-East Asian Nations) and SAARC (South Asian Association for Regional Cooperation); the Summit meetings of SAARC were the first to endorse the Convention at such a prestigious level. In all this activity, close cooperation was maintained with the Centre on Human Rights, whose administrative role vis-à-vis the Convention had to be duly respected. This was not a Unicef product, even if Unicef inevitably became the UN agency most visibly associated, given its mandate for children and its worldwide capacity for advocacy and social mobilization.

In 1988, the Working Group met for two extended sessions to complete the review of the text and the drafting process. Prior to these meetings, Unicef organized informal consultations that allowed NGOs and others not members of governmental delegations to make an input in the run-up to a finished text. The Article that caused the most friction during these final stages concerned the involvement of children in armed conflict, in particular the age of recruitment into the armed forces. In spite of some delegations' reservations about settling for weaker protections than those already enunciated in other international instruments simply in order to achieve consensus, the final text was adopted unanimously in the Working Group and therefore went forward to its formal procedural fate—through ECOSOC, the Third Committee (on social and humanitarian affairs) and to its final staging post in the UN General Assembly—without need for further debate. There is no question that it is a major triumph, one often overlooked, to achieve consensus among upwards of 160 nations on a text, particularly one due to pass into international law. The transcendence of children as an issue—their big political card—helped to work its magic.

During the months before the 1989 General Assembly, Unicef offices accelerated their promotion of the now definitive text and tried to pave the way for the adoption of the Convention in the General Assembly, and the subsequent ratification process. At Unicef headquarters, a rearguard diplomatic initiative was conducted to head off any threat by one or other government to reopen debate on the text, which—fortunately—did not materialize. After safe passage through the Third Committee, the Convention was adopted in the UN General Assembly on 20 November 1989, 30 years to the day on the anniversary of the adoption of the Declaration of the Rights of the Child. A huge party, attended by 300 children as well as UN delegates and officials and Convention-supporting NGOs, celebrated the victory.

On 26 January 1990, the Convention was opened for signature and 61 countries signed. This was the highest number ever to indicate an intent to ratify a human rights instrument at the very first opportunity. In February, Ghana became the first country to ratify the Convention. Over the next few months, as part of the lead-up to the World Summit for Children in September, a sufficient number of states ratified—20—to enable the Convention to come into effect as an internationally binding treaty.

What in fact had the nations of the world accepted on behalf of children? They had agreed upon a set of universal norms and standards to be upheld vis-à-vis the upbringing and care of children, by parents and guardians, by teachers and caregivers, by their substitutes where normal family and community mechanisms had broken down, in appropriate consultation with children themselves; these norms were to be sanctioned and pursued by ratifying states via national legislation and its implementation, and their performance in so doing was to be monitored by a panel of international experts constituting a Committee on the Rights of the Child.

Apart from general articles supporting non-discrimination and the 'best interests of the child' as overriding principles, the rights set out by the Convention fell essentially under four headings: survival, development, protection and participation. Survival rights included the rights to life and life-protective interventions (unspecified, but understood to mean GOBI-type interventions) and to assistance from the State in times of emergency. Development rights included those to nurture, love, food, health care and education; and the duty of the State to support parents' responsibilities in these contexts by social service provision. Protection articles established the child's rights not to be abused, neglected or exploited economically, sexually or in other ways. Participatory articles conferred on the child the right to be consulted in matters that affected his or her well-being, for example, in custody cases, and to have a voice in the wider society. Not only did the Convention place new obligations on adults vis-à-vis children, especially on the State; it took children a significant step away from the traditional view that the young not only are the dependants of parents (or adult substitutes) but are subject to their absolute control until they reach the age of majority.

In one or two countries around the world, the voice of child claimants to these rights had already made itself resoundingly heard.

Within Unicef, the rise of concern with children's rights was closely associated with the rise of concern surrounding street children. Although the protection of children in war- and emergency-related situations also fell within the scope of a rights rather than welfarist framework, these were situations in which Unicef had always been programmatically involved. To those who had difficulty understanding what the advent of rights meant for their work and the children's cause more generally, the need to develop programmes for children on and of the streets was the easy path to comprehension of the changes expected. As a result, for many years the misperception lingered in some parts of Unicef that issues of children's rights were exclusively to do with street children, who themselves were synonymous with CEDC. Although this confusion was irritating to those articulating a much more significant change in the concept of childhood and in adult-child relationships, the fact that it was so pervasive led in part from its substance.

Children who lived on the streets often suffered abuse at the hands of the police and in government institutions; many were unjustly deprived of their liberty and endured blatant violations of human rights. On their own side, they might yearn for love and affection, desire skills and education and deeply regret the childhood and protections they had lost; but few were willing or able to return to structured dependence on adult control after months or years of independent and unstructured living. The freedoms and protections in connection with children forced into a premature assumption of adult responsibilities and pitted against an unfriendly adult world have adult connotations inapplicable to the child growing up in the traditional household or 'modern', middle-class home. Not surprisingly, therefore, the issue of children's rights surfaced most prominently around confrontations between children on the streets and repressive—or protective, from which it is sometimes indistinguishable—adult authority.

Perhaps the first stirrings of this confrontation should be dated from the 1976 youth rebellion in Soweto, South Africa, but this uprising of school-goers against the injustice of an apartheid curriculum was too early to be analysed in terms of children's rights. So the story starts instead in Brazil a few years later[57]. During the early 1980s, the Brazilian military regime was preparing to make way for civilian rule after around 20 years in power. The epidemic of children on the streets was coincidentally reaching crisis proportions, and as a result the expression of demands for children's rights became integrally associated with the stirrings of legalized democracy. Apart from the numbers of children involved (not as many as the 30 million often then quoted but still a very large number) and extreme actions taken against some of them, including targeted murder, this connection occurred because of the organizational networking of those trying to support them. The process had been started by the 'Alternative Programme for Street Children' in which Unicef had been instrumental[58].

The street child in his or her twin guise of social menace and victim was a symptom of the ingrained poverty not only tolerated but structurally reinforced by the old patriarchal and militaristic order. To many Brazilians, this child appeared a potent symbol of a society in need of radical change. Boys and girls who had not passed school age, in many cases had not passed puberty, had been let down by their families and society and were now undergoing brutalization and criminalization on the streets. At a time of feverish political activity, the acutely deprived and socially damaged child became a burning issue, and one around which disparate groups rediscovering the joys and travails of democratic participation managed to coalesce.

In 1985, voluntary state bodies on behalf of street children elected the first National Commission of what was to become a National Movement for Street Boys and Girls. The following year, representatives from street and working children's groups assembled in Brasília for the First National Street Children's Congress. The event, which gave its participants a chance to voice their concerns, particularly the increase in violence against them, resulted in a blaze of publicity. For the first time, street children were projected in something other than a negative light—as potential contributors to society. The meeting also positioned the National Street Children's Movement and its progenitors within the ranks of popular forces claiming a democratic role in the redrafting of the Constitution, a process currently being advanced by a special Constituent Assembly. From the perspective of Unicef, the drafting of the new Constitution provided an ideal opportunity to secure democratic involvement in establishing a framework for children's rights; this would underpin the continuing need for major improvements in public policy towards children.

Unicef was making every effort at the time to use the democratization process in Brazil to open up a children's dimension within political debate[59]. This was vintage Jim Grant strategy: when a country is in a process of rapid transition in whatever direction—right to left, left to right, military to civilian regime or vice versa—new or aspirant political leaders are casting around for popular causes with which to identify themselves. A swift move and a persuasive presentation may enable children to advance rapidly up the domestic policy agenda. In Brazil, this strategy was enormously successful. Unicef's reputation in the country has been greatly enhanced by its championship of the child as the ultimate target of social policy, an idea which ever since the mid-1980s has struck a responsive public chord. Its political mileage owes much to the way in which the children's cause is seen as untainted and incorrupt; in Brazil, children have been powerful politically simply because they are above the political divide and disassociated from the type of adversarial politics synonymous with intrigue, scandal and sleaze.

In September 1986, a National Committee on the Child and the Constitution was created by interministerial decree[60]. Its purpose was to invite submissions on how problems facing children could best be tackled in the new constitution. Apart from six ministries, including those of Education and Health, a number of important non-governmental bodies were represented, including the National Front for the Defence of Children's Rights, the Paediatrics Association and the National Street Children's Movement. The Committee campaigned intensively to gather a wide spectrum of opinion and to make their concerns politically important to members of the Constituent Assembly. Unicef worked with the Committee in a number of ways, providing a secretariat and technical assistance, recruiting advertising and publicity support worth $1.8 million and helping widen the net of groups and organizations involved. National meetings took place, as well as public debates, mass gatherings of children in front of the National Congress and in major cities, public hearings, the distribution of pamphlets, and meetings with individual members of the Constituent Assembly.

Discussions held in schools all over Brazil and meetings with local and state chapters of national NGOs and the voluntary 'commissions' produced the substance of two constitutional amendments. These were presented to the Constituent Assembly accompanied by a petition signed by 1.4 million Brazilian children and adolescents, which had itself been endorsed by a petition signed by some 200,000 registered voters. These texts became the constitutional chapter on children's rights. A full year before the Convention on the Rights of the Child was passed by the UN, the principles it would establish formed the basis of Article 227 in the new Brazilian Constitution. Inspired by this success, the movement for children's rights launched another even more far-reaching effort: the drafting of new legislation that would replace the existing Minor's Code with something consistent with the new Constitution, abolishing the old corrective and anti-childhood national child 'welfare' policy. After a year of intensive lobbying and debate, during which considerable opposition was mounted and a number of revisions were introduced, the National Congress adopted the Act and it was signed into law by President Fernando Collor on Children's Day, 12 October 1990.

During this whole experience of collusion between the democratization process and the child rights movement, Unicef's office in Brazil was charting an entirely new—quite sensitive and complex—role for the organization. In a real sense, Unicef Brazil was obliged to pre-empt the evolution of organizational policy to suit the era of rights-dominated development thinking, the era of the post–cold war. This was a country in which Unicef programmatic resources had always been minuscule in proportion to the scale of governmental services and inputs, and it was a country, therefore, in which Unicef had already had to carve a pioneering role vis-à-vis policy advocacy and development. Now it had pioneered another sort of engagement: advocacy for, and engagement in, the development of reforming legislation on behalf of the child. The legal and institutional context within which policies and programmes for children operated was no longer to be seen as beyond Unicef's scope. It had to be included in the analysis of children's and women's situation, and it had to be addressed even if this meant steering a course that brushed up against the political process and invited intrusion on the actions of politicians and even of political parties.

Through building partnerships with government and NGOs and across the whole range of civil society, Unicef in Brazil had begun to indicate a new programmatic framework and set a new advocacy trend. Where Unicef Brazil had led, other Unicef country programmes were—in time—bound to follow.

Chapter 6

Global Shifts

In December 1980, the UN General Assembly formally declared the 1980s the 'Third Development Decade'. Within a matter almost of months, as countries throughout the developing world began to feel the full chill of global recession, such a title already seemed a misnomer. In his 1981 *State of the World's Children* report, James Grant commented bleakly: 'Not for a generation have expectations of world development, and hopes for an end to life-denying mass poverty, been at such a low ebb.'

In industrialized countries, growth had slumped and unemployment risen to higher levels than at any time since the Great Depression of the 1930s[1], a state of misfortune bound to reverberate in countries heavily dependent on richer trading partners. Their problems were compounded by a precipitous rise in interest rates on the loans they had been persuaded to take out on easy terms during the oil-euphoric 1970s. In 1982, Mexico suspended interest payments on an accumulating mountain of debt and sparked off the debt crisis[2]. In 1980, the debts of the developing world stood at $660 billion; by 1990, they had more than doubled to $1,540 billion, draining away some $1,620 billion in interest and repayments over the period[3]. In the middle years of the decade, the industrialized economies began to recover; at the same time, some developing countries were experiencing growth—a few in spectacularly successful fashion. But the process was highly selective. No fewer than 60 developing countries experienced declining per capita income over the decade[4]. By its end, whatever the advances in child survival, the 1980s had become known in certain parts of the world—especially in Africa—as a lost decade, a decade of development reversal[5].

It was also a decade in which the concept of an imagined community of nations undergoing an identical process called 'development'—a process that by implication had already been achieved in its alternate, the industrialized world—began to unravel[6]. The concept of a 'developing' world had emerged in the 1950s during the rush for independence and was an entirely post-colonial construct. In the 1960s—the First Development Decade—it had made some sense to lump together countries from different continents on the basis of their common predicament—previous subjugation to European imperial domination, backwardness and widespread poverty—and to prescribe 'development' as their common means of escape.

For a mixture of reasons—paternalistic, philanthropic, strategic and to support business and trading interests—resources from the metropolitan powers were to be harnessed to this grand design: this was the ambiguous genesis of 'aid'. The 'developing' world and 'aid' (or ODA, official development assistance) were therefore created as part of the new scheme of international relations associated with the post-imperial legacy. During the preparations for the Second Development Decade (the 1970s), an aid target of 0.7 per cent of the industrialized countries' GNP was set. Although this target was formally accepted internationally, very few countries—Denmark, the Netherlands, Norway, Sweden—reached it or, indeed, seriously attempted to do so.

By the advent of the 'alternatives' era of the 1970s, 'development' had accumulated an industry of government and intergovernmental institutions, university studies programmes and charitable initiatives. These had generated a lively debate about what 'development' actually consisted of, both as a means and as an end[7]. The essential dichotomy—which kept being restated in different versions from the 1970s on—boiled down to one of economic productivity versus social advance, or the creation of wealth versus the eradication of poverty. How did investment in the one interact with investment in the other? And what criteria—economic, as in the growth of GNP, or human, as in the extension of life expectancy—should be used to discover whether 'development' had taken place?

Jim Grant, then President of the Overseas Development Council in Washington, was at this time busy championing human yardsticks of 'development' rather than growth in per capita GNP: reductions in infant mortality, illiteracy and so on. At the Institute of Development Studies in Sussex, UK, Richard Jolly—later to become Grant's Deputy Executive Director for Programmes—was helping to articulate a different strategic convergence of economic development and anti-poverty targets: 'Redistribution with growth' and 'Meeting basic needs', with employment creation as the most important way of raising poor people's income.

As development analyses multiplied and grew more diffuse, so did economic and political experience in the newly created or newly defined states of the 'developing' world. As it retreated into the past, the common post-colonial inheritance became less cohesive a glue than it had been in the first flush of the development era. If it had not been for the cold war, which precipitated the formation of the Non-Aligned Movement at Bandung in 1955 as an umbrella for those countries that did not wish to ally with either superpower, the lack of communality between the countries, let alone the regions, of the 'developing' world would almost certainly have been exposed much earlier than it was. The cold war created the 'third world', a category that was neither the capitalist West (the 'first world') nor the communist East (the 'second'). This geopolitically defined 'world', whose most obvious common distinguishing feature was its poverty, not its non-alignment, was virtually interchangeable with the developing one. United Nations member countries developed a bloc known as the Group of 77 to attempt by weight of numbers to exert a third world political muscle of their own.

In 1973 came the successful OPEC cartel that hiked oil prices, held the oil-consumers to ransom and indicated that this other 'world' might be able to extort more on its behalf from the first and second worlds than the crumbs of 'aid' that were all rich countries were typically prepared to offer. The oil price hike also produced a body of suddenly super-wealthy third world states in the hitherto impoverished desert autocracies of Arabia. Even though all of these were backward according to most definitions of 'development', it no longer made much sense to classify the United Arab Emirates, with a per capita GNP of $13,000 (1975), in the same bracket as Pakistan, with a per capita GNP of $130[8]. Yet the UAE was still by many criteria a 'developing' country, even if it was resource-rich and could now join the club of 'donor' as opposed to 'recipient' nations (another version of the 'developed'/'developing' paradigm, couched in terms of 'aid').

After the mid-1970s, the Arab states, along with other oil-producing states such as Nigeria, Mexico and Indonesia, no longer strictly (or consistently) belonged to one 'world' or another. Accordingly, organizations involved in development cooperation began to refine their assistance criteria to take account of the new rich/poor country disparities. Unicef, whose overriding purpose was humanitarian, began to categorize the cooperation it offered according to relative per capita GNP, focusing the vast majority of material support on programmes in the very poorest countries, including those most seriously affected by the higher costs of imported oil.

The OPEC success was the moment when both the construct of a coterminous 'developing' world first began to crack and the geopolitical concept of a third world reached its apotheosis[9]. By the end of the 1970s, the prospect of further shows of united political muscle had faded. The proposal for a New International Economic Order (NIEO)—a proposal set out in 1974 with the purpose of giving the developing world more of a say in world markets and monetary systems—drew all of its other than moral force from the OPEC shock. In spite of endorsement of the NIEO at a 1975 UN Special Session, when it became clear that commodity-based third world unity had been a one-off, the proposal sank below the international horizon.

By the late 1970s, a number of countries other than those that were oil-rich had begun to take on the nature and colouring of 'developed' economies. These became known as the NICs—the newly industrializing countries—and included the four Pacific 'Tigers': Hong Kong, Singapore, South Korea and Taiwan. Brazil and Mexico, in Latin America, also had 'developed' features, as did—arguably—Colombia, India, Indonesia, Malaysia and Thailand[10]. Within a few more years, China would be included in this halfway category; with the end of the cold war, so would the ex-socialist states of Eastern Europe[11]. Thus by the end of the 1980s, some of the countries of the second world were joining the 'developing' queue and seeking aid, while some in the third world that had industrialized in such a way as to precipitate and profit from the increasing globalization of the world economy were now becoming a new kind of first and third world hybrid.

These NICs might not yet have reached the level of GNP per capita that ensured their triumphant entry into the 'developed' community of nations, but their development needs, patterns and accomplishments had little in common with those of much poorer countries in their own continents—contrast Brazil with Bolivia in Latin America, Thailand or Korea with Nepal or Bangladesh in Asia—let alone in regions far across the world. Once again, donors and donor organizations had to readjust. In Unicef's case, this meant for NICs a shift from the direct provision of goods and training for basic services, and more emphasis on social policy formulation, advocacy and child rights and protection issues. In one or two—Korea and Brazil, for example—it also began to embrace fund-raising from the general public.

Just to complete the picture of increasing 'development' diversity (or confusion), some second and third world countries—Sri Lanka, Cuba—had by this time managed to achieve all but 'developed' status according to criteria of human and social advance (low infant mortality rate, high life expectancy, high literacy, strong social service coverage), but still languished in the ranks of the poor and backward according to any application of standard economic criteria. During the 1980s, Unicef began to fashion its world perspective according to young child mortality rates and other social indicators. This was partly to help guide the level of programme expenditure, but was as much intended to draw attention to human values as the real measure and target of poverty reduction—with which, in Unicef's view, 'development' was synonymous. In the 1990s, Unicef even began to rank countries according to social performance indicators, thereby purportedly monitoring their governments' commitment to the goals of the World Summit for Children and to the principle of 'children first'. The results of this exercise were first issued in 1993 in an annual publication: *The Progress of Nations*[12].

Meanwhile, all the diverse examples of 'development' had little to show for themselves in the one region whose development conundrums were reasonably comparable: sub-Saharan Africa. Here, after two decades of rapid improvement, oil price increases, drought, rising debt, civil conflicts and other setbacks of the 1970s left many countries in a condition of disarray. Food production had failed to keep pace with population growth and, beset by environmental pressures and ill-conceived agricultural policies, was constantly falling further behind. In 1982-85, much of the continent suffered catastrophic drought; less catastrophically, drought hovered constantly over the Sahelian countries and in the Horn. Rare was the African country—Botswana was the outstanding example—that managed to maintain economic progress through such misfortune and provide stricken rural populations with any kind of effective safety net.

As the 1980s advanced, the situation in Africa drastically deteriorated, absolutely and in comparison with other parts of the world[13]. Commodity prices, tumbling since the 1970s, failed to recover; the price of oil and imports remained high, and many countries faced severe balance of payments problems. Their situation was worsened by a steep rise in interest rates, which forced them to spend much of their reduced export earnings on servicing their debts. From whichever direction it was examined, the overall result was profound and systemic crisis: declines in productivity, investment, health and nutritional well-being, and upsurges in conflict and social stress[14].

As the new orthodoxy of market supremacy took hold and the world economy became increasingly globalized, investors turned their backs on a continent of replaceable agricultural commodities and negligible profit. The idea of 'development' as a process that allowed poor countries to catch up, closing the gap between themselves and the rich, was abandoned in the case of Africa[15]. Where development should have been, an abyss was being created by the destruction of traditional economic and political systems and the failure to substitute viable alternatives. On top of all of this came AIDS, which spread faster and earlier in Africa than in any other region and whose impact was felt by men, women and children in all social classes. As tragedies compounded, the principal use of aid in Africa became to clear up the detritus of human pain[16]. From an early point in the decade, Africa was treated by Unicef and the international community as a continental 'special case'[17]. The Bamako Initiative to make health care systems functional (see Chapter 2) was one example of a special response to Africa's very special problems.

In his yearly *State of the World's Children* reports, Jim Grant always gave due recognition to movements in the international political and economic firmament affecting the development climate, which directly or indirectly affected the well-being of children. The 'child survival and development revolution' was itself conceived partly with an eye to its suitability for 'dark economic times' when social budgets in the developing world were under strain and donor countries were trimming 'aid'[18]. All the ingredients of the 'child survival and development revolution' were low-cost and technologically straightforward, as was the key strategy for getting them into widespread use: social mobilization or 'people power'. It was partly the very optimism of the 'child survival and development revolution'—an optimism uniquely created by Jim Grant's ability to infect a wide stratum of people and organizations with his enthusiasm, sometimes in apparent defiance of common sense—that carried its momentum forward. By 1990, around 3.5 million children's lives were being saved annually by mass immunization and diarrhoeal disease control[19]: for them the 1980s was not a 'lost' but a 'gained' decade.

The child survival progress was the more striking given that the efforts to achieve it took place during a period characterized by doubt, scepticism, economic set-back, retrenchment and the anti-internationalism of the Reagan-Thatcher years. The hope and the invigoration of the 'child survival revolution' came at a time in which 'development' both as a concept and as a crusade was at a nadir. Many of its practitioners were in deep despair, and as the Third Development Decade drew to its end, the international community had not the heart to declare a Fourth. By contrast, Unicef was busier than it had ever been, articulating goals and strategies for children in the 1990s, pushing countries to ratify the Convention on the Rights of the Child, elaborating the doctrine of 'first call' for children and wondering how to bring off the supreme coup of a World Summit on their behalf.

If in their different ways the special concern for Africa and the 'child survival and development revolution' were both responses to the exigencies of 'dark times', there was a third way in which Unicef responded to the challenge of the 'lost decade'. In the tradition established back in the 1960s by Dick Heyward, then its Senior Deputy Executive Director, Unicef in the early 1980s again took on the task of analysing and bringing to the world's attention the way in which trends far beyond the control of Unicef were affecting the world's most vulnerable human beings. In the 1960s, the need had been to position efforts on behalf of children within the great development crusade. Now, the focus shifted to a need to protect efforts on behalf of children from the great development debacle.

In the face of the world recession and the subsequent crises of debt and adjustment, economic and fiscal considerations had thrust social concerns to one side. In contrast with their preoccupation during the 1970s with 'poverty alleviation' and 'basic needs', the Bretton Woods institutions—the World Bank and IMF—had ceased to be interested in how incomes and services for people in the lowest echelons of society were to be minimally protected[20]. This trend was reinforced by the increasing hegemony of market forces within the Western political and economic system. Not only children, but the whole social agenda was under threat—a threat which could easily derail the 'child survival and development revolution'. It was therefore extremely opportune that Jim Grant brought into Unicef as his new Deputy Executive Director for Programmes a person well suited to initiate an international salvage operation on behalf of human-centred values: a development economist of the anti-poverty tendency, Dr. Richard Jolly.

Richard Jolly was known to Jim Grant through their common participation in many international fora, including the Society for International Development (SID) and the North-South Roundtable, an independent intellectual forum established by SID. Jolly began his career as a young community development officer in colonial Africa. But it was as an economic thinker that he rapidly gained a reputation, becoming a protégé of Dudley Seers, a pioneer of development theory—the new academic look for the post-colonial age. In the 1960s, Seers helped establish one of development theory's most prestigious think-tanks, the Institute of Development Studies (IDS) at Sussex University (UK). When Seers retired in 1972, Jolly took over.

Under Jolly's leadership, IDS was in the vanguard of 'alternative' thinking on development and was a mecca for development researchers. He helped some of the most important contemporary development creeds come into being: 'basic needs' (to which 'basic services' emerged as the programmatic response) and 'redistribution with growth'. Both of these critiqued the notion that the fruits of economic growth automatically trickled down to the poor and argued the need to build into development policy affirmative action on their behalf. Jolly wrote and travelled widely to promote debate around this theme. He was a regular adviser to the British Government on aid-related issues during the 1970s, but aid, development and everything related to them suffered political eclipse under the post-1979 Thatcher administration. The invitation from Jim Grant to join Unicef came at this time, triggered by the retirement of the previous generation of senior Unicef statesmen, notably the two Deputy Executive Directors, Dick Heyward (Operations) and Charles Egger (Programmes) at the end of 1981.

The first study commissioned by Jolly on behalf of Unicef was entitled 'The impact of world recession on children' and was published in 1983[21]. Its analysis was based on case studies from countries around the world including Brazil, Cuba, Chile, India and Sri Lanka. The study's purpose was to present factual data to show that the poor of the world, and among the poor the children, were suffering the worst effects of the current recession. Phenomena normally described in narrowly economic terms—inflation and interest rates, debt and deficit—were revisited from the perspective of nutrition levels, educational enrolment, child labour and abandonment. This was no easy undertaking because so few countries had information-gathering systems that permitted this kind of analysis, especially ones from which it was possible to extrapolate trends; and the less developed the country—as in Africa—the less developed the data collection system and the less complete a picture it produced.

The study focused principally on the two regions—Africa and Latin America—where earnings had been most eroded and spiralling interest rates had exacerbated the burden of debts contracted during the loan-addicted 1970s. In many countries, per capita output had significantly fallen between 1980 and 1982; data would later show that in 17 out of 23 countries in Latin America, and in 24 out of 32 countries in Africa, average incomes fell between 1980 and 1985[22]. Governments were being forced to retrench, cutting back on social services expenditure and allowing the prices of basic necessities—especially food—to rise. A country's poorest citizens found their survival margins painfully reduced. Labour market contraction meant that work was more difficult to find and earnings lower, while the smaller amounts of cash gleaned by petty trading or casual hire bought much less. Since the poor had less purchase on the means of subsistence, and since services were becoming scarcer and more expensive to use, their health and nutritional status were declining. Since families of the poor tended to have more children, their children were inevitably the hardest hit of all.

Although hard information about the hidden casualties of the recession was difficult to unearth, the report found clear evidence in some countries that the minds and bodies of young children were taking a disproportionate strain. In northern Zambia, the average height-for-age of children had declined; in parts of Brazil, average birth weight was going down; in Costa Rica, the number of children being treated for severe malnutrition had trebled over the past three years. These findings were nothing more or less than what had been regarded previously as strong supposition; but their documentation, and their presentation in economic form—and, in due course, in economic fora—was an important innovation. Unicef made two basic recommendations: adjustment policies must not neglect the need to preserve minimum levels of nutrition and household income; and countries should place a safety net under child health and basic education by concentrating resources on low-cost, high-effect interventions. Thus was the recommended response bracketed closely to the call for a 'child survival revolution' and to its successor, the principle of 'first call'.

At this time an increasing number of countries were becoming obliged to initiate 'structural adjustment programmes' (SAPs) as a condition of loans from the International Monetary Fund. In the 1970s, the number of countries undertaking adjustment or stabilization programmes, usually with IMF assistance, had been in the region of 15 a year; between 1980 and 1985, the average was 47[23]. Unable to pay for imports, and finding that a high proportion of export earnings was haemorrhaging away on debt repayment, countries had few other choices than to resort to these IMF rescue packages, whatever the Draconian nature of the SAP preconditions. Balancing the national books, no matter what the human cost, was the name of the policy-making game. By the mid-1980s, the enforced austerity of SAPs, especially in Africa, was attracting humanitarian outrage in both North and South. President Nyerere of Tanzania demanded: 'Must we starve our children to pay our debts?'[24]

The problem with the standard recipe for adjustment was that it had the effect of discriminating against the poor and vulnerable. Thus, not only the recession but the remedies for the havoc it had wreaked on vulnerable economies were compounding the miseries experienced by people at the bottom of the ladder. That structural adjustment programmes were leading to austerity, reducing economic activity and ruining custom was understood even by the most modest itinerant vendor: 'We are SAPped,' complained the women in a West African market town[25]. And independently of their contribution to the rise of the numbers of people in poverty, many of the adjustment programmes had failed even in their own terms. In a number of 'SAPped' countries, there had been no resumption of growth; balances of payments were no healthier; governments were looking increasingly shaky and services increasingly threadbare[26].

Consensus was gradually gathering around the view that Unicef and the like-minded on the academic and NGO network were working hard to promote: the need for a broader approach to adjustment policy in which the protection of women, children and vulnerable groups was accepted as an integral part of its operation—ideally, of its objective. There were encouraging signals from some in the mainstream of international policy-making, including members of Unicef's Executive Board. At the request of the IMF and the World Bank, a policy dialogue started[27]. Unicef consultants and country representatives began to be invited to interact with World Bank missions to discuss the parameters of adjustment packages. The first occasion was in Ghana in 1985[28], after which measures to ease the burden of adjustment on the most vulnerable groups as well as to involve small producers—male and female cultivators and traders—in the regeneration of growth were introduced into the adjustment planning process for the first time.

Gradually, mainstream economic opinion began to shift. In July 1986, addressing the UN Economic and Social Council, the Managing Director of the IMF, Jacques de Larosière, conceded: 'Programmes of adjustment cannot be effective unless they command the support of governments and of public opinion. Yet this support will be progressively harder to maintain the longer adjustment continues without some pay-off in terms of growth and while human conditions are deteriorating. Likewise, it is hard to visualize how a viable external position can be achieved if large segments of the workforce lack the vocational skills—or even worse, the basic nutritional and health standards—to produce goods that are competitive in world markets. *Human* capital is after all the most important factor of production in developing and industrial countries alike.'[29]

Other resolutions and statements in international fora followed. To capitalize on this momentum, Jolly organized a larger and more significant study whose title, when it was published in 1987, quickly took on the force of a slogan: *Adjustment with a Human Face: Protecting the Vulnerable and Promoting Growth*. Once again, a number of case studies from countries involved in adjustment were commissioned; once again, the main emphasis was on Africa and Latin America. Although the study was conducted under Jolly's overall direction, its main authors were two development economists: Giovanni

Andrea Cornia, then Senior Planning Officer at Unicef, and Frances Stewart of the University of Oxford. The report was divided into two parts: a review of the impact of recession and adjustment on child welfare, and the presentation of a policy framework for 'adjustment with a human face' covering both economic policy areas and social sectors.

The first part confirmed the findings of the previous study: namely, that standards of health, nutrition and education among children—as measured by changes in IMRs, birth-weight trends, school enrolment and completion rates and the re-emergence of epidemic diseases—were stagnating or deteriorating in a number of countries. (Once again, these findings were necessarily limited by the shortage of data from many of the hardest-hit countries, a problem that itself demanded political and strategic redress.) The second part of the report spelt out the range of economic and other policy measures comprising 'adjustment with a human face'. Drawing on the country case studies, the report illustrated that letting the poor and vulnerable go to the wall was not a *sine qua non* of reducing public expenditures, controlling domestic inflation and balancing the books. The assumption underlying the SAPs of the early 1980s had been that if a short, sharp shock could be delivered, the resultant stabilization would naturally lead to a resumption of growth. In a number of cases, the short, sharp shock had been so devastating that productivity had plummeted, leaving the patient even flatter on its back.

The report was unequivocal in stating that programmes of adjustment were necessary. At this time some international NGOs were condemning structural adjustment as yet another form of neo-colonial aggression against countries that had been dealt a bad hand both by history and by contemporary economic trends. This was a position from which Unicef carefully disassociated itself. While supporting the need for adjustment, it argued that balance of payments stabilization should be sought within a much broader and longer-term framework, within which the use of short, sharp and potentially devastating shocks was avoided. The two other key elements of the approach were to promote conditions that favoured economic growth (by maintaining investment flows and by using constrained resources with the kind of efficiency uncommon in the spendthrift 1970s) and to operate adjustment policies in such a way as to preserve ordinary people's well-being. This could be managed by reallocations within the social sector (for example, from high-tech hospitals to primary health care) and by providing the kind of short-term relief usual in the case of humanitarian disaster: food supplements and public works employment. After all, if the whole purpose of development was to promote human well-being, it was an act of contrariness verging on the absurd to leave human well-being out of all policy calculations.

In the not-so-distant past, deep distress among society's least well-off following an economic downturn had been regarded as inevitable, almost a part of natural law. Now Jolly, Cornia and Stewart were claiming that principles that had been established in the industrialized world during the post-Depression 1930s and with the creation of the European welfare state should be equally applicable to international adjustment policies in the late 20th century. This was an argument already partially won in the international political sphere, where a degree of international responsibility for the welfare of the victims of wars and natural disasters was accepted—perhaps not always willingly or generously, but at least accepted. 'Adjustment with a human face' applied the same argument in the economic sphere. By contemporary moral standards, it could not be acceptable for those drawing up the terms of adjustment packages to treat national balance sheets as if tidying them up had nothing to do with the human condition, or as if such 'soft' considerations were outside the range of their responsibilities.

The authors of *Adjustment with a Human Face* went further. Theirs was not simply a pious plea, an exercise in hand-wringing by the well-intentioned, but a realistic proposition backed up by solid examples of workability. Brazil and Zimbabwe were cited as examples of countries whose recession had been relatively short because their economies had not been allowed to contract. Zimbabwe had also pursued other 'human face' tactics, targeting agricultural credit specifically at the small farmer, as a result of which the volume of marketed maize and cotton had soared[30]. The success of this policy was cited to show (as were some other examples from Bangladesh and India) that to target public and private investment towards small-timers, male and female, was sound from the growth point of view as well as from the perspective of poverty redress.

A number of examples from the 'child survival and development revolution' were quoted to indicate that the spread of basic services was compatible with retrenchment: Indonesia's *posyandu* programme (see Chapter 3), which supplied preventive health to the country's under-fives at a cost of only $5-6 per child per year; Tanzania's basic drugs programme, whereby a core list of essential drugs were procured in generic form with funds from DANIDA via a WHO- and Unicef-sponsored scheme at a cost of only $0.45 per head of population. And as safety-net examples, public works employment schemes, usually on the basis of food-for-work, were cited: the deployment of landless or marginal farmers on road building and irrigation in India; a temporary income-support programme for 150,000 marginal urban dwellers in Peru. In drought-ridden Botswana, the same safety-net objective was met by supplementary feeding for preschool and primary-age children. The Botswana example was striking because of the nationwide nutritional surveillance that allowed the food supplementation programme to be focused on those in need at any particular time. Putting an effective information-gathering system in place to monitor fluctuations in the well-being of vulnerable groups, especially children, was the last element in the 'human face' package.

The publication of *Adjustment with a Human Face*, coupled with strenuous promotion of its theme[31], made a significant international impact. Unicef's level of dialogue with arbiters of national economic and financial policy rose, and the organization began to be treated with more respect in non-welfare contexts. Although when it came down to it there was little real willingness to undertake a fundamental redesign of SAPs according to different first principles, the notion that there must be some cushioning of the poor and vulnerable was at least accepted. In many cases this merely meant that a safety-net provision was added to an existing SAP: the same set of antidotes was prescribed for the problems of the ship of state, but a lifeboat would be provided to pick up drowning passengers. But that there was an appreciation for the need for safety nets was a significant change. The report and the publicity surrounding it also won Unicef allies in the anti-SAP non-governmental movement now seeking—for example—rescheduling or outright cancellation of debts on behalf of the worst-affected countries[32].

In 1990, the re-emergence of gross poverty as a serious issue for the Bretton Woods institutions to address was signalled in the annual *World Development Report* of the World Bank, which took poverty as its central theme. The report paid tribute to Unicef for having steered adjustment in new directions: 'Many observers called attention to [evidence of declines in incomes and cut-backs in social services], but Unicef first brought the issues into the centre of the debate on the design and impact of adjustment. By the end of the decade the issue had become important for all agencies; it is now examined in many adjustment programmes financed by the World Bank. As Unicef advocated, attention is focused both on the effect of adjustment policies on the poor and on specific measures to cushion the short-term costs.'[33] In spite of the continued supremacy of free-market orthodoxies and trade liberalization, poverty alleviation was beginning to re-emerge as a necessary as well as a humanitarian target of development policy.

The *State of the World's Children* reports annually revisited 'adjustment with a human face'. But Unicef's own role at the cutting edge of adjustment research declined as the issue became more widely owned. In the context of Africa, Unicef continued to conduct an independent and vocal analysis of the structural adjustment process and the prospects of recovery; adding, after the watershed year of 1989, analysis of economies in a different kind of transition, in Central and Eastern Europe. In the field, operational support for 'adjustment with a human face' grew, and increasing numbers of Unicef country offices took part in initiatives by government and the World Bank to include safety-net measures for the vulnerable within adjustment packages. Meanwhile, at the global level, Unicef began to shift its advocacy message from 'adjustment with a human face' to 'development with a human face'. This provided an intellectual scaffolding within which the goals for children in the 1990s, eventually endorsed at the World Summit for Children, could be positioned.

In 1990, UNDP issued the first of its *Human Development Reports* under the supervision of Mahbub ul Haq, previously Minister of Finance and Planning in Pakistan and a long-time member of the international development aristocracy. His report took on to the next stage what Unicef had begun: a reassertion of humanity as both lodestar and pilot of the development process. The 'human development index' it presented contained an echo of the 'PQLI'—the Physical Quality of Life Index developed by Jim Grant and his ODC colleagues during the 1970s. Fifteen years later, a full member of the international economic establishment had produced a set of indicators that embraced the social (and political) dimensions of life. These formally articulated a vision of development—in a phrase of E. F. Schumacher's from the alternative 1970s—'as if people mattered'. What had once been alternative had, after several reworkings and a strong dose of officialization, become mainstream.

As the 1990s arrived, the twin crises of adjustment and debt rumbled on. And as the Asian 'Tigers' forged ahead and certain Latin American economies began to recover and grow rapidly—albeit unreliably—the crisis location narrowed. It became more or less confined to that ill-starred continent that had come to symbolize all the misery that the term 'third world' could conjure: Africa.

The problems of sub-Saharan Africa had already begun to merit extreme concern by the early 1980s. A seemingly endless succession of emergencies—mostly caused by or at least associated with drought—emanated from what was becoming a regional special case. In Sahelian West Africa, pastoral societies were being destroyed by the remorseless advance of the desert; in the Horn and in Angola, Chad, Mozambique, the Sudan and Uganda, drought intermingled with civil disruption and warfare to produce a tide of human misery and displacement. Only in a few southern countries, notably Zimbabwe, whose long state of insurrection finally ceded to majority rule and independence in 1980, did the new decade bring markedly better prospects than the old.

A watershed came in 1984. Throughout that year, drought deepened in its familiar transcontinental path across the Sahel and into the Horn, as well as in countries far to the south. In spite of a great ringing of international alarm bells, food relief was not activated on an even remotely appropriate scale. The result was famine of the biblical variety. In what had become the mode for the exposure of mass tragedy in the late 20th century, a televised news report from northern Ethiopia finally managed to bring home to the world the fact that starvation was engulfing millions of people. The BBC news item broadcast on 23 October 1984 and subsequently screened throughout the world had an impact that must rank as one of the most far-reaching in television history, both in its immediate effect—producing massive assistance for sick and dying people—and in triggering sustained public and official scrutiny of Africa's immense problems[34].

At the United Nations, Secretary-General Javier Pérez de Cuéllar set up a special Office for Emergency Operations in Africa (OEOA). This initiative owed much to Jim Grant, who was anxious to come up with a creative way for the UN to respond to humanitarian crises without depending on Unicef or another UN body to become lead agency for the entire UN system. This had the effect of diverting immense amounts of time and energy away from the main task currently within an organization's mandate—in Unicef's case, the 'child survival revolution'. The OEOA proved very effective, and in time, paved the way for a restructuring of the manner in which the United Nations system responded to emergency relief[35]. In Ethiopia itself, 7 million people were provided with rations via an effectively coordinated UN and NGO operation in which Unicef was an active participant. A huge outflow of food aid, funds and supplies was also sent to 19 other countries throughout the African continent[36].

But the impact of the Ethiopian famine did more than launch a thousand mercy ships. Mainly thanks to a remarkable effort led by the popular singer Bob Geldof, it brought consciousness of the African continent to a generation who had not been born at the time when the cause of African freedom had inspired the world. By rallying his colleagues from the music industry and launching 'Band Aid' (a rock industry charity), 'Live Aid' (a global television concert event) and 'Sport Aid' (a fund-raising drive among athletes), Geldof and a number of celebrities from the worlds of show business and sport helped to raise large sums of charitable money and put the saving of lives in Africa onto the popular political agenda.

From early in the 1980s, sub-Saharan Africa had been singled out by Unicef's Executive Board as requiring priority attention. New country offices opened and activity expanded continuously, up to the end of the decade and beyond. By 1990, over one third of Unicef's human and financial resources were deployed in Africa[37]. But in spite of their rhetorical concern, many governments did not dedicate serious resources to Africa's predicament until the public outcry in the 'donor' world surrounding the crisis of 1984-85. The popularity of Geldof's mega-events suggested that, in the era of celebrity and media power, there were new heights of public attention and action to be commanded on behalf of the developing world if the right buttons could be pushed.

This diagnosis of the public mood appealed strongly to Jim Grant, who saw in these portents an opportunity for 'social mobilization' on a larger scale—not just for operationalizing immunization but for expressing global solidarity with the poor, especially with children. The network of Unicef National Committees, whose financial contribution Grant had not previously regarded as justifying a claim to major organizational significance, now came into their own. The Africa emergencies gave the Committees an opportunity for visibility and fund-raising that they took with both hands, boosted by the visits of Unicef's Goodwill Ambassadors—notably Harry Belafonte, Liv Ullmann and later Audrey Hepburn—to disaster-stricken countries. In the early 1980s, the Committees provided around 17 per cent of Unicef's income; by the early 1990s, the amount was to surpass 25 per cent[38]. In the case of Sport Aid, the Unicef tie-up through the National Committees (and field offices) helped to transform the event into a worldwide success involving 83 countries and raising $30 million[39].

Unicef was also improving its links with the highly professional NGO coalitions burgeoning in both North and South. In the wider world, 'people power' was beginning to make its muscle felt not only on behalf of the victims of drought and disaster in Africa, but on behalf of environmental issues and in political contexts: 'democratization' had become a force in the Philippines, in Central America and in Africa itself, where it was even beginning to snap at the heels of apartheid. Unicef now set itself the task of enlisting 'people power' into a 'Grand Alliance for Children'[40].

'People power' in the form of NGOs, trades unions, mothers' clubs and youth associations represented only one stratum of allies, however. The 'Grand Alliance' also needed figures of national importance and those occupying the seat of power. Mechanisms and special campaigns were developed for enlisting all conceivable species of the influential: artists, writers and intellectuals; the media; parliamentarians; mayors; church and spiritual leaders, and—of course—Heads of State. Much of the pace-setting for this new chapter in Unicef external relations was pioneered in Africa. The reason was partly because of the continent's immense human need and the priority attached to Africa by Unicef; it was also because of the need and the popular sympathy it evoked.

Within Africa itself, initiatives that were upbeat and hopeful provided a breath of fresh air amidst the prevailing gloom. In early 1987 came the first of a series of symposia for different groups: a meeting for African artists, writers and intellectuals in Dakar[41]. Such meetings provided a recruitment ground for new adherents to the cause of child survival and new members of the 'Grand Alliance'. The Dakar meeting, with its 'Dakar Declaration' on behalf of the African child, was the curtain-raiser to a more ambitious stroke. This took place at the annual Assembly for the Heads of State and Government of the Organization of African Unity at Addis Ababa in July 1987. Through the mediation of President Abdou Diouf of Senegal, the OAU adopted a resolution proclaiming 1988 the 'Year for the Protection, Survival and Development of the African Child,' with the target of 75 per cent immunization of infants by 1990. This led to an invitation to Grant to address the 25th anniversary meeting of the OAU in Addis Ababa in July 1988, an occasion on which he dumbfounded his audience by bringing to the rostrum to speak on his behalf a young Ethiopian girl, Selamaweet[42]. As a four-year-old, Selamaweet's face had adorned a Unicef poster calling for child survival, and now she spoke as witness to the benefits of Unicef's campaign.

For a UN organization to develop a sophisticated lobbying technique for regular use at intergovernmental fora was unprecedented. Unicef's contacts with delegations and the secretariat before and at OAU meetings led to the tabling of such proposals as the setting of dates for immunization targets, the banning of trade in non-iodized salt or the termination of advertising for breastmilk substitutes. Grant used the meetings to consolidate his personal relations with Heads of State as well as to ease the path of his country representatives to the topmost echelons of government once they returned home[43]. Unicef's investment in this kind of 'summit' advocacy was justified less by its measurable benefits for programme delivery than by the way in which it brought issues affecting children into the common parlance of regular international discourse. Statesmen who might initially be surprised to find themselves examining immunization tallies and becoming conversant in the virtues of mother's milk began to accept such conference items as a normal part of the agenda.

Unicef efforts to affect debates at intergovernmental meetings were not confined to Africa; in fact, they originally grew out of Asia. The creation of the South Asian Association for Regional Cooperation (SAARC) provided an opportunity to place children on its first Summit agenda, at Bangalore in November 1986; this was the first time Heads of State had addressed such an item in such a gathering[44]. The second SAARC Summit in Nepal in October 1987 endorsed the acceleration of expanded programmes on immunization[45]. Many other regional initiatives took shape over the late 1980s: there were resolutions at Islamic conferences, at the Organization of American States, even at a Gorbachev-Reagan summit—all of which helped to legitimize the presence of children's concerns in international affairs. Without this preparation, the seed of the Summit might well have fallen on stonier ground. And Grant was correct in believing that Africa—whose myriad cultures had a common trait of child-centredness—would be especially receptive to a children's agenda. He had a knack of heartening Africa's leaders with his message of 'doability' and the popular appeal of child-friendly policies. It was at a West African Heads of State meeting that the idea of a World Summit for Children first saw formal expression, and it was the African delegates to the Unicef Executive Board who kept the idea on track[46].

As the decade progressed, the spate of climatic emergencies in Africa temporarily abated and there were even signs that economic growth might return. But in many countries the combined force of adverse terms of trade, debt, past debilities and economic stagnation was proving impossible to transcend. The prestige projects once so pleasing to international financiers and their African clients—show-piece buildings, cement factories, airports and highways—now littered the landscape as monuments to inappropriate investment and unpayable debt. And as the pillars gave way under a political economy that had chosen to leave out of its calculations the need to maintain the typical rural household, the reverberations of economic collapse and environmental depletion penetrated deep into the fabric of traditional life.

The multiple predicaments of Africa posed an acute challenge to development analysts, and Unicef was among the organizations to address the challenge. Jolly and his economist team's first contribution to the debate was published in 1985, under the title *Within Human Reach: A future for Africa's children*. The study pointed out that for women, above all, and for the children they bore and raised, the burdens of development failure were heavy. Women's key role in family food production having been consistently ignored by policy makers, the margins within which they were able to grow or procure such essentials as food, water and fuel were steadily eroding. In the rapidly expanding urban areas, where unemployment was rising and the value of wages eroding fast, the situation was if anything worse than in the countryside. Women, young people wanting to enter the job market and children forced to drop out of school and enter 'street' employment were worst affected by the increasingly difficult task of putting food in the family pot and keeping a tin roof over the family head.

The ongoing Unicef analysis of Africa's predicament and the necessary policy reaction continued to echo and reinforce the thesis presented in *Adjustment with a Human Face*. The evidence that the 1980s represented a 'lost decade' for many of Africa's children continued to pile up. By 1990, the enrolment rate in primary education had fallen in 20 sub-Saharan countries. The regional average had dropped from 80 per cent to 70 per cent—often the outcome of SAP-induced expenditure cuts and impositions of fees that parents could not afford—in Tanzania, for example[47]. The prevalence of underweight children had risen from 29 per cent to 31 per cent between 1980 and 1985 and stagnated for the rest of the decade—in contrast to every other region in the world[48]. Close to half of Africa's population was still beyond the reach of even minimal health services, and resurgences in tuberculosis, yellow fever, cholera and chloroquine-resistant malaria were exerting extra pressures on weak and underfunded health infrastructures, bent to breaking under the growing burden of AIDS. Only in a few middle-income countries—Côte d'Ivoire, Mauritius, Senegal, Zimbabwe—was the record less than acutely discouraging[49]. Given the stresses they were enduring, the remarkable resilience of so many of Africa's people deserved profound admiration.

As if Africa's economic and social ills were not enough to bear, parts of the continent were experiencing a mounting toll of violence, as civil strife displaced drought as the mainspring of African distress. Ethnic conflict, dampened during the pre-independence nationalist struggle, had re-emerged progressively during the post-colonial aftermath. And the cold war battle for hearts and minds had not neglected to ply its discords and sell its guns along Africa's social fissures. In some countries—the Congo and Nigeria—the political clothing of nationhood had ripped apart soon after the national flag was unfurled. In others—Burundi, Rwanda, Chad, Uganda—upheaval came a little later. In the 1970s and early 1980s, ideological confrontation in the Horn both masked and hastened the disintegration of carefully constructed webs of kinship and dynastic alliance among the Ethiopian and Somali peoples. And away in the southern cone of the continent, the long struggle for majority rule continued. In the 1980s, the tactic of fomenting proxy wars among antipathetic neighbours Angola and

Mozambique was used by the white South African rearguard to postpone their own loss of power.

By 1989, a combination of apartheid, social and civil unrest, military incursions and cross-border engagements had created at least 6 million refugees and 35 million displaced people within their own countries, and caused untold suffering, dislocation and disability among millions more[50]. Under the circumstances, Unicef country programmes were remarkable in managing to advance the child survival campaign as effectively as they did. Some interventions—measles vaccination, ORT and vitamin A, for example—were particularly appropriate as part of emergency relief measures since infectious diseases on top of nutritional deficiencies typically caused far more deaths in famine and refugee camps than did starvation. But beyond increased child survival programming and 'Grand Alliance' building, Unicef also began to move in other directions.

One initiative concerned children affected by war. Following the 1986 Executive Board review of 'children in especially difficult circumstances', Unicef representatives in the nine countries of Southern Africa—Angola, Botswana, Lesotho, Malawi, Mozambique, Swaziland, Tanzania, Zambia and Zimbabwe—decided to take a stand on behalf of children affected by apartheid and destabilization. South African policies were impoverishing ordinary families caught in their backlash, and—as with recession, as with adjustment—their impact could be measured in terms of children's declining health and nutritional status. This was most marked in Angola and Mozambique, where the highest rates of young child mortality in the world now prevailed: between 325 and 375 per thousand live births[51].

The underlying cause might well be underdevelopment, exacerbated by the usual litany of adverse terms of trade, rising debt and past mistakes in domestic policy. But of this death toll, as high a proportion as 45 per cent was attributable to South Africa's attempts to undermine these countries' political, economic and social fabric. Unicef's successive reports on *Children on the Front Line,* first published in 1987, represented an attempt to use the political neutrality of the children's issue to make a strong anti-war and anti-apartheid statement on their behalf[52].

Another initiative was an attempt to help countries swamped by debt to discharge some of it by substituting, through Unicef, action on behalf of children[53]. The scheme was based on the fact that some of this debt had become worth so little that the creditor bank had little to lose by writing it off as a charitable donation. This idea was originally proposed by Marco Vianello-Chiodo, Director of Unicef's Programme Funding Office[54]. In exchange for an agreed equivalent in local currency, which would be made over to an approved programme of Unicef cooperation, a commercial bank would cancel an amount of debt owed by a debtor government or sell it at a heavily discounted rate. Outstanding debt obligations would thereby be converted into local currency contributions for Unicef programmes. These programmes would, of necessity, have to be already approved and contain a high local cost component. Typically, they included programmes to support women's income generation, primary education and water supply and sanitation[55].

The country where this experiment was pioneered was the Sudan; the beneficiary programme was the water supply programme in southern Kordofan. By 1991, six commercial banks, two in the United Kingdom, two in Germany and two in the United States, had donated to Unicef outstanding debt obligations valued at $20 million, in cooperation with the Bank of Sudan and the Unicef National Committees in the countries in question. In return, the Sudanese Government had contributed the equivalent of $2 million in Sudanese pounds (an amount three times the value of the debt on the secondary market)[56]. 'Debt relief for children' helped to generate more resources for social programming, and—as important—it also helped project children's issues into the extensive debt relief and cancellation debate. By late 1995, Unicef had carried out more than 20 separate debt conversion transactions in Madagascar, Senegal, the Sudan and Zambia (as well as in Bolivia, Jamaica, Mexico, Peru and the Philippines). Debt with a face value of $199 million had been converted into local currency worth $53 million for an expenditure of $29 million[57].

And then there was AIDS, whose impact on Africa was in a class by itself. By the late 1980s, it was becoming clear that AIDS—elsewhere associated almost exclusively with adult males engaging in particular high-risk sexual behaviours and with blood transfusion—would have an unexpectedly profound impact on African children[58]. Sub-Saharan Africa was hit worse than any other region by the worldwide epidemic. In 10 countries of Eastern and Central Africa around 5 per cent of adults aged 19 to 45 were already thought to be infected with HIV; in some urban areas, the proportion was much higher—between one quarter and one third[59]. The virus was being transmitted overwhelmingly by heterosexual relations and was as common in women as in men[60].

Some of these women—the probability was between 25 and 40 per cent—would transmit HIV to their newborns, in the womb or at delivery. But a high case-load of paediatric AIDS was only a part of the picture. Since all adults infected were in the prime not only of their reproductive but their economic life, and since birth rates in Africa tended to be high, dying parents were leaving behind large numbers of orphaned children. When Unicef first calculated in 1989 that within 10 years, 4 million African children would have been orphaned by AIDS, the figure was greeted with disbelief. Before long, WHO had upped the estimate to 10 million[61]. These children would all become dependent on the traditional African safety net: the extended family. How would their elderly relatives, deprived of their grown sons and daughters, conceivably manage the strain?

In the rest of the world, the turn of the decade was accompanied by the euphoria stemming from the end of the cold war. Unicef, like everyone else, envisaged the release of new resources from the relaxation of the long East-West confrontation and the end of the arms race. This 'peace dividend' could be applied, it was hoped, to the noble effort of building a more equitable, prosperous and healthy world, a world fit not just for the inheritance of some but of all the members of the coming generation.

Nowhere in the world was a latter-day Marshall Plan of investment in sustainable human and physical development more needed than in Africa. But any such hopes were quickly dashed. The resources released from reductions in arms and military expenditure found their way mostly into deficit reduction in industrialized countries. Meanwhile, it was the countries of Eastern and Central Europe, emerging from their own long subjugation to a rather different kind of colonial rule, to which 'development' attention now turned.

Between August 1989 and the end of that year, communist administrations that had held sway for over 40 years abdicated or ceased to exist in Bulgaria, Czechoslovakia, the German Democratic Republic, Hungary, Poland and Romania[62]. Soon afterwards, the regimes of Yugoslavia and Albania also collapsed. Except in the case of Romania, this extraordinary political shift—a virtual abandonment of power by what had appeared to be utterly entrenched systems—took place without a shot being fired. The USSR had, since 1985 when Mikhail Gorbachev assumed its leadership, embarked on a liberalization and reform process. It had left the hard-liner regimes in its European orbit to do the same or perish. In 1989, most perished.

The resurgence of political freedoms and democratic rights in countries so long sequestered behind the iron curtain caused such celebration in the first world that the implications of such sweeping change were not at first apparent. So stunned was the world by the extraordinary implosion that felled one of its main network of alliances—the Warsaw Pact—and then the superpower at its centre that it took time for international institutions to take in what had happened. The conventional ordering of world affairs had been altered past telling. As difficult to foresee were the effects on the well-being of citizens, including children, in the countries involved.

Yet these were bound to be severe. At the heart of the process of change was the long falling behind of the economic performance of the USSR and its satellites, which had been in train since the early 1970s[63]. The abrupt dismissal of long-cherished command economies and socialist safety nets came not from a political movement riding a crest of success, but as a statement of lost confidence in a system of economic and social management that had conspicuously failed to produce the decent quality of life for all on which its legitimacy depended.

In the 20 years before the post-1989 reforms, life expectancy in many countries was declining and poverty was increasing[64]. Thus, as in the case of the developing world's deteriorating fortunes in the early 1980s, in the period of post-communist transition the people of the second world had to face both the effects of a poor economic record and the dose of medicine now required to put it right. Here was a familiar recipe for hardship, especially among the vulnerable: children, women, the disabled, the elderly, large families, the unemployed—those whose condition it had been a principle of socialist regimes to cushion and protect.

Although as ill-prepared as everyone else for the transformation of the international landscape, Unicef had long-standing ties with countries in the Eastern bloc, some of which were historically deep-rooted. Following the creation of the UN International Children's Emergency Fund in December 1946, the destination of much of its help for children still suffering the aftermath of the Second World War had been the countries of Central and Eastern Europe[65].

The first four countries ever to receive Unicef supplies—3 million pounds of powdered milk dispatched by sea from New York in mid-1947—were Austria, Greece, Poland and Yugoslavia. Longer-term assistance had followed: campaigns for disease prevention, including BCG vaccination; paediatric equipment and training fellowships for MCH health professionals; milk conservation equipment for the incipient dairy industry in Bulgaria, Czechoslovakia, Poland and Yugoslavia. With Poland, in particular, Unicef always had a special relationship. Unicef's founder and father figure, Dr. Ludwik Rajchman, was Polish; Maurice Pate, the first Executive Director, spent many years in Poland between the wars.

Before long, the growing antagonism of the cold war had closed Unicef's offices in Eastern Europe, and with their closure came the end of most programmatic assistance. But already a new type of relationship had begun. In

1947, the first Unicef National Committee in Europe was formed in Yugoslavia. In the same year, the first Unicef greeting card was produced from a picture drawn by a Czechoslovakian child. After the Polish Unicef Committee was set up in 1962, its chairman, Dr. Boguslaw Kozusznik, toured Central and Eastern Europe to export the idea of establishing such Committees, and by 1974, Bulgaria, Czechoslovakia, Hungary and Romania had followed suit[66]. The Committees were sponsored officially and attached either to a ministry or to a mass organization, but in other ways they operated like typical National Committees: raising money by selling Unicef greeting cards and running information campaigns on the needs of children in the developing world.

After 1989, most Eastern European Committees regrouped and assumed the character of independent NGOs. As with other Unicef National Committees, the newly passed UN Convention on the Rights of the Child became a platform from which the Committees of the countries of Central and Eastern Europe could champion the cause of children not only in the developing world but within their own shell-shocked societies. These two events—the passage of the Convention and the sudden collapse of the three-world divide of the cold war period—hastened Unicef's own gradual organizational transition from exclusive concern with children of the 'developing' or third world, to concern with child victims of mass deprivation—especially that attendant on development failure—in whatever 'world' it was found. The 1991 (post-Summit) *State of the World's Children* report for the first time included a commentary on the children of the industrialized world. The cause of children was beginning to transcend not only the political but the 'development' divide. And the reverberations all over the world of the movement for democratization meant that 'development' and 'rights' perspectives were also beginning to merge.

Unicef's first post–cold war involvement in the problems of children in Eastern Europe was precipitated by the downfall of the Ceaucescu dictatorship in Romania at the end of 1989[67]. This revealed to a horrified world the fallout of state policies emanating from a twisted mind-set towards families and child care. The regime had been pronatalist in the extreme—banning contraception and taxing the childless, but at the same time it had pursued policies that curbed household incomes, dislocated extended family networks and allowed the price of food to soar. It had virtually forced parents to bring into the world children they did not want and could not support. Many mothers resorted to abortion: around 40 per cent of Romanian pregnancies (1985) were illegally terminated in spite of the high risks of complication, even death, and of punitive state reprisal. Others handed over their newborns to dreadfully inadequate state 'orphanages'. As a result, 150,000 children were living in appalling conditions, without proper food, warmth, clothing, medical care or affection. Over 1,000 of the youngest had contracted AIDS from transfusions with HIV-contaminated blood[68].

Television footage of these children's misery caused a spontaneous outpouring of public sympathy from around the world. Unicef was among the earliest international organizations to respond to what was palpably a child emergency[69]. In collaboration with the Romanian Unicef Committee, supplies of basic drugs and medical equipment were provided for 200 children's institutions and hospitals, as were disposable syringes for use throughout the child health care system. But questions quickly began to arise about longer-term Unicef involvement on behalf of children in countries long considered 'developed'. The 1990 Executive Board decided that programmes of assistance for Central and Eastern European countries would have to be funded out of special contributions. In the case of Romania, $4 million was provided by two governmental donors and seven National Committees and a programme was launched in 1991; in the same year Albania—by far the poorest country in Europe—also became a Unicef recipient. Former Yugoslavia also began to receive emergency help from Unicef as part of the UN humanitarian response to the outbreak of war in late 1991[70].

The components of these programmes—even where practical in war-torn ex-Yugoslavia—were similar to approaches evolving in some of the 'newly industrializing' countries of the developing world: technical assistance for training health and social workers; surveys into the situation of children; the establishment of nutritional monitoring surveillance systems and other data-gathering mechanisms to facilitate analysis of children's well-being; help in developing national programmes of action (NPAs) to meet the goals pledged at the World Summit for Children; policy discussion on street children or other children in especially difficult circumstances; information exchange and coordination to make good the lack of it between NGOs (local and international) and government bodies; promotion of the substance of the Convention on the Rights of the Child and of its ratification[71].

In Romania the programme was supported by a reorganized National Committee, which undertook fund-raising and advocacy on behalf of children's rights and needs domestically and internationally. This was the first occasion in which a Unicef programme and a National Committee functioned alongside one another in the same country. Here, as in other countries of Central and Eastern Europe, the time of transition was seen as an opportunity to etch into the post-communist order the idea that children are entitled to 'first call' on society's resources[72].

As the new decade got under way, misgivings that the course of the social and economic transition would not come easy gave way to downright alarm. Warfare in the former Yugoslavia and its threat elsewhere were the most visible problems. But there were terrible strains almost everywhere. Adherence to a communist development model might well have been an obstacle to political and economic health, but destroying it did not on its own repair the structural faults in the system—rather the reverse. The free market orthodoxies that were substituted, sometimes traumatically, had effects similar to the 'SAPping' of Latin America and Africa in the 1980s. And just as, in the 1980s, Unicef had taken upon itself the measuring and the publicizing of the impact of macro-economic policies in the developing world on the well-being of children, now in the 1990s it was to undertake the same role vis-à-vis the transition in Central and Eastern Europe[73].

The International Child Development Centre (ICDC) in Florence began to assemble data and instigate inquiries into the social fallout of countries' transition to the market economy[74]. This activity took place along lines parallel to the continuing inquiry into crisis and adjustment in Africa and elsewhere. The work involved economists, social statisticians and policy specialists from countries of Central and Eastern Europe, and was designed to help countries emerging from the long socialist experiment to develop tools for social analysis in the new policy formulation climate. The first product of the inquiry—*Children and the Transition to the Market Economy: Safety Nets and Social Policies in Central and Eastern Europe*—was published in 1991. In 1992, the ICDC set up a special project, called 'MONEE', to monitor the transition on a continuing basis, in partnership with statistical offices and policy centres.

The 'MONEE' project began to publish regular reports in 1993, and the overall picture it painted was grim. As in so many countries of the developing world, the 'therapy' of adjustment to bring balance of payments deficits into line—wage control, price rises, exchange rate devaluation, the elimination of inefficient industry, and cuts in social services—had acted less as a spur to economic renewal than as a blanket stifling the embers of economic life. Prices for food and other essentials spiralled upward as subsidies were removed; meanwhile, jobs—previously universally guaranteed—vanished as ex-state-monopoly industries went under, unable to compete in the brutal world of open markets and advanced Western technology. Families facing the double shock of runaway inflation and loss of earnings found themselves hopelessly worse off. In Bulgaria, for example, the purchasing power of wages fell by 40 per cent in 1991. In Poland and Hungary, the share of family income spent on food rose by 50 to 60 per cent. In most countries, well over 20 per cent of the

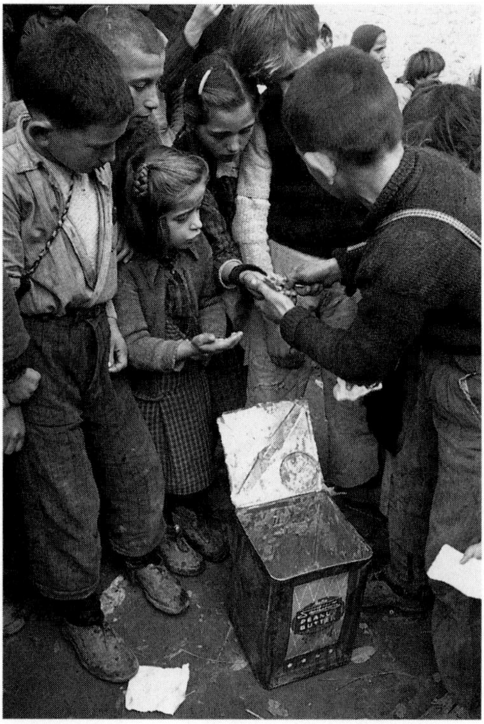

UNICEF/ICEF-0244

Based on the principle that children are above politics, UNICEF was created to provide food, clothing and other support to children in both victorious and defeated countries devastated by World War II.

In the 1950s, school children in Athens, Greece, were among the millions of children whose nutrition was improved by UNICEF's distribution of dried milk.

UNICEF/ICEF-0355

UNICEF's third Executive Director, James P. Grant, addresses a press conference at the start of the World Summit for Children, the unprecedented gathering of 71 Heads of State or Government, who met at United Nations Headquarters on 30 September 1990 to commit themselves to meet basic health and education goals for children by the year 2000.

Unicef Goodwill Ambassadors Sir Peter Ustinov, Liv Ullman, Audrey Hepburn and Julio Iglesias pause for a moment after the official closing of the World Summit for Children.

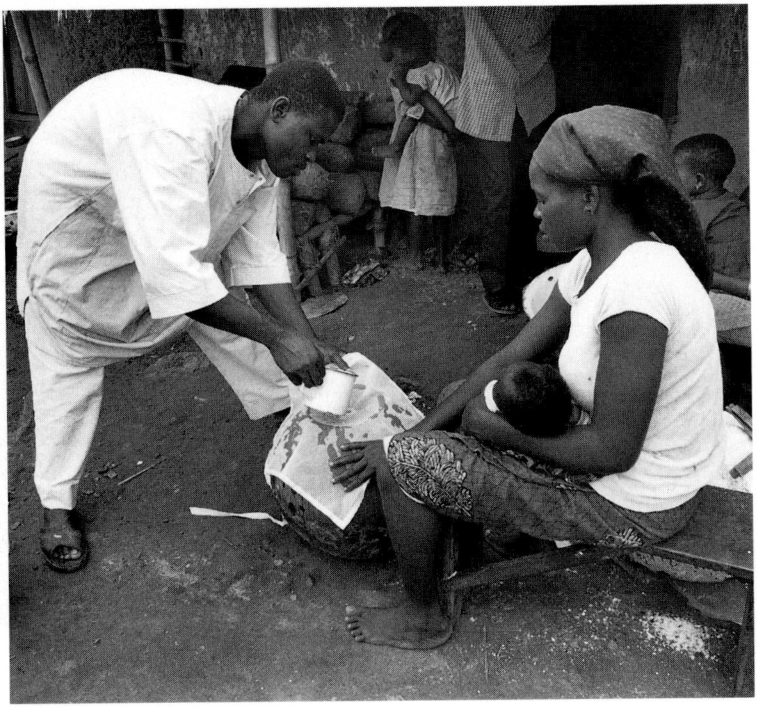

UNICEF/92-0090/Giacomo Pirozzi

A UNICEF-trained village health worker in Nigeria demonstrates how to filter water to prevent guinea worm disease.

A girl with goitre, caused by lack of iodine, is examined in her classroom in Bangladesh, through a UNICEF-assisted programme promoting the use of iodized salt to eliminate iodine deficiency disorders.

UNICEF/93-0050/Maggie Murray-Lee

A baby receives a regular check-up at a health centre in Bogota, Colombia. Monitoring of a child's growth is a vital tool for detecting early signs of malnutrition and preventing other health problems.

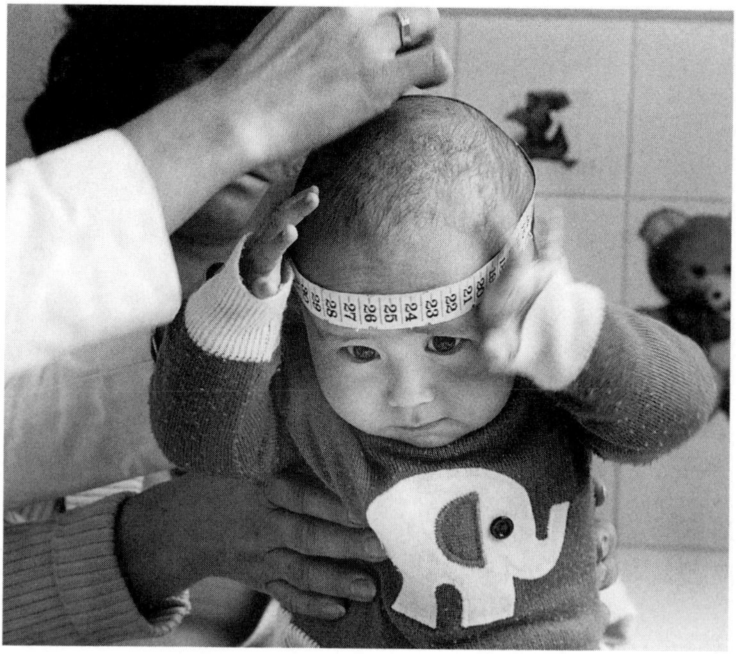

UNICEF/88-0006/Ellen Tolmie

Children at a UNICEF-assisted daycare in Harare, Zimbabwe, receive nutritionally balanced meals as part of a programme to ensure their physical, emotional and social development.

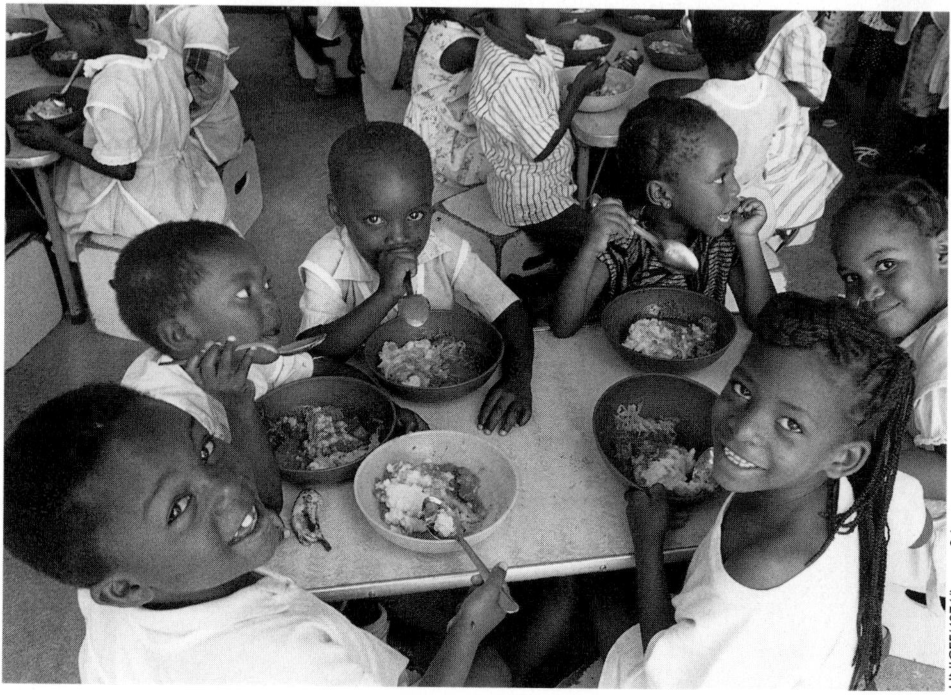

UNICEF/4974/Jorgen Schytte

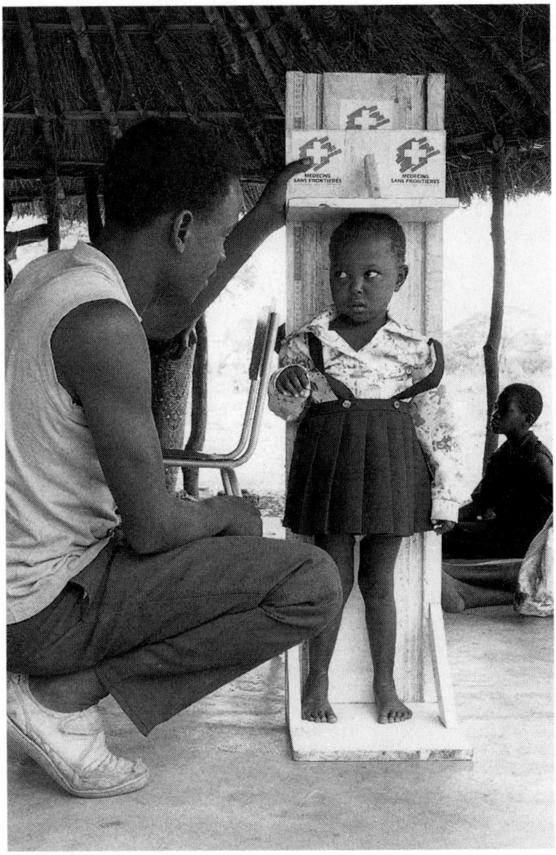

UNICEF/2621/Carolyn Watson

UNICEF partners with such non-governmental organizations as Médecins sans Frontières to deliver basic health services to children in all situations, including this Mozambican refugee girl who had her height measured in a camp in Zambia in 1989.

A Nigerian mobile health team staffed by women health workers travels to the south-western village of Odolan to deliver basic health services for children and women.

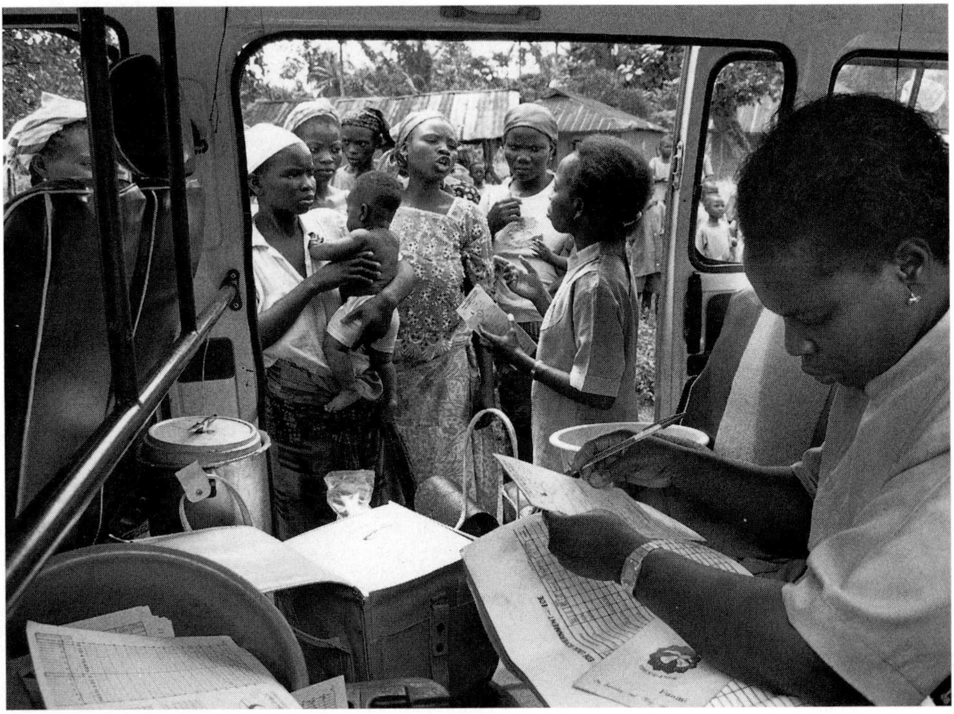

UNICEF/92-0088/Giacomo Pirozzi

In 1985, Turkey's national immunization drive vaccinated 80% of the country's children under five years old against TB, diphtheria, pertussis, tetanus, measles and polio. By 1990 the global goal of immunizing 80% of the world's children under one against the six diseases had been achieved.

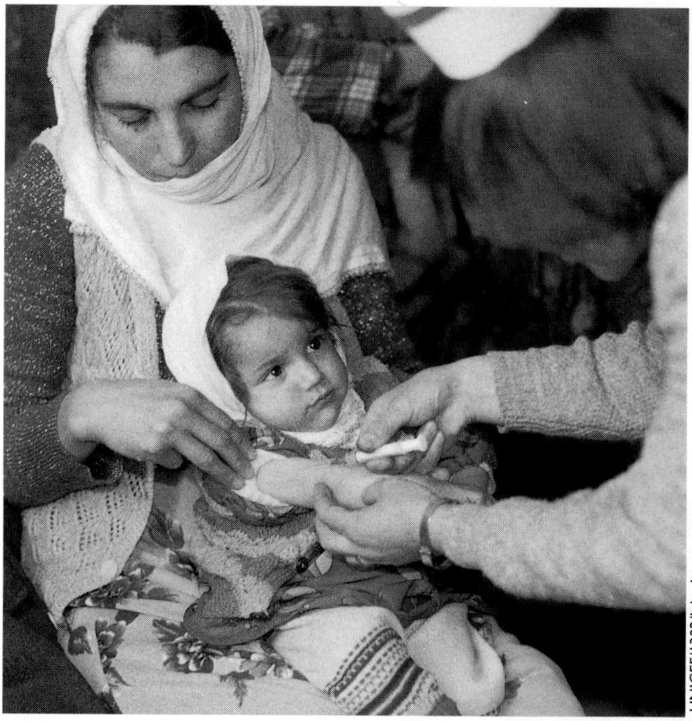

UNICEF/1302/John Isaac

A woman breastfeeds her newborn at a maternity hospital in Shanghai, China, one of thousands of hospitals throughout the world certified as 'Baby-friendly'—meaning that they follow the 'Ten Steps to Successful Breastfeeding', encouraging mothers to exclusively breastfeed their infants for at least the first six months.

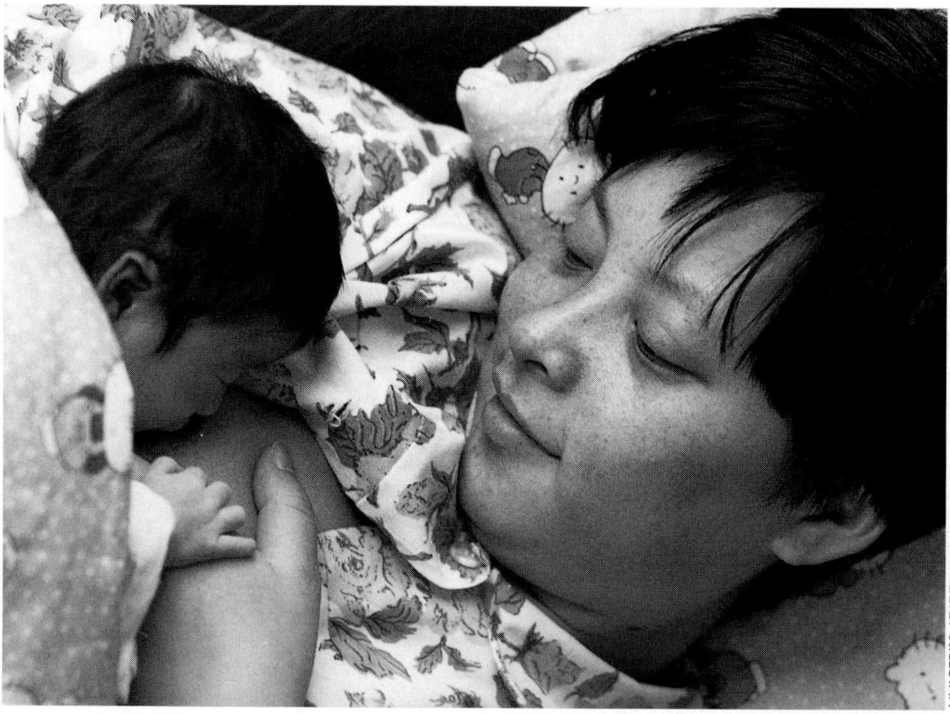

UNICEF/93-1767/Roger Lemoyne

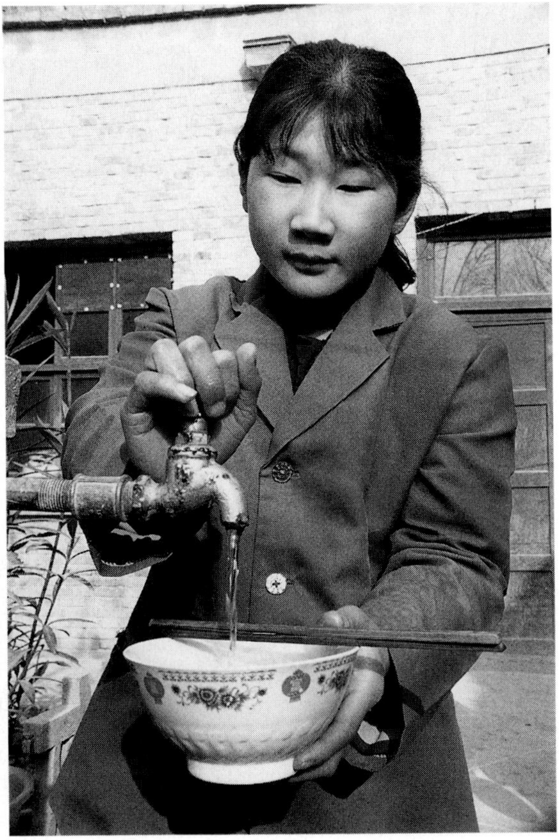

UNICEF/93-1710/Roger Lemoyne

UNICEF assists with the provision of safe water and sanitation in China, especially in distant or disadvantaged rural communities.

Safe water is collected at a UNICEF-supported conservation project near Mauritania's capital. Upgrading water points in poor neighbourhoods, training communities in maintenance and providing hygiene education are components of comprehensive water and sanitation programmes throughout the developing world.

UNICEF/5750/Lauren Goodsmith

Girls learn to write in an informal class held in a squatter community where there is no primary school in Bogota, Colombia.

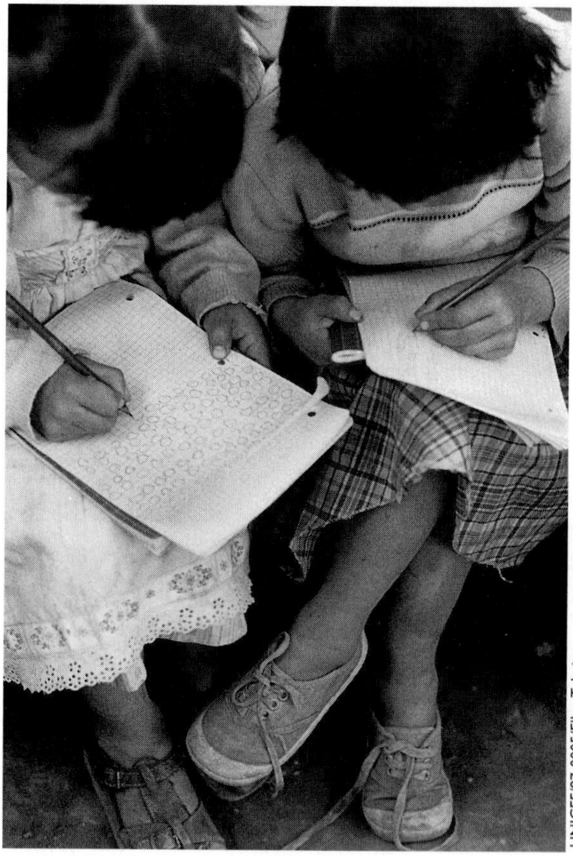

UNICEF/87-0005/Ellen T

A girl helps with the household chores at her home in the Lebanese village of Akroum—many other children in the country have had their lives disrupted by war.

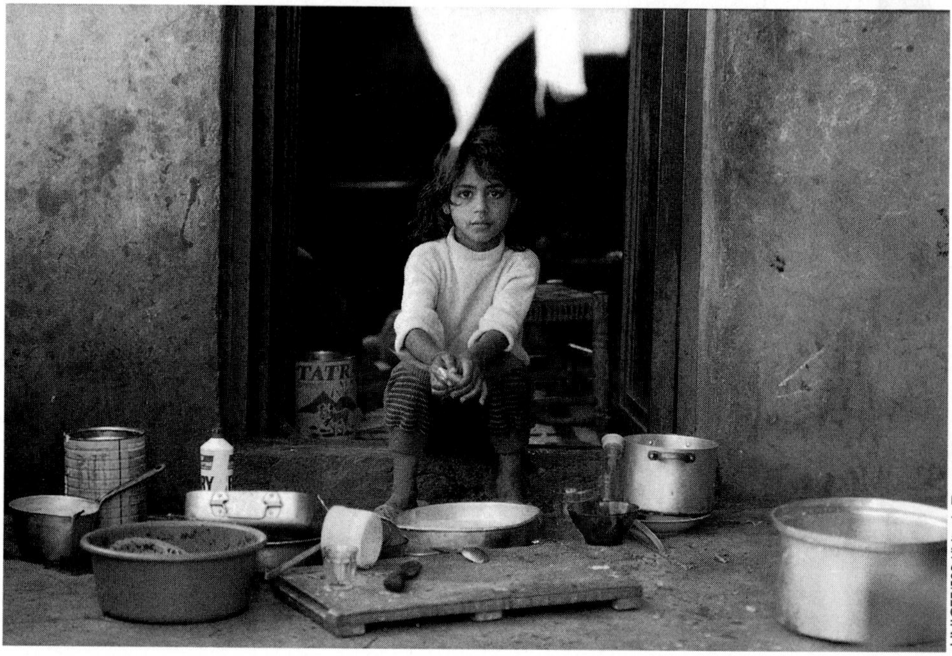

UNICEF/5234/Nicole Toutounji

Girls and boys share rudimentary desks and writing materials in an outdoor class at a village school in Benin. In 1993, only 65% of eligible children were enrolled in primary schools in Benin, one of the world's poorest countries.

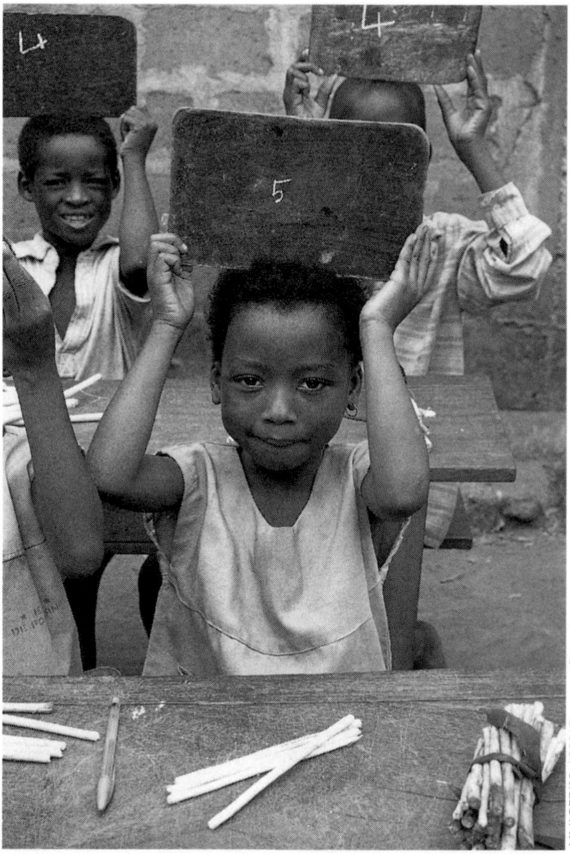

UNICEF/93-1992/Giacomo Pirozzi

Educating girls is a good social investment. Increased national economic productivity, lower infant and maternal mortality rates, reduced fertility and increased life expectancy have all been linked to higher educational achievements by women.

UNICEF/2243/Jorgen Schytte

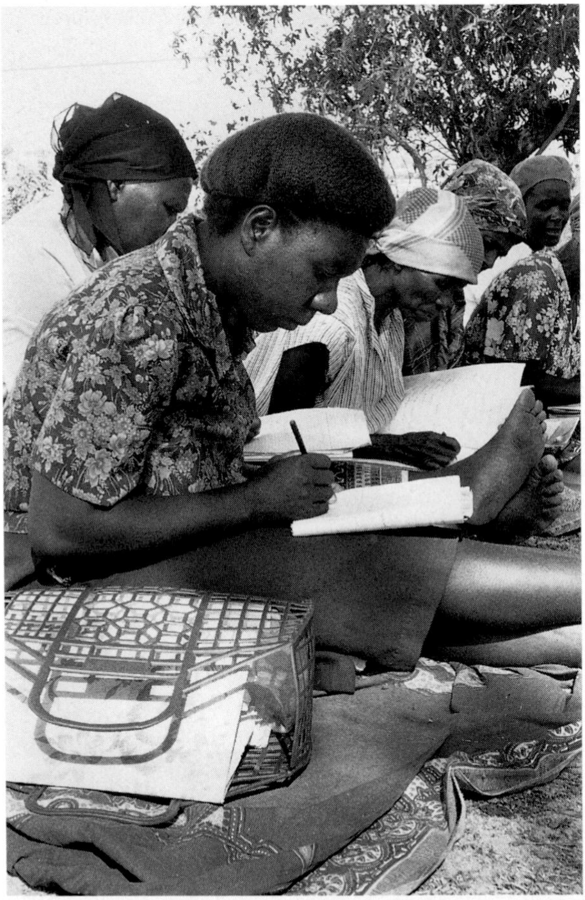

UNICEF/3139/Carolyn Watson

Women in Zimbabwe learn to read and write in their language, Shona, in a UNICEF-supported literacy programme for women.

A woman journalist interviews women in Nepal, during a journalism training course co-sponsored by UNICEF to increase knowledge about, and coverage of, development issues by the mass media.

UNICEF/93-1278/Maggie Murray-Lee

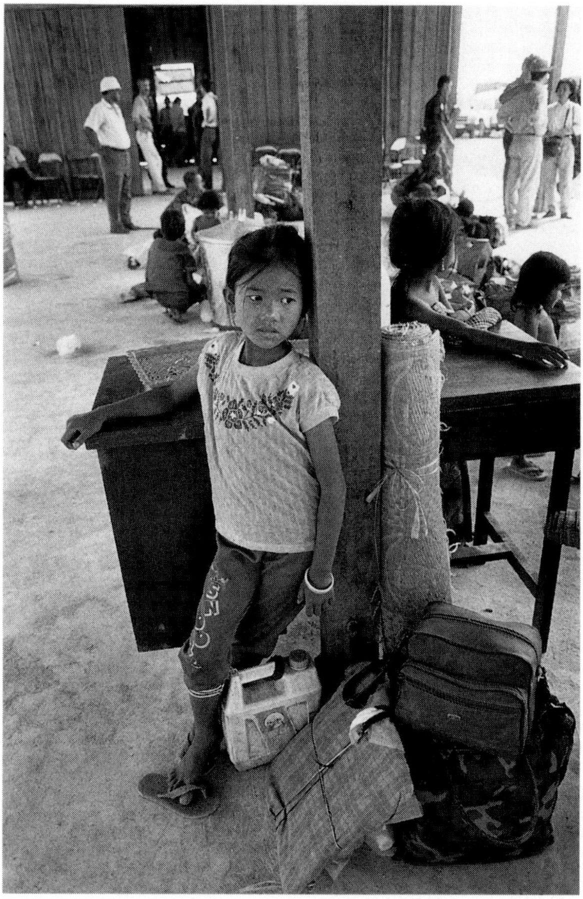

UNICEF/5879/Roger Lemoyne

After years of exile in refugee camps in neighbouring Thailand, a girl waits in a repatriation centre, one of thousands of children returning with their families to Cambodia in 1992 in a massive UN-supported inter-agency effort to consolidate peace in that country.

Children open a shop gate under the watchful eye of a UN peacekeeper in Mogadiscio, Somalia in 1993. The continuing conflict in that country has highlighted the limits of effective emergency operations in the virtual absence of national government, forcing UNICEF and other relief organizations to find new ways of meeting the needs of children surrounded by war.

UNICEF/93-634/Betty Press

Since 1975, more than a million civilians, many of them children like this Cambodian boy, have been killed or maimed by land-mines, an estimated 110 million of which are now strewn across 64 countries. UNICEF's 1996 Anti-War Agenda calls for a global ban on the production, use, stockpiling, sale and export of anti-personnel mines.

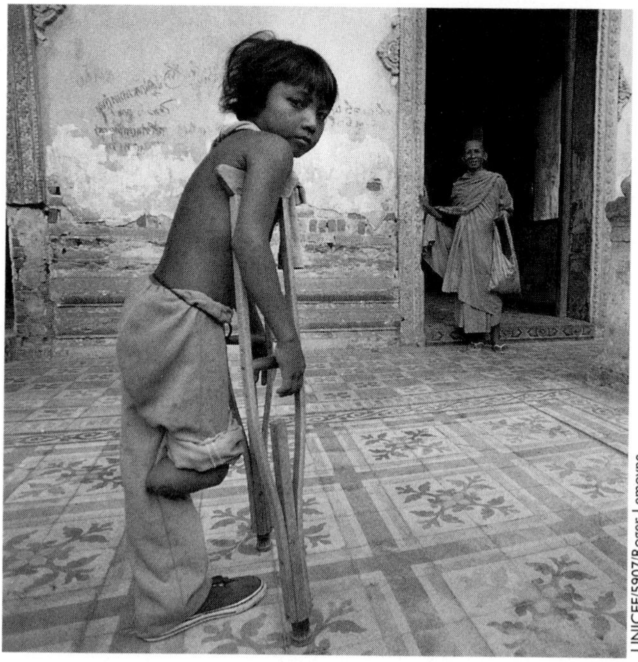

UNICEF/5907/Roger Lemoyne

A family of Rwandan refugees arrives in Tanzania in April 1994, among the 300,000 fleeing the slaughter of hundreds of thousands in their country. Three months later, a million more Rwandans, including 100,000 unaccompanied children, crossed into Zaire in one week, creating an unprecedented humanitarian crisis and leaving a devastated and traumatized nation that will need generations to recover.

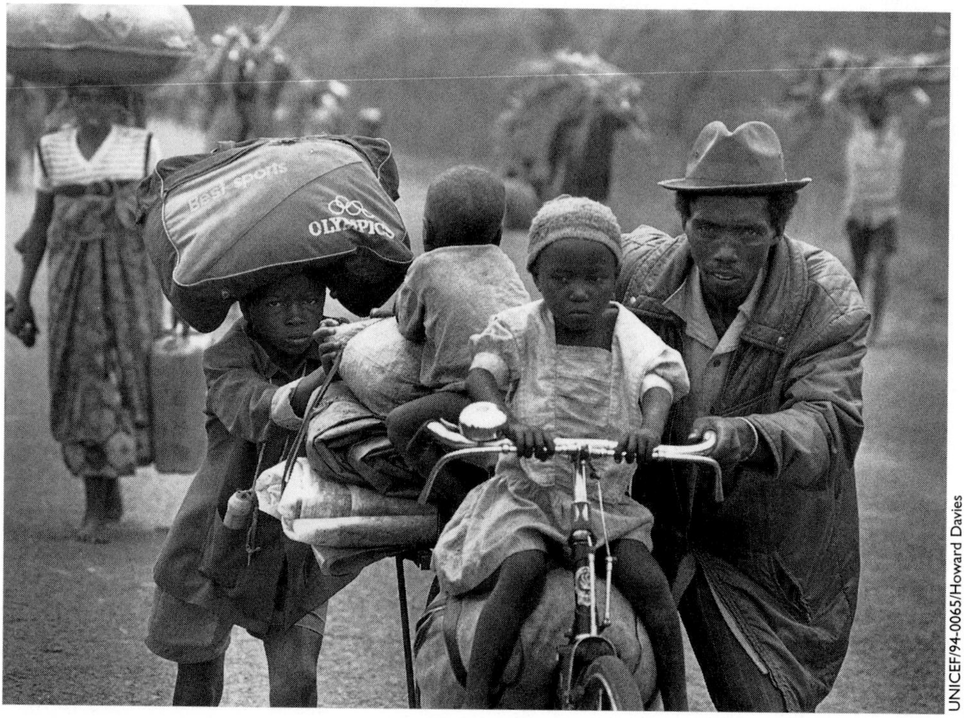

UNICEF/94-0065/Howard Davies

In the 1990s, war continues to be part of daily life for millions of children. Soldiers visit a kindergarten for displaced children in Croatia, where some 50% of the 1.2 million people displaced by the fighting that followed the break-up of former Yugoslavia, were temporarily settled.

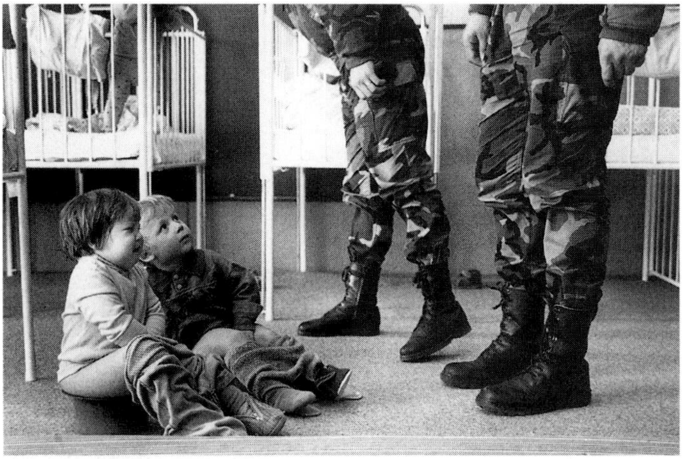

UNICEF/5549/Darko Gorenak

UNICEF/94-0877/Roger Lemoyne

A boy in Sarajevo mourns the loss of his older brother, killed in the war in Bosnia and Herzegovina. In addition to emergency, health and education support, UNICEF has trained a network of health workers and teachers throughout former Yugoslavia to recognize and treat child trauma.

At a UNICEF-assisted centre for unaccompanied children in Rwanda, children act out the killings they have witnessed, part of a trauma treatment programme to help them cope with their war experience.

UNICEF/94-0588/Betty Press

A woman with AIDS embraces her daughter in Malawi, one of several African countries where the spread of HIV/AIDS now threatens the reduction of infant and child mortality—achieved over several decades—as well as leaving thousands of children orphaned when their parents succumb to the disease.

UNICEF/93-1229/Cindy Andrew

Two boys sleep on a street in Rio de Janeiro, Brazil. The plight of street children and others in need of special protection worldwide helped lead to the creation of the Convention on the Rights of the Child, which became international law on 2 September 1990.

UNICEF/5262/Jeremy Horner

UNICEF/0111/Peter Tacon

The Convention states that children have the right to basic health and education, free expression and protection against exploitation. For thousands of children who must work to survive, UNICEF supports programmes to ensure their working conditions are safe and that they have access to education and other basic services.

In Bangladesh, UNICEF collaborates with the Government and employers to find alternatives to employing children in strenuous work such as breaking stones at brick factories, which threatens their physical, mental, emotional and social development.

UNICEF/93-0024/Maggie Murray-Lee

On assuming her position in 1995, UNICEF's newly appointed Executive Director Carol Bellamy visited several countries in Africa—and met these displaced children in Liberia—reasserting the organization's continuing priority attention to that continent.

UNICEF/95-0196/Giacomo Pirozzi

Equal opportunities for all girls and women, especially in education, is another priority for UNICEF—as it continues its work as the international representative of children, guided and energized by the now almost universally ratified Convention on the Rights of the Child.

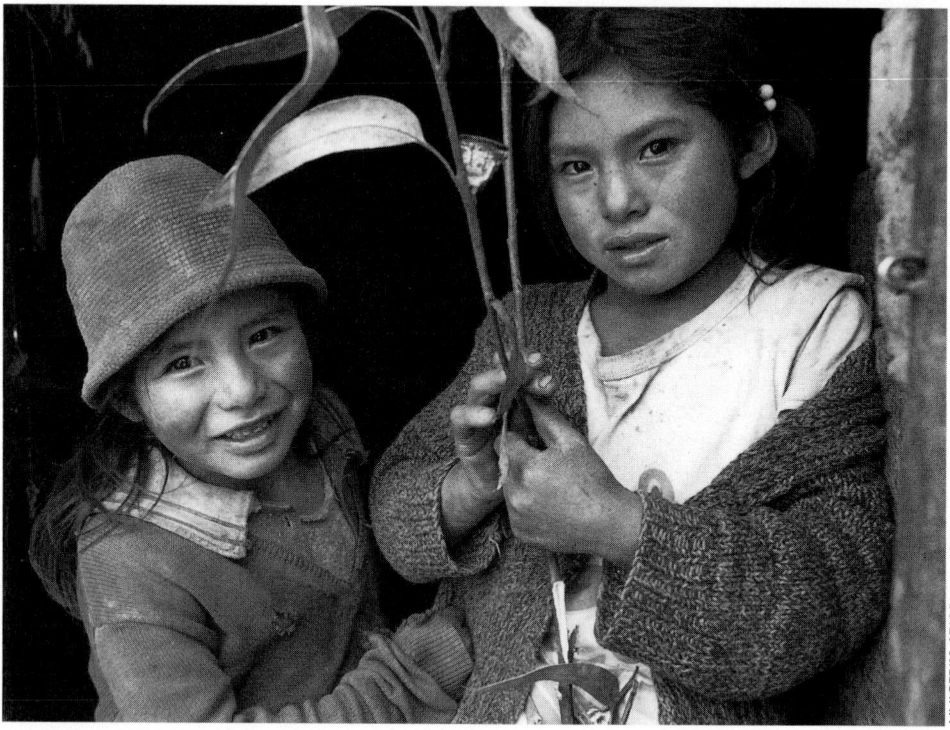

UNICEF/93-0712/Jeremy Horner

population was living in poverty, rising to 40 per cent among large families and in the worst areas[75].

Those hardest hit by the process of economic and political change were children, pensioners, young (often single-parent) families with small children, and ethnic minorities—some of whom became the target of pent-up frustration stemming from the extraordinary upheaval that had brought people used to lifelong certainties face to face with deteriorating living standards and profound insecurity. Government spending on health, education and other social services had been severely cut. Families with working parents who depended on public nurseries were forced to withdraw their children due to prohibitive fees, and the provision of preschools dwindled. Charges for school meals became exorbitant. Infectious and vaccine-preventable diseases were rising. Drugs were increasingly scarce, and health and medical facilities were forced to close due to equipment failure. Although some countries introduced some cushions for vulnerable groups as part of the reform process, they did so half-heartedly; the scope of such cushions was limited and their value quickly became eroded.

In no way could the need for drastic social and economic reform in the ex-second world be challenged: there was even less choice than there had been for the adjustment process in the third. But the extent, the speed and the suddenness of the process within a whole geopolitical network of more than a score of states and aspirant national entities was unprecedented. Even the most prescient policy adviser could not have foreseen all the implications of not one, but a whole succession of leaps in the dark. It takes time to assume and grow into new political and economic clothing (as many ex-colonies had amply proved); to establish new institutions and reorient existing ones; to substitute individual rights for state control—in the case of property ownership, for example; to develop the rule of democratically constructed laws and administration; and to change individual outlooks and behaviours.

The trauma of the restructuring process was leading to high social costs. These showed up in infant mortality and child nutrition rates, as might have been expected, but their impact on families, especially on adult males and therefore on women family providers, was very much more severe. Death rates were escalating, marriage and birth rates falling, school enrolments decreasing and the mounting crime wave, especially among unemployed and disaffected young people, was becoming unstoppable. Such characteristics of the transition were themselves a threat to the reform process and to its public acceptability.

Unicef avoided describing its proposed remedy by the obvious term: 'transition with a human face'. But this was essentially what it once more suggested: a system of safety nets—unemployment benefits, minimum income guarantees, child allowances, subsidized school meals, free maternity, health care and schooling—for vulnerable groups and careful monitoring of social policy. While accepting that it was right not to divert aid from developing regions, Unicef believed that the international community must show more support for social welfare activities connected with the transition[76].

Responding to its own dictum, in 1992 the Unicef Executive Board made a more vigorous commitment to react to 'worsening circumstances that have triggered acute human need'; this commitment included the countries of Central and Eastern Europe, but in the forefront of minds were the 'new independent States' of the suddenly collapsed ex-USSR. Criteria were agreed (low per capita income, high IMR) whereby certain countries qualified for non-emergency programme assistance; in others, only policy advice and advocacy were to be offered. The 'qualifying' states were Albania in Europe and Armenia, Azerbaijan, Kazakhstan, Kyrgyzstan, Tajikistan, Turkmenistan and Uzbekistan in the ex-USSR. However, technical assistance would be available to 'non-qualifying countries' in special circumstances, and extra resources—$2 million in both 1993 and 1994—were provided to support the data-gathering and monitoring activity in the region and the social policy analysis into which it was feeding[77].

At the same Board meeting, it was agreed that Unicef National Committees in Central and Eastern Europe could from 1992 onward reserve all their proceeds from the sale of greeting cards and other fund-raising events and apply them to the benefit of children in their own countries. Many Committees were already playing a policy-influencing role, having been instrumental in organizing situation analyses of the condition of children. They had also successfully pressed for ratification of the Convention on the Rights of the Child and for the adoption of the 'Baby-Friendly Hospital Initiative'[78]. The Unicef determination to ensure that social policies affecting children would have a place on the transitional agenda was well on its way to being realized.

If 1992 was a critical year for the evolution of policies towards children in crumbling parts of the industrialized world, it was also an important year for children in the even more frangible states of Africa. Once again, parts of the continent—27 million people in 14 countries—were suffering severely from drought, and certain countries—Liberia, Sierra Leone, Somalia—were approaching the ultimate in post-colonial breakdown: the 'failed State'. The collapse of consolidated forms of authority and administration and their replacement by armed groups equipped with modern weaponry presented a severe challenge to the forces of international humanitarianism, let alone development, in the late 20th century. This was a far cry from the arcadia of the 'new world order' that the end of the cold war was supposed to usher in.

Elsewhere the tide of democratization was not running smoothly. The implosion of the USSR and the growing ethnic and nationalist turmoil in former Yugoslavia and other 'new independent States' were unwelcome features of a world freed from the rigidities of superpower stand-off. The 'peace dividend', dented heavily by the Gulf War, was yielding little extra to invest in the fight against world poverty. As far as Africa was concerned, the industrialized powers no longer had any strategic purpose in cultivating allies on the continent. They began to hedge assistance packages with conditionalities concerning political and economic reform, often as a pretext for aid reduction. And if the politicians' and diplomats' interest was mostly absorbed elsewhere, the bankers' and businessmen's was virtually non-existent.

The long chapter of poor performance had landed all but a handful of Africa's economies in an investment desert as parched as the Sahara. Only the humanitarians—international and NGO—kept their energies and outlook tuned to Africa, and they were becoming dismayed by the degree to which they were devoting themselves to emergency relief and the maintenance of health and welfare services from which impoverished governments were retreating. Apart from a surprising degree of success in reaching vaccination targets—by 1992, two thirds of African countries had met the goal of 75 per cent immunization coverage[79]—the health and nutritional condition of children appeared again to be deteriorating[80].

Having acted as a strong impetus behind the World Summit for Children, Africa's leaders looked to Unicef for a quid pro quo: help in remobilizing international concern behind their continuing battle with debt and decline. The result was Unicef's co-sponsorship of an OAU 'International Conference on Assistance to African Children'. The purpose of the meeting, held in Dakar, Senegal, in November 1992, was to solicit new international resources and energize national political will behind policy reorientation towards women and children[81]. By September 1992, 44 African countries had signed the Children's Summit Declaration, but few had yet prepared national programmes of action (NPAs) to translate this commitment into policy and practice[82]. Unicef wanted the Conference to provide a framework within which African countries would work hard to develop NPAs and set their policies on a child-friendly track; in response, donor countries would, it was hoped, be willing to provide extra funds to put these programmes into effect. The imperative of meeting children's needs and promoting their rights would help launch an optimism offensive to combat the prevailing Afro-gloom.

Optimism was sorely needed. There were a few promising political signs—democratic elections in Zambia, new-broom leadership in Ethiopia, Ghana and Uganda, the release of Nelson Mandela from prison in South Africa—but not many equivalents on the economic front. Africa was still staggering under the cross of its external debt, which by 1992 approached $200 billion[83]. Each year, Africa struggled to pay around one third of the interest that fell due; the rest was simply added to a bill that no miraculous discovery of mineral wealth, no economic great leap forward on the Asian pattern, no transformation of the investment climate would ever enable Africa to pay. In spite of persistent calls to cancel the debts of the poorest countries, forgiveness exercises—the Toronto Agreement, the Brady Plan, the Trinidad Terms—had managed to wipe only $7 billion off the African slate.

In October 1992, Unicef's ICDC in Florence published a follow-up study to *Adjustment with a Human Face*, this time focusing on Africa alone. The study was wishfully entitled: *Africa's Recovery in the 1990s: From Stagnation and Adjustment to Human Development*[84]. The picture it constructed of the situation of Africa's children according to the usual social indicators offered little that was either encouraging or new; but, the study insisted, the 'adjustment decade', however painful and unpromising in many countries, had not been without its successes. Of the four SAP objectives—stabilization of balance of payments, removal of structural bottlenecks, economic growth, and protection for vulnerable groups—three had been achieved in five countries: Guinea-Bissau, Mali, Mauritius, Senegal and Zambia. Most countries had met at least one or two. But no one could pretend that results had been better than 'limited'. Only Mauritius, a relatively small island State in the Indian Ocean, had managed a four-star performance.

Real and sustainable recovery, the analysis suggested, must come out of the evolution of a new development strategy for Africa. This must be 'food-led', based on investment in smallholder agriculture and smallholder manufacturing enterprise. A redistribution of resources—land title, training, credit—towards these groups was needed; so were favourable pricing policies for their goods and an infrastructure—roads, market-places, crop storage facilities—to serve them. There must be a determined abandonment of the prestige industrial installations and luxury buildings that had been the graveyard of African hopes. As well as increased international flows, funds for the rejuvenation and expansion of educational and health care services could be generated by domestic reallocations, away from defence and from capital intensive schemes, towards activities that engaged the energies and creativity of—as well as served—people.

The International Conference on Assistance to African Children (ICAAC) also adopted an avowedly upbeat tone. Taking as its theme 'Africa's Children, Africa's Future', the Conference provided an opportunity to 'refocus the development dialogue between Africa and its development partners onto children and women'. In the 'Consensus of Dakar' adopted by the Conference, the 46 African countries represented not only recommitted themselves to the World Summit for Children's 27 goals, but also agreed to certain intermediate child health and nutritional goals by the mid-decade—1995. The Conference did succeed in catalysing the process of NPA preparation in Africa. By 1993, 23 sub-Saharan countries had finalized their NPAs, a proportion higher than in any other region except Latin America[85].

Worldwide, by this time 105 countries had either finalized or drafted their NPAs, covering a total of 88 per cent of the world's children[86]. In many, the preparation of these NPAs had been an opportunity to bring together many different sectors of society—government and non-governmental, religious and secular, public and private, national, subnational and local—in a joint endeavour to plan and programme on behalf of children. In some large federal countries—Mexico, Brazil, the Philippines, Egypt and India, for example—this process was also being undertaken at state, and sometimes at municipal, level.

In September 1993, on the third anniversary of the Children's Summit, a round-table meeting entitled 'Keeping the Promise to Children' was held in New York[87]. Heads of State or Government, Ministers, and representatives of 77 countries and many UN agencies met to reiterate their commitment to reduce child mortality by one third, malnutrition by one half, and to extend schooling to 80 per cent of children before the end of the century. They also undertook to speed up action on behalf of children by adopting a set of 10 'mid-decade goals', selected because they were thought to be achievable by 1995, or because they provided stepping-stones in terms of increased service coverage towards the goals for the year 2000.

Apart from universal ratification of the Convention on the Rights of the Child, these 'mid-decade goals' were all related to the control of specific diseases and nutritional deficiencies: increased immunization coverage and use of ORT; elimination of neonatal tetanus, polio, and vitamin A deficiency; eradication of guinea worm disease; reduction of measles; universal iodization of salt; and promotion of 'baby-friendly' maternity facilities. The funding strategy outlined for the attainment of these goals was described as the '20/20 vision': a call for developing countries to allocate at least 20 per cent of their public expenditures to basic social sectors: primary education, primary health care, family planning, nutrition, water and sanitation; and for industrialized countries to earmark 20 per cent of their development assistance for the same purpose. The 20/20 idea—which was essentially the brainchild of Jim Grant, Richard Jolly and Mahbub ul Haq—was supported in a number of regional meetings over the next two years.

Three years after the World Summit for Children, the momentum it had generated was still continuing to build. And this had occurred in spite of the negative global climate and the insecurities of the 'new world disorder' that was now presenting such a contrast to the old certainties of East and West, North and South. The subsequent international summit agenda for the 1990s had already been distractingly crowded: environment (Rio de Janeiro, 1992) and human rights (Vienna, 1993) had already occurred; population (Cairo, 1994), social development (Copenhagen, 1995), women (Beijing, 1995) and cities (Istanbul, 1996) were still upcoming.. But in an important way the Children's Summit process differed from these much larger talking and negotiation shops.

In their cases, the UN system provided the opportunity and the organizational context in which international norms of principle and policy behaviour could be established, but its job then virtually ceased. Few UN organizations had an established capacity at country and sub-country level that enabled them to enjoy an instrumental role in ensuring that rhetorical pledges were translated into action. This was the task of sovereign governments, according to all internationalist principles. But however sincerely made on the rostrum at Rio or Vienna, Cairo or Copenhagen, promises were easily forgotten once the delegates went home. Some governments might not have the capacity or the will to pursue new commitments with urgency unless pushed into doing so by activist campaigns of 'organized shame'. Their promises might well not be revisited until whatever UN Commission entrusted by the Conference to pursue its follow-up agenda convened yet another international meeting.

The case of the World Summit for Children was unusual in that a UN organization—Unicef—with a strong field presence in almost every developing country, and a National Committee in many industrialized ones, existed to take the post-Summit agenda forward. Under Jim Grant's leadership, this network had developed a considerable capacity for mobilizing a wide range of partners within the countries concerned and a credibility at high levels of government. In the wake of the Summit, Unicef representatives were able to chase—politely, tactfully, expertly—senior government figures and provide technical and financial assistance to enable national programmes of action to come into being. Never before had a national-level process stemming directly from an international meeting been facilitated to this extent by the local offshoots of a UN member organization. This was mainly because no other UN organization (with the exception of UNDP in the developing world) had the breadth and range of presence and governmental access; it was also because no other UN organizational head had conceived the idea or the strategy to promote his or her organizational mission in such a far-sighted and comprehensive way. Unicef's country-by-country support for the elaboration and implementation of NPAs not only helped accelerate action on behalf of children but offered a model of how an international body in the UN system could promote real grass-roots progress as an outcome of commitments achieved at the international level.

During the late 1980s and early 1990s, at a time of international change more significant in historical terms than any period since the end of empire, Unicef had managed to establish the principle that how children's well-being was affected by macro-events was an important part of their observation and interpretation. The Summit had been the imprimatur, and its follow-up the reinforcement, of this idea. Within restructuring, adjustment and debt relief; within sustainable development and democratic reform; within the maelstrom of movements and 'isms' converging on the international agenda, Unicef had persistently asked: 'And what about children?' The task of examining their condition, it insisted, had to be undertaken in a scientific, not a sentimental, kind of way, and it helped to develop techniques for so doing.

The condition of children and their families had always been accepted as a barometer of change; now it was beginning to be seen as a determinant of policy, not a residual effect to be examined when the main task of adjustment, or political and legal reform, had been accomplished.

The elaboration during 1993 of the 10 mid-decade goals was a tactical manoeuvre to sustain the energy of the post-Summit process. Opening the Keeping the Promise round-table, UN Secretary-General Boutros Boutros-Ghali declared: 'Of all the subjects of development, none has the acceptance, or the power to mobilize, as does the cause of children.' But children had not done it on their own. Many organizations, but especially Unicef, had been their instrument. Their well-being had become identified with a particular vision of sustainable, human-centred development. That vision was helping to keep the cause of development alive. In the name of children and under their cover, Unicef was playing its special part in keeping aloft a somewhat tattered development banner.

Chapter 7

The Gender Dimension

From the moment of its own birth, Unicef accepted as a matter of course that the well-being of children was inseparable from the well-being of those in whose wombs they were conceived, at whose breasts they were suckled and in whose care they traversed the dangerous passages of early life. The primacy of the mother in a child's well-being was regarded by all child development specialists as axiomatic, and Unicef was anxious from its earliest days to assist women, especially those who were poor or disadvantaged in some special way, in their maternal roles.

To embrace maternity within the concept of public health was one of the early Unicef's central tenets. Some of its most important postwar assistance in Europe and later in the developing world was for the training and equipping of midwives, both the white-coated variety and the village 'auntie' who supervised childbirth in traditional settings[1]. The midwifery 'kit' for the TBA (traditional birth attendant)—hygienic gloves, clean razor blade, forceps, gauze, scissors and other essentials for delivery—was a standard Unicef item, updated and replenished over the decades. Unicef also promoted low-tech gynaecology and paediatrics, or MCH (maternal and child health) services, which were still embryonic in the early 1950s in most countries of the ex-colonial world.

Within a very few years, Unicef also began supporting women in their socially delegated, as opposed to biological, maternal roles as the upbringers of children. Mothers' clubs in Brazil and Egypt were seen as conduits for health and nutrition education and home economics; in India, day care provided an opportunity to feed and stimulate the young child and release mothers' time for other responsibilities[2]. In the 1950s and 1960s, the range of domestic activities Unicef assisted was widened to include 'mothercraft' and 'homecraft' in countries such as Kenya. Here, as in many other ex-British colonies, the women's movement of the day was fashioned after the needlework and cake-baking conventions of the imperial alma mater. In West Africa, women were a prime target of *animation rurale*, a popular thrust of the worldwide community development movement.

As awareness rose about the heavy domestic load carried by many women in the rural third world, support for their role as hewers of wood and drawers of water was added. Clean water supplies close to home reduced the time and energy women spent on supplying the household's utilities, as did fuel-efficient stoves. Milk production, poultry-keeping and vegetable gardening could all be seen as support for child nutrition if they were carried out by women in a family labour context. And if women collectively pursued these activities on behalf of the community, this was applauded as an adjunct to their nurturing role. As the 1970s dawned, basic services schemes—soon to become the centrepiece of Unicef's 'alternative' approach—began to rely heavily on women volunteers as their front-line care-in-the-community workers. They were trained to become 'health promoters', 'village-based workers', 'handpump caretakers'—the outer arm of primary health care (PHC)[3]. And within urban basic services programmes, activities for and with women—to reduce the difficulties of raising children amidst urban squalor and brutality, to ease their lack of access to water and other utilities, and to help them earn money and organize for community improvement—were absolutely central[4].

The movement for women's rights that gathered momentum in the early 1970s concerned itself with the situation of women from a very different perspective. Far from seeking greater support for the safe accomplishment of maternity and domesticity, women were refusing to be defined by these roles and were demanding equality with men in other spheres of life. Their protest was against entrenched male domination of power, property, pay, educational and job opportunity, and the discriminations and disadvantages women suffered in these contexts. These discriminations were concomitants of their political and economic dependence on men, which in turn was based primarily on their role in reproduction and family care. Now they were insisting on gender equality as a right independent of maternity and child-raising—activities that, in the industrialized world, no longer occupied the long drawn-out and pivotal role in many women's adult careers that they had customarily held[5]. So determined were women activists to avoid being legally and socially defined by their reproductive organs—over which modern contraception had dramatically increased their control—that emphasis on other-than-motherhood and non-wifely roles was a distinguishing characteristic of the movement.

There was no permanent organization in the United Nations system for women as there was—by a historical quirk—for children. As some of the new champions of the women's cause began in the early 1970s to seek international linkages, they looked to Unicef for help. But they were disappointed. Not surprisingly, given the radical climate surrounding 'women's liberation' and the contemporary lack of recognition that low status of women interacted with poor family well-being, there was deep resistance within Unicef—male-dominated, as were all bureaucracies at the time—to the idea that an organization created in the name of children should be concerned with women in capacities other than child-bearing and -rearing[6].

This view was legitimized by the reality that changes in laws affecting women's status and the articulation of policies to promote equal gender opportunity would have little immediate effect on the lot of women in the developing world with which Unicef was most concerned. The kind of disadvantages experienced by women caught in the trap of poverty, illiteracy and unremitting toil were not easily susceptible to the passage of laws. 'Basic services' to improve a woman's and her children's health, relieve her worries and reduce her domestic drudgery seemed to Unicef at this time more appropriately 'liberating' for most such women, though the degree to which these services depended on the willingness of women to give unpaid service in pursuit of goals that did not necessarily mesh with their own was widely underappreciated. Some in positions of responsibility at Unicef believed that opening up women's horizons and granting them access to the workplace would distract them from their domestic roles and thereby lead to child neglect. Although no statistics, then or since, have ever been produced to support the idea that the children of women who are educated, employed and fairly paid suffer commensurate health and nutritional disadvantages—invariably the opposite is the case—this attitude has often since seemed teflon-coated[7].

Gradual conversion to the idea that women might have a significant role to play in development was inspired initially less by the movement for women's rights than by the mounting panic about population growth and the growing pressure of human numbers on planetary resources[8]. In the lead-up to the first World Population Conference in 1974, those who had managed to think of the women of the third world only as the mothers of its children began to view their child-bearing activities in a new and alarming light. Women were suddenly important because they were the progenitors of all the human statistics that were preoccupying planners with their future requirements for health and education services, jobs and housing, and jeopardizing economic development by their unprecedented profusion. Modern contraception, the technological response, was mostly designed to inhibit female, not male, fertility. Therefore the potential mothers of the next generation must be persuaded to bear children 'responsibly', in numbers and at intervals that would not overwhelm either their own or their State's fragile resources. On the question of what went on in the womb of a woman living in the third world countryside or in one of its shanty towns, the protagonists of women's rights and of development had, for the first time, found themselves on common ground.

This was the reasoning behind the appointment in 1974 of Unicef's first 'family welfare adviser' ('family welfare' was a contemporary euphemism for 'family planning') with a brief that explicitly included 'programming for women'[9]. The position was initially financed by the UN Fund for Population Activities (UNFPA). This continued until 1976, when Unicef decided to institutionalize a post for its senior policy specialist on women's affairs (though it was not prepared to call her that until 1983). In 1975 came the first UN International Women's Conference and the launch of a Decade for Women, 1975-85. These events played a critical role in boosting Unicef's commitment to women, both in terms of programming for 'women in development' and in terms of female advancement within its own ranks. In turn, this made Unicef more sensitive to the way in which a core of influential women thinkers were speaking up on behalf of women in the developing world and recasting perceptions about their role in economic life[10].

Up till the mid-1970s, women in the pre-industrial communities of Africa, Asia and Latin America had not been perceived as making any significant contribution to the family economy. Assumptions about the distribution of tasks within the household had echoed the norms of middle-class industrialized society—namely, that family resource procurement was carried out largely or exclusively by male breadwinners and that anything women might additionally earn was pin money for the purchase of extras. In many parts of the world, these assumptions were highly flawed. The domestic load carried by many third world women had been noticed as consuming time and energy that could otherwise have been spent on mothering. But when the workload was examined and described from a quite different point of view, it turned out to be not really 'domestic' at all, according to norms operating in most Western societies, but economically highly significant.

In Africa, women undertook almost every task connected with growing and processing food, including planting, weeding, hoeing, harvesting, winnowing, tending small livestock, milking all milkable beasts, storing crops and pounding, grinding and sieving them into cookable ingredients. Out of a 16-hour day, around 11 hours were spent on these tasks[11]. Women were responsible for between 60 and 80 per cent of agricultural work, 50 per cent of animal husbandry, all food processing and almost all the market-place trade in household food[12]. In Asia and Latin America, their agricultural burden might not be as heavy, but even the most casual inspection showed that nowhere was it light—even in a country such as Bangladesh, where rural women were secluded from society. In Africa, women produced most of the family food supply[13], and they also had to provide—not just manage as in industrialized societies—supplies of water and fuel. And when families from a peasant background migrated to town, women normally had to go on providing household utilities, even though they could no longer draw upon the natural environment, and buckets of water and bottles of kerosene now had to be paid for with cash.

On top of these responsibilities came other household maintenance and subsistence tasks. Many African women were expected to repair and replaster the family hut annually; in most pre-industrial societies, women manufactured household items: clothing, baskets, mats, charcoal, salt, rope, pots and kitchen utensils. In societies where female seclusion was not the norm, women regularly traded their production surpluses of these items as well as vegetables and food snacks in the 'informal sector'—the only context for engagement in commercial life open to them. Since everything to do with children's upbringing was traditionally left to women, many used the fruits of these transactions to pay the costs of schooling, and medicines if their children were sick. The 'breadwinning' male typically produced only one half of household income[14], and he rarely assumed tasks in support of his partner's domestic work, which invariably included waiting on him, his parents and other relatives.

Where women's work was so central to the household economy, it was unrealistic to compartmentalize women into two quite different creatures—the (economically significant) worker functioning outside the household, and the (economically insignificant) dependent home-maker and child-bearer—and engage with only one of them. In most of the third world, such a division was entirely artificial. The long obsession with economic production as the gauge of development, and—even more important—its definition as something with a monetary value in an officially recognized national or international market had obscured the fact that all the functions required of a woman in traditional society, including bearing and raising children for the family workforce, were economically important. Women's work had been marginalized in standard development analysis mainly because women did it and therefore—the presumption went—it did not count; since it was marginal, the circular argument continued, no one need bother to count it[15]. But once the full scope of women's role in the household economy began to be appreciated, it became clear that any effort to help women as mothers would be handicapped by a failure to take into account the entirety of their roles. A woman who had to hoe a field or ply a trade to keep her family afloat could not waste time on skills such as embroidery and cake decoration—those typically taught in contemporary home economics courses. Even mothercraft lessons on subjects like bathing the baby had to be considered contextually, with the cost in energy and time of collecting, and heating, the water taken into account.

By the time 1980—the mid-point in the Decade for Women—had been reached, a great deal of effort had gone into a new analysis of the situation of women in the developing world[16]. Although there was still resistance in Unicef to picking up the cudgels on behalf of women qua women, the resistance was at least beginning to crumble: in the report prepared for the Mid-Decade Women's Conference in Copenhagen, recognition was given for the first time in a Unicef document to the fact that women were individuals in their own right, and that instead of trying to separate out their roles as child-bearers, nurturers, domestic workers and managers, Unicef should address their multiple roles—as wives, mothers, economic providers, citizens and leaders—in totality[17].

The need for something more than 'women's projects' was also beginning to be recognized. In some programme contexts—water and sanitation, for example, and urban basic services—there was already an important degree of recognition that women's involvement was central to programme implementation. Not only would their special needs have to be considered, but women would have to be allowed to express those needs to programme designers and managers and take part in decisions such as where a handpump should be placed and how its upkeep should be paid for; or which women in an urban neighbourhood should be regarded as eligible for business loans or help with school fees[18]. The projects that Unicef had initially supported under the rubric of 'homecraft' because they taught handicraft or horticultural skills were now reclassified as 'income-generating'. Networks of women's clubs and associations were given advice in marketing and business skills: their capacity to yield viable income was now seen as a more serious, less peripheral matter[19].

But there was another side to the analysis of women's impact on development: the effects of its impact on them. Evidence was beginning to show that the changes that modernization had wrought in the landscape over the past two decades had tended to increase, rather than relieve, women's drudgery. Population growth had meant a heavier pressure of people on the land, which made it harder to grow enough food, further to walk to gather fuel and water, and longer to fill the pot from the trickle of water in the well. It also swelled the casual workforce, increasing the difficulties faced by landless or land-short families and swelling competition in the informal sector. Seasonal agricultural work was harder to come by, impelling menfolk to migrate to the city in search of a living. Although this brought occasional remittances from afar, marital bonds tended to loosen and families fragment. As the world entered the 1980s, a growing number of both urban and rural families were depending on women as their sole or main provider. Women were losing the security provided under traditional marriage and social systems, and at the same time they were working longer hours and life was becoming more expensive and harder.

This was because most of the opportunities offered by development had gone the way of the few, and these few were mostly men. Agricultural development tended to mean cash crops, crops that could be sold by a national marketing board to pay the national import bill. Cash was for the male heads of household, the supposed providers, so agricultural extension workers visited the men, not the women, with advice about hybrid seeds, tools and fertilizers. One study in Africa showed that women—despite their vital role in food production—received less than 10 per cent of extension contacts[20]. Improved technology, training courses, credit to set up a mechanized mill or processing business were automatically appropriated by men. Those who set off for town, or were drawn into the labour market by mines, factories and the industrialization process, gained a precarious entry to the 'modern' world while their womenfolk languished back in the rural home. Women were being left further behind, losing status rather than gaining it. 'Development' was playing a trick on women: it augmented their role in the economic life of their families while failing to include them in its benefits.

The 1980s was the decade in which not only Unicef but the whole network of international development institutions was forced to come to a reckoning with the way 'progress' was treating women.

When the 'child survival and development revolution' was launched in late 1982, the paramount contribution of mothers to child well-being was given due recognition. Not only did growth monitoring, oral rehydration, breastfeeding and immunization require mothers' full understanding and active participation, but GOBI in its fullest form had two 'F's suffixed: food supplementation (later changed to food security) and family planning; a third 'F'—female education—was added in 1983. These were the other three predeterminants of major improvements in child survival, according to the group of experts advising Jim Grant. Thus the total 'child survival and development revolution' package was supposed to consist of GOBI-FFF, even though the three 'F's were never given equivalent weight.

These 'F's were an acknowledgement that there was a close link between the social aspects of a woman's situation and her family's condition. This had first been revealed by analyses of the disappointing results of many of the family-planning campaigns of the 1970s, notably the massive promotion of contraceptive technology and sterilization in India. Women in most poor societies did not step forward with alacrity to swallow pills, be fitted with IUDs or terminate their child-bearing possibilities. In large parts of the world—all of sub-Saharan Africa and much of Asia—a woman's status, her own sense of her value and her role in life were intimately associated with her child-bearing career, especially with the number of sons she bore[21]. Unless it was clearly in the family's interests—interests guarded by husbands, fathers and mothers-in-law—she was not likely to curb her reproductive behaviour. Besides which, the unlettered mother regarded child-bearing—its products and its intervals—as something over which the Almighty rather than the human will presided.

However, in some Asian countries—for example, in Sri Lanka, Taiwan and Thailand, and in Kerala state in India—family planning had proved relatively acceptable. These were all places where women's educational attainment was high in relation to their socio-economic status. And as demographers began to correlate drops in the birth rate with women's state of learning, child health specialists followed in their wake. A World Bank study of 1980 showed that each additional year of a mother's schooling reduced the chances of her newborn child dying in infancy by 9 chances in 1,000—even when key differences between families, such as income levels, were taken into account[22]. Thus, increasing the number of years spent by girls in school from—for example—three years to nine could reduce high infant mortality rates (above 100 per 1,000 live births) by as much as 50 points.

The reason for this very important sociological connection between women's education and improved child survival was not difficult to detect. Women who were better educated were likely to buy, and prepare, better-quality food for their children and to know how to handle common childhood ailments. Not only had they gleaned such information in school, but the experience of learning had imbued them with a sense of individuality and powers of choice. An educated woman was a woman with a belief in her ability to take decisions on her own, a woman inclined to step out from under the heavy layers of fatalism that had characterized her mother's and grandmother's attitudes to life and break the mould of ingrained and unquestioning submission, and a woman whose opinion and actions deserved—at least potentially—the respect of her husband.

Although the contribution that women's education could make to child survival was acknowledged in the rhetoric of the 'child survival and development revolution', in the campaign's early, fundamentalist phase no serious emphasis was given to expanding programmatic support in this area, or indeed in other 'women in development' contexts. Unicef's annual expenditure on formal and non-formal education, for example, was $36 million in 1987, compared with $40.4 million in 1983[23]; during the mid-1980s, while expenditures on child health shot up, this category of assistance remained virtually static. In the run-up to the International Women's Conference in Nairobi in 1985, Unicef echoed the latest jargon of women's rights by talking about the need for 'women's empowerment'. But in reality, there had been a retreat to a position in which women were perceived as important because of their role in infant and young child nurture. When Jim Grant talked about 'empowering' women[24], he cited—with his extraordinary capacity for single-mindedness—the need to provide mothers with the necessary knowledge and motivation to monitor their children's growth, use ORT to treat diarrhoeal illness, breastfeed and take their infants to be immunized. The presentation of GOBI as a formula for women's empowerment caused some anguish among senior women in Unicef. Grant did redeem the analysis a little by suggesting that knowledge in such important child health contexts could give women confidence to do more for themselves in other spheres of life[25].

As for access to family planning—one of the three 'F's affixed to GOBI and a quintessential element of women's rights—here Grant ducked the issue entirely. He wanted Unicef to have no part in promoting contraception either on grounds of women's reproductive rights or for the sake of population control. At the same time, he wanted to avoid criticism that Unicef was advocating the saving of millions of children's lives without appearing concerned about the extra numbers of mouths to feed that this would necessarily entail. On the connection between child survival and fertility, Grant took a very particular line: 'Fewer child deaths means fewer births'. According to this logic, child survival was itself a means to reduce family size—despite the obvious truth that more children surviving in one family could not mean that the family would be smaller. This apparent contradiction was explained by a phenomenon known as the demographic transition: a country with high mortality and high fertility rates had first to reduce mortality before parents would be convinced not to have 'spare' children to offset those who would die young; once mortality rates had dropped, a reduction in births could be expected to follow[26].

Although no demographer could prove a causal effect, there was an observed connection between declining infant mortality and declining fertility, and the pace of fertility decline accelerated once infant mortality rates had dropped to below 100 per 1,000 live births[27]. By emphasizing this 'family planning' effect of the 'child survival and development revolution', Grant had reversed the usual formula, whereby family planning was regarded by WHO, UNFPA, the World Bank and the leading international population and family planning NGOs as important because it contributed to child health and survival, not because child survival contributed to it. In Grant's scenario, Unicef was contributing to fertility decline because child survival was a kind of delayed-action contraceptive—although he would not have used those words.

This was, for example, the theme of Unicef's contributions to the 1984 International Conference on Population in Mexico City[28] and to the Better Health for Women and Children through Family Planning Conference in Nairobi in 1987[29]. It was popular neither with the international health and family planning community nor with those active on behalf of women's rights. Besides adopting this line for reasons of strategy—which was to repeat child survival messages under any and every umbrella—Grant was determined not to let Unicef become overidentified with advocacy of family planning because of the controversies surrounding contraception and abortion. These controversies were reflected in the contrasting views held by different members of the Unicef Executive Board, by official bodies in countries where Unicef had programmes, and by governmental and non-governmental donors Grant was naturally anxious not to offend. Whatever his personal convictions on the subject of family planning, he therefore did his best to keep his 'child survival and development revolution' away from this contentious arena. He wanted to keep child survival squeaky clean.

In 1985—the last year of the Decade for Women and the year of the culminating international conference on women—Unicef's Executive Board reviewed its programmes and policies towards women for the first time since 1980. The paper lamented: 'The reality that women are the key actors in the child survival strategy has not yet been internalized throughout Unicef. This factor, together with the current weak linkages between women's socio-economic programmes and the child survival and development revolution, has led to a depreciation of the significance of women's socio-economic standing in relation to child health activities. Recognizing the important role women play remains a challenge for Unicef.'[30] Although the policy review explicitly pointed out the need to improve women's socio-economic status per se because of the knock-on effect this would have on social development and on child well-being, the fact remained that this was a challenge that a Unicef obsessed by child survival was unwilling to face.

Some senior policy and programme staff still believed in their heart of hearts that there was a dichotomy between the interests of women and the interests of children, and that direct support for the former would siphon away resources from the latter[31]. However, given the growing international influence of the women's cause, and the increasing presence of women in senior Unicef positions, the pressures—from the Executive Board, from some Unicef country offices and from UN and other partners—began inexorably to mount.

Although there was little backing from headquarters throughout most of the 1980s, the decentralized character of Unicef came to the rescue of 'women in development'—as for other programme areas not embraced by the 'child survival and development revolution', such as water and sanitation and urban basic services[32]. Activity went ahead in the field as a result of pressures felt on the ground and therefore reflected in the country programme.

Much pioneering work was under way in Latin America, and Unicef country offices wanted to play a role. In 1976, in the wake of the first International Women's Conference in Mexico in 1975, the Unicef Regional Programme on Women in Development for the Americas and the Caribbean was set up in Bogota, Colombia. In time this became a dynamic venture with a respectable impact on women's programmes in the region. It began by undertaking studies, situation analyses and workshops at the national and international level, and followed up with assistance to women's projects in several countries: Bolivia, Ecuador, Mexico, Peru, and others[33].

In 1982 a major evaluation was undertaken, as a result of which the programme was upgraded. (By this time, the Unicef Regional Office for the Americas and Caribbean in Bogota was headed by a woman Director, Teresa Albañez, an ex-Minister in the Government of Venezuela.) Instead of being seen as project 'recipients' with all the welfarist connotations that implied, women were henceforth to be regarded as 'participants' in projects and partners in development. Two lines of programme action were identified: support for basic services and support for economic activities. In the latter context, there was a determined rejection of the old 'homecraft' approach, which had never seriously addressed the issue of women in poverty[34]. In Eastern Africa, where the women's programme was also strong and where the Regional Director was also a woman (Mary Racelis), similar thinking was afoot[35].

As a result of the recession and debt crisis of the 1980s, the predicament of women already disfavoured by the development process was progressively worsened. If adjustment negatively affected children, it did so partly because of its impact on women's and household income, as well as because of cuts in health, education and social services—which themselves threw back onto women an increased nurturing burden. The debt and adjustment crisis that descended on Latin America after 1982 disproportionately affected women who were already poor[36]. Both their numbers and their degree of poverty grew, while at the same time the survival of almost one third of the entire population of Latin America and the Caribbean came to depend on their statistically all-but-invisible labours, as well as their social contributions in the absence of service care[37]: care for the sick, for example, in families that could not afford a doctor's fee or hospital visit; child-care services, growth-monitoring sessions, literacy groups, community kitchens and other mutual support.

By the end of the decade, 86 million women in the region were estimated to be living in absolute poverty, of which 40 per cent were 'heads of household'[38]. Both culturally and economically, women had been relegated to marginal and underpaid occupations; their entrenched disadvantage in terms of education and the employment market meant that many had to fall back on commercialized versions of domestic work, in which low pay and instability of employment reduced their situation to near-servility. (Some solved these problems by entering prostitution.) A Unicef-sponsored study in Argentina found that women's incomes had dropped to a level less than half that of men; in Jamaica, the proportion of households dependent on women had risen to 45 per cent, and 40 per cent of these were in the lowest income group. Typically, women in poor Latin American environments were working longer hours—an average of 13—at lower wages than they had done a decade before[39]. Where many commentators talked of the 'feminization of poverty', Unicef in Latin America began to argue not only for 'adjustment with a human face', but for 'adjustment with a female face'.

At the same time, support for women's economic activities in the region was stepped up. The 1982 evaluation had showed that where women remained the beneficiaries or quasi-employees of what were essentially handicraft projects, the termination of start-up financial assistance quickly led to project bankruptcy. Genuine commercial viability, personal growth and eventual autonomy for women 'participants' needed to be built into the conception of a project if any real and sustained increase in income was to ensue. Experience suggested that credit, with the skills to handle personal savings and finance, had to be the mainstay of any long-term programme to improve women's economic situation in such a way as to improve their families' well-being. The main difficulty was that conventional banks and lending organizations were not prepared to give loans to people who were poor, let alone to people who were both poor and female.

In Colombia, Unicef set about breaking this log-jam by persuading various state agencies to handle lines of credit for various networks of women's groups if Unicef itself first established a guarantee fund. One programme set up in the very poor southeast sector of Cartagena in 1983 through the Centro de Desarrollo Vecinal 'La Esperanza' (the La Esperanza Neighbourhood Development Centre) worked with women street vendors whose previous means of credit was from usurious 'financiers' charging 10 per cent interest a day. Under the scheme, they joined solidarity and savings groups and received low-interest credit and support. In 1984, Unicef signed an agreement with the National Vocational Training Service (SENA) to systematize the programme and replicate it throughout the country. By 1987, 225 solidarity groups with 750 members had been established and 10,000 family members had benefited indirectly[40].

By 1985, the experiences in Latin America and others elsewhere were encouraging Unicef to talk about 'infiltrating' women's issues into mainstream national programmes, 'emphasizing activities that are both income-saving and income-generating'[41]. The most striking example of a nationwide programme to help women overcome their lack of access to resources was the Grameen Bank of Bangladesh, set up in the mid-1970s by Professor Muhammad Yunus of Chittagong University. Yunus wanted to prove to himself and his students that those normally shunned by institutionalized moneylending—the rural poor—were entirely 'bankable'. In 1976, he set up a credit scheme for local villagers in which the only eligible applicants were the very poor: those with almost no land—less than 0.5 acres—and almost no possessions. Grameen had a policy of no collateral, relying instead on membership in local groups and peer pressure to guarantee loan repayment. Loans might be given for a milch cow, a food-processing device such as a rice-husker, poultry and even home improvements such as a handpump. The success of this experiment attracted support from external donors, and by 1985 the Grameen Bank had over 220 branches serving 170,000 borrowers in 3,600 villages across the nation[42].

Unicef was a keen supporter of Grameen, providing funds to help train women 'branch managers' and group leaders, and helping integrate motivation for child survival activities and family health improvements into local group pursuits. The bank focused increasingly on women savers: they came to constitute 89 per cent of Grameen clients, and their repayment rate on a cumulative loan disbursement of around $185 million (1990) was an extraordinary 98 per cent. Average per capita income in borrowers' households rose by over one third[43]. These results, obtained in a Moslem country where women were in purdah, therefore did not play a visible role in the market past the age of puberty and had been erroneously assumed incapable of commercial undertakings, did much to change attitudes—not only in Bangladesh but around the globe—towards women as efficient users of credit. Grameen inspired a number of similarly modelled user-group savings and credit schemes for women in countries as diverse as the Dominican Republic and Nepal.

Although a growing number of Unicef programmes of cooperation were actively involved in pursuing the cause of women as a coterminant of child survival, the Executive Board remained far from convinced that there was a real organizationwide attempt to give efforts on behalf of women what had been internationally established as their due[44]. Instead of leading the field for women, the UN's organization for children now appeared to be dawdling in its rear, still regarding 'women in development' as some kind of extra, not as central to everything Unicef was about. Senior women policy advisers began to feel that things had reached a nadir. In 1986, Board members expressed their concern; the result in 1987 was an implementation strategy agreed by the Board to make sure that policies already laid down in 1980 and 1985 became fully operationalized. The review was not supposed to make policy so much as to make policy stick.

The 1987 policy paper spelled out uncompromisingly that Unicef regarded women's development as integral to the social and economic mainstream. Women's needs were to be considered not only in the context of bearing and raising children but in the whole range of their interconnected roles. The woman vendor of pots and pans was to be given the same consideration as the woman at the antenatal clinic, the woman bringing her child for vaccination, the woman in the literacy class and the woman community worker: they were all the same woman. Not only should programmes cease to compartmentalize women's roles, but the whole logical process of examining women's developmental role should be reversed. Women were not in some ghetto of their own; they were a part of every picture. Therefore within each programme and sector, women's roles needed to be analysed, and the inequalities stemming from gender had to be made a target of affirmative action. From then on, every Unicef situation analysis and country programme must fully incorporate the gender dimension, and programme staff should be gender-trained and gender-oriented systematically so as to help this come about. Programmes that favoured women within the health, education, agricultural, labour, housing and water and sanitation sectors could support a holistic strategy that addressed nurturing, poverty and equity issues at the same time.

In subsequent years, the Executive Board sternly asked for annual updates on the implementation of the 1987 strategy. The abandonment of 'women's projects'—seen as an essential conceptual leap in redefining Unicef's approach—needed to be carefully monitored; there was justifiable fear that in the more recalcitrant field environments it might lead not to the mainstreaming of women in the development process but to their convenient oblivion. And still there was a sense in many parts of the organization that the forward-looking policy was barely connected with its actual realization. However, it was not so much the nagging of the Board as the arrival into view of a hitherto unnoticed person that finally propelled the genderization of Unicef forward. This was the 'girl child'.

For every 100 female babies delivered into the world, at least 105 males are born[45]. The female human being is more biologically durable, and the surplus of boy infants is nature's way of balancing the sex ratio in the population. Ordinarily, the number of surviving girls soon overtakes that of boys; if given the same degree of care and nurture throughout the passage of infancy, childhood and adolescence, females should outnumber males and live longer.

Yet there are parts of the world where this male-female rebalance never occurs; where, instead, human intervention—in the form of girl neglect—favours the survival of males. In India, for example, there are only 957 females aged 0 to 4 years for every 1,000 males in the population, although official statistics indicate that 112 males are born for every 100 females[46]. Preference for sons is most marked in South Asia and the Middle East, where many traditional proverbs attest to the undesirability of daughters: in Bangladesh to have a daughter is described as 'watering a neighbour's tree' because the benefit of her upbringing will accrue to someone else. But the evidence of relative discrimination is by no means confined to those regions. In Colombia, 75 deaths of boys between the ages of 1 and 2 occur for 100 deaths of girls; in Mexico, 86; in Senegal, 99. Only in some countries of Africa, the Caribbean, and Central and Latin America is there equal preference for girls and boys[47].

Cultural attitudes stressing the value of sons against daughters are so much a normal part of traditional codes that they were long simply taken for granted. That they might significantly influence parental behaviour towards the health and nurture of the young girl began to draw scientific attention only in the mid-1980s. The impact of son preference on child well-being was first documented by Unicef in the Middle East and North Africa, where a series of country studies described the cumulative disadvantages suffered by girls from birth until age 14, by which time many were married and about to precipitate a similar cycle in their own offspring. Discrimination began with the lack of enthusiasm—even insults—greeting the birth of a girl, the mother's early abandonment of breastfeeding to attempt another pregnancy, the girl infant's extra susceptibility to diarrhoeal and respiratory infections, and her relative lack of food and clothing[48].

This analysis was important not only for its findings but for the setting of indicators to guide the collection of gender-sensitive data about child survival and development—an aspect of the necessary ingredients of the CSD revolution that up to this point had been ignored. It also illuminated the discriminatory predicament of girls not only in their earliest years—from birth to five years of age—but until the mid-teens. The concentration by Unicef on child survival on the one hand, and by WHO and others on 'safe motherhood' (see later in this chapter) on the other, had led to a serious neglect of the young girl and adolescent by researchers. Concern about the girl child implied, therefore, not only a gender approach to childhood but concern about the whole period of childhood, including the precocious onset of maternity. In the Middle East, this typically occurred to the girl-woman, married off in adolescence.

In the late 1980s, similar concern about the girl child began to be expressed in the Indian subcontinent, largely by women's rights activists. There were increasing reports of girl infanticide in states where dowry prices had become inflated, and of the use of amniocentesis tests for foetal sex determination and the subsequent abortion of unwanted female embryos. The use of modern gynaecological techniques to support age-old son preference raised a hue and cry, and in 1988, Maharashtra's state legislature became the first to ban the use of prenatal technologies and techniques for this purpose[49]. However, the publicity given to this extreme form of discrimination against girls helped bring to light other more insidious discriminations. Studies showed that, especially in lower income groups, malnutrition tended to be both more common and more severe among girls than boys; that girls were breastfed less often and taken less frequently to the health centre when sick[50]. In the Punjab, one study among underprivileged children showed that 50 per cent of girls were seriously underweight for age compared to 15 per cent of boys[51].

In 1988, the South Asian Association for Regional Cooperation (SAARC) declared that 1990 would be the Year of the Girl Child. In 1990, they declared 1991-2000 the Decade of the Girl Child, and proposed an SAARC Plan of Action incorporating appropriate recommendations from the World Summit for Children Declaration[52]. With Unicef assistance, Bangladesh, India, Sri Lanka and Nepal set about compiling gender-disaggregated data on children and developing a profile of the comparative situation of girls. With the exception of Sri Lanka, there turned out to be a consistent pattern of discrimination in parental and health service care in every country, combined with an extra household working burden and a lack of schooling compared with boys.

In Bangladesh, for example, it was found that twice as many girls aged between one and two years suffered from nutritional wasting as boys. The report coolly stated: 'A poor family with many children just cannot give everyone as much food as is wanted and the girl has to sacrifice for her brothers.' When it came to schooling, girls were similarly disadvantaged. Only 10 per cent of girls aged 10 to 14 years attended school, compared with 23 per cent of boys. In spite of laws restricting child labour, the participation of girls in paid work had increased, while that of boys had declined; meanwhile, a great deal of girls' work, whether paid or unpaid, was in domestic households other than their own, which was invisible in official statistics[53]. A Unicef-assisted study in Nepal found that girls spent almost twice as many hours a day working as boys, and that by age 10, 7 per cent of Nepalese girls were married; 40 per cent were married by age 14[54]. In Bangladesh, by age 15, 20 per cent of girls had borne their first child[55].

From 1989 onward, Unicef became an important advocate for the girl child, including the gender perspective on childhood in its annual reports to the Executive Board on the implementation of Unicef's 'women in development' policy[56]. In industrialized countries, where that part of the women's movement concerned with such issues had begun to regard Unicef as a reactionary force, its pioneering role in adopting the cause of girls did much to re-establish its credentials as an organization concerned about gender inequality. In its turn, Unicef's advocacy did much to persuade the women's movement that they should engage with children's concerns from this much neglected direction: so concerned had some women's activists been to avoid typecasting in maternal roles that they had overdistanced themselves from the children's cause[57]. The genderization of childhood coupled women and children together in a new kind of way. The recognition that discrimination against the female sex had to be fought from before birth and throughout infancy and childhood added a new dimension to the campaign for gender equality.

Meanwhile, in a number of Asian countries, public education initiatives supported by Unicef set out to persuade parents that girls were as valuable as boys. The most striking of these was the development in Bangladesh of a cartoon series for Asia-wide distribution based on the adventures of a small girl called Meena. The Convention on the Rights of the Child was beginning to spawn a number of national and local fora to promote children's rights and review existing legislation relating to childhood protections, and these mechanisms were useful contexts in which to affirm the childhood gender equality called for in Article 2. In 1990, Unicef published a booklet: *The Girl Child: An Investment in the Future*. The wide currency this publication enjoyed among NGOs, partner organizations, Unicef National Committees and others indicated that here was an issue that had captured the public imagination. Within Unicef itself, many who had not been committed to women's rights within the context of development happily embraced the rights of females in the context of childhood.

If the true scale of gender imbalances in nurture, nutritional well-being and health care provision were being systematically revealed for the first time, the differentials in educational access had long been noted—and deplored because of the correlation between a woman's lack of schooling and her family-planning and child-care behaviour. During 1989, preparations were under way for the International Conference on Education for All, sponsored by UNESCO, UNDP, UNICEF and the World Bank, to be held in Jomtien, Thailand, in January 1990. This helped to refocus Unicef's attention on educational disparities suffered by girls: two out of three of the world's 300 million children who were not in either primary or secondary school were female, as were two thirds of the world's 960 million illiterates[58]. From this point onward, closing the gender gap in education re-emerged as a Unicef concern, and increased resources were dedicated to education as a category of assistance (see Chapter 8).

But 'girl child' issues did not stop at questions of equal access to family care, health and education throughout the whole infancy and childhood period. Girls as compared to boys were doubly in need of special protections because of their extra physical and sexual vulnerability. Their perceived inferior status not only laid them more open to exploitation, but they were also more vulnerable to its consequences. The Bangladesh Decade for the Girl Child Action Plan stated: 'Disadvantages facing the girl child are compounded by an apparently increasing incidence of violence against girls and women, such as abduction and rape, assault, kidnapping and immoral trafficking. Despite the existence of laws and penalties, social attitudes towards women's status seem to permit these behavioural aberrations.'[59] Similar phenomena were occurring in Nepal and in the northern provinces of Thailand.

On the one hand, women's activists were struggling to bring an end to practices that constrained women's opportunities, self-awareness and participation in society: early marriage, and practices that protected an adolescent girl's chastity by enforcing her seclusion (purdah) or sealing her genital area (circumcision). On the other, these systems of girl protection were vanishing under the pressures of 'development' and nothing was being put in their place. All over the developing world, the growth of a rich, mobile, industrialized middle class had created new types of moneyed demand; the simultaneous creation of a pauperized underclass produced the corresponding supply of vulnerable young people. Poverty and rapid urbanization were eroding behavioural codes and forcing girls to venture out to work They were young, sexually mature, undereducated and ill-prepared for adult life, and their options were limited. They entered the world of earning without the necessary preparation or resources to negotiate their path through the minefield of adult exploitation. The result was a foregone conclusion. According to the Norwegian Government: 'Every year, one million children are either kidnapped, bought, or in other ways forced to enter the sex market.'[60]

Gradually, under the rubric of the Convention on the Rights of the Child, Unicef began to expand its advocacy role in relation to issues affecting girls and women under the age of 18 in contexts that had previously been taboo. No fewer than 14 Articles in the Convention covered special protection, of which 8 specifically or indirectly covered sexual and other types of exploitation. Given their prominence in the Convention, and the emphasis they commanded within the child rights lobby, an organization that wished to maintain its position in the international vanguard for children could no longer neglect the issue of children involved in sexual trade. The context in which Unicef initially became involved—as in other child protection issues—was that of 'street children'. In Kenya, in the Philippines, in India, in Brazil[61], in almost all countries where increasing numbers of children were working and living around market-places and shopping malls, some proportion of the children were girls. These girls, often runaways from violent homes and sometimes from sexually abusive stepfathers, were easily seduced, or reduced, into selling sex to make a living. Given that the returns were infinitely higher than for selling flowers or chewing-gum, once they had started prostituting themselves, it was extremely difficult for them to stop.

In the Philippines, Brazil, Bangladesh and a number of countries, Unicef began to network with NGOs, assisting the process of capacity-building and financing research. In Thailand, where under-age prostitution was of a high order of magnitude and the sex industry very commercialized, Unicef embarked on a special programme related to children and teenagers in prostitution. The Police Department believed that there were 400,000 prostitutes altogether throughout the country, of whom around 40 per cent were below the age of 16 (1992)[62]. This figure indicated not only the very high number of young girls in prostitution—160,000—but the high preponderance of teenagers in an industry in which youth and freshness command a high premium. That premium had now become enhanced in the era of AIDS: Thai men, a high proportion of whom visited prostitutes as a form of entertainment, were now seeking out younger girls in the belief that they were less likely to be HIV-infected[63].

The young employees in the bars and massage parlours of Bangkok and Thailand's resorts all came from the poor provinces in the north and north-east, whose inhabitants were hill-tribe people. Traditionally, girls from these areas were expected to provide economic support to their families before they were married, and the modern way to do this was to go to town to earn[64]. Private agents functioned as middlemen between poor rural parents and placements for their daughters in the country's booming tourist and entertainment industry. Recruiters offered parents 'advances on wages', and their poverty and their value system enabled them to accept this money without feeling that they were 'trading' their children in a morally reprehensible exchange[65]. NGOs, many of them religiously motivated, took a different view, and staged rescues of young girls effectively enslaved in brothels. This helped to create international notoriety around the issue.

After strong NGO campaigning, the Thai Prime Minister announced in 1992 that child prostitution would be eliminated and set up a special task force to carry out this policy. Since that time, Unicef has been actively engaged in a programme designed to prevent the mass entry of hill-tribe girls into the commercial sex industry[66]. Reading materials, videos and radio messages in hill-tribe languages have been introduced into primary schools to familiarize girls with the hazards of prostitution, suggest job alternatives and explain their rights. Unicef has also assisted the 'Daughters Education Programme', a residential leadership training centre for post-primary girls from villages where recruitment agents for the sex industry are highly active. The girl scholars become change agents in the communities they come from, helping to transform the social and economic conditions to which girls like them would otherwise become victim.

Commercial exploitation was only one framework within which Unicef was by the early 1990s actively beginning to address the risks posed by sexual activity to young teenage girls. Almost everywhere in the world, the age of first sexual encounter has recently been declining. Precocious sex frequently leads to early motherhood: in the Caribbean, for example, 60 per cent of first babies are born to teenagers, many of them unmarried. It also poses the age-old problem of sexually transmitted disease, whose potential threat to health and life have been dramatically multiplied by the advent of AIDS. Sexual and reproductive health, especially in teenagers, became therefore the lens through which Unicef in the late 1980s began to refocus its attention on its very earliest historical female concern: women's biological role in reproduction.

For the first time, in 1989 *The State of the World's Children* published a specific set of statistics about women: an indication that the pressure to heighten Unicef's attention to womanhood was gaining ground. The statistics illustrated gender disparities in life expectancy, literacy and school enrolment, and women's access to family planning and maternity services.

Their most striking feature was that, of all disparities between life chances in the industrialized and developing worlds, the widest gap was in rates of maternal mortality. Of the 500,000 women who died from causes related to pregnancy and childbirth every year, 99 per cent were in the developing world. Well over half the deaths occurred in Asia, where every year over 300,000 women died, most of them in Bangladesh, India and Pakistan. Of those remaining, 150,000 were in Africa, where a woman's lifetime chances of dying of pregnancy were 1 in 21 as compared with 1 in several thousand for women in Europe[67]. As significantly, 25 per cent of maternal deaths were among teenagers[68].

The causes of these deaths were identical to those that had made childbirth a risky, even life-threatening, undertaking for women in the industrialized world not so long ago. They included haemorrhage, infection, toxaemia, obstructed labour and complications following unsafe abortions[69]. As many as 200,000 women were estimated to lose their lives annually as a result of illegal abortions—a reflection of unmet need for family planning[70]. In the modern world, antibiotics and obstetric technology had reduced the risk of dying from childbirth to almost zero for women within their reach. However, for many millions of women in the developing world, supervised delivery in a modern maternity ward with drugs and emergency care on hand was beyond the bounds of possibility.

In some African and South Asian countries, up to two thirds of women—especially those who lived in the countryside—still gave birth in the privacy of their own or their mother's home with only the village 'auntie' in attendance. This *dukun*, as she was known in Indonesia, *dai* in India and Pakistan, *matronne* in French-speaking West Africa, belonged to one of the oldest professions known to humankind. Her skills were passed down through many generations, and she usually learned at her mother's side how to tend a woman in labour and bring her baby into the world. Although the traditional birth attendant might be capable, her instruments were crude and her hygienic standards not the highest; more important, if something went severely wrong, she might not be able to see mother and child safely through their joint moment of jeopardy.

Ever since the 1950s and 1960s, Unicef had supported the training of traditional birth attendants (TBAs) and provided trainees with basic midwifery kits. Instead of treating her as an illiterate crone to be swiftly displaced by a fully trained alternative, Unicef had confirmed the TBA's importance in birthing, but had attempted to add 20th-century knowledge and public health equipment to her armoury. During 1977-86, training had been given at Unicef expense to some 250,000 TBAs[71]: this form of cooperation in maternal and child health (MCH) services was still a prominent feature in a large number of country programmes. But improving the TBAs' performance was not always easy: many were unused to learning in a classroom setting and without persistent supervision easily reverted to old habits. Many countries in Asia and Latin America were therefore now developing a new, better-trained auxiliary midwife cadre. China—the cradle of so many public health innovations—had made spectacular progress in reducing maternal mortality by promoting three 'cleans': a clean surface for the mother in labour, clean hands and clean cutting of the umbilical cord.

Unicef also supported the distribution of iron folate, vitamin A and iodine in antenatal and postnatal clinics to improve maternal health and nutrition. These supplements—the first 'F' of GOBI—helped to reduce the incidence of low birth weight (affecting 22 million babies a year[72]) and fortified women physically for the stress of pregnancy and breastfeeding. Mainly because of their heavy workload, around two thirds of all pregnant women and one half of all other women in the developing world suffered from anaemia. This lowered their resistance to disease and increased their fatigue and their chances of miscarriage. The reduction of micronutrient deficiencies was therefore an important element of better maternal health[73].

In early 1987, the 'Safe Motherhood Initiative' was launched by WHO with strong backing from the World Bank and support from other UN agencies. This emphasized a number of strategies for reducing maternal mortality. Although over one third of pregnancies in the world could be considered high-risk simply on grounds of age, only around one half of women in the developing world made one or more visits during pregnancy to a health facility[74]. Screening out the high-risk cases and advising such women to give birth under professional supervision would help to reduce obstetric emergencies. Other ingredients of 'safe motherhood' were to increase the use of family planning services and to reduce the prevalence of sexually transmitted diseases (STDs), especially HIV. The Initiative set the target of reducing the maternal mortality rate by half by the year 2000, a target reconfirmed at the 1990 World Summit for Children.

During the early advocacy of 'safe motherhood', Unicef supported most strongly those parts of the package that had the greatest bearing on child survival. Apart from regular contributions to TBA training and MCH, this largely meant an increased emphasis on immunization with tetanus toxoid: 750,000 infant deaths were annually attributed to tetanus soon after birth. With all the emphasis on *childhood* vaccination, maternal vaccination still languished at 30 per cent. Unicef's other focus remained that on 'empowering women to breastfeed'[75]. In the late 1980s, Unicef's support for 'safe motherhood' could still only be described as lukewarm. Gradually, the threat of HIV to young women, and the new consciousness of issues relating to the sexual exploitation of girls, pushed Unicef into a new appreciation of the need to promote reproductive health and to defend girls' and women's rights in this context.

Pressure from Unicef country offices in AIDS-affected parts of Africa and the Caribbean was critical to this process. In the very early stages of the worldwide AIDS epidemic, the threat to children appeared to come mainly from the risks associated with the use of hypodermic needles and blood transfusion, in immunization campaigns and hospital treatment. But in the mid-1980s, a special AIDS threat to mothers and children began to emerge. It transpired that HIV-infected women could pass on the virus to their baby in the womb or at delivery. Such children, born with an agent in their blood that thwarted the body's every effort to construct routine defences against infection, failed to thrive. By age five, almost all had died[76]. To begin with, WHO calculated that the risk of maternal HIV transmission was 50 per cent; as studies accumulated, this was reduced to 30 per cent. This percentage still represented a very high risk to healthy child-bearing in places where infection was widespread.

Unlike in Europe and North America, in Africa, the Caribbean and Asia the overwhelming means of HIV transmission was by heterosexual relations. From the outset of the epidemic in Africa—where by far the highest number of infections were to be found—the number of female cases was equivalent to, or slightly higher than, the number of male cases. The highest concentration of HIV infection occurred in women at the height of their child-bearing years, usually between the ages of 20 and 29. Therefore, if the spread of HIV in women remained unchecked, it posed a significant threat to the continuing gains of the 'child survival revolution'. Demographers calculated that young child mortality rates in seriously affected countries would rise by amounts estimated between 10 and 50 per cent[77]. Unicef estimated that before the end of the century, 2.7 million children would have died of paediatric AIDS, more than 90 per cent of them in Africa[78].

In 1988, at the prompting of the Executive Board, Unicef began to articulate at a policy-making level how it could contribute to the WHO-led global effort to combat HIV[79]. Already, some country offices had begun to engage in programmes to prevent the spread of HIV, especially among young women and girls. Uganda was the pioneering country. The subject of sex education in the classroom is one everywhere fraught with controversy. However, Uganda was willing to accept that the importance of protecting the generation yet to embark on a sexual and child-bearing career overrode all other considerations. With support from Unicef, in the late 1980s the Ministry of Education totally revised the science curriculum in primary and secondary schools. Teachers were trained in a new syllabus that included health education and AIDS prevention; classroom materials and extracurricular activities were developed. By the end of 1991, over 2,000 Ugandan teachers had been trained and 30,000 primary school textbooks produced[80]. Meanwhile, the Ugandan schools programme had become a model for others to copy. In Zimbabwe, an AIDS action programme for schools was introduced under the title 'Education for Life'. The first book off the production line in 1993 for Grade 7 pupils talked about friendships, sexuality, resolving personal conflict and how to live kindly towards yourself and others in a world with AIDS. In a number of countries, educational programmes tried to help schoolgirls learn how to say 'no' to sex.

Unicef programmes also attempted to reach children and teenagers who were not in school. Organizations such as the Undugu Society of Kenya, which catered to working children on the street, began to develop programmes for sexual awareness and self-protection. In the Caribbean, comic strips and videos targeted teenagers fond of partying and disco life. In Trinidad and Tobago, Unicef supported a six-part television series about AIDS called *Body Beat*[81]. In Thailand, hot-line services, including telephone and radio outreach, were set up for students. In Nepal, a theatre group toured villages throughout the countryside to provide entertainment with a strong anti-AIDS message. In Zambia, where a Unicef study showed that one quarter of all perinatal deaths in the country were a consequence of syphilis in the mother, Unicef supported a programme to increase awareness about STDs[82].

In some countries, Unicef also supported women shouldering the socio-economic fallout of AIDS: those taking in the orphaned children of daughters,

daughters-in-law, sisters or co-wives. Many such women needed income support, either by help with agricultural tasks or by jobs or credit for small business enterprises. Unicef's role was usually a coordinating one, helping bring together NGOs and community organizations involved in helping the AIDS-affected, backing them with materials and training, and acting as an intermediary with government departments and international donors.

As the epidemic progressed, and epidemiological knowledge of the reasons for HIV's spread increased, it became clear that—in Africa especially, but in the developing world as a whole—AIDS was a disease of the predominantly young and the predominantly female[83]. The age profile of AIDS tended to be younger in women than in men: HIV infection peaked in young women aged 15 to 25, and did not do so in men until age 25 to 35[84]. This was partly attributed to the physical immaturity of young women's genital organs, which increased the chance of the virus' transmission, a risk that compounded the relative ease of the male-female passage of infection. But much more influential were the social practices surrounding sexual relations and reproductive life. By the age of 19, 60 to 70 per cent of women in many African countries were married and respectably engaged in sex[85]. Meanwhile, those who remained unmarried and were continuing with their education—whether in Africa, the Caribbean or elsewhere—were members of a society in which urban and 'modern' life had had a profound effect on personal behaviour. One survey in Nigeria found that 43 per cent of schoolgirls aged 14 to 19 were sexually active[86]. The rises in prevalence of STDs, particularly among 16- to 24-year-olds, were causes of alarm to public health officials everywhere. This had a particular connection to the spread of HIV, because the presence of another STD increased by tenfold the chances of contracting the AIDS virus[87].

For many women in developing countries, the threat of AIDS was deepened by the social inequality between men and women. Women lacked control over their sexual lives and over the sexual lives of their husbands outside marriage. As well as forcing out into the open the neglected subject of sexual health, the AIDS epidemic prompted inquiries into sexual mores—inquiries that many found distasteful. It transpired that many African and Asian women had little negotiating power over sexual relations, and were conditioned to expect none inside or outside marriage. This meant that the vast majority were unable to refuse sex or demand the use of a condom. And the accepted pattern of sexual behaviour in men in certain cultures did nothing to improve matters. Those who demanded unprotected sex and had it with multiple, casual partners increased the powerlessness of women to protect themselves from HIV[88].

Girls who had embarked on an independent or semi-independent life—often because economic circumstances obliged them to earn—were particularly vulnerable. In Zimbabwe, HIV infection among 15- to 19-year-olds was six times higher in girls than in boys[89]; in street girls and women involved in sexual commerce it could be as high as 80 per cent. Even those in relatively sheltered situations were subject to sexual pressure. In Uganda and Zambia, schoolgirls were often enticed into sex by promises from 'sugar-daddies'—teachers or employers; in the Caribbean, peer pressure was as much to blame. All of these sociocultural discoveries reinforced Unicef's involvement in educational programmes for young people's and women's self-protection, not only by imparting knowledge but also by equipping them with the skills and with the acceptance that they had a right to negotiate the terms of their sexual engagements.

Its support for AIDS prevention confronted Unicef anew with its reticent attitude towards contraceptive devices—in this case, prophylactics, which could block the transmission of HIV. As a result of the AIDS crisis, contraceptives began to assume a new—or forgotten—role in STD control and public health. Condoms in particular were seen as an important means of physically preventing the spread of the AIDS virus. But Unicef was focusing its attention almost exclusively on trying to encourage behavioural change—abstinence or monopartnership. The case Unicef presented for its lack of emphasis on prophylactics stressed the fact that, in many countries of Africa especially, the supply of condoms could be erratic and their consistent use beyond the financial means of the average couple. Operational considerations were also a factor: Unicef did not want to devote the energies of its procurement system to becoming a leading world supplier of low-cost condoms (as it had for vaccines); it was willing, however, to act as a purchasing agent for them on a reimbursable basis if other donors could find no better source of supply.

The course steered by Unicef was a delicate and controversial one. In the background was Unicef's reluctance to be publicly associated with advocating the use of contraceptives for fear of becoming embroiled in religious and cultural controversy. At the same time, it was anxious to disassociate itself from the idea that it opposed their use as a self-protective or 'safe sex' measure. Although it was not willing to supply condoms itself for AIDS prevention programmes, it by no means decried their use or tried to prevent them from being mentioned in the AIDS awareness literature it was helping to spread.

Whether for family planning or for disease control, contraception was still implicitly a 'no-go' area in Unicef. But as the 1980s drew to an end, both the AIDS epidemic and growing activism over reproductive rights within the international women's movement were gradually forcing Unicef towards adopting a public position on family planning. Over the decade, in spite of its place within the three 'F's suffixed to GOBI, family planning was barely mentioned in Jim Grant's annual *State of the World's Children* reports. This was in spite of the well-established contribution to child survival of reducing births in the categories of 'too young', 'too old', 'too many' and 'too frequent'.

The 'Safe Motherhood Initiative' had pointed out that spacing births at least two years apart, and avoiding pregnancies under the age of 18 and over the age of 35, could reduce maternal deaths by as much as 25 per cent. Spacing births also redounded to the health of a woman's existing and future children, as the international family planning and health community consistently underlined: a mother preoccupied by the birth of a new baby was less able to give a newly weaned child the necessary time and care that the vulnerable toddler required. Nevertheless, despite all the evidence that family planning services were a vital part of improved maternal and child health, Unicef only ever spoke of giving women the *knowledge* to avoid at-risk pregnancies; never did it speak of the low-cost technological means that would enable them to do so, nor except in the context of general support to MCH did it support family planning services. Not surprisingly, therefore, it was often criticized for not being sufficiently active in family planning.

Pressure on Unicef from certain members of its Executive Board and partner agencies in the UN system began to mount. In 1990, a number of delegates stressed that readily accessible family planning was an essential part of any strategy to improve maternal health, and sent a clear signal that they wanted more attention to family planning. In the 'Strategies for Children in the 1990s', a goal for family planning for the year 2000 was established: access by all couples to information and services to prevent unwanted and risky pregnancies. This goal was later reasserted in the World Summit Declaration and Action Plan. The Board also asked the Executive Director to submit to its 1992 session a report on its collaboration with the UN Population Fund; this led to the preparation of a Unicef policy paper on family planning for 1993. The position it outlined would provide the basis of Unicef's contribution to the International Conference on Population and Development to be held in Cairo in 1994.

An important indication that Jim Grant was now less reluctant to avoid the association of Unicef's name with any pronouncement on family planning came in the 1992 *State of the World's Children* report. This set out 10 propositions for a 'new world order' to favour children; one proposition was on 'planning births', which was described as 'one of the most effective and least expensive ways of improving the quality of life on earth'. For the first time in more than a decade, the case for supporting family planning as a measure to improve maternal and child health and survival had been prominently spelled out in a Unicef document. The arguments were those consistently advanced over the years by UNFPA, the World Bank, WHO and leading international NGOs.

When the Unicef policy review on family planning was published the following year, it repeated the case in favour of family planning as an aid to maternal and child health[90]. The review added that reductions in under-five mortality and in fertility had a 'powerful synergistic effect': smaller family size improved the prospects of child survival, and improved child survival motivated couples to want fewer children. Unicef was, as usual, anxious to defend itself against the charge that child survival added to the problem of population growth, and underlined that support for MCH and family planning together could do more to solve the population problem than either activity by itself.

When it came to the specific actions Unicef proposed to take, however, the policy review essentially reiterated the existing contexts in which Unicef supported women and described these as constituting a family planning policy. These included the enhancement of women's socio-economic roles and status; support for mothers as bearers, breastfeeders and rearers of children; support for girls' education and female literacy; and the spread of information via traditional and modern communications channels. The emphasis was placed on Unicef's role in the 'improvement of knowledge' category, given its expertise in social mobilization and IEC (Information, Education and Communications). Support for actual family planning services 'integral to MCH' was mentioned, with the proviso that Unicef did not supply contraceptives and under no circumstances supported abortion as a family planning method[91].

The wheel had come full circle. Where in the early 1970s, Unicef enhanced its support for women's programmes as an adjunct to what was then called 'responsible parenthood', now it paraded its support for women's programmes as its contribution to family planning. Yet the fact that it had linked its name firmly with the issue after a long period of silence was welcomed in the international health and family planning community. It was even argued—as if Unicef were somehow responsible—that the holistic approach to population policy adopted at the International Conference on Population and Development in Cairo in September 1994 was closely in line with Unicef's own position. Whatever the record, the important point was that a real consensus had been reached and Unicef and its international partners in reproductive health were singing the same tune.

Meanwhile, Unicef was beginning to grasp the more awkward nettles of reproductive health, such as the exposure of young girls in prostitution to HIV and AIDS. In some of the worst-affected countries, notably Thailand, Uganda and Zimbabwe, concerns about the disproportionate impact of HIV infection and of AIDS' social damage on the young led for the first time in Unicef to serious policy-making concern with adolescent health at the international level[92]. Pro-active work in schools and the use of the media and youth organizations to spread sexual health awareness became part of the Unicef pro-child public health menu. If this happened *sotto voce* to begin with, in the wake of the 1994 Cairo Conference it received a real organizational boost[93]. Unicef was finally beginning to include sexual and reproductive health frameworks within the mainstream of its support to children and girls.

By the early 1990s, the importance of women's role in social and economic development had gained widespread recognition, not only on grounds of equity and justice but for much more hard-headed and practical reasons. Evidence had accumulated from all over the developing world that there was a close link between a country's commitment to the advancement of women and improvements not only in social indicators but in economic productivity and overall development advance[94].

Fortified with this extra ammunition, the international women's movement was increasingly managing to transcend the 'women's programmes' and 'women's issues' ghetto. Recognition was growing that gender was a fundamental organizing principle of society, and that profound inequities stemming from its application were inhibiting progress in every area of human life. This perspective began to emerge strongly on agendas other than the women's alone—in *Agenda 21*, for example, the product of the Earth Summit at Rio; and it dominated the international conferences on human rights at Vienna in 1993 and on population and development at Cairo in 1994.

The mounting visibility of the women's cause, and the prominence of the 'gender' framework within which governments and donors were now—theoretically at least—addressing all their policies concerning development and human rights, could not fail to rub off on Unicef. The Unicef medium-term plan for 1992 to 1995 identified the status of women and girls, their participation in development and their empowerment as a central focus of Unicef cooperation[95]. Without progress in these areas, the plan stated, the fulfilment of commitments made by governments in the World Summit for Children Declaration and Plan of Action would not be possible.

Such formulations in Unicef documents had become familiar to those who had fought long and hard to gain recognition for the centrality of women's disadvantaged status to the prospects for the world's children. Politically correct sentiments of this kind were expressed in policy documents galore, but their import had still not been internalized throughout the organization or its programmes, as the report of the 1992 Multi-Donor Evaluation of Unicef pointed out[96]. Although 'mainstreaming' of women's issues had been the key Unicef 'women in development' strategy since 1987, few of the necessary institutional changes and approaches to programming had been introduced, at least in the countries studied by the Multi-Donor team. Instead of being an antidote to the marginalization of women, mainstreaming had sometimes been used as a pretext for failing to allocate increased resources to gender-related action. Gender analysis was not being universally applied, and therefore the need for specific affirmative activity on behalf of women was not being revealed. Even programmes for the girl child—so prominent in Unicef advocacy—were conspicuous by their absence in the countries studied.

The Unicef record vis-à-vis women was undoubtedly patchy, but at the same time, partly because of organizational backing and partly in spite of it, the importance of the gender dimension in children's concerns had become much better appreciated, both inside and outside Unicef. By the early 1990s, it was being given more than token respect in sectoral programming in health, water and education; in situation analysis and data collection about children; in programmes for 'adjustment with a human face' and in programmes for countries in post-communist transition; latterly, also in schemes for emergency relief and rehabilitation. More offices were backing gender-based employment and economic studies; in some countries—the Dominican Republic and Zimbabwe, for example—legal reforms affecting women's property rights in marriage were on the Unicef country menu[97].

These changes had come about partly because Unicef had made efforts to increase the proportion of women employed in its professional categories and their representation at senior levels. By 1994, 39 per cent of professional employees in Unicef were female[98], a level above the one third targeted for the UN but still some distance from parity. Since 1987, one of the three Deputy Executive Directors (for Operations) had been a woman, Karin Sham Poo, who had done much to promote the greater representation of women in senior management positions[99]. In 1995, on the death of Jim Grant, Carol Bellamy was appointed as Executive Director[100]. Bellamy was only the second woman to be selected to head a major UN Fund: the first was Nafis Sadik of the United Nations Population Fund.

Not all the most striking Unicef initiatives on behalf of women—in programmes, in advocacy or within its management culture—could be attributed to women officers and representatives, but the necessary sensitization of the country office or headquarters department often could be. One such example was the attempt in Bangladesh to base the 1992 situation analysis and country programming strategy on the life cycle of girls and women[101], an approach that was later adopted for widespread use in Asia[102] and echoed in organizational thinking.

From 1993 onward, Unicef began to deploy a 'women's empowerment framework' in gender analysis workshops. This was a serious effort to overcome the organization's failure to internalize the gender dimension. Programme staff were taught to use an analytical hierarchy that allowed them to distinguish between welfarist activities that treated women as passive recipients; those that opened up their access to resources; those that promoted their participation in society; and those that enabled them to achieve parity with men. A policy review in 1994 in preparation for the 1995 International Women's Conference in Beijing elaborated further plans for Unicef's self-genderization and expressed the hope that 80 per cent of staff would have been trained in gender-awareness by 1995[103].

During the 1980s, Unicef had strenuously championed the techniques of social mobilization and 'empowerment' as a means of reaching child survival goals. In the 1990s, the challenge still remained of putting these techniques at the service of women for their own advancement. Women who were marginalized and refused equal opportunities were likely to fail in every role and in every area of their lives. If they so failed, women—who were half of the people—were bound to drag back their children and the rest of humanity with them. For years, Unicef had pointed out that child survival and development depended on 'women's empowerment'. Although in the mid-1990s it was still unclear whether Unicef fully understood throughout its fabric the real implications of such a statement, the signs that it was finally doing so were distinctly more promising.

Over one issue there was widespread agreement. If there was one key above all others that could unlock women's potential to transform their lives, that key was schooling. With education came not only knowledge and qualifications but the independence of spirit that enabled women to take their place in the world as fully fledged individuals and to resist male oppression and exploitation. The right to basic education was the theme of Carol Bellamy's statement to the 1995 International Women's Conference in Beijing[104]. This statement was as much a signal about Unicef's new level of commitment to education as it was about its commitment to women. As the main mission of the organization, 'child survival' was now beginning to take a back seat, and 'child development'—not only physical development, but intellectual, psychological and emotional development—was steadily gaining ground.

Chapter 8

Learning for All

During its early existence, Unicef took the view that children's needs could be divided up and compartmentalized. The founding resolution defined the Unicef mission beyond emergency relief as to do with physical well-being: 'for child health purposes generally'. As the years went by, this was treated very much as a *tabula rasa* on which the Executive Board might write what it chose, and the definition proved reasonably elastic. But it was not stretched to cover activities that contributed to the child's knowledge, understanding, moral or spiritual health, or social behaviour.

Although the school was the social institution outside the family with the most influence on the formation of the child, assistance with education—whether in the form of items such as blackboard, textbook or desk, or of teacher's training—was off limits. The only knowledge that Unicef was willing to help impart—either to adult or to child—was that concerning child health and nutrition. And the only learning 'institutions' that Unicef was willing to assist were the informal gatherings where mothers met or where young children were deposited in a minder's care.

A change in this position was first mooted in the late 1950s by certain delegates from the developing world to the Executive Board[1]. But it was resisted by those who regarded Unicef as having a deliberately narrow humanitarian focus that must be defended from the proposition that children's needs were indistinguishable from those of the wider society. These objections gradually dissolved in the currents of contemporary opinion. One influence was the mounting evidence that education was a key to economic advance: in the era of development, many countries were not able to absorb technology and financial investment because they did not have enough administrators or trained manpower. Education would solve this by building up the 'human capital'. The idea that people were a natural asset, like a rich lode of ore waiting to be mined, was central to development thinking at this time. 'Children are a country's most precious resource' was the version of the idiom to infiltrate Unicef's ideology. Logically, to champion the interests of the child required investing in the intellectual, psychological and social as well as the physical needs of this 'resource'.

Other interconnected influences were at work. Many African countries came to independence at the beginning of the 1960s, and their hunger for education echoed the pressures from others for a wider range of options concerning the type and content of cooperation available from the Unicef shelf[2]. A desire to respond to the recipient voice and react to changing times led to Unicef's landmark Survey on the Needs of Children. This was conducted worldwide between 1960 and 1961, and received major inputs from WHO (on children's health needs), FAO (on their nutritional needs), UNESCO (on their educational needs), ILO (on their training needs) and the UN Bureau of Social Affairs (on their social welfare needs).

The report on the survey, reviewed by the Executive Board in 1961, revolutionized Unicef's outlook on how to help the world's children, presenting the case for addressing the needs of the 'whole child' within the context of national development plans[3]. During the discussion by the Board, many delegates stated that education was as vital an aspect of children's needs as were health and food, and that this field of potential assistance should not be overlooked.[4] From this point onward, it would not be. The compartmentalization of children's needs was over; the 'whole child', within the context of both the family and the community, set the new parameters within which Unicef assistance would be provided. 'Elementary education', 'agricultural education' and 'vocational training' were now eligible for Unicef aid.

In many of the countries arriving at independence, the educational inheritance from colonial times was meagre, to say the least. In some African countries, only a tiny élite had finished secondary school, let alone university. At primary level the picture was often of more children out of school than in. In Africa, no more than 37 per cent of primary-age children were enrolled in school; in Asia, the figure was 50 per cent; in Latin America, 60 per cent. Of these, only in Latin America did girls constitute nearly half; in Africa and Asia, only a third of schoolchildren were female[5].

These figures disguised the disappearance of many children from the classroom—one third of boys, one half of girls—long before the primary school cycle was complete[6]. Nor did they indicate the quality of the education provided, some of whose inadequacies were legendary: geography syllabuses that required children to know the names of towns and rivers in Europe but nothing of their own continent; history that taught about the campaigns of Gauls, Romans and conquistadors but nothing of the ancient Inca or Maasai. Modern educationalists also complained about the rote learning, the autocratic teacher-pupil style and the lack of attention to analytical and problem-solving skills. Worst of all was the acute lack of teacher training, the disastrous conditions of buildings and equipment, and the shortages of textbooks on every subject.

During the early 1960s, UNESCO convened a series of regional conferences so that African, Asian, Latin American and Arab countries could set their own timetables and priorities for the growth of education over the next two decades[7]. In all regions, ambitious targets were set for expansions across the board, but at primary level the goal was the ultimate: universal primary education—UPE—by 1980 (in the case of Latin America, by 1970). As close as possible to 100 per cent of children in the primary-age cohort should have classrooms and chairs, and be sitting in them facing a trained and well-equipped teacher, in less than two decades. This was a very tall order; quite how tall, given the demographers' continued innocence about the suddenly accelerating rates of child survival, and therefore of the increasing numbers in the age group coming up to educational entry, was not then realized.

The next decade or so saw a historically unprecedented rate of classroom growth in all the developing regions. At primary level, enrolments doubled in Asia and Latin America over the two decades to 1980, and in Africa they tripled[8]. Although Unicef's contribution was bound to be modest, its decision in the early 1960s to support 'elementary education' in response to rising demand was timely. Between 1960 and 1970-71, Unicef aid to education rose by three and a half times (from $3.4 million to $14.1 million) compared with that allocated to child health, which rose only by 50 per cent[9]. In 1970-71, assistance to education accounted for nearly one quarter of all Unicef cooperation, while health accounted for just over half. Most support went to educational supplies and equipment, with teacher training, science education and vocational institutions absorbing much of the rest.

By the early 1970s, it was becoming evident that the great leap forward in primary school provision fell far short when measured against the increasing numbers of children entering their school-age years. For all the energy with which Ministries of Education were opening new classrooms and filling them with pupils, they were failing to keep pace with the growth of the five- to nine-year-old age group. The result was an increase in the absolute numbers of the unschooled, and in illiterates, especially girls and women. The figures, moreover, did not reveal the vast social waste represented by high numbers of dropouts, failures and 'repeaters'. Instead of presenting a time-bound challenge to the leaders of the newly independent countries, the quantitative and qualitative shortcomings in educational opportunity now seemed to constitute an unfillable gap. Leading commentators described a 'world educational crisis': the need and demand for learning was rapidly outstripping the capacity to provide it[10].

The experience in educational progress had mirrored that in the social and economic sphere: there had been rapid advance, but its benefits had failed to filter down, further entrenching the poor in their state of disadvantage. This outcome of the development crusade of the 1960s led to the quest for 'alternative' strategies in the 1970s, emphasizing social equity and poverty alleviation. Within Unicef, one of the earliest manifestations of this quest was a radical overhaul of its policy on education. In 1972, the Executive Board decided that it would cease to offer more de-luxe inputs such as sophisticated vocational training and science education in secondary schools; Unicef would now focus specifically on those children deprived of basic education by poverty, especially in rural areas. No longer was 'building up the human capital' the priority; improving the lives of the poor and remedying educational disadvantage had taken its place.

One of the strongest criticisms of contemporary school curricula was that they were inappropriate to the future lives of the vast majority of primary-school leavers. A small minority were destined for secondary education and salaried jobs in town, but around 80 per cent were left stranded in the pre-industrial rural economy, equipped not with ideas and methods for its transformation but with the mark of failure by the standards of urban society. The cities of the developing world were full of young people with half a school certificate and few prospects of gainful employment, whose only ambition was not to go home to the constricted horizons and predictability of life on the land. Accordingly, 'alternative' educational thinkers were full of ideas for amending the curriculum to match the exigencies of future rural life. Unicef's new policy attached importance to reforms of this kind, which could mean introducing goat-raising and poultry-keeping as school subjects or teaching sanitary conduct and disease control in the science classroom. In Tanzania, for example, Unicef was a strong backer of President Julius Nyerere's *ujamaa* (community) schools and helped provide practical support for making operational his philosophy of 'Education for Self-Reliance'[11].

As well as reordering its priorities for conventional schooling, Unicef was also keen to explore what might be done outside the formal system to help prevent the waste represented by the millions of half-lettered children who had dropped out of school, and those who had never managed to get there. It therefore commissioned a major research study from Philip Coombs, a leading international expert, and his team from the International Council for Educational Development (ICED) into schemes for 'non-formal education'. Such schemes had long been a target of Unicef cooperation, often under the label of health education or women's programmes. They ran the gamut from mobile training schools for teenage drop-outs (Thailand), to radio schools for remote *campesinos* (Peru), to 'village polytechnics' (Kenya), to preschool arrangements and literacy training for mothers' clubs in a large number of countries.

In 1973 and 1974, ICED reports were presented to the Unicef Executive Board. They drew heavily upon 'alternative' pedagogic ideas and on a landmark UNESCO report entitled *Learning to Be*. According to contemporary wisdom, what education gave to a person in terms of ability to take on new challenges and engage with new ideas could be as important as the actual content of the syllabus. Coombs and his ICED colleague Manzoor Ahmed took as their starting-point the recognition that education was a lifelong process in which what people learned as children at their parents' knee, and what adolescents learned as they found their way in the adult world, was as significant as the prescribed chunk of their lives spent in the classroom. They identified a 'minimum package' of attitudes, skills and knowledge needed by every young person, including a positive attitude towards learning itself; basic literacy and numeracy; a scientific understanding about the environment; and functional knowledge about raising a family, running a household and earning a living[12]. The most important category of clients for the delivery of this package were those who had missed or dropped out of school, the great majority of whom were, of course, female. Here was the genesis of 'basic education'.

During discussions on these reports, some reservations were expressed by members of the Executive Board that non-formal education was being overhyped as a panacea for the shortcomings of the formal primary system. This was a period during which radical educational thinkers such as Paulo Freire in Brazil and Ivan Illich in Mexico were going so far as to debunk standard schooling systems altogether, describing them as instruments for reinforcing structural inequity[13]. According to this perspective, schooling could not be a valid learning experience unless it not only imparted knowledge but helped people to become 'conscientized' about the forces operating in their lives and to be able to take some control over them. (The use of knowledge to 'empower' people was the less revolutionary version of the same idea current in the 1980s.) Such critics tended to be in favour of alternative systems of learning as a substitute for contemporary primary schooling systems; other supporters of non-formal programmes simply felt that some countries were too poor to secure a reasonable primary education for all their young citizens, and that in such circumstances, a shorter, cheaper alternative imparting relevant skills for rural life would be better than nothing.

Unicef side-stepped the politicization of the education issue by expressing its support for education in both formal and non-formal contexts and by refusing to join in condemnation of the former. But this somewhat artificial debate, in which formal and non-formal educational approaches were wilfully presented as a dichotomy, rumbled on within the international educational establishment for many years, its various protagonists vying for funds and ideological favour and generally clouding the educational sky. As far as Unicef was concerned, the ICED reports marked the systemization of what it meant by non-formal education, and a commitment to future support, including support for adult literacy schemes, especially among women, and to educational activities for out-of-school youth. Unicef was careful to point out, however, that enthusiasm for 'learning to be' should not be allowed to substitute for reforming the mainstream educational system and providing more standard schools. These were ultimately the only long-term answers, and graduates from as many non-formal schemes as possible should be able to cross over into the educational career pathway that proper schools existed to provide.

By 1980, public expenditures on expanding networks of schools and colleges—with the exception of oil-rich developing countries—had levelled off. By now it was becoming evident that although the growth rates for primary schooling recommended by the UNESCO regional conferences of the 1960s were almost miraculously on target, few countries were anywhere near being able to provide enough places for universal enrolment. In Africa alone, they had underestimated the need for places by around 11 million[14]; as in so many other development contexts, population growth persistently scuppered their plans. Moreover, the enrolment figures continued to mask the high number of drop-outs and 'repeaters'. Enrolment could not be trusted as a measure of whether universal primary education had been reached in any given setting. The capacity of a country's school system did not necessarily indicate either the way it was used or its quality—which, in turn, affected parents' decisions about whether or not to send their children to school.

The benefits of educating their children were not always obvious to poverty-stricken rural or slum-dwelling families. Some parents could not afford to do without their children's—especially their daughters'—help in minding younger siblings, tending livestock, fetching water and firewood, and other tasks essential to family well-being. Others might skimp and save to put a boy or two through school in the hope that he would be one of the lucky ones to make it to a big desk in town: even where school was nominally free, uniforms, shoes, a school bag and bus fares usually represented a major investment. But if the school was far away, the teacher negligent, the girls' modesty and even chastity insecure, parents might feel that the benefit was not worth the cost, especially for girls, and especially if their children were among the 'repeaters' whose chances of respectable graduation receded every year. As far as non-formal alternatives were concerned, parents often felt that the sacrifice they had to make was pointless if the education their children received was inferior and failed to provide a passport out of the life of drudgery they themselves had known.

As the 1980s dawned, therefore, the promise of UPE remained unfulfilled. Just over two thirds of all 6- to 11-year-olds in the developing world were enrolled in school as compared to 92 per cent in industrialized countries[15]. In Africa, the figure was well up from one third plus at the start of the 1960s to nearly two thirds, but this still left over one third of school-aged children unprovided with basic education.

Worse was to come. Under the impact of debt and adjustment, educational expenditures plummeted. In sub-Saharan Africa, public spending on education per inhabitant fell by one half between 1980 and 1987, and in Latin America, by 11 per cent over the period[16]. At the same time, the combination of currency devaluations and the depression of public sector salaries reduced the value of teachers' earnings to a point where they were forced to moonlight—even to sunlight—and work elsewhere. In many countries, teachers became demotivated and demoralized by their deteriorating working conditions and standards of life[17]. In some countries, many lost their jobs: in 1984, as part of Zaire's austerity plan, 46,000 teachers in primary and secondary schools (20 per cent of the total) were laid off[18]. The quality of the schooling service in certain countries was undermined to a point where the very viability of the educational process could be called in question[19].

During most of the 1980s, Unicef was deeply engrossed with the child survival revolution. Although 'female education' was one of the three 'F's suffixed to GOBI, the Unicef mission had become heavily concentrated on technologically doable elements of the primary health care agenda. The 'child survival revolution' never squeezed out education as it did much of the non-medical basic services programme agenda, although expenditure on education rose very little over the decade; instead, it more or less co-opted the education programme on behalf of child survival. New materials produced for primary schools and primary school teachers' training emphasized child survival messages: the value of immunization, growth monitoring and the use of ORT[20].

Outside the school setting, the story was repeated. Women's groups and literacy classes were natural targets for a curriculum revision emphasizing information that was compelling and precious because it was about child health and child survival—matters that touched them deeply. It often contrasted favourably with the childish and irrelevant texts borrowed from the primary syllabus that often alienated adult learners. As the decade progressed, a degree of fusion developed between efforts to promote non-formal adult education and the social mobilization process, steadily gaining ground as the Unicef-recommended tool for building momentum behind services for child survival at all levels of society.

This fusion between the propagation of information among adults via non-formal educational channels, and social mobilization for child survival, was dramatically advanced by a particular initiative emanating from Unicef. This was jointly backed by UNESCO and WHO and gathered support from over 100 other organizations concerned with the health and condition of children. It was the brainchild of Peter Adamson, Jim Grant's collaborator on the annual *State of the World's Children* reports. Its name encapsulated its quintessentially simple purpose: *Facts for Life*.

The first line of attack in the child survival campaign was the promotion of disease prevention via simple medical technology. Among the prescriptions that made up GOBI, only breastfeeding had no scientifically modern, 'quick fix' characteristic. But in spite of their technological prowess, all of them—even immunization, the most proximate to a magic bullet—required the willing cooperation of parents, especially mothers. In other words, people had to understand their value in order to use GOBI techniques, willingly join in community efforts to promote them or demand that they be provided. And if knowledge was a critical ingredient of the propagation of GOBI, this was even more the case in matters such as personal hygiene, the spacing of births or the avoidance of HIV infection. In cases such as these, the use of technology might be incidental and the application of knowledgeable behaviour all-important.

The *Facts for Life* initiative was based on a simple premise. Every year, 14 million young children's lives were lost and millions more were permanently impaired almost entirely as a result of preventable causes. The information that, converted into knowledge, could prevent this waste of life was readily available, and was easy to grasp and put into practice. Therefore, all parents and all communities should have access to the information as a right. Clearly, on the basis of past experience, the fulfilment of this right could not be left to the health sector alone: the transformation of beliefs, attitudes and behaviours that the spread of information was supposed to effect demanded reinforcement from many different directions. The promotion of health, especially child health, had to become the concern of all parts of the community.

To make this happen, two types of actions were necessary. First, the information should be reduced to its essentials and packaged in an easily understandable, non-controversial and distributable form. Hence, an 80-page publication with key facts under 10 child health and survival headings: timing births, safe motherhood, breastfeeding, child growth, immunization, diarrhoea, coughs and colds, home hygiene, malaria and AIDS. The messages contained under these headings were to be the simplest and most authoritative expression of contemporary scientific consensus. Second, the material contained in the *Facts for Life* publication had to be communicated by every conceivable channel and organizational partnership in such a way as to make the information part of the basic child care knowledge of every family. *Facts for Life* activity could be seen as a way of shortcutting the educational process that would normally put this knowledge at the disposal of people still excluded from standard information and communications channels or alienated by the messages they carried.

The process of distilling the world's child health expertise into a handful of dos and don'ts was by no means straightforward. Information is not neutral, nor can it be divorced from context: within different cultural settings and depending on different behavioural codes, the priority and aptitude of messages—about child feeding, for example—changed. Nonetheless, some essential information about child health remained constant: the desirable minimum age of child-bearing, for example; the desirable duration of breastfeeding; the necessary immunization routine; the importance of washing hands before eating. Adaptations and prioritization could be made *in situ*, by health educators and communications professionals with intimate knowledge of the audience's attitudes and beliefs.

More problematic was the achievement of consensus within the health and practitioner community about what the messages should say. There might be areas of disagreement among medical researchers about matters such as the role of home-brewed ORS in dealing with childhood diarrhoea and the child-spacing properties of breastfeeding, for example. For this reason, the technical supervision of *Facts for Life* was undertaken by WHO, and a large array of child health experts in many disciplines were fully consulted. If something appeared in the booklet that gave any senior health policy decision maker a reason to dismiss its contents as inaccurate, the chances of its use in that setting would be negligible. These 'facts for life' must be ownable by everyone, not least by those who would decide upon their fate.

Having gone through an exhaustive consultative process to produce a deceptively simple text, the even more difficult task began: that of enlisting all types of communications personnel and machinery to make *Facts for Life* penetrate barriers of understanding and behaviour that had previously remained impervious to health education advice. This was the subject of lengthy discussion during 1988-89. Experience showed that only frequent and varied repetition of new information, over a long period and from sources that could be trusted, could truly succeed in putting health information at people's disposal in such a way that they actually used it to supplant old habits. This was particularly the case for an illiterate mother who had learned how to raise her children from senior family women whose diktat was not lightly flouted. Unless the weight of information surrounding her—from media, community leaders, health workers, trusted friends, shopkeepers, visiting relatives—endorsed what she learned in her mother's club, she might easily assume that curious ideas about child sickness and mothering behaviour did not apply to her.

Facts for Life was launched in 1989. It was published in tandem with a resource book, *All for Health*, which provided myriad examples of communications ideas, vehicles and partners. Teachers and primary health care workers were leading candidates: *Facts for Life*, ready-made, could be incorporated into classroom syllabuses and health education courses. But the essence of the project was to extend the spread of health education via the kind of partners the 'child survival revolution' had called upon for immunization drives. The same principle of social mobilization was to be put to work to create alliances; the only difference was that this was a campaign to spread knowledge rather than the use of medical technology. Religious leaders could disseminate *Facts for Life*; so could employers, trades unions, journalists, community leaders, NGOs and entertainers. The aim was not only 'health for all', it was also 'all for health'.

The first print run of 275,000 copies of the booklet in five languages went out of stock within a year. Already versions had been brought out in Chinese, Burmese, Swahili and six Filipino languages and dialects[21]. By the end of 1991, *Facts for Life* had been published in 138 languages and distributed in 97 countries. Altogether, 4 million copies had been produced[22]. The worldwide response had been everything that could be hoped for, and more. In around 25 countries the slim volume had entered the school curriculum. In as many, its messages had been adapted into leaflet and poster form for use in clinics, health centres and consulting rooms. A number of countries had developed training programmes based on *Facts for Life* so that teachers, health volunteers and agricultural extension workers had a confident and professional grasp of how to communicate the basic messages.

A number of Unicef country offices had created video and audio versions of *Facts for Life*, and in many, these were being used for TV and radio 'spots'. Newspapers, journals and magazines carried articles, cartoons and competitions. In some countries, communications and marketing media other than standard TV and radio had been used. For example, in Brazil, a major supermarket chain had put 'facts for life' messages on 120 million plastic shopping bags; in Kenya, they were carried on 10 million matchboxes; and in Turkey, they appeared on 2 million milk cartons[23].

One of the most obvious settings in which localized versions of *Facts for Life* could be used was programmes for women. One organization to take up this idea with enthusiasm was the Viet Nam Women's Union. Initially, this national movement intended to propagate 'facts for life' throughout its 11 million members and ensure their sustained application. The Women's Union had a dynamic secretariat at national, provincial and district levels and its outreach was therefore assured. But it soon transpired that adjustments were necessary. At this time, Vietnamese women were having to weather the profound social changes accompanying the process of economic transition. In the late 1980s, the commune-based system of production and social management was replaced by one based on the family unit. Suddenly, Vietnamese women had to shoulder far more economic responsibility for family well-being and take up the slack of social services cut-backs. The Women's Union felt called upon to help them.

In 1990, with support from Unicef, the Women's Union launched what was to become a countrywide project based on two components: *Facts for Life* and credit for rural women. *Facts for Life* was translated into Vietnamese and the five main ethnic minority languages. Teams of communicators—25,000 altogether—were trained to put across the top 10 messages, both in public meetings and in one-on-one discussions during household visits. The respect in which the Women's Union was held meant that their training carried authority. Team members learned fast and were susceptible to such new ideas as family limitation and the need to breastfeed the baby immediately after birth (which went against local custom).

One of the promotional activities introduced in a number of Vietnamese provinces was *Facts for Life* contests. These were first conducted at village level. On the appointed day, women who wished to enter came to the village hall. The audience sat on one side, and participating mothers with their children on the other. On the platform stood a paper tree covered with questions folded and tied to look like blossoms. Each mother plucked a question from the tree, and when her name was called, gave her answer. Then all the babies were weighed and their growth and appearance checked to see which mothers were putting *Facts for Life* into effect. The judges then chose the winning 'couple' who received a prize—usually of clothes—and the right to progress to the next round at district level. These contests became celebrated provincewide events.

The credit scheme enabled women to put into practice what *Facts for Life* had taught them: without this component, many women struggling to make ends meet in the new market economy would not be in a position to put into effect the information communicated to them. Viet Nam's most significant child health problem was malnutrition, from which around half of the under-five population suffered in one degree or another[24]. With the modest loans of $30 provided under the scheme, most women bought small livestock, piglets, ducks and laying hens. This would not have been permitted in the old days of communal production, and their knowledge of livestock raising was rusty. But Vietnamese women quickly recovered the necessary skills. Many became poultry and piglet mini-entrepreneurs, enabling them to abandon menial jobs—porterage and haulage are common traditional occupations for Vietnamese women[25]—and spend more time with their children. Diets, as well as child-care skills, improved as a result. One small-scale study in a commune in Hai Hung province found that out of 187 families, only six had not managed to make significant improvement at home as a result of the programme[26]. 'Facts for life', promulgated within a structured and well-run campaign, were providing a genuine inspiration to Vietnamese women.

Such was the worldwide success of *Facts for Life* that, in 1993, a second edition was brought out. By this time, more than 9 million copies of the first edition had been published and the text had been translated into 176 languages. Fears that the text would prove too universalist had been dispelled: in many instances, the messages had been recrafted and retailored. Chapters had been added or substituted, following the advice of local experts, on subjects ranging from smoking and drug abuse to dental hygiene, accidents and sexually transmitted disease. The second edition of the booklet took advantage of experience gained with the first. Its co-publishers included a new sponsor, UNFPA, which joined the original trio of Unicef, WHO and

UNESCO. Over 160 international NGOs signed up as partners in the venture[27]. By 1995, more than 10 million copies of *Facts for Life* in over 200 languages were in circulation[28].

The new edition of *Facts for Life* contained only one major change: the addition of a new chapter, on early childhood development. This subject—the cognitive and psychosocial growth of the young child—had been eclipsed in Unicef during most of the past decade by the campaign for child survival. The movement for 'basic education', gathering momentum in the run-up to the 1990 World Conference on Education for All, managed for the first time to inscribe early childhood cognitive growth on the child survival and development agenda.

The impetus for this Conference came, perhaps surprisingly, from the foremost champion of child survival and of the technological 'fix', a person often derided for his 'mono-focus': Jim Grant of Unicef.

Jim Grant had never overlooked the need to respond to the glaring educational needs in the developing world. Before he became head of Unicef, he had been as interested in examples of low-income countries with high literacy rates as he had in those with low child mortality rates. He believed that these 'positive deviants' in education and primary health care provision offered blueprints for achieving reductions in the worst manifestations of poverty without having to wait for the conquest of poverty itself. For this reason, he had appointed as his head of programming worldwide Dr. Nyi Nyi, an ex-Minister of Education in Burma responsible for a renowned mass literacy campaign.

Early in 1982—before the development of GOBI—Grant made a determined but vain attempt to persuade UNESCO to collaborate on a major initiative to promote 'primary education for all'[29]. Without a positive response from the key international partner, education had to wait. By 1987, cognizant that child survival gains could only be sustained by an informed population, Grant was again beginning to cast around for ways of accelerating progress in basic education. He looked for an equivalent to GOBI: low-cost, doable interventions that would work on a mass scale. In his Annual Report to the Executive Board, he gave an indication of the way his mind was working: 'Social mobilization was the principal means for the unprecedented expansion of primary education and literacy in Burma and the United Republic of Tanzania in the 1970s. Unicef is now examining ways in which the rapidly growing experience in social mobilization can contribute to more effective educational activities.'[30]

Grant believed that there must be strategies that could short cut the long, slow, intergenerational process of inculcating new knowledge, new ideas and new attitudes into people via the classroom or its close equivalent. But in order to find out what these might be, and to create a sense of international agreement and momentum behind them, he believed that a common international platform had to be constructed. UNESCO was now headed by Dr. Federico Mayor, whose attitude towards a major international initiative on basic education was positive. In 1989, a Joint Committee on Education consisting of representatives of the Executive Boards of UNESCO and Unicef was set up to promote collaboration between the two organizations[31]. With support from Mayor, Grant then set about persuading the heads of UNDP and the World Bank to commit themselves to a joint inter-agency venture. In February 1989, the heads of these four organizations announced their proposal for a World Conference on 'Education for All' to take place in Thailand early in 1990[32].

Twelve years earlier, an international conference at Alma-Ata had tackled the world crisis in health and come up with the primary health care strategy and goals for 'Health for All by the Year 2000'. Grant was determined that the international conference on 'Education for All' would similarly confront the world crisis in education. He was prepared to commit considerable time and energy—his own and Unicef's—to trying to make this happen.

Under the impact of structural adjustment programmes and the drain of debt repayment, this crisis had continued to deepen. UNESCO pointed to a 'dangerous erosion of human resources that . . . might set back the countries of the South by a whole generation or even more'[33]. Cut-backs in educational expenditures were striking most damagingly at the foundation of the educational pyramid, in primary schooling and basic literacy. The proportion of 6- to 11-year-olds enrolled in primary schools was falling in many countries, especially in sub-Saharan Africa where, by the late 1980s, average educational expenditure per person had more than halved since 1980, from $33 to $15 dollars per head[34]. In many countries, capital spending had virtually ceased, and recurrent expenditures were often confined to teachers' salaries alone. The impact on school operations and quality could be devastating. A survey of schools in rural Mozambique, for example, found that only 3 per cent of pupils had seats or desks, and only 17 per cent of classrooms had a desk for the teacher[35].

Despite their sorry state, the main problem facing children of school-going age was not that they did not have classrooms to go to. By 1990, over 90 per cent started school; the more serious continuing problem was that the rate of school drop-out was still so high that almost one in two disappeared long before completing primary education—often before reading and writing skills had been properly absorbed. Children's absence might well be connected to parents' lack of conviction that demoralized teachers in dilapidated buildings could confer much of value on their youngsters, but more significantly, family economic circumstances were making it increasingly difficult for parents to afford schooling costs. The combination of rising expenditures on fees and incidentals, the lack of useful qualifications gained and the need for older children to contribute to household income at the earliest opportunity made a chilling recipe for the reinforcement of educational deprivation among the truly poor. The consequences for social stress and progressive alienation of young people could only be imagined.

If the 1980s had seen a further deterioration in the world educational crisis, they had also produced an impressive array of data confirming the economic value of education. World Bank studies consistently showed that returns from education were higher than from most other types of investment: four years of primary schooling, for example, led to an average increase in farming productivity of 10 per cent or more[36]. Furthermore, the growing emphasis on gender-based inequalities had amplified this aspect of the educational picture. The World Bank found that nations that had invested heavily in female primary education also benefited from higher economic productivity than did countries whose women remained educationally deprived. Countries with a large 'gender gap' in education—meaning a wide discrepancy between male and female enrolment rates—tended to be less economically productive than countries whose capital investment and labour-force situation was otherwise similar[37]. These advantages of investing in girls' primary education were additional to their already well-known social benefits: lower infant and maternal mortality, raised life expectancy and considerably reduced fertility. Female education was therefore becoming a potent and proven influence not only on child survival but on development as a whole.

Yet, one decade from the end of the century, nearly 1 billion people—of whom two thirds were women—could not read or write. Over 100 million children—of whom two thirds were girls—had no chance of going to school[38]. All these were people whose basic learning needs would not be met under prevailing economic and educational circumstances, and whose prospects in life would be correspondingly curtailed. This was the situation the World Conference on Education for All set out to tackle. Its aim was not only to set educational goals for the year 2000 and mobilize new financial resources to meet them, but also to forge a world consensus on a feasible concept of 'education for all'. A new vision of basic education was heralded on which to construct national plans and strategies to reach the educational goals for the year 2000. The most important of these were that 80 per cent of 14-year-old children should have attained a nationally designated level of learning and that adult illiteracy should be reduced to half its 1990 level, at the same time closing the literacy gender gap.

The new vision of basic education circumvented the time-worn contest between the merits of formal and non-formal educational systems. Unlike in the case of primary health care, commitment to basic education implied less a commitment to a particular curriculum delivered by a particular type of learning institution than to the twin principles of 'learning for all' and 'learning as an essential ingredient of equitable and sustainable development'. Basic education was seen as the learning foundation for all citizens, in which fundamental knowledge and skills for life were acquired. It was also regarded as the foundation on which—depending on their resources and needs—societies built further learning opportunities for as many people as possible. The normal venue for acquiring basic education was the primary school, which should be within reach of every child; however, non-formal programmes could substitute and supplement where necessary. All other possible channels of communication and social action—traditional and modern—should also be harnessed to the basic educational cause[39]. Here was the emphasis on social mobilization on which Jim Grant set so much store.

How these principles were to be put into practice on national and local scales was not specified in the 'Framework for Action to Meet Basic Learning Needs' developed during the pre-Conference consultative process. The conference organizers deliberately chose to set up a 'Framework for Action' rather than a 'Plan of Action' because it was considered inappropriate to designate one global plan for the great diversity of situations and stages of development among the countries concerned. The idea was that countries should develop their own plans within a framework that reflected an international sense of solidarity behind the educational cause. Therefore, the Framework drew together a wealth of practical experiences from all over the globe for the inspiration of policy makers, educators and communicators. Among the programmes described were many supported by Unicef, including examples from Bangladesh and Colombia.

The non-formal educational programme run by the Bangladesh Rural Advancement Committee (BRAC) was known as an outstandingly successful experiment in recuperating children left out of the primary system. The country's literacy record was among the lowest in the world; only a third of those aged 15 years and over could read, write and understand numbers at a functional level—skills that were denied 85 per cent of rural women[40]. In 1985, in response to requests from landless villagers, BRAC initiated a primary education programme with experimental schools in 22 rural communities[41]. By late 1989, when the Education for All conference was under preparation, the programme had expanded to 2,500 schools. From its inception, the programme's objective was to develop a replicable basic education model, which in three years could provide basic literacy and numeracy to the child of the poorest family. To redress the disadvantages suffered by girls, they were to make up 70 per cent of the pupils in every school.

BRAC adapted the learning procedure to the circumstances of the child, rather than requiring the child to adjust to the conventional rules of the primary school. For example, the school building was a modest thatched hut with walls of bamboo slatting and a packed earth floor constructed by the community at a convenient location. School timing—three hours per day—and school terms were coordinated with the requirements of the farming season and the domestic chores that all children, especially girls, were expected to shoulder. The typical BRAC teacher was a young married woman from the neighbourhood. She received an intensive two-week training, regular supervision and an extra day of group training every month. The running of the school was in the hands of a village management committee, and parent-teacher groups met regularly to discuss the children's progress.

The overwhelming response to the programme debunked the myth that poor and illiterate rural parents were apathetic—even hostile—towards their children's prospective education. The drop-out rate was almost negligible, and among the younger age group (8 to 10 years old), over 90 per cent joined the fourth or fifth class in the regular primary school after having completed three years with BRAC[42]. The cost of BRAC schools was extremely modest: only $18 per child per year, or one quarter of the cost of the state primary system. (Following the Education for All conference, and in the wake of 1990 legislation for compulsory primary education passed by the Bangladesh Government, the BRAC programme rapidly expanded. By 1992, it had mushroomed to 12,000 schools reaching 360,000 children, and continued to grow exponentially[43].)

Unlike BRAC's programme, the Escuela Nueva—new schools—programme in Colombia was designed not as an alternative to the formal primary system but as an alternative within it. It was intended to redress the educational disadvantages suffered by rural children, whose chances of attending schools of reasonable quality were much more restricted than those of their counterparts in town. Rural schools were short of teachers, textbooks and equipment, and although the curriculum was designed to be taught by one teacher per grade, the majority of schools were multi-grade but had only one or two teachers. As a result of these schools' many deficiencies, the situation in the early 1980s was that only around 65 per cent of rural children enrolled, and only one in five completed the full five-year primary cycle[44].

The roots of the Escuela Nueva programme extended back into the 1960s, when the concept of the 'unitary school' was introduced in parts of the country with low population density. In this experimental type of school, only one teacher was needed, and his or her main function was to help children to teach themselves rather than to give lessons in the traditional way. This meant that the teacher could work with several groups of pupils at once, with each group following a subject guide and proceeding at their own pace. The greater autonomy in learning conferred on the pupil meant that the timetable was flexible, allowing children to absent themselves for agricultural tasks at planting and harvest time. It also enabled one teacher to supervise five different grades. This methodology owed much to the enthusiasm of the late 1960s for radical pedagogical approaches.

The unitary school experiment was not as successful as it could have been because the necessary changes in teachers' training and curriculum revision were not introduced. These shortcomings were systematically addressed by the Escuela Nueva programme, launched in 1975. Practical problem-solving and the application of knowledge within the community rather than performance in tests became the hallmark of the methodology. Teachers were given a much fuller training in the philosophy and content of the programme. They were also encouraged to use popularly elected students to help run group work and to call upon parents and local officials to help with school management. Links between the school and the community were fostered. Stories and songs from the local culture were used in the classroom, which also became a conduit for information about health, nutrition and hygiene.

During its first few years, the programme was extended relatively slowly, but by 1985 there were 8,000 Escuelas Nuevas across the country. At this point, the Colombian Government decided to adopt the approach as the means to achieve universal rural primary education[45]. From 1987, with assistance from Unicef, a period of rapid expansion began. By 1989, nearly 18,000 of the 27,000 rural schools in the country had been embraced by the programme. Within three to four years, the expectation was to reach the entire rural primary school cohort. Studies undertaken in the late 1980s showed that Escuela Nueva students scored as well as or slightly better than students from traditional rural schools in terms of self-esteem, civic and social behaviour.

And they scored consistently higher in academic achievement tests, notably in mathematics and Spanish. Among teachers, 90 per cent believed that the new schools were superior[46].

These educational experiences, and many others that similarly aimed to provide a basic education efficiently and at low cost, came under close scrutiny during 1989 in the run-up to the World Conference on Education for All. Unicef helped a number of Ministries of Education to conduct investigations into their schooling situation and to hold preparatory seminars and workshops. The Conference itself, co-sponsored by UNESCO, Unicef, UNDP and the World Bank and hosted by the Thai Government, took place in Jomtien, Thailand, in March 1990. It attracted nearly 1,500 delegates and observers from 156 countries, four Heads of State, over 100 Ministers of Education, heads of several international organizations, professional teaching bodies and NGOs from all over the world. The participants unanimously adopted a World Declaration and a Framework for Action to meet the basic learning needs of every person—child, youth and adult—in the world.

The 'vision' of a basic package of knowledge and skills—a 'basic education'—to which everyone had a right was accepted. It would be up to countries to define their own version, but at a minimum, access to primary schooling should be universal[47]. Countries committed themselves to planning a strategy for achieving this access by the year 2000—although Jim Grant had to use all his powers of persuasion to have this date included in the conference Declaration—and to using this goal as the cutting edge in a broader 'Education for All' offensive. Also accepted was the principle that enrolment levels could no longer be used as a gauge of primary educational progress, and that assessment systems should be devised in each country to give a more accurate measure of how both pupils and educational programmes were faring.

The Conference also stressed that priority was to be given to girls and women, and to other disadvantaged groups: ethnic minorities, children in remote rural areas and children in 'especially difficult circumstances', notably those caught up in war, those with disabilities and those obliged to live and work on the streets. These emphases reflected the current concern with children's rights: the Convention on the Rights of the Child had recently been passed in the UN General Assembly. Finally, the Conference emphasized that the other elements of basic education, including early childhood development, adult literacy and basic knowledge for living, needed widespread promotion through all conceivable communications channels. This legitimization of the 'third channel'—the informal as opposed to the formal or non-formal educational route—was seen by Unicef as recognition of the important developmental role of social mobilization, both as a means to achieve other development goals and as a knowledge-conferring end in itself.

The stage had been set, just six months before the World Summit for Children, for the generation of new resources and action towards the goal of 'learning for all'.

In the original plans for the Conference, the concept of basic education did not include early childhood development. Only as a result of regional discussions and pressure from NGOs was the importance of special attention in the earliest years of life recognized as critical to the child's later educational attainment[48]. Children who took part in some kind of preschool programme where they learned the alphabet and took part in structured activities were more likely to go to school and to do well than those who did not. The effects of early childhood programmes on enrolment and school performance therefore captured the attention of policy makers seeking to cut the numbers of 'repeaters' and drop-outs. However, the argument connected to education was only one part of an impressive case for making early childhood care much more widely available.

Down the years, Unicef had been ambivalent about the degree of support it should offer the mental and psychosocial, as opposed to physical, development of the young child. Preschool centres in a number of countries had long been a target of Unicef assistance, but the rationale usually presented was the opportunity to provide a nutritious meal for youngsters, monitor their physical well-being and provide substitute care arrangements for overburdened mothers. While all child development experts were agreed that early stimulation improved the infant's and youngster's learning potential, the feeling persisted that many preschools were head-start programmes of a luxury kind for better-off children, and therefore had a less compelling claim on Unicef cooperation than did those attempting to ensure survival and physical well-being. The ideas of child development experts such as Piaget and Montessori seemed destined only for application in the industrialized world.

The 1979 International Year of the Child prompted new enthusiasm for early childhood development, and a number of countries instigated new preschool programmes[49]. Many borrowed ideas from the basic services approach, and set about helping communities run their own simple centres by providing training, backup and equipment to local volunteers. A typical example of such a programme was that launched in 1979 in the Dominican Republic, where a preschool department was created in the Ministry of Education. Its staff worked with local communities to select and train preschool *promotores*, build rudimentary thatched shelters, make playthings out of local materials and operate the centres. The community response to the scheme was enthusiastic, and within two years 20,000 children had been enrolled[50].

Similar programmes could be found in a number of Latin American countries, and early childhood care was a common feature of area-based and urban basic services programmes in Indonesia, the Philippines, Zambia and other countries in Asia and Africa. One of the most renowned was the Integrated Child Development Services programme in India, which, by 1985, had established networks of *anganwadis*—day-care centres for children aged three to six—in around 100,000 villages[51]. Although in the *anganwadis* provision of a nutritious meal was still seen as important, much more emphasis was now given to the young child's psychosocial development through play and interaction with peers.

Despite the success of this and other similar programmes, within Unicef the spotlight on early childhood development dimmed during the 1980s. The takeover by GOBI of Unicef's infancy and early childhood agenda meant that the policy focus—if less so the practice—was once again, as in Unicef's early years, virtually confined to the child's physical well-being. With few exceptions, little attention was given to psychosocial development as an integrated component within 'child survival and development revolution' programming. A policy review on early childhood development[52], which came before the Board in 1984, performed a useful function in reviewing the state of the programming art, but its recommendation that psychosocial concerns should be fully incorporated into health-promoting activities barely ruffled the child survival surface. Over the next few years, UNICEF put considerably more energy into incorporating child survival activities and messages into preschool programmes than into extending child survival to include mental, psychological and social well-being.

By the late 1980s, with the Education for All Conference on the horizon, moves were afoot to refocus attention on the non-physical components of the child development picture. Independently of Unicef's main priorities, the decade had witnessed mounting interest in early childhood, not only in the industrialized but in the developing world. This was in part a reflection of profound social and demographic changes. The urbanization explosion and the monetization of all aspects of life, the rising number of women raising children on their own—30 per cent of households in Latin America and the Caribbean were female-headed[53]—and the increasing entry of women into paid employment had turned custodial day care of their children into an essential need for millions of struggling families. Unlike her rural sister working in the fields, the poor urban mother could not easily take her toddler with her to the workplace. Nor did she have older female relatives living nearby with whom she could safely leave them. Under the pressures of contemporary life, family structures were changing, and traditional arrangements for early childhood care were vanishing.

The impact of these changes was manifest not only in Latin America and the Caribbean, which in the developing world had set the pace in organized early childhood care, but more strikingly in Asia. For example, in Korea, the percentage of children attending preschool programmes had risen from 8 to 57 per cent between 1982 and 1986; in Thailand, 24 per cent of children between ages three and six spent part of the day in a non-formal educational setting, and in the Philippines 19 per cent of this age group enjoyed 'early childhood enrichment'[54].

The scientific evidence accumulated from these experiences provided powerful ammunition for arguments that this kind of childhood enhancement should not be postponed until age five, when survival was more or less assured. Children in disadvantaged groups appeared to gain even more from it than the better-off. Structured care and stimulation at each developmental stage were far from being a luxury. Cognitive and social growth began automatically on the child's entry into the world. If neglected or actively hindered, this could have as profound a negative effect on the child's future well-being as—for example—the lack of a nutritionally optimal diet or the absence of clean water and sanitation. Child survival and child development—in all its guises—were interdependent.

The debates surrounding the Convention on the Rights of the Child also helped to underscore the fact that inadequate care in early childhood was an important predisposition not only for poor school performance but for landing up at an early age begging or working on the streets. Over the longer term, a poor start in childhood could lead to delinquency, unemployment and the intergenerational perpetuation of failure and poverty[55]. The Convention claimed on behalf of children the right to 'develop to their full potential', and Article 18 gave expression to the right of children of working parents to 'benefit from child-care services and facilities'. The need for an expansion of low-cost family and community-based services was reiterated in the World Summit Declaration and Plan of Action.

The 1989-90 series of landmark international commitments to a new vision of fulfilled childhood—the Convention, the Education for All Conference and the Summit—therefore marked the moment at which a degree of fusion finally occurred between the concepts of biological and other types of healthy growth. As a result, in the 1990s, a subject now redefined as 'early childhood care and development' (ECCD) entered a new phase of creative life.

Within Unicef, the new commitment to ECCD led to an effort to synthesize the wide range of experiences stemming from programmes all over the world and to draw the insights from them into future programming directions. There was still a need to counter the narrow, institutional, elitist and expensive image associated with preschools. A formula along the GOBI lines would be inappropriate; instead, a menu of different but complementary types of intervention was developed. One approach could be to educate caregivers. In China, for example, at the instigation of the All China Women's Federation, over 200,000 communities organized 'Parents' Schools', designed in part to help people adapt to parenting in the one-child family[56]. Included in the curriculum on child development was a Chinese version of *Facts for Life* produced by Unicef.

Another example of the 'educating caregivers' approach was the 'Child-to-Child' concept developed by the Institute of Child Health in London. This was pioneered in a number of countries, including Jamaica and Uganda, and was eventually adopted in 75 countries, including Romania and the UK[57]. The programmes were designed for school-going children aged 8 to 15, who could take health-promoting messages and actions back into the home. The normal parental and social expectation was that these children helped to look after their younger siblings as part of their household duties. The Child-to-Child syllabus helped to ensure that they performed their duties—bathing or feeding the baby, playing with him or her—in ways best designed for the child's development. Adult members of the family, it was hoped, would learn from them and follow their example.

The Child-to-Child curriculum taught growth monitoring, sound health and nutritional practice, and how to play with brothers and sisters, and included skills such as toy-making and ORS preparation. The programmes proved very effective in supporting the conventional GOBI package and in reaching beyond it to a fuller picture of stimulation and cognitive and social growth. In 1991, the Child-to-Child Trust won Unicef's annual award, given in memory of Maurice Pate, its first Executive Director, for what was described as a 'new, effective and revolutionary idea' in working with children for better health. In 1993, a publication called *Children for Health* was developed by the Child-to-Child Trust in association with Unicef for use by teachers, youth leaders and others working with children and young people. It contained an adaptation of *Facts for Life* messages, along with ideas on how to communicate them to children and ways in which to incorporate them into Child-to-Child: the two concepts thus became mutually reinforcing.

A different kind of approach towards early childhood development was support for the more typical village-based centre. Some of these—such as UPGK in Indonesia and Programa de Alimentação de Pre-escolar in Brazil—were originally inspired by the need for nutritional improvement, and later added cognitive skills; others—like the 'Entry Point' scheme in Nepal—were intended primarily to enable women involved in credit programmes to organize child care collectively and make better use of their time. All such programmes supplied a complementary environment to the home for part of the child's nurture and upbringing. Other approaches emphasized the strengthening of national institutions, developing national family policies or proposing changes in laws and regulations to protect the infants of working mothers or other children in difficult circumstances.

Last but not least, there was a need to inform parents and all those professionally concerned with children about the benefits to be gained from well-rounded early nurture. Hence the importance of the new chapter on early childhood development in the 1993 revision of *Facts for Life.*

In the wake of the Jomtien Conference, Unicef made strenuous efforts to ratchet up the level of human and financial resources committed to basic education, and—alongside UNESCO, the World Bank, and many other national, international, NGO and corporate partners—to make the 1990s as significant a decade for learning as the 1980s had been for child survival. At its first meeting after the Conference, the Unicef Executive Board approved a plan whereby allocations to basic education would rise from the level of 10 per cent in 1990 to reach 25 per cent by the year 2000—at which point they would equal the allocation to child health[58]. A team of senior advisers on education was recruited for Unicef headquarters and for the regional offices, and a number of country offices began to expand their capacity to support educational programming. In his own public statements, Jim Grant made it clear that though he was still as committed as ever to the child health agenda in the Children's Summit Declaration, he regarded education as critical in leading to and sustaining the achievement of all other Summit goals[59].

The idea that the universalization of primary education should be the cutting edge of Education for All was endorsed by the Joint Committee on Education (UNESCO and Unicef) in October 1991. By this time, Jomtien had already inspired a worldwide mobilization: governments, international agencies and NGOs had collaborated in holding over 100 conferences and round tables on Education for All issues, and an Education for All Forum had been established, based in UNESCO. Unicef had played an active role in these activities, encouraging and supporting the formulation of plans of action and other follow-up activities in over 70 countries. In 1993, a previous Minister of Education in Zimbabwe, Fay Chung, was invited to head Unicef's Education Cluster, and new energy was devoted to Unicef's own strategic thinking for the sector. A policy review in 1995 strongly reiterated Unicef's commitment to primary education as the most important component of basic education—whether in a conventional primary school or a more flexible schooling environment. 'Second chance' equivalents of primary education for youth and adults and early childhood care and development were regarded as important in helping to reach the EFA goal, as well as in their own right[60].

The twin thrusts of Unicef support to primary schooling were to make the classroom more accessible, especially to girls, and to increase schooling efficiency. This was to be achieved by promoting greater flexibility in the organization of the school and its management. Teaching and learning practices were to be geared towards making the school better fit the child's circumstances. At the same time, Unicef would support non-formal programmes in order to provide immediate places in the classroom to those whom the formal system would take many years to reach. This was described as a 'Bailey bridges' approach, indicating that it was meant to be a temporary but serviceable stopgap. Certainly, there was an immense task to be undertaken if there was to be any hope of meeting the goal established at Jomtien—Education for All by the year 2000. This goal had been endorsed by the World Summit for Children, with special emphasis not only on access to schooling, but on completion of the primary school cycle by 80 per cent of children. The mid-decade 'stepping-stone' goal for education adopted in 1993 was to promote primary education 'with gender equality'. Education was to be the main context in which Unicef pursued affirmative action on behalf of girls.

The part of the world in which Unicef was most active in this context was South Asia, mainly because of the attention the SAARC countries had decided to devote to the 'girl child'[61]. In this part of the world, girls' primary school enrolment trailed that of boys by 29 per cent[62]. The main reason for girls' absence was the time-honoured parental belief in the value of investing in sons rather than in daughters. Experience showed that resistance to sending girls to school dwindled where the classroom was nearby, and the opportunity cost to parents was reduced. In Bangladesh,

Bhutan and Nepal, enrolment rose when each community had its own small school and girls did not have to travel far to the classroom. This was especially important in societies where girls past puberty were not allowed to walk about the neighbourhood, or where they were at risk of sexual harassment. In Pakistan, girls were kept out of mixed schools and schools without separate washrooms. Providing separate facilities so as to be able to maintain sexual distance made a significant difference.

So did an active policy to train more women teachers. In Nepal, where the female teaching force rose from 3 per cent in 1971 to 10 per cent in 1980, girls' enrolment rose tenfold. In both Africa and the Middle East, advocacy on behalf of girls also began to pay dividends, if more slowly. Tanzania similarly focused on bringing more women into the teaching force, assigning 'female coordinators' to train underqualified girl teachers on the job. Within five years girls' enrolment jumped from 74 to 95 per cent of boys' enrolment[63]. Altogether, Unicef identified nine different types of approaches that purported to reduce the 'gender gap', including the provision of scholarships to compensate parents for the loss of household help and adjustments to the curriculum to make it relevant, practical and gender-neutral.

Another large group of children for whom accessibility to schooling was an issue consisted of those who lived in remote, mountainous or arid regions where population was scattered. For these settings, an increasing use was made of multi-grade schools, similar to those developed under the Escuela Nueva programme in Colombia. Multi-grade methodology was used in many poor and mountainous areas of Viet Nam, where a teacher learned how to instruct two classes in the same room simultaneously, each facing opposite ends and receiving the teacher's attention alternately. One-teacher schools were also used in the marginal rural areas of many Latin American countries other than Colombia: Bolivia, Mexico and Peru, for example.

Many indigenous peoples living in these areas—such as those in the high Andean *altiplano* in Bolivia and Peru—had suffered centuries not only of economic and social neglect, but of cultural oppression. For Aymara and Quechua children, accessibility to schooling not only meant the need for its physical presence, but for instruction in a language they could comprehend, and in terms that did not denigrate their own culture. In Bolivia, growing demand for cultural recognition by the 60 per cent of the population made up of indigenous peoples prompted the national Teachers' Union to insist upon educational reform. In 1988, with support from Unicef, a special unit was set up by the government to take this forward. In 1990, a new intercultural bilingual educational syllabus in three languages—Aymara, Quechua and Guarani—was introduced into the first grade in 114 schools. Each year, another grade was added so that by 1994, the original intake was in its fifth grade of bilingual instruction.

Evaluation of the programme showed a notable improvement in school performance, particularly in the lower number of 'repeaters'. Children who had learned Spanish as a foreign language were actually more proficient in it than those for whom Spanish had been the exclusive language of instruction. In the more developed Aymara and Quechua areas of the *altiplano*, there was some resistance to the programme from teachers and communities steeped in the old Spanish-driven ways, but among the Guarani of the Amazonian basin, the programme was enthusiastically received. Here it became a rallying point for the preservation and promotion of the Guarani cultural identity and the rights of indigenous people in general. In accordance with the tenets of the Convention on the Rights of the Child, intercultural and bilingual education in Bolivia had become an expression of the right of the child to be educated in the context of his or her own language and culture[64].

The need to improve primary schooling efficiency prompted an equally wide range of response. Some programmes focused on the quality of instruction, some on syllabus content, some on community management of schools and many on all three. All were designed to reduce drop-outs and repeaters and ensure a certain level of attainment at an economic cost per child. One outstanding programme was the Shikshak Samakhya or Teacher Empowerment Project (TEP) in the Indian state of Madhya Pradesh.

In this state, the largest and one of the least developed in India, the obstacles to reaching universal primary education seemed truly insuperable before the TEP programme was introduced. A low rate of school enrolment, particularly among girls and among scheduled castes and tribes, reflected all the usual problems prevalent in backward and remote rural areas, plus the extremely dysfunctional condition of their primary schools. Teachers did their best not to be posted to schools in such areas, to the point of irregular twisting of officialdom's arms, and those who were appointed often simply failed to turn up. If they did, the order of the day was rote learning and scolding by turns. The teachers' low motivation and negligible professional commitment was the product of poor training and lack of orientation towards the needs of children from backgrounds regarded as socially and culturally inferior[65].

Shikshak Samakhya set out to revive regard for teaching as a noble profession whose practitioner—the guru—was a person of high status and self-esteem commanding the trust and respect of pupils and parents alike. One-day reorientation courses for teachers were conducted in a typical classroom, transformed overnight by the painting of bright pictures and a three-foot-high blackboard all around the room. The training emphasized children's participation, stimulation and gaining their attention through teacher-child interaction, singing, dancing and learning-by-doing. Teachers were expected to use these techniques in their own classrooms, to make their own materials and to be creative in inventing songs and games. At the end of the session, teachers pledged their continuous commitment to their work and to their school for a minimum of five years. They were expected to gain the same commitment from their pupils to attend. They also received a small grant with which to brighten up the classroom. As members of associations of newly trained peers, they met regularly and received follow-up from the educational authorities.

By late 1994, more than 50,000 teachers of Standard I children had been reoriented. Plans had been made to complete the reorientation of all 160,000 such teachers in Madhya Pradesh by the end of 1995. Each year, another class has been added in a phased, incremental way so that all five primary grades are gradually moving over to an action-oriented curriculum and teaching style. The designers of the approach, which include staff from Unicef's Bhopal office, have developed a monitoring system that allows them to measure its capacity to attract children to school, keep them there and enable them to master specific knowledge and skills. By early 1995, in Dhar district, where the programme was first introduced, enrolment in Standard I had risen substantially, and in a number of schools the performance of children in Standard I had overtaken that of children in Standard II[66]. Progress towards UPE was being achieved in a sustainable way at very low cost.

In December 1993, the international movement for Education for All gained a boost in momentum. An Education Summit of the nine most populous nations in the developing world (dubbed the E-9)—Bangladesh, Brazil, China, Egypt, India, Indonesia, Mexico, Nigeria and Pakistan—was held in New Delhi. Heads of State and their representatives pledged commitment to the goal of reaching universal basic education. Between them, these nine countries accounted for 2.7 billion people, half the world's population, and almost three quarters of its illiterates. It was in these countries, seven of which had a good chance of reaching UPE by the year 2000, that the main battle for basic education would be lost or won. In his statement to the New Delhi Summit, Jim Grant described Education for All as 'at the centre of the revolution in human development'. He continued: 'Progress towards the EFA goals must be accelerated with both national and international resources if we are not to fall further behind in the struggle to narrow the rich-poor chasms in the global society.'[67]

While recognizing the many initiatives that gave great cause for hope, UNESCO sounded a similarly apocalyptic note. Despite all the progress of recent years, rising numbers in the school-going age group were still making quantitative achievements appear negligible. An estimated 162 million children, 70 per cent of them girls, would be excluded from primary school in the year 2000 unless a breakthrough in basic education was managed within the next few years. Of these, 72 million would be South Asian children, and 52 million, sub-Saharan African[68]. The 'world crisis in education' was still far from being solved.

Early in 1994, the four organizations that had backed Jomtien—Unicef, UNESCO, UNDP and the World Bank—began to consider a special African Education for All Initiative, complementary to the already launched E-9 programme, which included Egypt and Nigeria. Some African countries, notably two of the Southern African countries that had gained internationally recognized independence in the 1980s, Namibia and Zimbabwe, were investing heavily in primary education. Zimbabwe had managed to double primary school enrolment in the almost unbelievable time-frame of two years by a variety of measures: double-session teaching, training teachers *in situ*, rationalizing the curriculum and devolving financial and managerial responsibility for schools onto the community[69]. But this tremendous public policy commitment was very much a reaction to the long years of white minority rule and the skewed schooling investment of the past. The story of Zimbabwe's success contrasted sadly with the situation in countries without so strong a political impetus for educational reform and with fewer resources. In many African countries, the long years of debt and structural adjustment had led to heavy reductions in educational expenditures and eroded the physical fabric and quality of schooling. In 1990, it was estimated that one half of school-age children in Africa were not in school, and all the signs in the first part of the decade were that this negative trend was continuing[70].

Worse still, the eruption of wars and civil conflicts, many of them symptomatic of the 'new world disorder' to which the end of the cold war had given birth not only in Africa but elsewhere, meant that millions of children were being deprived of anything resembling a normal, structured, regular school-going childhood. In this climate, two new themes began to emerge. The first was attention to children's educational and psychosocial well-being as an important element of emergency relief, often by setting up schools in relief camps and among displaced populations. An example of this was the 'school in a box' project introduced in the aftermath of the 1994 Rwandan emergency, whereby

11,500 teachers were trained in using a portable kit that enabled them to set up a classroom anywhere[71].

The other new theme was 'Education for Peace'. In countries such as former Yugoslavia and Lebanon, Unicef began to support programmes for children who had been brought up among violence, communal hatreds and factionalism, and who might well carry such attitudes forward into adulthood were they not replaced with ideas of mutual understanding and a belief in the virtues of peaceful coexistence. In the humanitarian as well as the development context, education was undergoing a renaissance.

Chapter 9

Children at the Front Line

When the 'ICEF' was created by the UN General Assembly in 1946, it was to provide emergency help to children in Europe and elsewhere suffering war-induced deprivation in the aftermath of World War II. When the organization achieved permanence in 1953, its remit was broadened to include children suffering the effects of more general poverty and deprivation, and the word 'Emergency' was dropped from its title. But the imperative to respond to children in special need as a result of war or other disaster was already indelibly stamped in Unicef's genes.

In the 1950s, the era of the disease campaign, there was a strong desire to place prevention ahead of cure, and in the 1960s, the era of the development crusade, an even stronger urge to give priority to the lasting solution. In 1960, the Swedish delegation to the Executive Board even proposed that Unicef should drop out of emergency first aid altogether[1]. But this idea provoked considerable opposition. It was neither desirable nor practicable for the leading international organization for children to ignore the 'loud' as opposed to the 'silent' emergencies.

However distracting emergencies might be from the ongoing preventive and developmental task, the provision of help for child victims of major tragedies was a crucial part of the organization's mandate: this was the expectation of the public, the media, donors, Unicef field staff, National Committees and secretariat. To leave all such action to the responsibility of others would have been incomprehensible. The organization's reputation and credibility depended upon being active, and being seen to be active, at times when the sufferings of those it existed to help were bathed in the glare of publicity. This was reinforced after it became routine for disasters, even in remote places, to be paraded on the nightly television news. Besides which, Unicef was an organization invented to provide 'material assistance'—the goods in the hand so sorely needed in emergency circumstances—and over the years had developed an expertise and capacity in supply procurement unparalleled in the rest of the UN system.

But the degree of involvement, and the disaster relief role of a children's as compared with other types of humanitarian organization: these issues beset Unicef almost from its inception. The question of how much organizational time, energy and resources should be spent on relief as opposed to development is one that has been frequently revisited over the course of Unicef's history. On the one hand, Unicef has always been jealous of its—usually—high reputation for swift and impartial humanitarian action, and aware of the publicity and fund-raising opportunities emergencies provide. On the other, its organizational culture has persistently marginalized emergency work, treating it as inferior to—sometimes as a diversion from—long-term programming for development[2]. If development efforts would only be successful, the argument ran (not just in Unicef but in many NGOs), disasters would not occur. Or if they did, not at least on a scale beyond the capacity of the country in question to handle without inviting or having to accept assorted ranks of international relief warriors rushing to their assistance.

During the 1970s, when the basic services strategy and the country programming process were being developed as the purpose and framework for Unicef cooperation, the question of how to respond to emergencies and what priority should be attached to emergency activity was left out of the process[3]. The problem of how to bring emergency action back into the Unicef mainstream was not subsequently satisfactorily resolved. Questions surrounding Unicef's role in emergencies were supplied with answers on an entirely ad hoc basis. In exceptional circumstances an emergency programme might become an organizational priority: the Bihar famine in India (1966), for example; the Nigerian civil war (1967-70); the Bengal cyclone (1970) and the subsequent creation of Bangladesh (1971); to a lesser extent in the African droughts and famines of the 1970s and in the countries of Indo-China throughout the Viet Nam War period[4]. In some of these situations, especially those that were politically sensitive, the Unicef Executive Director took a prominent role in negotiating or leading the relief programme. For example, Maurice Pate, Unicef's first Executive Director, was asked by the then UN Secretary-General—Dag Hammarskjöld—to help initiate a UN humanitarian operation in response to famine in the Congo in 1960; Henry Labouisse, the second Executive Director, was the key UN humanitarian negotiator in Lagos during the famine crisis associated with the Nigerian Civil War[5].

When Jim Grant took over at Unicef in 1980, he inherited the largest and most complex humanitarian relief operation the organization had ever shouldered. Twelve months before, the Vietnamese army had invaded and conquered Cambodia (then Kampuchea), ending the four-year reign of terror conducted by the Khmer Rouge under their leader, Pol Pot. The disruption of agriculture and ordinary economic life under the Khmer Rouge between 1975 and 1978, followed by their further disruption by the Vietnamese 'liberation', led to severe food shortages and a threatened famine. But the political complexities of the situation all but mired international efforts to come to the rescue of the Cambodian people.

Because Viet Nam had committed an aggression against its neighbour, an aggression excoriated by all its usual opponents—the Chinese, the ASEAN countries, the US and its Western allies—the regime installed in Phnom Penh was denied international recognition, no matter how preferable it was to the one it had replaced. Most of the UN system was therefore unable to interact with the authorities in Phnom Penh. But Unicef had developed ways of navigating around such insuperable obstacles to UN diplomacy as 'international recognition' and 'sovereign inviolability'. The Secretary-General, then Kurt Waldheim, had therefore turned to Henry Labouisse at Unicef, and asked the Children's Fund to act as 'lead agency' for the entire UN system inside Kampuchea. The relief operation both inside the country and on the Thai-Kampuchean border was to be run in conjunction with the International Committee of the Red Cross (ICRC).

The request to act in such a linchpin humanitarian role derived from Unicef's success in upholding over several decades the principle that children are above the political divide. At the time of Unicef's creation, Maurice Pate had insisted that no child should be seen as an 'enemy' and thereby disqualified from receiving Unicef assistance. At the beginning of the cold war, at the moment when the US was refusing to help victims of war in Europe via the existing UN mechanism because its aid went impartially to people in both Eastern and Western Europe[6], this was a more exceptional stand than it appears today.

The critical phrase in Unicef's founding resolution was that assistance should be dispensed 'on the basis of need, without discrimination because of race, creed, nationality, status or political belief'. Thereafter, by applying a certain elasticity of interpretation, Unicef had behaved as if this clause meant that it was not held up to quite the same rigorous rules of diplomatic conduct in respect of sovereignty as other UN bodies. A record of working on both sides of civil wars had been established since 1948, in the earliest instance in the conflicts in Greece, in China and in the Middle East, even though this meant working through de facto authorities unrecognized as legitimate by other UN Member States. In 1965, Unicef's record on behalf of victims of armed conflict had been given international recognition with the award of the Nobel Peace Prize.

The principle of 'children above the political divide' gradually gained weight with use. It had reached a new level of acceptance and operationalization—despite all attendant political difficulties—during the 1967-70 Nigerian Civil War. Alongside the International Committee of the Red Cross, the organization that epitomized the idea of international humanitarian neutrality in wartime, Unicef had functioned as the conduit into rebel-held 'Biafra' for a major input of UN and international relief. Henry Labouisse had undertaken a mission to Lagos in mid-1968 and—with great difficulty—obtained the tacit agreement of the federal authorities in Nigeria to a relief operation that crossed what they regarded as enemy lines[7]. During the Nigerian conflict, with all its inter-ethnic hatred and accusations of genocide and atrocity, Unicef had never lost the confidence of either side—a tribute to the quiet negotiating skills of Labouisse and to the transcendence of the children's cause. A few years later, Labouisse managed to obtain agreement for Unicef to send aid to children on both sides of the Vietnamese conflict. In this instance he had to overcome both the isolationism of a communist regime suspicious of a UN, and therefore Western-tainted, organization, and the extreme displeasure of the US government, a major Unicef backer[8].

In the case of Kampuchea in 1979, the 'aid on both sides' principle was upheld with the gravest difficulty. The authorities in Phnom Penh demanded as a condition of receiving aid from Unicef and ICRC that none be provided to women and children at the Thai border still under the control of the Khmer Rouge. The two organizations' representatives found Kampuchean officials completely unable to comprehend that in order to meet this demand, Unicef and the Red Cross would have to abandon sacrosanct principles of humanitarian neutrality. To this they could not agree[9]. Matters came to a head in October 1979 and a formula was accepted whereby neither the agencies nor the authorities conceded the other's point of view. After this, a massive airlift of emergency supplies from Bangkok into Phnom Penh finally went ahead[10]. By the time Grant took over at Unicef in January 1980, Unicef and ICRC were not only leading a huge supply and logistic operation inside Kampuchea to stave off famine, but also—alongside UNHCR—running a major relief programme on the Thai-Kampuchean border for 500,000 refugees fleeing the Khmer Rouge.

For the next two years until the end of 1981, Unicef was obliged to continue to carry the UN 'lead agency' role in Kampuchea. This was because the political sensitivities surrounding the status of the Phnom Penh regime proved intractable as long as Vietnamese troops remained in the country, shoring up the security situation and the regime. Over the two-year period, the joint UN and ICRC programme, in which Unicef shouldered the lion's share of the administrative burden inside Kampuchea and much of it outside the stricken country, delivered some $634 million in assistance[11]. Grant himself was obliged to devote a considerable amount of his own time and energy to heading up 'lead agency' activities, and was deeply conscious of the diversion of organizational resources—especially of some of the brightest and best of his staff.

This experience had a major influence on Grant's attitude towards Unicef's role in emergency relief during his forthcoming leadership. However visible and popular prominence in a major emergency might make Unicef, the price in terms of the rest of the organization's agenda was much too high in his opinion. Being 'lead agency' included coordinating UN appeals and providing all-around support for the Secretary-General's representative and other UN agencies' programmes on the ground. Grant was not primarily a relief impresario. He was, on the contrary, deeply committed to the human development agenda, having already spent his lifetime's career in its service. From the outset at Unicef, he made it clear that his principal mission was to help combat the 'silent emergency' of child ill-health and poverty in the developing countries. He therefore resolved that he would in future try to prevent Unicef from being nominated as 'lead agency' for the UN system in a humanitarian crisis. This explains why, in 1985, at the height of the Ethiopian famine, he strongly backed the establishment of a special Office for Emergency Operations in Africa (OEOA) within the UN Secretariat[12]. He was very aware that lending staff and loaning facilities to a separate operation would be much less organizationally draining than shouldering all the responsibility. It was his constant worry that child survival initiatives would falter if Unicef became sucked remorselessly into the bottomless pit of relief provision.

However, there was an important context in which Grant promoted Unicef action in emergencies. The principle to which Unicef had been committed since its earliest years—that children are above the political divide—was one that Grant heartily embraced. In the early 1980s, he began to search for ways to exploit this principle on behalf of the 'child survival and development revolution'.

* * * * *

The idea that children had a special claim to be protected from the scourge of war had first been articulated by the Save the Children Fund (UK) during the First World War and had gained ground in public consciousness steadily throughout the century. During the early 1980s, this idea began to accumulate new force. Civilians rather than armed soldiers appeared to be bearing an increasingly heavy burden of death and injury during war. Around 20 million people had lost their lives in conflicts since 1945, and among these the civilian proportion had risen from around 50 per cent to 80 or even 90 per cent in more recent wars. The overwhelming majority of deaths were among poor families in the developing world, and especially among women and children[13].

At the 1983 session of the Unicef Executive Board, Nils Thedin, the leading delegate of Sweden and a long-time Unicef elder statesman, proposed what at first hearing sounded like an old man's dream: that children be declared a 'neutral, conflict-free zone in human relations'[14]. This call came from Thedin's lifelong commitment to finding ways of protecting children from the fallout of man's inhumanity to man—especially in a more violent world, a world in which military strife and conflict were increasingly intruding into ordinary people's lives. In the past, the innocence and vulnerability of children had been cited as a pretext for shielding them from warfare and as a justification for humanitarian efforts on their behalf. Thedin now took this idea further forward, advancing the notion that where children were, there should warfare cease.

This call, repeated with force during the 1984 Unicef Executive Board discussion on 'children in especially difficult circumstances'[15], resonated with Grant, never one to be deterred by a good idea's apparently hopeless impracticality. Later that year, at a meeting in the office of UN Secretary-General Javier Pérez de Cuéllar with President Napoleon Duarte of El Salvador, Grant glimpsed an opportunity to put Thedin's idea into effect[16], at the same time combining it with his current main objective: the 'child survival revolution'.

At the time, civil war was raging in El Salvador. Grant proposed a unilateral cessation of hostilities on both sides—army and rebel—to allow a period of what Duarte called '*tranquilidad*' so that parents could take their children to be immunized. After protracted negotiations with guerrilla leaders by senior bishops of the Roman Catholic Church, both sides agreed to a series of daylong lulls in the fighting early in 1985. These were not to be called cease-fires or truces: neither side wanted to appear to be showing a white flag.

Thus was born the idea of 'days of tranquillity': days on which a war was stopped so that something so comparatively mundane as a children's vaccination programme could take place. On three days in consecutive months, the Salvadoran conflict gave way to a programme in which 3,000 health workers immunized nearly 250,000 small children against polio, measles, diphtheria, tetanus and whooping cough. At the instigation of Unicef, and with considerable help from others—including ICRC and the Vatican—Thedin's concept had been realized. The significance of the achievement was far greater than its tally of around two thirds of Salvadoran children immunized—somewhat lower than the target of 80 per cent. 'This reconciliation for progress and the common good announced loudly El Salvador's commitment to a positive future and has been an inspiration to the rest of the world,' wrote Pérez de Cuéllar in a letter to President Duarte[17].

The 'days of tranquillity' experiment was repeated in El Salvador regularly every year until the end of the civil war six years later, by which time the 80 per cent target had been reached and consistently sustained. The Pan-American Health Organization (PAHO) had used the opportunity to introduce other activities—nutrition education, family planning advice and supplies—under the banner of 'Health: a bridge for peace'[18]. As importantly, the Salvadoran 'days of tranquillity' had set a precedent for similar experiments elsewhere.

In 1986, independent negotiations with the Ugandan government of Milton Obote and with the Ugandan National Resistance Army under Yoweri Museveni led to the establishment of 'corridors of peace'—also for a countrywide vaccination campaign. In the case of El Salvador, parallel campaigns had been run on both sides of the battle lines; in the case of Uganda, the parties agreed to allow the campaign machinery to cross over from one side to the other. Vaccines, personnel and equipment were funnelled into the war zone through special air and land corridors. The first flight along a 'corridor of peace' in Africa took place on United Nations Day, 24 October 1986.

A few months later, in March 1987, following negotiations with the warring parties in Lebanon, a similar exercise took place in Beirut. In 1988-89, vaccination teams operated in Afghanistan in both government-controlled and *mujahidin*-controlled areas and succeeded in raising immunization coverage levels to 80 per cent in some areas[19]. To what extent these exercises helped to create the preconditions for an overall reduction in hostilities can only be speculative, but that they began to etch in the international consciousness an acceptance that children could—and should—be treated as a 'zone of peace' seems certain. When, after a few flights into the Ugandan venture, the 'corridor' nearly broke down, it was reinstated with a public declaration by the government that 'we all have children and we are all Ugandans'[20].

Every occasion on which warring parties could be persuaded to put down their guns to give priority to children's future well-being not only helped to build up a case-load of precedent, but added force to a principle incipiently taking on the character of an international moral norm. Ironically, the enforcement of this norm could be managed only by the exercise of great political acuity. To be non-political—to put children's health momentarily above all political considerations including the waging of a war—required being highly political; engaging with the political process, even on behalf of children, entailed taking considerable risks. Any subsequent opprobrium that might descend on the leadership in question might tarnish even actions they had taken—apparently disinterestedly—on behalf of children. Some of the more daring Unicef representatives faced these challenges willingly; many took their cue from Grant, whose skills as a negotiator with Presidents and leading officials they built upon and emulated.

It was Grant's track record in this context that led to his appointment by UN Secretary-General Pérez de Cuéllar as the leader of Operation Lifeline Sudan (OLS). During 1988, a disastrous famine had caused the loss of 250,000 lives and led to the displacement of nearly half the 6 million inhabitants of southern Sudan[21]. This tragedy was the outcome of many years of civil war exacerbated by drought, which had driven people from their homes and caused a complete breakdown in traditional food security systems[22]. By January 1989, it had become clear that unless a massive effort was made before the rainy season to move supplies to strategically placed depots throughout the country, a similar tragedy would ensue over the coming months. An estimated 2.25 million people were in need of emergency assistance, of whom 600,000 were in imminent danger of starvation.

Accordingly, a joint government and UN meeting at the highest level was convened in Khartoum in early March to come up with a relief and supply delivery plan. Jim Grant led the UN delegation on behalf of the Secretary-General, and the meeting was attended by senior representatives of the Sudanese Government, UNDP, WFP (World Food Programme), FAO, ICRC, NGOs and bilateral donors. The meeting took place in an atmosphere of widespread scepticism. Since 1983, the Government had been locked in combat with the Sudan People's Liberation Army (SPLA), and both protagonists in an ugly civil war had persistently obstructed relief efforts mounted on behalf of civilians outside their control[23]. The SPLA was not represented at the 'high-level meeting' and predictably denounced it as 'illegal and a deep conspiracy'. To win approval in such a climate for a plan that involved delivering large supplies of food through 'peace corridors' or their equivalent to civilians on the enemy side of the fighting lines required great delicacy of negotiation.

So as not to antagonize the Government, all references to SPLA-held territory in the conference documentation were suitably oblique, but for the first time in UN relief assessments in the Sudan, projections of the needs in such areas were explicitly included. In order to make arrangements to reach such areas, it was suggested that the responsible UN officials should deal directly with the insurgents. Obtaining agreement to this provision was the vital breakthrough for it enabled humanitarian needs throughout southern Sudan to be addressed. The principle of humanitarian neutrality—that aid should be given not only to children but to all civilian non-combatants independently of whose control they were under and that relief programmes should not be regarded as weapons of war—was given official recognition. As a result, the SPLA decided to give the plan its support.

The Government agreed to an initial month of tranquillity during which relief efforts could proceed without fear of military action; the SPLA also accepted this idea with the proviso that only specified 'corridors of tranquillity' should be used for the safe passage of relief personnel and goods. These were to be negotiated through the mediation of UN officials, which effectively meant the mediation of Grant. The all-around consent to the plan was described by Grant with some hyperbole as 'historic'; certainly, it was in a different league from obtaining agreement to a vaccination campaign, which, unlike food supplies, could have no military or strategic usefulness[24]. The establishment of Lifeline was certainly a major achievement. It was also one for which a great deal was owed to Grant, both personally and because his position at the head of Unicef allowed the UN to overcome its normal inhibitions about working on both sides of a civil war and the invasion of sovereignty that this implied.

OLS was thus brought into being as a special UN operation, staffed by personnel seconded by Unicef and other UN organizations. Time was not on their side. Convoys of food supplies had to be dispatched and delivered by air, train, barge and truck to some of the most remote and worst-affected towns in the south, in some cases arriving no later than mid-April. Altogether, an estimated 120,000 metric tons of food and non-food supplies had to be delivered by September 1989—just six months away—through terrain that was hostile in every sense of the word. In order to keep things moving and iron out operational difficulties concerning the 'tranquillity corridors', Grant paid eight visits to the Sudan during this period and injected considerable energy into OLS. He also projected the suffering of the Sudanese people onto the world stage in such a way as to garner international publicity and financial support. By the end of September, when Grant handed over the leadership of OLS to Michael Priestley of UNDP, 88 per cent of the relief supplies—or 103,000 tons of food and 4,000 of medical and other non-food supplies—had been delivered to their many destinations.

Much of the donkey work of organizing depots and actually distributing food and other supplies to the population was carried out by NGOs, many of which had been conducting relief programmes in SPLA-held territory from bases in Uganda and Kenya for the past few years. Unicef itself, which had previously been prevented by the Khartoum Government from working in areas under the control of the SPLA, now began to supply cold-chain and other EPI equipment for immunization. By October 1989, vaccination clinics had become operational in all garrison towns and camps for displaced people, and had reached 90,000 children in SPLA areas.

The many organizations operating under the Lifeline umbrella continued to conduct their programmes autonomously; the contribution of Lifeline was to provide them—Unicef included—with an overarching political framework, mutually accepted by the warring parties, in which these relief efforts could take place. Lifeline also brought about a reduction in the level of fighting, at least along the 'corridors of tranquillity', and therefore temporarily enabled some of the people of southern Sudan to resume a lifestyle approximating to normal. Above all it gave people hope. Even though Lifeline's operations were interrupted at times when government forces and rebels intensified their military operations, never again did civilian despair become so widespread or intensive. A second phase of Lifeline was negotiated and began in March 1990, and with stops and starts Lifeline has been running ever since.

Operation Lifeline Sudan was an important milestone in the opening up of 'humanitarian space'. The provisioning of beleaguered populations in time of war can never be detached from its strategic and military implications; nevertheless, both sides in the Sudanese conflict recognized that to deny food to innocent people, especially children, who happen fortuitously to be under an enemy's control is to breach an international moral code. In the media age, actions that induce widespread human suffering cannot long be kept from public attention and tend to call down an unwelcome degree of international opprobrium. Among other political and military considerations, this one may not always win the day, but at least in the Sudan—as elsewhere—it is among the factors to be put in the balance. In elevating the rights of ordinary humanity to be treated as if they were something more than the pawns of warring parties, OLS set an important precedent on the African continent and helped to advance the humanitarian cause worldwide.

In Unicef, involvement with OLS represented a high point in the organization's identification with the principle of 'children above the political divide'. Since that time, there has not been a concerted effort to codify the principles involved or identify where next to take the concept. Although this is a cause of regret, it is perhaps inevitable. The nature of some of the conflicts in the recent past—notably those in Rwanda and Burundi—has set back the moral and legal extension of what, up to 1991-92, was a fledgling 'new humanitarian order' designed to protect innocent civilians, especially children, and has left its advocates floundering in horrified disbelief.

Within the international humanitarian community, including among the most active and experienced emergency-oriented NGOs such as Médecins sans Frontières and Oxfam, relief operations in the Sudan opened up an important debate on 'humanitarian neutrality'[25]. This debate, which has remained ongoing, gained force during the flight of Iraqi Kurds into Turkey in early 1991 after their uprising in the wake of the Gulf War. Questions were repeatedly raised about the degree to which the sovereignty of a government over all the peoples it claims to rule ought to be respected in cases where there are gross breaches of civil rights, especially where a civilian population is the intended victim of military action by the government in question. The 'safe havens' established by the international community in Turkey in 1991 can be said to have exemplified the notion of 'children and innocent civilians as a zone of peace'. They were justified *ex post facto* by what was called the 'right of humanitarian intervention'[26]. Whatever the subsequent advances and retreats surrounding this new grounds for international military action, the creation of 'safe havens' turned out to be a precedent unlikely to be much repeated. It could only occur because of all but global unanimity among the nations concerning the actions of a joint enemy.

The complexities surrounding such issues became ever more tortuous as the 1990s advanced and certain countries in Africa and the ex-USSR descended into chaotic inter-ethnic and internecine turmoil. In the post–cold war world, the question of how to expand and uphold 'humanitarian space' has become ever more pressing.

The increase in emergencies over the decade of the 1980s, especially in Africa, led to a new consciousness of their effect on child victims. This consciousness mainly emanated from countries such as Afghanistan, Angola, Mozambique and Uganda, where a fluctuating state of emergency, interspersed with military action, was ongoing for a period of years.

At headquarters, Unicef was very preoccupied with the 'child survival revolution'. In the context of disaster response, it was inclined to stress the suitability of GOBI interventions for children's health and physical well-being in relief camps and against cholera, measles and other epidemics[27]. The 'GOBI in emergencies' approach was an extension of Unicef's traditional view of children as the most vulnerable members of any population caught up in emergencies both 'loud' and 'silent'. But on the ground in places where emergency had become a way of life, an additional perspective was emerging.

With the growth of interest in children in their own right had come a new awareness that disasters had specific impacts on children and childhood, and that these impacts needed their own responses. This was particularly the case in emergencies associated with war. When the 1984 Unicef Executive Board asked for a review of 'children in especially difficult circumstances', one of the categories of children to be included in the CEDC definition—largely thanks to Nils Thedin and his promotion of 'children as a zone of peace'—was 'children in situations of armed conflict'[28]. This decision was a symptom of a renaissance of national and international interest in a group of children whose particular problems had tended to slip from view since the end of the immediate postwar period in Europe and Asia. The pioneers in raising these child protection issues—both as advocates and in programming terms—were, as usual, the NGOs, especially those within the Save the Children international alliance.

The special Unicef study prepared for the CEDC review not only examined the consequences of war on children in terms of death and injury, but drew attention to the profound psychosocial problems children were liable to suffer in an armed struggle in which a high proportion of the casualties were civilian. As Unicef had discovered in many earlier emergency settings, including those affecting the children of Viet Nam in the early 1970s and Kampuchea in 1979-80[29], children who had become caught up in conflict often bore hidden psychological scars that could take a lifetime to erase.

The earliest studies of the effects of armed conflict on children were undertaken in combat areas during the Second World War and among concentration camp survivors. From these it emerged that war had an all-embracing impact on a child's development, attitudes, experience of human relations, moral norms and outlook on life. Facing violence on a continuous basis created deep-rooted feelings of helplessness and undermined the child's trust in others[30]. The most common form of damage resulted from a child's separation from one or both parents because of their death or 'disappearance'. A child who had seen a parent or close relative being murdered or tortured, who had witnessed the wanton destruction of the family home, who had been forced to participate in acts of violence or who had been abducted, kidnapped or driven into flight from home bore psychological scars that could manifest themselves in disturbed behaviour for a long time afterwards.

From the mid-1980s onward, following the pioneering work of NGOs such as the UK Save the Children Fund, Unicef began to develop programme approaches to help children overcome fears and terrors that had become deeply implanted in their subconscious. One of the countries in which this was an early Unicef preoccupation was Mozambique. Many outrages of almost unbelievable cruelty were committed against children by the Mozambican National Resistance (Renamo) during the South African–backed insurrection of the 1980s. Significant numbers were abducted and taught to show no fear or sympathy, then forced to kill other children, even their own family members. By 1987, Renamo was believed to have murdered 100,000 people and committed widespread atrocities on ordinary civilians, including many children. Estimates of children traumatized, orphaned or abandoned ranged from 250,000 to 500,000, up to 10 per cent of the age group[31]. Unicef conducted surveys into the effects on children and published the results in its series of reports on *Children on the Front Line* designed to bring attention to the plight of children in southern Africa (see Chapter 6). Unicef also began to support programmes for the mental and emotional rehabilitation of Mozambican children. Primary-school teachers were trained in counselling techniques to enable children to express their feelings of terror and anxiety through drawing pictures and writing essays.

These techniques also began to be applied by Unicef in other theatres of East African conflict such as Uganda and the Sudan. Assistance was sought from a Norwegian child psychologist, Magne Raundalen. A stronger emphasis also began to be placed on education within emergency assistance as a vehicle for the social rehabilitation of children and for their emotional repair. In Mozambique, Unicef paid for the reconstruction of primary schools, 2,500 of which had been destroyed by armed attack[32]. In other settings, such as Sri Lanka, workshops or 'talk-shops' were organized to help young people explore their feelings about conflict and its resolution and share their experiences through structured discussions and exercises[33].

A remarkable effort to enable children to shed the hatreds and social divisions experienced in a wartime upbringing took place in Lebanon. 'Education for Peace' was initiated by the Unicef office in Beirut early in 1989 at a time when a mounting wave of violence had closed the schools and confined children to their homes and bomb shelters. Unicef had long been aware that because of the country's state of armed division, the children of Lebanon were growing up in separate enclaves with no physical chance to meet. So it was decided to remedy this situation by running a 'peace camp' where the children from different cultural and religious backgrounds could meet and get to know each other.

As a start, a group of young people aged from 18 to 25 with scouting and similar experience were trained by Unicef as camp monitors. The first camp was planned for July 1989 in a village far away from the scene of hostilities. After the rival militias and their various factions were advised of Unicef's intentions, buses carrying the Unicef flag drove the children through the Beirut checkpoints. The two weeks spent living together dissolved misunderstandings and created firm friendships. Unicef staff were surprised less by the happy intermingling of the smaller children than by the lack of mutual distrust displayed by the monitors, who proved able to discard attitudes absorbed from their elders and confirmed by a lifetime surrounded by violence.

So popular was the idea of bringing together children from the different communities that before the first camp was over, other organizations had begun to operate day camps under the Education for Peace banner at playgrounds, schools and community centres. Unicef managed the curriculum and training of all monitors and provided transportation as well. It was a rule that the participating children—including those in Palestinian refugee camps—must come from more than one area of the country. By the end of the 1989 summer season, around 29,000 children aged between 5 and 12 had attended peace camps of one kind or another. During the following year more than 240 NGOs collaborated with Unicef to promote the programme, and 40,000 children altogether took part. In the next phase of the programme, Unicef developed a curriculum for use in schools and a series of weekend events that took place throughout the year[34].

Many Education for Peace activities developed for use in Lebanese classrooms were subsequently incorporated—along with others from Liberia, Northern Ireland and Sri Lanka—into classroom projects in industrialized countries under the rubric of 'Education for Development'. This entailed the promotion among young people in both industrialized and developing countries of values such as global solidarity, peace, tolerance and environmental awareness. This attempt to educate the coming generation for world citizenship took its cue from the statement in the Convention on the Rights of the Child that a child's education should prepare the way for 'responsible life . . . in the spirit of understanding, peace, tolerance, equality of the sexes and friendship among peoples'. Not only in the classrooms of Lebanon and Sri Lanka did young people need to unlearn entrenched attitudes about the 'alien other'; they needed to do the same in Europe and North America—as became more conspicuous after the outbreak of hostilities in former Yugoslavia[35].

The wars of the 1980s brought into view another abuse of childhood prompted by armed conflict: the use of children as soldiers. This phenomenon first came to widespread international attention during the Iran-Iraq war, when half a million Iranian boys aged between 12 and 18 were recruited into the armed forces and thousands were reported to have lost their lives functioning as human mine detectors[36]. The recruitment of children who had become orphaned or lost contact with their families into the ranks of Museveni's Ugandan National Resistance Army was another notorious incidence of child soldiering. During the 'corridors of peace' initiative in 1985-86 to vaccinate children on both sides of the fighting line, Unicef representative Cole Dodge took the opportunity of protesting both to Museveni in person and through the international media the carrying of arms by children[37].

Once the issue of 'child soldiers' had been brought to light, it became obvious that boys in their early teens were a common feature in fighting forces around the world, regular and irregular. In environments where children's engagement in economically significant work was regarded as normal, the employment of under-age teenagers in military activity in communities engulfed by war was similarly part of the normal inculcation of children into adult life. In Afghanistan, Cambodia, El Salvador, Ethiopia, Liberia, Peru and Sri Lanka, children took part as combatants, not necessarily as fighters but as cooks, cleaners, messengers and porters. The total number of 'child war workers' was estimated in 1988 at 200,000 worldwide[38]. Some engaged in military life willingly, others under heavy duress. In some cases, as in Mozambique, refusal to cooperate with armed captors could lead to children being deliberately killed so as to prevent them being of use to the opposition forces.

The increasing attention given to the many impacts of war on children was reflected in the debates during the final drafting stages of the Convention on the Rights of the Child. The age at which teenagers could be permitted to enter the armed forces became a stumbling block for some countries in the drafting group, who felt that 16 should be the lower limit. However, Article 38 finally specified 15 as the minimum age of military recruitment, with the proviso that among those aged 15 to 18, 'States Parties shall endeavour to give priority to those who are oldest'. The Convention also stipulated that, in accordance with their obligations under international humanitarian law to protect civilians, States Parties should make special efforts to care for children affected by armed conflict, including promoting their physical and psychological recovery and their social reintegration.

Since the passage of the Convention, other issues concerning wars and children have been precipitated onto the international agenda. One of the most important of these is the residual damage caused to human beings by uncleared land-mines. An estimated 100 million mines have been laid as part of military action in more than 60 countries[39], and even when the fighting they are part of is long since over, these mines have the capacity to kill and maim people innocently going about their daily lives. Over 1 million people, most of them civilians, have been killed or injured by land-mine explosions since 1975.

Many of these casualties are children. This is because they are particularly at risk: they tend to run about and play in a carefree way, without an adult's in-built sense of caution. They are also inquisitive, and mines come in a variety of shapes and colours that attract children to them as playthings. When a mine goes off in the hand or under the foot of a child, the child has more than a 50 per cent chance of dying outright; those who survive usually face the prospect of amputation. Angola has more than 20,000 amputees, including many children; Cambodia has more than 35,000—one in every 230 members of the population[40].

The cost of demining averages between $300 and $1,000 per mine. In a country such as Cambodia, where there are 7 million mines and the annual per capita GDP is $150, the costs involved reduce to nil the prospects of clearing all the country's land-mines[41]. Apart from programmes to rehabilitate children with disabilities, which are conducted in many war-affected countries as a part of primary health care services, Unicef has begun to promote mine-awareness schemes. In El Salvador, the 12-year conflict that ended in 1992 left large numbers of uncleared mines and unexploded ordnance lying around in the countryside. When children began to be killed and injured by these devices, Unicef enlisted the help of the Salvadoran army, the ex-rebel forces and the UN Peacekeeping Mission to develop a mine-awareness project[42]. Teachers, health workers and community leaders were trained to point out the dangers of mines to children in affected communities through posters, leaflets and educational media. By the time the programme had been completed, a significant decrease in the number of children injured had been noted.

Unicef has also consistently maintained that the use of anti-personnel land-mines violates core provisions in the Convention on the Rights of the Child, including the child's right to life and the State's obligation to ensure the 'survival and development of the child'. The ultimate solution to the land-mine issue is to remove mines already laid, and to prevent their further use as weapons of war. In 1993, the UN General Assembly unanimously adopted a moratorium on the export of land-mines—a moratorium yet to become fully respected. Even this moratorium is only a first step. Unicef, along with ICRC and increasing numbers of NGOs, maintains that the rights of children demand a complete ban on the use of land-mines; it has recently announced that it will no longer deal with companies manufacturing or selling mines[43]. The opportunity to obtain agreement to an international law on land-mines arose in October 1995 at a UN conference dedicated to the control of 'inhumane weapons'. Unfortunately, the proposal failed to gain international endorsement, but undoubtedly the campaign will go on[44].

Another variation of international conflict whose special impact on children has inspired humanitarian protest is the imposition of political and economic sanctions. These are usually applied as a substitute for military intervention in an effort to bring a regime regarded as an international pariah to its knees, as in Iraq; or to subject a regime to heavy international pressure, as in the case of former Yugoslavia. But measures that are intended to deprive a country of trading opportunities, ruin its economy and—by implication—its services, may have a disastrous impact on civilian populations. In non-democratic societies especially, these civilians have played no part in installing the regime and cannot be held responsible for its policies or practices. Since children are the most vulnerable members of the population, the negative impacts of sanctions fall hardest upon them. In Iraq, for example, five years of sanctions meant that by late 1995, infant mortality had doubled and mortality in children under five had risen by five times; 20,000 new cases of child malnutrition were being reported every month[45]. The International Red Cross and Unicef were among those calling for ways to be found of reducing the humanitarian disaster that sanctions constituted for Iraqi mothers and children.

A similar experience befell the children of Haiti, especially the children of extremely poor families, between the coup of 1991 and the ousting of the military regime by US-led international action in 1994. Over the three years that UN sanctions were imposed, the rate of malnutrition for children under five in health institutions increased from 27 per cent to over 50 per cent[46]. In mid-1993, a team from the Harvard Center for Population and Development Studies visited Haiti. Their study, with which Unicef was closely associated[47], recommended that in future, international sanctions be imposed in such a way as to target specifically the military and their élite supporters, and that safeguards on supplies of food and medicines be built in to protect the poor and vulnerable. In early 1994, Unicef began to call within the UN system and outside it for increased child-awareness in the application of sanctions[48].

In late 1995, in the annual *State of the World's Children* report written for 1996, its 50th anniversary year, Unicef took as its main theme the subject of 'children in war'. A 10-point 'anti-war agenda' to reduce the specific impacts of warfare on childhood was proposed. This was a recognition that, 50 years after Unicef's creation to relieve the postwar predicament of children in Europe, the issue was as compelling as it ever had been. It also marked an increasing awareness in Unicef of the abuse of childhood suffered as a result of an upbringing in the midst of violence and armed hostilities, particularly where atrocities were widespread. The 'new world disorder' unleashed by the end of the cold war was one of the dynamics inexorably driving Unicef towards acceptance of a rights perspective, in addition to a development perspective, in its worldwide work for children.

The illusion of 'peace in our time' that accompanied the end of the cold war proved short-lived. The closing two years of the 1980s were ones of optimism, with the UN universally acclaimed for its role as peace-broker. Iran and Iraq declared a halt after eight years of hostilities; Soviet troops withdrew from Afghanistan; Vietnamese troops withdrew from Cambodia; Namibia inched towards independence; and countries such as Cyprus, El Salvador and South Africa, which were embroiled in long-running internal confrontations, seemed closer to resolving their tensions. But the prospects of a peace dividend and the sense of a more unified and harmonious world quickly receded. First came Iraq's invasion of Kuwait and the 1991 Gulf War. Then came a contagion of nationalist and ethnic strife, much of it apparently unleashed by the removal of superpower rivalry as a controlling influence over threats of national destabilization.

In the different hemispheres and continents, even in the countries within them, the thaw in East-West relations had different implications: in much of Latin America and in South Africa, for example, it raised the stakes for the advent of democratic rule. But in many fissiparous environments previously ruled by authoritarian regimes bolstered by links to one or other hegemonic adversary, sectarian or inter-ethnic passions boiled to the surface. The regions most affected by this phenomenon, despite their very different histories, conditions of 'development' and political cultures, were the ex-USSR and Eastern Europe, and sub-Saharan Africa. The long economic crisis and the crushing effects of transition in one region and structural adjustment in the other added a further destabilizing influence[49]. In Africa, certain nation States whose contours had been artificially imposed in colonial times and were sustained by cold war dynamics now showed a propensity to disintegrate. No region was, however, exempt: in Asia, Afghanistan continued to implode; and in the Americas, Haiti was in a state of almost perpetual crisis.

The year 1992—the year in which the UN Secretary-General issued his policy document *An Agenda for Peace*—saw a further significant escalation in the number of emergencies involving the UN system, especially the number in which conflict was the principal characteristic. The UN's twin roles as broker between warring parties and as main international supplier of humanitarian relief to their victims were simultaneously coming under intense pressure. As a result of loud complaints from donor countries and the international NGO community about the shortcomings of the UN's humanitarian response, a new Department of Humanitarian Affairs (DHA) was set up following a UN General Assembly resolution late in 1991. Therefore 1992, the year in which the Somali famine crisis confronted the world with the new phenomenon of the 'failed State', can be seen as a year in which international humanitarianism was confronted with the grim realities of the post–cold war era once the honeymoon was over.

For Unicef, as for many other organizations involved in emergency relief, the Somalia crisis in particular represented a defining experience for post–cold war emergency operations[50]. At the end of 1990, during the fighting that led to the overthrow of President Mohammed Siad Barre, the UN organizations and NGOs, with the exception of a very few including ICRC and Médecins sans Frontières, had evacuated Somalia[51]. During 1991, most NGOs returned; but the UN, including Unicef, did not; some supplies were provided but there was no international presence. Only in December 1991 did Unicef obtain permission from the UN Secretary-General to send in some resident staff and re-establish its operational base[52]. Part of the reason for the absence of the UN was the atomization of power in the country and lack of a clearly constituted government—the body with which all organizations operating under a UN umbrella must formally deal. The lack of concerted international action led to a deterioration in the compounding political and economic crisis in the country. All order disintegrated in the face of violence and chaos, while famine took hold.

From late 1991, Unicef built up its presence in Somalia, putting in place—like other agencies—increased logistics, supply, communication, transport and security systems to make up for the absence of normal government infrastructures. However, its actions at this time were later perceived by an internal assessment to have fallen into the category of 'too little, too late'[53]. During 1992, a cease-fire was brokered by the UN and a relief operation involving the UN system was developed. But in the chaotic political and security circumstances, it took time for the programme to become effective. The creation of DHA early in the year did not initially do much to ease the problems of relief and rehabilitation under the UN umbrella[54]: the modalities for DHA operations and lines of command within the new-style UN humanitarian response were still embryonic. In the meantime, the children of Somalia starved. Unicef rightly felt in retrospect that it could and should have done more on their behalf.

The problem was that the organization's energies were engaged elsewhere. During 1992, while hundreds of thousands of Somali lives were lost or in peril, Unicef had still not elevated the famine crisis to a level of major corporate priority[55]. Staff in the Somali office were not given adequate support; the programme was not fully geared to the emergency circumstances, and many actions were undertaken on an ad hoc basis in response to a rising crescendo of NGO and media criticism[56]. In October 1992, a UN mission to Somalia headed by Jim Grant and Jan Eliasson, the new Under-Secretary-General for Humanitarian Affairs, finally brought about the necessary transformation of organizational concern. The mission led to the formation of a 100-day UN action programme for accelerated humanitarian assistance[57]. After this, things rapidly changed, but for too many Somali children the organizational commitment had come too late[58].

Within the new UN programme, Unicef was to provide survival assistance to displaced populations, help them return home and re-establish access to basic services, including health, nutrition, and water and sanitation[59]; significantly, although it had much the largest UN presence in the country, it did not take on the 'lead agency' role. The 100-day plan did much to restore—temporarily—the credibility of the UN's humanitarian response. But it did not do enough to ease immediate distress. In December 1992, a UN General Assembly resolution paved the way for the US-led military intervention 'Operation Restore Hope'. During 1993, this was handed over to UN leadership, but the humanitarian neutrality of the mission subsequently became compromised[60].

Amidst these difficulties and a continuing state of lawlessness and insecurity, Unicef and the other humanitarian organizations—UN and NGO—continued their programmes. For this, some relief workers—notably Sean Devereux and several other Unicef staff—paid with their lives. Others lived in a constant state of fear and anxiety for protracted periods, sometimes losing all faith in the fundamental decency of human relations and paying a high psychological price[61]. The need to provide counselling and other types of special support to staff serving in such settings as Somalia was recognized as a result of these experiences. This was among the emergency management reforms that Unicef began to introduce around this time.

Criticism of UN humanitarian operations had begun well before the Somalia crisis and was coupled with contemporary calls for UN reform—especially for better inter-agency coordination. The Save the Children Fund was one of the NGOs most actively calling for improvements in the UN emergency response, and among other studies into UN reform, that of the Nordic UN Project was highly influential[62]. The creation of DHA early in 1992 was in large part a response to calls for reform dating from the post–Gulf War emergency in Iraq[63]. But the first few years of DHA's existence were extremely fraught as it tried to contend with the long list of accusations levelled at the UN's humanitarian record and achieve a viable *modus operandi* with powerful members of the UN system already on the humanitarian block.

DHA was not expected to take over the functions of existing UN organizations with their various mandates for humanitarian activity—principally Unicef on behalf of children, UNHCR on behalf of refugees and WFP as organizer of food aid, but also UNDP (as field-based system coordinator) and the specialized agencies FAO and WHO. DHA's purpose was, rather, to run consolidated fund-raising appeals so that the different organizations were not constantly appealing to donors in competition with each other for the same emergency victims, and to provide a mechanism for avoiding waste and duplication by coordinating the various programmes on the ground. From the outset, Unicef was a keen supporter of DHA. Grant saw its creation as useful not only for the UN system as a whole, but as a welcome bulwark against the increasing strain exerted on Unicef's resources—financial and human—by 'loud' emergencies.

In the early 1990s, UNICEF's annual emergency assistance expenditures rose dramatically year by year: from $49 million in 26 countries in 1990, to $111 in 50 countries in 1991, to $167 million in 54 countries in 1992, to $223 million in 64 countries in 1993[64]. The huge jump in expenditures was accounted for mainly by the programmes in Iraq, Somalia and Sudan, and by 1992-93, in former Yugoslavia[65], but the African continent as a whole was the most crisis-ridden. Major emergency programmes were under way in Angola, Ethiopia, Kenya, Liberia and Mozambique as well as in Somalia and the Sudan. As a proportion of annual programme expenditures, the increase in emergency spending was from less than 10 per cent during the 1980s to more than 20 per cent[66]. There were policy implications in this change—a change that in spite of the creation of DHA, which might have been expected to de-emphasize Unicef's role in emergency relief, was consistent year to year. Inevitably, the switch in the destination of an important share of Unicef resources and human effort recalled the long-standing sense of competition between the emergency and the development roles of an organization that had always embraced both within its humanitarian mandate.

For several years, Unicef had been building momentum behind the idea of saving millions of children's lives unnecessarily lost to the 'silent' emergency of common childhood ailments. The growing clamour surrounding the loss of children's lives in emergency situations was becoming a distraction from the main task Unicef had set itself for the decade: of helping countries develop and realize national programmes of action in the wake of the Children's Summit. It was true that, compared to the 13 million children who died from easily preventable disease, the fewer than 1 million who died in 'loud' emergencies was comparatively modest[67]. But the sight of children suffering and dying on the nightly television news in an increasing list of major emergencies imposed its own demands. In the public mind in countries around the world, organizations such as Unicef existed to respond to such predicaments. The crises of the 1990s left Unicef with little alternative than to bite the emergency bullet with greater intensity than ever before.

So soon after the false dawn of international peace and prosperity, with all its promise of 'peace dividends' and human development progress, it was with some initial reluctance that Unicef began to address the changing emergency world. The first major step came when, in 1991, Unicef commissioned an evaluation of its emergency activities in an effort to draw upon the lessons of the past, especially vis-à-vis emergency preparedness and institutional capacity[68]. The subject of Unicef's involvement in emergency relief was revisited by the Multi-Donor Evaluation of Unicef, conducted during 1992. The report commented on the need to resolve what were described as the organization's 'contradictory signals about the position of emergency response activities in the organization' and the need to develop a clear Unicef policy at the global level on how to deal with emergencies[69]. Within the next year, Unicef had begun to address these issues as a matter of priority, establishing a new Office of Emergency Programmes and instituting various structural and policy changes. These included enhanced staff training and capacity for emergencies, improved security provisions and new arrangements for rapid response to emergencies[70].

Gradually, the way in which the crisis landscape was being remoulded in the post–cold war world was emerging into view. Not only was there no longer a clear-cut dichotomy between disasters classically described as 'natural' and 'man-made'. Even emergencies that appeared to be of recent inception—those in Rwanda and Burundi, for example—were the product of long-term processes in which ethnic hatreds were one element among others: environmental degradation, human displacement, population pressure on land and declining terms of trade. These emergencies were, therefore, essentially ongoing. They were not temporary phenomena, breakdowns in the state of regular affairs. Turmoil in such countries had become the context of normal life, as much a manifestation of the development process—or its failure—as of a short-term halt within it[71]. The 'loud' emergencies had merged with the 'silent', or more accurately, had become ongoing acute silent emergencies that sporadically attracted loud attention. No longer was there a sense that in such environments aid for relief and aid for development were separate and competing.

Emergencies had once been characterized by images of hungry children, soup kitchens, ration bowls and teams of emergency helpers, many in medical uniform, trained to run camps and carry out emergency first aid. But this approach to dealing with population flight, the disruption of farming and subsistence life, the destruction of service infrastructure, and outbreaks of nutritional shortage or epidemic disease was clearly less than adequate. Increasingly, the humanitarian relief environment was becoming dominated by the need to find new techniques to respond to the 'complex' emergency.

The changes introduced into Unicef's emergency management system during the 1990s were a response to the evolving nature, and the expanding scale, of contemporary disasters. The word 'complex' embraced both causes and effects.

Complex emergencies were defined as those 'on a major scale, usually involving multiple causes with more than one political entity directly involved'[72]. Often, especially in Africa, drought as well as conflict contributed to mass population movement and serious food shortage, and was part of the layered complexity of cause and effect. In some cases the state of emergency became permanent as formal economic and civic structures collapsed, and dominant groups plundered whatever assets the general population retained by violence and thuggery[73]. In early 1993, out of around 50 ongoing emergencies, 10 were classified by the UN as 'complex': those in Afghanistan, Angola, Azerbaijan, Cambodia, Iraq, Liberia, Mozambique, Somalia, the Sudan and former Yugoslavia[74]. In 1994, Rwanda and Burundi were added.

However, the designation 'complex' for an emergency was to some extent tautological; since when had emergencies been simple? The use of this term by the UN had as much to do with the intricacies of political breakdown in the post–cold war environment as to compounding emergency causes. Most conflicts were no longer between nation States, nor even between two clearly defined political parties using weaponry rather than words to contest an existing national territory. They were, rather, a violent manifestation of clashing and overlapping tensions—ethnic, religious, ideological—by groups vying for control over some part but not necessarily all of an existing State.

Fighting did not take place on a battlefield, nor was it primarily conducted by armies constituting the military wing of coherent political groups capable—should they win—of instituting effective government. It bore a strong resemblance to forms of warfare and civil upheaval common in the pre-modern era and long relegated to history, now being hideously revived with the addition of modern arms. Therefore, a set of organizations such as the UN, which had been designed exclusively to deal with relations between nation States—or, at a pinch, aspirant 'national' entities—had some difficulty in describing such situations, let alone in devising mechanisms to respond to them[75]. In the new era of internalized and deformalized warfare, the machinery of international humanitarianism faced challenges it was ill-prepared to meet.

With its long track record of elevating children's needs above the political divide, and more recently of negotiating 'corridors of peace' and 'days of tranquillity', Unicef appeared better rehearsed for negotiating humanitarian access with 'illegitimate' warring groups than UN organizations only used to interacting with recognized authorities. In its 1991 emergency evaluation report, this characteristic of Unicef's de facto mandate was described as one of its 'comparative advantages'[76]. However, where armed conflict was endemic among a number of groups—as in Liberia, Somalia, the Sudan and former Yugoslavia—it was difficult to negotiate stable understandings with the various factions. A Unicef attempt to bring about a 'week of tranquillity' in Bosnia-Herzegovina so that supplies could be brought in before the winter of 1992-93 was only partially successful because the parties involved did not hold to their agreements.

The new type of conflicts had special implications for their civilian victims. Combatants did not confine themselves to destroying enemy forces. They also set about winning over parts of the population and demonizing others, using high levels of brutality and collective violence, including against children. This phenomenon had already been witnessed in the 1980s in the Iran-Iraq war and in Mozambique. In the 1990s, it became more widespread. In the besieged cities of former Yugoslavia, for example, children were shot at by snipers as a macabre form of target practice[77]. In the Philippines, children brought up amidst armed insurrection frequently became guerrilla fighters in their teens, having absorbed from elders the idea that killing people was a normal kind of activity[78]. In Rwanda and Burundi, youngsters of the alternate ethnic group might be specifically targeted by genocidal gangs in an effort to destroy the next generation.

There were other more general ways in which children suffered from what ought to be an anachronistic type of warfare. Combatants often pursued a scorched-earth policy, destroying homes, social networks, community infrastructure and people's means of livelihood. In Angola, for example, the combined consequences of 10 years of warfare and drought contributed to a significant deterioration of children's nutritional condition, with between 25 and 40 per cent of children suffering from moderate malnutrition[79]. Similarly, in southern Sudan, a 1993 nutritional survey found that in areas with a recent influx of displaced families, malnutrition rates among the under-fives were 56 per cent[80].

As the 1990s advanced, upholding the UN's guiding principles of humanitarian relief—'impartiality, neutrality and humanity'[81]—in environments characterized by indifference to human rights and the collapse of civil administration and of normal economic life became increasingly difficult. Some NGOs preferred to adopt a stance of solidarity since at least this gave them access to the civilian population under the control of the 'illegitimate' side[82]. In circumstances where the humanitarian writ simply did not run, NGOs became increasingly the conduits for inputs of bilateral or international assistance to those inaccessible to the formal machinery of intergovernmental cooperation.

It proved, for example, extremely difficult to sustain Operation Lifeline Sudan in the face of a refusal by the embattled parties to respect the neutrality of humanitarian assistance and its practitioners. In 1994, conditions of insecurity caused 50 temporary evacuations of relief workers stationed in southern Sudan[83], and the destruction of compounds and looting of relief supplies in their absence. Practical expression of the original acquiescence gained for humanitarian principle frequently collapsed, but it also never entirely dissipated. In 1995, the SPLA became the first 'illegitimate' combatant group in dispute with a recognized national government to commit itself to the provisions of the International Convention on the Rights of the Child.

In the circumstances of certain complex emergencies, particularly those where genocidal activity was involved, the concept of 'innocent civilians' seemed to evaporate. Yet this was the concept on which the laws and conventions surrounding humanitarian assistance had all been erected, as had the idea of 'children as a zone of peace'. In some environments—the Rwandan crisis of 1994, for example—civilians, including children, were so systematically brutalized that it was almost impossible to separate the 'guilty' from the 'innocent'; in early 1995, an estimated 300 children were held in Rwandan prisons as suspected war criminals. In the case of these children, Unicef was a provider of food and medical help, and a defender of the basic human rights of the imprisoned, especially of those accused of genocide[84].

In circumstances fraught with hatred, aid to civilians could itself become a weapon of war. Combatant respect for symbols such as the Red Cross or the blue UN flag became less reliable. Instead of enjoying immunity from the contest, international relief became something protagonists admitted or withheld from adversary populations according to their current strategic purpose: witness the fate of many relief convoys in former Yugoslavia. Whether or not aid was allowed to pass through barricades might depend on military strategy or on whether a combatant party currently wished to present itself in an internationally favourable light. The media have become part of the armoury of warfare, wooed and manipulated by adversaries to pursue outcomes that guns, shells and international diplomacy have failed to bring about. In the humanitarian context, the media have often been 'played' to provoke international public sympathy for civilian victims, especially in the countries of powerful and important potential allies.

In the effort to create or maintain 'humanitarian space', the world's leading powers have taken unprecedented actions in the emergencies of the 1990s. The first occasion was in early 1991, when military forces were used to secure physical space in northern Iraq—the 'safe havens'—in which international assistance would be distributed to Kurdish refugees. This breach of the principle of national sovereignty—the idea of a 'right to humanitarian intervention'—was widely applauded at the time as a symptom of the world's growing insistence on the duty of the international community to protect human life. But subsequent deployments of troops under UN auspices in Somalia and former Yugoslavia to protect relief operations were more ambiguous in their outcomes and much more controversial. There are now serious questions about whether the militarization of international assistance in the deformalized and 'illegitimate' wars of the post–cold war is to the advantage of effective humanitarian practice[85].

Such viewpoints form part of the debates surrounding the ethics and principles of humanitarianism thrown up during recent crises. The removal of transcendent superpower interests in the causes and outcomes of emergency situations produced naïve expectations that a UN system driven only by the purest of motives could intervene successfully simply because its efforts were uncluttered by ideological and strategic rivalry. When this vision first came into view, the UN's image benefited enormously from the prominence it gained in the new diplomatic and relief climate. But its institutions and member organizations quickly found themselves—literally and metaphorically—in the firing line.

All parts of the UN system involved in any way with diplomatic and humanitarian affairs have suffered intense scrutiny and criticism for their performance in the face of the new world disorder. Unicef has not been immune to such criticism, as the Multi-Donor Evaluation of 1992 clearly illustrated. At the same time, some Unicef staff members have had to put their lives on the line in order to carry out the emergency relief mandate in extremely difficult circumstances. Over the past five years, more than 20 national and international staff members have lost their lives in conflict situations, to random violence, to genocidal attack (in Rwanda in 1994) and by deliberate murder.

Unicef as an organization has been protected from controversy in some degree by its mandate for children, whose helplessness and innocence gives some protection to efforts made on their behalf. Since the rise of children on national and international agendas, and the passage of the Convention on the Rights of the Child, the fate of children in the contemporary world carries an increasingly forceful moral charge. Even among the most brutalized of armed combatants, the desire to relieve the suffering of children where the conscience can still be touched continues to count for something. The power of the children's cause to advance humanitarian space should not be underestimated, nor can it afford to be: there are few similar means of leverage at humankind's command.

Meanwhile, Unicef has continued the process of reform and streamlining of its emergency mechanisms. It is now more common for Unicef programmes in countries where emergencies are ongoing to interface regularly between emergency relief, rehabilitation and longer-term development. Although funded under separate headings, cooperation frequently takes identical forms: support for immunization, control of diarrhoeal diseases, repair or construction of water supply and sanitation systems, support for household food security and income-generation among women.

The fact that Unicef has been engaged long term in many naturally disaster-prone countries—such as Bangladesh, and in Africa—has meant adapting local operations to circumstances of sudden or creeping emergency. Unicef's decentralized character on the ground, coupled with the capacity of its supplies procurement operation, UNIPAC, based in Copenhagen, has the potential for flexibility and speed of response. However, all these 'comparative advantages' have felt an intense degree of strain, and more needs to be done to make them fully 'advantageous'[86].

In the meantime, new policy issues relating to emergencies have crowded the agenda: what to do for the growing populations of the internally displaced—25 million at end 1994[87]—who do not carry the status of refugees because they have not crossed an international frontier; how to promote a ban on land-mines; how to lessen the impact of sanctions on children; what to do about mass rape and the special human rights violations experienced by women in warfare. Relatively new areas of emergency programme activity also required policy definition: best practice in the context of psychosocial counselling; how to demobilize and detraumatize child soldiers; how to deal with conditions of social breakdown in the 'failed State', including the problem of increasing numbers of orphaned and unaccompanied children. And still there are questions as to whether Unicef has truly been willing to accept that emergencies will play a central part in its programme activities until the millennium and probably well beyond.

When Unicef first came into existence, the response to the emergency needs of children was 'some milk, and some fat...on bread'[88]. Supplies of drugs and vaccination equipment were later added, but there was no idea of extending relief and rehabilitation programmes beyond support for children's physical well-being. The subsequent 50 years have seen a metamorphosis in humanitarian activity, both in the techniques applied within the traditional response areas of food, shelter and medical first aid, and in the evolution of new types of programmes to respond to aspects of emergency-induced damage. They have also seen a sea change in attitudes in most parts of the world, hastened by the advent of the television era and the visual evidence of cruelties and inhumanities that remained under wraps in the past.

Although the new world disorder and the phenomenon of the 'failed State' sometimes seem to have ushered in a new age of barbarism, it is not the case that wartime atrocities against 'innocent civilians', including children, are previously unknown; the pages of history are riddled with them. What has changed even more than the rules of wartime engagement in the late 20th century is our level of awareness of warfare's many forms of human damage, and a concomitant change in values that demands that this damage be prevented or repaired. Fifty years after it was founded, Unicef's evolving approach to children affected by complex emergencies reflects that change in values at the international level, and tries to influence them further.

In many emergency circumstances—in Angola, for example, and in Mozambique—Unicef still provides today's protein-rich equivalent of dried milk for traditional programmes of supplementary child feeding. Immunization campaigns, water supply repairs and rebuilding the primary health service infrastructure are also *de rigueur*. But the initiatives of the 1980s and 1990s—psychosocial counselling, the maintenance of schooling, land-mine awareness, efforts to reunite lost children with their families and 'Education for Peace'—are also becoming regular components of emergency country programmes. Programmes of today, unlike their cruder predecessors of 50 years ago, undertake much more than physical first aid. They aim to repair the psychological capacity of children and families, and to protect the state of childhood itself.

The existence of the Convention on the Rights of the Child now provides a basis for advocacy on behalf of emergency-affected children. In the face of wide-scale human rights abuses, it may prove impossible to hold governments to the commitments they have made on behalf of children by appending their signatures to this international treaty[89]. Nevertheless, the Convention provides a legitimate basis for shaming warring parties over their disregard of children's well-being and for advancing the proposition of 'children first'. Programmes for 'Education for Peace' emphasize the provisions of the Convention as a basis for building mutual respect and understanding between children of all races, and between children and adults.

In 1994, in response to a General Assembly Resolution, the UN Secretary-General appointed a Special Rapporteur, Graça Machel of Mozambique, to head a worldwide study on the impact of armed conflict on children, with support from Unicef. The report on this study will go before the UN General Assembly close to the date of the 50th anniversary of the resolution that conjured into existence a UN 'International Children's Emergency Fund'. It is to be hoped that the coincidence will prove prophetic for the children's cause.

Chapter 10

Towards 2000 and Beyond

It is a cloudless day in northern Mexico in May 1994 and a grand public occasion is under way. In a ruined church containing dignitaries, politicians, mayors, officials and a children's choir, Governor Arturo Romo de Gutierrez of Zacatecas is launching his 'new State policy in favour of the child': better health care, more rural schools, more popular participation. 'We must build a new world, a society of peace, democracy and progress in which all can live well, especially the children.'[1]

This language of political commitment to children, echoed in strikingly similar speeches on platforms in places as far apart geographically and politically as Brazil and Bangladesh, South Africa and Senegal, the Philippines and India, could be easily traced to its source. It had travelled four years and several hundred speeches from the World Summit for Children. Mexico was one of the first countries to lay out a national programme of action to put into effect the promises made at the Summit.

The then President of Mexico, Carlos Salinas de Gortari, called his first 'Meeting for Monitoring and Evaluating Summit Commitments' in early November 1990, barely a month after the Summit was held. Jim Grant of Unicef attended this 'national evaluation' and others that followed: the seventh evaluation meeting in October 1994 was one of the last public engagements Grant's failing health allowed him to undertake. At these events, as in the ruined church at Zacatecas, health, social affairs and education officials recounted their achievements on behalf of Mexican children to prolonged and much-publicized applause. After the end of his presidential term, Salinas' name became besmirched in ill-repute; a commitment to the politics of childhood is not a guarantee of sainthood. But it was due to Salinas' commitment to Grant's vision that Mexico lowered its 1990 infant mortality rate by one third, six years ahead of the target date set at the Children's Summit[2].

When UN Secretary-General Pérez de Cuéllar asked Unicef to follow up on countries' Summit commitments, he could never have envisaged how assiduously it would do so. Between 1990 and the end of 1994, Jim Grant and his country representatives held over 100 meetings with Presidents and Prime Ministers to promote the Summit goals[3]. Nearly 100 countries had prepared and launched national programmes of action (NPAs) to 'keep the promise to children'. Even more impressively, in 76 countries, such programmes had been started or were in preparation at state, provincial or municipal level[4]. By 1995, this 'decentralization of the NPA process' was relatively far advanced in 50 countries, according to a survey conducted by the International Child Development Centre in Florence[5]. Among those to join the Governor of Zacatecas in calling for improvements for children were 24 state governors in Brazil, 60 city leaders in the Philippines and 13 mayors of West African capitals[6].

All this activity, and Unicef's direct and indirect role in it, was exemplary by comparison with most national and local outcomes of lofty resolutions passed in international fora. Some of these programmes of action, perhaps, were not much more than glossy documents expressing good intentions. But a large number were important instruments, developed painstakingly by a range of national and local officials, for reshaping and streamlining health and education services and remotivating their staffs. Some were introduced in tandem with new systems for collecting data to measure health, nutritional and educational progress. These were systematically encouraged by Unicef, with advice and funds as part of the Summit follow-up and NPA process.

During the early 1990s, Unicef's organizational culture became dominated by 'the goals'. In the 1980s, the central mission—expressed as the 'child survival revolution'—had been the reduction of young child mortality. Following the Summit, it had become a broader extension of the same idea: reductions of children's rates of death, disease, malnutrition and illiteracy with reference not to one, but to several, key social indicators. As with young child mortality, these indicators were regarded not simply as measures of a population's state of poverty but as key symptoms of its plight that should themselves be attacked in the name, and on behalf, of children. Improvements in these indicators were seen as contributing to the reduction of poverty itself.

This emphasis on measurable and time-bound goals—an emphasis reinforced in 1993 by the setting of the mid-decade goals (see Chapter 6)—led to charges in some quarters that Unicef was more interested in what was described as 'targetitis' than in 'sustainability'[7]. Such criticism failed to take into account the importance attached by Unicef over the past decade to improving techniques for measuring how programmes were faring, especially in the field of public health. New methods using cluster surveys had first been developed to help measure progress towards universal child immunization, and were introduced into many countries with Unicef's help. After the Summit, a quick and comprehensive survey methodology for measuring progress towards all 'the goals' was developed, with support from WHO, UNFPA, the UN Statistics Office, Unicef and the Centers for Disease Control in Atlanta. Its widespread use meant that the degree of precision with which many countries were now collecting data in the social sector was unprecedented. As well as the reporting benefits, such techniques provided quick feedback to communities and authorities on how well they were performing programmatically[8]. The investment Unicef made in helping authorities understand what was going on in the poorest 20 per cent of communities was regarded not just as a means of measuring whether targets were being reached, but as an important element of Unicef cooperation in its own right[9].

Unicef also placed a strong emphasis on 'the goals' as a public relations exercise to mobilize and maintain forward momentum towards them. But to dismiss this as 'targetitis' was unfair. The scale of NPA preparation, the volume of child-related rhetoric it produced and the degree of serious attention paid in many countries to monitoring and evaluation as an essential part of programming were counterweights to the occasional provocative critique. Many directors of social sector services found that the new political backing they enjoyed opened up new vistas. In some cases, the setting of targets induced the very shake-up and redirection of health and educational services, which everyone agreed was at least as important as the goals themselves. Even the fact that the 'goals-led strategy' generated controversy—as selective primary health care had done a few years before—showed that the post-Summit process was making its mark in elevating children and social objectives on the policy-making agenda.

In 1993, in addition to its annual *State of the World's Children* report, Unicef published the first in a new series of reports entitled *The Progress of Nations*. This was principally devised as another boost to the goal-driven process. *The Progress of Nations* set out to monitor countries' rates of minimum human needs satisfaction by bringing together statistics on the progress each was making in health, nutrition, education, family planning and progress for women[10]. Its controversial characteristic was to list countries in their order of performance in these areas, implicitly criticizing those whose performance fell behind that of others whose GNP was similar. The digest of information the report contained was valuable in its own right, but the publication's wider purpose was to use global statistical comparison to influence national policy-making in the child's direction. This was taking social number-crunching a step further than Unicef had ever taken it before.

The report also took the opportunity to highlight the fact that if countries were sincere in wanting to achieve progress towards measurable improvements in human well-being, they would have to put in place the means of essential data collection. More, and up-to-date, information was needed about disease case-loads, service delivery figures, even births and deaths. This was a theme reiterated in subsequent editions of *The Progress of Nations* in 1994 and 1995. The need for better data—one of the themes of the 1990s—was the flip side of the emphasis on targets and goals.

As the mid-point of the decade drew near, Unicef began to exert the maximum leverage at its disposal to encourage countries to meet the mid-decade goals. In late 1994, *The State of the World's Children* for 1995—the last of these reports to be issued during Jim Grant's lifetime—reviewed in detail the practical accomplishments so far. The verdict was that more than 100 of the developing nations, with over 90 per cent of the developing world's children, were making significant progress[11]. According to Grant: 'Overall, it is clear that a majority of the goals set for 1995 are going to be met by a majority of the developing nations. This means that, by mid-decade, about 2.5 million fewer children will be dying every year from malnutrition and disease. And at least three quarters of a million fewer children each year will be disabled, blinded, crippled or mentally retarded.'[12]

Rarely, if ever, had so many nations in the world rallied behind a common social programme and made such progress towards its accomplishment. To a degree that Unicef could not and did not lay claim to because its organizational impetus was only one element among many, this had happened because of Jim Grant. Not only had he had the vision of a Summit and Summit goals; he had thought out a subsequent strategy for creating national and local bandwagons to transform the rhetoric produced by the Summit into reality. And the momentum for this process had been sustained for several years after the event itself had paled into the past.

One of the most outstanding successes was the progress being made against iodine deficiency disorders (IDDs). Following the Children's Summit, all 94 countries whose populations were affected had agreed to aim for 95 per cent iodization of common salt—the simplest method of mass IDD prevention—by 1995. By 1994, 60 were on target. Other notable successes included the promotion of breastfeeding by the establishment of baby-friendly hospitals, improvements in immunization tallies and significant advances towards polio eradication in 43 out of the 55 countries that had set themselves a 1995 deadline.

This round-up of post-Summit achievement in the *State of the World's Children* report concluded by commenting that to maintain momentum towards the year 2000 goals, more support was needed from the industrialized nations. At the time of the Summit, only a small proportion of all aid—around 10 per cent—was being allocated to social investment. The industrialized countries had promised to review their aid programmes with a view to helping the developing countries meet the Summit goals. In the four-year interim, little had happened towards a comprehensive revision of donor priorities. Not only the quality of aid, but its quantity was unimpressive: as a proportion of donor countries' GNP, official development assistance (ODA) had been declining since the early 1980s, and in 1993 had reached an average of 0.29 per cent—the lowest for 20 years[13]. Moreover, the share of United Nations resources being devoted to relief and emergency work had increased from 25 per cent of the total budget in 1988 to 45 per cent in 1992[14]. This was perhaps inevitable given the spate of crises—in the Persian Gulf, Rwanda, Somalia, the Sudan, former Yugoslavia—that had erupted in recent years, but it was an unfortunate indication of a transfer of resources from causes to cure, the report concluded.

In early 1995, the World Summit for Social Development in Copenhagen was looming. Here was a new opportunity for those countries that controlled three quarters of the world's wealth and dominated the international machinery of trade, aid and finance to commit more investment to sustainable human development. In early 1995, Unicef—now temporarily under the directorship of Richard Jolly following the death of Jim Grant in January—made its presentation for this latest World Summit. Children and youth, Unicef claimed, should be at the heart of the new international social pact called for by UN Secretary-General Boutros Boutros-Ghali.

Since the Children's Summit, Unicef claimed, the world had already made considerable progress in meeting those needs, 'and the potential exists to make that progress truly global'[15]. To accomplish this, concrete goals for the reduction of poverty should be set and the necessary resources allocated. The 20/20 formula—the donor nations to provide 20 per cent of ODA and the developing countries to allocate 20 per cent of their government budgets to the social sector—was developed under the auspices of UNDP and strongly promoted during the Summit by Unicef, UNDP, UNESCO, UNFPA, WHO and a number of NGOs.

For much of the last four decades, no matter how strongly the problem of world poverty had been presented as one for which the richer nations of the world must shoulder their share of responsibility, the necessary commitment—moral and financial—had not been forthcoming. Their failure was a central theme of Grant's last *State of the World's Children* report, which had further stated that time was running out. In the early decades of the post-colonial inheritance and with the cold war raging, there had been both an economic and a strategic—not to mention a humanitarian—case for the investment of public funds into the notional equivalent of an international welfare state. Not only had the basis for that case gradually changed in the intervening years, but the strategic need to win 'third world' allies with a judicious use of aid was disappearing rapidly into history. The whole nature of internationalism, and the mechanisms by which it was expressed, were suffering acute strain as an outcome of their liberation from superpower stasis.

The Social Summit that took place in Copenhagen in March 1995 attracted 116 Heads of State: the largest number until then ever to attend an international meeting. The brightest hope of its anti-poverty agenda—the 20/20 initiative—was diluted during negotiation[16]. Many donors were unwilling to commit themselves to spending a fixed proportion of their aid on social needs; developing countries were equally unwilling to commit themselves to spending one fifth of their GNP the way the world told them to. This was understandable, given the indignities to which they had been subjected in the recent past over programmes of structural adjustment. However, many country delegations brought to the Conference achievements in poverty reduction—accomplished against the odds of the 'lost development decade' of the 1980s. Unicef itself issued a special report entitled *Profiles in Success*, detailing the social progress achieved by countries that were not necessarily high earners, but that had adopted development strategies targeted at the poor[17].

Whether or not the Social Summit could regenerate the cause of 'development' as an international anti-poverty crusade was the question underlying its ambitious agenda. Of all the problems in the world, decades of 'development' had shown that poverty was the least susceptible to universal characterization or a composite solution. Joblessness, widening economic divides and social alienation were not issues that were easy to address other than rhetorically at an international level.

Given the tensions and distractions of the 'new world disorder', it was difficult to see early in 1995 where the cause of international development was headed. Twin themes important to Unicef—a focus on human well-being on the one hand and on sustainability on the other—were continuing to gain ground, but the space occupied on the international agenda by the cause of 'development' generally was shrinking. It was certain that for as long as there was an international anti-poverty agenda, Unicef would promote the cause of children as its leading edge. Equally, it would champion the elimination of poverty as a leading edge of action on behalf of children. But the development framework was no longer the only, nor perhaps even the main, context in which the children's cause was now moving forward.

The role of the Convention on the Rights of the Child in the post-Summit pursuit of 'goals' was not immediately conspicuous. Unicef was pledged by the Convention's terms (Article 45) to assist in its implementation, complementing the work of the Committee on the Rights of the Child, a 10-member body of experts elected by States Parties[18]. However, in most Unicef country offices, as in headquarters, support for the Convention was largely perceived as an external relations exercise whose main purpose was to gain country ratifications. Grant fervently supported the ratification of the Convention by as many countries as possible, and put considerable personal and organizational energy into promoting these ratifications. Beyond this, Unicef advocacy concerning the Convention was intended to inform governments, citizens, NGOs and children themselves about the concept of child rights and their expression in international law.

In 1990 the Convention was, therefore, still regarded by much of Unicef—with the notable exception of Latin American country offices—as peripheral to its own child-centred human development mission. From 1991-92 an alternative school of thought began to develop. The theme of complementarity between the Summit goals and the Convention articles came to the fore, largely due to the International Child Development Centre in Florence[19]. Commentators wove their way between two perceptions of the Convention: one, that it could help achieve 'the goals'; the other, that the implementation of the Convention itself was the most important goal of all and ought to be the basis of all Unicef action. The Convention, as a relatively timeless international treaty, legitimized the goals[20]; meanwhile, a country's determined pursuit of 'the goals' was an indication that it was actively trying to honour the rights designated in the Convention[21].

By a process of comparison and fusion, therefore, the Convention and the goals became interlinked. Gradually the Convention began to be perceived less as some separate manifesto for children on parts of which Unicef was active than as an overarching statement expressing values and norms that should inform everything that Unicef was doing. In spite of increasing lip-service paid to this perspective, however, there continued to be a weak manifestation in practical terms—programming guidelines, policy documentation, budgetary allocations—of Unicef commitment to the Convention as an ultimate frame of reference. Over the natural course of organizational absorption of such a major international statement of standards concerning childhood, and with help from key individuals, this was to change. But for the meantime, for all practical purposes, 'the goals' continued to hold sway.

While Unicef country offices in the developing world were caught up in post-Summit activity, the Unicef National Committees in the industrialized countries were also gazing out over enlarged horizons. For them, too, a new chapter had opened. Before the Summit, some had feared that it would be a spectacular 'global event', largely without substance. In its wake, their doubts dissolved. The Summit had given both children and Unicef a profile much enhanced by the *gravitas* conferred by top-rank political participation. It had caught a ground swell of increasing public concern about childhood in the industrialized world; Unicef had built a Summit wave, and had used that wave to carry forward the children's agenda. However, there were many other items on that agenda—child neglect, child abuse, single-parenting, preschool education, drugs, juvenile crime, the State's reduction of services—that were not prominently mentioned in the Summit Declaration or Plan of Action but were very prominent in industrialized countries' preoccupation with their children.

Although the Summit helped to reinforce the advocacy platform, 'the goals' did not carry the same dynamic force in the industrialized countries as they did elsewhere. This was not surprising given that they were mainly designed to deal with classic problems of child malnutrition, hunger, illiteracy and ill-health experienced in the countries of the developing world. The role of the industrialized countries in meeting the Summit goals was essentially that of donor, although efforts were made to encourage them to prepare NPAs, and many did so[22]. But there was not the same need to secure governmental commitments to targets that bore little relation to contemporary manifestations of poverty in the fully industrialized State.

Yet the post-Summit atmosphere increased the growing feeling that the situation of children in the industrialized world ought now to command some degree of Unicef's concern. For the first time, the subject was tackled in *The State of the World's Children* for 1991[23]. During the 1980s, the report stated, the proportion of children living below official poverty lines had increased in many Western countries, paralleling the situation of children in developing countries mired in debt and economic crisis. The countries in which this had happened included Canada, Germany, Ireland, the United Kingdom and the United States. In the United Kingdom, for example, the proportion of children living in families whose income was less than half the national average had more than doubled during the decade, from 12 per cent in 1979 to 26 per cent in 1989[24]. In the US, one child in five was estimated to be living in poverty. According to Marian Wright Edelman, President of the Children's Defense Fund, a leading anti-poverty voice for children in the United States: 'The inattention to children by our society poses a greater threat to our safety, harmony and productivity than any external enemy.'

Unicef was beginning to feel its way towards a role vis-à-vis all the world's children rather than those exclusively in the developing world. The difficulty was that while it remained locked into a definition of child distress borrowed from models describing poverty solely in terms of classic survival, health and education indicators, there was no clear basis of legitimacy for a broader concern. Within the Unicef world-view, countries were divided into donors and recipients; although over historical time, some countries had switched camps—countries in Eastern and Central Europe, for example, moving across the divide in one direction, and Hong Kong, Korea and Singapore crossing in the other—the broad axis remained that of rich world versus poor.

All Unicef's programmatic and policy advisory work took place in the 'poor' world: essentially the world of low per capita GNP, but also the world that performed badly according to the classic survival, health and education indicators. Therefore, although Unicef might fund research into child poverty in the 'rich world'—and tentatively began to do so—there was nowhere for Unicef to go with such research. Thus a 1993 study[25] made interesting and important points about the way the market-led drive for prosperity in the US and UK was discriminating against children. But other than by attracting a *frisson* of media attention, there was no mechanism whereby its conclusions could be fed into any policy-making apparatus.

If a rights perspective was superimposed on the poverty perspective, these problems fell away. Many of the concerns relating to children and childhood in the industrialized countries centred on child protection, or what Unicef had described since 1986 (see Chapter 5) as CEDC—'children in especially difficult circumstances'; invariably, most CEDC were children of the poor, or of racial or ethnic minorities. In some countries, one child in three suffered family breakdown[26]; the number of children raised in single-parent households was rising everywhere. So were reported cases of child abuse: in Britain, these were three times more numerous in the early 1990s than in 1970[27]. There were other signs of childhood and adolescent dislocation. In the US, figures both of suicides and murder cases showed a rising proportion of child and adolescent victims[28]. In many industrialized and industrializing countries, young people were becoming disaffected by their inability to find work and join the social mainstream. The results showed up in crime statistics, teenage pregnancy and the relatively high level of HIV infection among the young[29]. Like counterparts on the streets of Nairobi, Rio and Bombay, certain young people in New York, Paris and London were retreating into a world of homelessness, violence, sex and drugs.

The National Committees—the bodies that represented Unicef in industrialized countries and whose traditional role was fund-raising and public information—were unsure how to engage with children's issues in their own societies. But they increasingly found themselves forced by the weight of public interest to comment on the international dimensions of issues such as child labour, children victimized by war and conflict, child slavery and prostitution. A framework now existed for their involvement. The Convention was not only a relatively timeless instrument; it was truly universal in its conception and application. Its articles required adherence in West and East, North and South, independently of a country's per capita GNP and social indicators performance.

A process different from the familiar one of running fund-raising and information programmes in the industrialized world to meet children's needs in the developing world was required. In developing countries, responding to children's needs included monitoring the situation of children, advocacy on behalf of disadvantaged groups, policy debate and legislative change; all these were equally relevant in industrialized countries. The Convention opened up new possibilities for Unicef National Committees[30]. It gave them licence to campaign on child protection issues—such as the restriction of infant formula marketing, for example, or a ban on the production and sale of land-mines—which concerned children in 'developing' and 'developed' settings alike. The North/South dichotomy was anyway becoming increasingly blurred in the post–cold war world. Even while National Committees in industrialized societies were beginning to take up advocacy for child rights, some Unicef country offices—such as the Brazil office—were undertaking fund-raising and information among the general public.

The new visibility of the children's cause increased the Unicef National Committees' sense of self-confidence. This was a time when the prominence of the voluntary and non-governmental sector was generally increasing, partly because it was regarded as having an important role to play in the evolution of civil society in the post-communist world, and partly because, both as resource- and service-provider, more was demanded of private philanthropy in a climate politically and economically hostile to bureaucracy and the State.

A combination of these factors, together with the outbreak of emergency situations in the early 1990s, led to a substantial increase in the overall proportion of funds provided to Unicef by the Committees and other partners in the private sector. Between 1990 and 1992, National Committee and NGO contributions rose by over $80 million, a proportion of 40 per cent[31]. In 1994, the non-governmental income from the Committees, greeting cards and private sector income was $327 million out of a total Unicef income of $1,006 million[32]. Significantly, at a time when multilateral aid volumes were under threat, Unicef's income was buoyant and private contributions were increasing.

The National Committees' contribution of nearly one third of Unicef's resources led to changes in the relationship between them and the Unicef secretariat. Many of them gained in self-confidence, and their increased resources allowed them more room for manoeuvre in their own programmes of advocacy and 'education for development'. Their professionalism regarding Unicef issues increased along with their autonomy. They benefited, too, from the fact that they were NGOs, a breed of organization whose star in international circles was rising, while the UN generally was struggling to maintain a positive image in the eyes of governments and the general public. This network of autonomous Committees helping to put Unicef's cause constantly before the public throughout the industrialized world was an asset unique within the UN system and much envied. Their increased importance was formally recognized by many of their governments. By 1988, 21 out of 33 National Committees were represented in their government delegations to the Unicef Executive Board[33]; their leaders were also represented on Unicef delegations to UN meetings such as the International Nutrition Conference in 1993 and the Social Summit in 1995.

The expanding 'Grand Alliance' on behalf of the children's cause was also reflected by the number of distinguished artists, celebrities, intellectuals, sportsmen and sportswomen who had become Goodwill Ambassadors for Unicef. For most of its life it had been 'represented' by only two core Goodwill Ambassadors: Danny Kaye (1953 until his death in 1987) and Peter Ustinov, who by 1995 had served for over 25 years and undertaken countless television and personal appearances. In 1980, Liv Ullmann—the first woman Ambassador—had similarly become a highly committed emissary, visiting Unicef programmes in a number of countries[34]. In the late 1980s came a sudden spate of new Goodwill and Sports Ambassadors: Richard Attenborough, Harry Belafonte, Tetsuko Kuroyanagi, Roger Moore, Edmund Hillary, Vanessa Redgrave, Judy

Collins, Imran Khan, Johann Olav Koss, Julio Iglesias, Mario Kreutzberger, Youssou N'Dour, Neon Nai and Nana Mouskouri[35].

But the gentle actress whose dedication to Unicef from the late 1980s conferred upon her a starring ambassadorial role was Audrey Hepburn. Appointed in 1988, Hepburn travelled widely on behalf of Unicef, especially to famine-stricken African countries—Ethiopia, Somalia and the Sudan—which she visited at considerable risk and discomfort. The sufferings of the children of Africa affected her deeply and were those with which she closely identified in her new career as international children's champion. On her death in January 1993, an Audrey Hepburn Memorial Fund was set up to benefit specific projects for African children in crisis[36]. The contribution of Ambassadors such as Belafonte, Hepburn, Ullmann and Ustinov was significant not only in publicizing the plight of children and helping to raise money. They also used their prestige to engage with national leaders on the issues behind the scenes, helping build political momentum behind 'the goals' and the Convention.

As Unicef devoted more energy to advocacy, information activities in both developing and industrialized countries began to draw upon the latest in communications and marketing expertise. The redefinition of 'development education' as 'education for development', an activity equally appropriate for North and South, was one example of the changing world-view. Another was the staging of events in both North and South with local dignitaries and celebrities on such occasions as the 'Day of the African Child' (June 16).

Towards some of these allies—the media, for example—special efforts were made. Unicef country offices organized seminars, study tours and training fellowships for journalists so that they could be given in-depth familiarization with issues[37]. Special associations of artists and intellectuals were formed so that creative people could offer their skills on behalf of children outside their formal professional lives. The idea of forming media groups was pioneered in industrialized countries to encourage better coverage on human development and children's subjects. After 1991, following the establishment of a special Unicef support fund for global communications, these were set up in developing countries. The purpose of this kind of advocacy was to build up nuclei of informed people among those who set trends, acted as role models or influenced opinions in the hope that they would take up the children's cause less in the 'lady bountiful' tradition than as a professional concern.

Another communications initiative very much in the mode of transworld thinking set out to explore how visual entertainment—especially animation—could be put to use for children's issues. The attraction of animation was its capacity to convey messages in a way that was visually appealing to a wide audience[38]. Unicef's first involvement was in Nepal during the 1980s, where simple cartoon features were developed for use in remote villages to put across health messages entertainingly[39]. In 1990, Unicef hosted an Animation for Development Workshop in Prague. This started the ball rolling on joint projects between Unicef and key members of the industry, including Hanna-Barbera Cartoons. The earliest of these to reach fruition was the *Meena* series in Bangladesh (see Chapter 7).

The Unicef attempt to reinforce partnerships on behalf of children in the volatile climate of the post–cold war placed great emphasis on the role of NGOs. As the 1990s progressed, NGOs increasingly found themselves not only at the front line in emergencies, but also stepping in to substitute for cut-backs in social services in all parts of the world. In some European countries, in Latin America and in some countries of Asia and Africa, they also carried much of the impetus for democratic change. They were pioneers of alternative programme models and creators of popular movements; they enjoyed a growing reputation as the unofficial conscience of nations and as critics of international action. They also became an increasingly important source of human development funds in the face of ODA cut-backs. By the early 1990s, the total contribution of NGOs to the development process worldwide was estimated to be around $5 billion a year[40].

From the late 1980s onward, both in the field and at headquarters, Unicef began to give NGOs a weightier voice and a larger role in both its programmatic and its advocacy work. It began to invite NGOs to participate in meetings on child-related issues about which they were particularly concerned. These included female rights, especially the right of girls to education—the subject of a special NGO symposium held in New York in November 1991—and children's rights generally. As far as child protection issues were concerned—those connected to 'children in especially difficult circumstances'—the pressure coming from the NGOs in developing countries, and from NGOs and Unicef National Committees in industrialized countries, was still the most influential dynamic behind Unicef's own programmatic involvement.

For NGOs both national and international, the passage of the Convention on the Rights of the Child had been a watershed. Not only was the Convention something they had fought for and won, it provided an internationally endorsed framework for child-related action and a new legitimacy for their work. The Convention also provided a neutral umbrella under which they could find common ground with National Committees for Unicef and promote child-related issues collaboratively. In the UK, for example, a Child Rights Development Unit was set up as a joint Unicef National Committee initiative with a group of children's NGOs to monitor the implementation of the Convention in the UK. Altogether, NGO coalitions to promote and monitor the implementation of the Convention were formed in over 50 countries.

As the new decade progressed, it gradually became clear that the landscape vis-à-vis child-related issues had permanently altered. Child consciousness as a feature of public policy was on the rise. And although the NPAs and 'the goals' were playing an important role, it was ultimately the language of childhood protection and children's rights that most accurately expressed the changing mood of public concern.

If the 1980s was the decade when the cause of children was propelled into view, the 1990s became the decade in which it never vanished from sight. In the developing countries, this owed much to the orchestrated pursuit of NPAs, 'decade goals' and Convention ratifications. At the international level, it owed something to the effort made to ensure that children's concerns were addressed within the discussions on others—the environment, human rights, population, poverty and women—now taking their turn in the international sun. In the industrialized world, the children's cause was rising as a result of the cumulated fruition of political and social trends. In certain industrialized countries, notably the US and the UK, troubling stories of youthful drug addiction, homelessness, teenage pregnancy, child murder, school-ground violence and social alienation constantly captured media headlines. A moment of profound psychological shock came in 1993 when two 10-year-old British boys were found guilty of the murder of a two-year-old they had apparently abducted for the purpose. This event was perceived—not just in the UK but elsewhere—as a symptom of deteriorating moral and spiritual values among the young[41].

If childhood was in difficulty in the West, an equally distressing picture emerged from other parts of the globe. In the past decade, conditions of conflict in Africa, Asia, Central America, the Middle East and former Yugoslavia had produced 2 million child deaths, 4 million to 5 million children permanently injured by bombs, bullets, land-mines and other weapons, 1 million orphaned or separated from their parents, and many millions more traumatized, homeless or living in refugee camps[42]. At the verge of Unicef's 50th year, in the words of its *State of the World's Children 1996* report: 'To an organization born among the detritus of war, it sometimes seems as if the historical wheel has come full circle.'

Arguably, as great a level of damage was being inflicted on childhood by economic stress. According to the International Labour Office (ILO), as many as 200 million children around the world were working in jobs that were dangerous, unhealthy or inhumane[43]. Increasing numbers of children—especially in Asia, notably in India, Nepal, the Philippines and Thailand—were being sold or enticed into prostitution[44]. Human rights campaigners regularly reported new instances of gross violations to childhood: six-year-old boys abducted to the Middle East to work as camel jockeys[45], girls barely past the age of puberty sold into sexual slavery in Thai brothels[46], 11-year-olds engaged as partners for paedophile tourists in the Philippines[47]. The sensational nature of these accounts conferred on them a special commodity status, which ensured their public airing even if it did not always lead to a sober understanding of the social and economic dynamics surrounding the phenomena.

Whether damaged childhood was really becoming more prevalent as a product of the Western-led modernization process and the erosion of traditional value systems, or whether it was simply more noticed because the fate of children generally was more noticed, it became increasingly a subject of comment. Many reactions were confused: horror on behalf of child 'victims', and equal horror against child 'criminals'—two categories that frequently overlapped. There was equal ambiguity about who and what was responsible for the destruction of childhood. The divorce rate, the fragmentation of family life and the number of single-parent households—factors blamed for all manner of social ills—implied parental responsibility. Not only parents, but employers—and by implication legislators and law enforcement agents—were responsible for the engagement of children in exploitative, servile or dangerous work, including sexual services[48]. But parents, too, were victims of forces beyond their control—landlessness, unemployment, conditions in the workplace, media-fed consumer expectations, lawlessness and crime—which the State had some duty to regulate. Meanwhile, many employers of children saw themselves not as exploiters, but as saviours and benefactors: without their jobs, the children would starve. And children themselves might see an employer, even their procurer or regular sexual client—a woman or man who had won their affection and trust—in a similar light[49].

All these areas of damaged childhood, and those associated with political turmoil and the collapse of society into violence and warfare, fell into the category of 'child protection' issues. Unicef had first begun to address these issues in its extensive 1986 policy review on 'children in especially difficult circumstances' (see Chapter 5). The difficulties of any global analysis of such problems and of developing a unified prescription in response to any one of them, let alone to CEDC as a group, had already emerged. This was one reason—in addition to the familiar one of government sensitivity—why the green light given to activity in this area had at the time been somewhat pale. There was no instantly applicable technical solution, nor a single responsible sector—as, broadly speaking, was the case with public health—with which to address such problems. This made them less 'doable', in Jim Grant's inimitable phrase. More experience of the type pioneered in Brazil (see Chapter 5) was needed in how an international organization such as Unicef could best respond to problems traditionally tackled on a very localized scale by churches, NGOs and social welfare departments.

It was also the case that in the mid-1980s Unicef's top priority had been the 'child survival and development revolution' and, within that, universal immunization by 1990. The 1986 CEDC policy review had legitimized country-level action and suggested some 'situation analysis' and 'advocacy', but no priority was placed upon CEDC as yet. Not only would emphasis in this area require quite a different standpoint about the nature of deprivation in childhood, but it would require a shift from the recent Unicef focus on infants and the very young child, to the whole passage of childhood up till age 18, and from physical survival and well-being to personal development in all its manifestations—intellectual, social and emotional. In the late 1980s, the time for such a shift was less than propitious.

Nevertheless, the pale green light in favour of child protection activity provided in 1986 was all many country offices needed. In Bangladesh, Ecuador, Egypt, India, Kenya, Mexico, Myanmar, the Philippines, Thailand and some West African countries, Unicef began to carry out situation analyses and develop programming and advocacy skills around CEDC. Initially, the focus was mainly on street children, but gradually and inevitably—since street children were invariably working children, and might be abandoned children, sexually exploited children or child criminals—they began to embrace other categories of deprivation and risk. NGOs working on behalf of exploited and abused children exerted local pressure, and their allies in the broader human and child rights community did so internationally. Media exposure of the issues also prompted Unicef's deepening involvement, as did interest emanating from the concerned public in industrialized countries via Unicef National Committees.

Some country offices commissioned special surveys. Many focused on networking relationships and coordination. In Bangladesh, Brazil, India and the Philippines, Unicef encouraged—and funded—the establishment of 'child rights fora': umbrella bodies within which NGOs at national or local level could develop a common agenda and voice on child protection issues. These also provided a setting for seminars, training workshops and the running of national advocacy campaigns, as well as a context in which to invite the participation of children and young people themselves in the debates. In countries such as Brazil, organizations of this kind were regarded as manifestations of the new democratizing civil society.

Other parts of the UN system were also beginning to respond to the new climate of opinion concerning children's rights. Graça Machel, appointed to head a UN study into Children and Conflict in 1994 (see Chapter 9) was not the first special appointee of the UN Secretary-General on an issue concerning children. The number of shocking exposures of damaged childhood during the run-up to the passage of the Convention on the Rights of the Child had led in 1990 to the appointment of a UN Special Rapporteur on the Sale of Children: Vitit Muntarbhorn of Thailand[50]. His area of concern included the exploitation of children in prostitution and pornography—the subject of activist campaigns by the International Catholic Children's Bureau, Redd Barna (Norwegian Save the Children), End Child Prostitution in Asian Tourism (ECPAT) and other NGOs. Many of these had published reports cataloguing abuses and seeking programmatic and legislative response[51].

Muntarbhorn's annual reports to the Commission on Human Rights, together with renewed media attention prompted by the spread of AIDS, helped to lift the issue of children's sexual exploitation out of the minority concern of moralist campaigners into a matter of serious policy interest. In the Philippines and Thailand, this led to legislative change banning under-age prostitution; some European countries—notably Sweden—brought in legislation to prosecute their own nationals for paedophile acts committed abroad and began to apply it. A World Congress on Commercial Sexual Exploitation will take place in Stockholm in August 1996, sponsored by the Swedish Government, Unicef, ECPAT and the NGO Group for the Convention on the Rights of the Child.

The exploitation of children in the workplace also attracted a new level of attention in the early 1990s. In some settings the recruitment of youngsters into the organized workforce was connected to the process of economic globalization. The attraction of cheap labour led to the increased establishment of garment, toy and other light manufacturing export industries in countries such as Bangladesh, China, the Philippines and Thailand. This in turn fuelled the process of urbanization and social transition. Women and youngsters were absorbed into the 20th-century Asian equivalent of Europe's 19th-century sweatshops; in Latin America, into plantations and mines. The workplace was often hazardous, working hours long, and breaks for rest, leisure or schooling inadequate or non-existent. In his 1992 report to the Human Rights Commission, Vitit Muntarbhorn commented: 'Much of the exploitation of children arises precisely because material values have overtaken those which place a price on human life and development. Shamefully, the human rights of the child may be violated because the child is viewed as a factor of production... rather than an entity vested with substantive rights and inherent dignity.'[52]

An important influence on the re-emergence of child labour as an international issue after a long period of dormancy was the growth of the movement for social responsibility in trade. This set out to emphasize the exposure and elimination of child labour as an abuse of worker's rights[53]. The employment of under-aged workers was seen by consumer groups and labour unions in Europe and North America as unethical, partly because their use dramatically reduced labour costs and gave products made by them an unfair competitive edge. In 1992, legislation was proposed in the US to ban the import of products from foreign industries in which children under 15 years of age were employed. The Harkin Bill—as it was known—caused shock waves throughout the developing world and became the subject of heated international debate.

One of the countries specifically targeted was Bangladesh. In 1992 around 10 per cent of the 750,000-strong workforce in its garment industry—garments were Bangladesh's most important source of export income, and its most important customer was the US—were alleged to be under 14 years old[54]. At the time, schemes were being introduced by some socially aware garment industry employers to phase out child work in a humane and appropriate manner. But from 1993, so alarmed did the industry become at the prospect of international reprisals that these were abandoned in favour of sudden mass dismissal. All parties, including industry and government, agreed that this was not in the interests of the young workers involved. Pleas from a variety of sources, including child workers themselves, have since softened the manufacturers' policy. A national Child Labour Working Group including employers, the Department of Labour, ILO and Unicef has been formed to develop an appropriate response to the issue, not just in the garment industry but in the country as a whole[55].

This illustration of the way in which international action, however well-intentioned, can have an unfortunate impact on the children involved is a salutary lesson in basing policy initiatives in complex areas on simplistic assumptions. There are real dilemmas concerning the reduction of child labour. The abolition of child work may, in certain settings, lead to worse distress or worse exploitation of children. If their own and their parents' situation obliges them to work, they may then be forced to earn illegally, invisibly, in circumstances of greater vulnerability. Only if school-going and a more economically and socially secure life can be guaranteed to the working child is his or her total removal from the workplace desirable. The first step is the removal of children and teenagers from hazardous workplaces and the provision of education for working children. This type of response—unlike a boycott of goods made with child labour—is difficult to effect through international mechanisms. Bearing these complexities in mind, after considerable internal reflection, in May 1995 Unicef issued its own guidelines for procurement of goods on national and international markets to ensure that its own purchasing policy was entirely consistent with its stand on child exploitation and the provisions on child work set out in the Convention on the Rights of the Child[56].

Another country where Unicef devoted considerable attention to the issue of child labour was India. Since the early 1980s, there had been increasing exposure of child labour in the rapidly expanding hand-woven carpet industries of South Asia. The plight of these children, many of whom were 'bonded' to employers by parents manipulated into a position of unrepayable debt, was brought to national and international attention during the 1980s by organizations such as the Indian Bonded Liberation Front and Anti-Slavery International[57]. During the early 1990s, activists demanded legislative change and stronger penalties against perpetrators of bonded child labour. A German group working with Indian NGOs is trying to achieve an export ban on all rugs not carrying a 'Rugmark' seal of approval that the product was made without child labour. Unicef's country office in New Delhi was closely associated with this initiative, especially with programmes for the rehabilitation of children released from the carpet industry[58]. By 1995, the Indian Government had also begun to develop its own scheme to monitor labour practices in the industry[59].

One of the major problems in responding to the predicaments of CEDC was the lack of good data. Whatever the inadequacies of contemporary health and educational statistics, they were nothing in comparison with the gaps associated with hazardous child work, sexual abuse, child servitude and the impact of warfare and violence on children. Even in the organized labour sector—as for example in the Bangladesh garment industries—accurate information was hard to come by because factory owners were reluctant to release it. In the informal workplace, figures were even more elusive: as casual labourers in agriculture, fishing or on construction sites; in bars, restaurants and massage parlours, workers—adult or child—were rarely registered and their numbers fluctuated widely. Child workers in these occupations and in domestic service—which together constituted the majority of child workers in developing countries[60]—were to all intents and purposes officially non-existent. If this was the case for child labour, even more problematic was accurate information on even more sensitive categories, such as bonded labourers or the sexually abused.

While Unicef country offices grappled with these difficulties, other parts of the policy-making apparatus were helping to shed light on the ways in which pressures of all kinds and at all levels of society were fracturing childhood and family life. In 1990-94 the International Child Development Centre in Florence carried out a four-year international inquiry into the 'urban child in difficult circumstances'. This project brought together research from five countries—Brazil, India, Italy, Kenya and the Philippines—in an attempt to identify common features of childhood under stress both from old forms of poverty and from the 'new poverty' emanating from the economic reversals of the 1980s[61]. The Centre was also fostering policy-making debate around children's rights. Not only was it actively trying to bring the concepts of human development and human rights closer in Unicef thinking, it was helping to extend understanding that the doctrine of children's rights expressed by the Convention was not simply about protections and CEDC, but contained far broader implications. This point of view was strongly reinforced in Unicef's senior management team by Guido Bertolaso, Deputy Executive Director of External Relations from 1993 to 1995, a leading exponent within Unicef of the Convention as the legal and ethical framework for the organization's entire range of work.

In certain country offices, the full implications of the Convention for Unicef's programmes not only had been understood but were already being acted upon. In the vanguard, as ever, was Brazil, whose Unicef Country Programme for 1994-2000 was entitled: 'Children and adolescents: the right to have rights'. In other countries of Latin America, notably Bolivia and Ecuador, the Convention was similarly seized upon as a basis for advocacy on behalf of social and legal reform. This type of stance had previously been regarded as outside Unicef's mandate, or had simply been shunned for reasons of sensitivity. Now this began to change.

Reinforcement came from another part of the UN system. In February 1991, the 10-member Committee on the Rights of the Child was set up under the terms of the Convention. It included figures such as Thomas Hammarburg of Sweden, Marta Pais of Portugal and Hoda Badran of Egypt (an ex-Unicef staff member) who were internationally respected and deeply committed to the children's cause. The creation of this body was designed to give the Convention at least some teeth: no powers of legal enforcement are attached to any international human rights instrument. Within two years of ratifying the Convention, States Parties were obliged to report to the Committee on the steps they have taken towards implementation. The Committee's task was to review and critique these reports, taking into account the evidence of independent groups such as NGOs. As increasing numbers of countries ratified the Convention, Unicef offices began to find themselves drawn into this reporting process, as facilitators, as technical advisers and as allies of those agents—government and NGO—trying to maximize the Convention's potential.

Although the Committee is a watch-dog whose purpose is to monitor and, where necessary, criticize States Parties' child rights performance, its policy has been to foster a constructive dialogue with governments. Since all implementation of the Convention in terms of legislative and policy change has to be carried out at national and subnational level, persuasion rather than confrontation is seen as its most practicable strategy. The principal instrument at its disposal is the States Party reporting process. This can be used as an opportunity to raise sensitive or 'invisible' issues with the country concerned and encourage moves towards the vision of childhood encompassed in the Convention[62]. Both in the period leading up to the presentation of the States Party report and in the post-reporting phase, Unicef has been an active partner of the Committee in a number of countries.

A case in point was Viet Nam. One of the earliest countries in Asia to ratify the Convention, its report fell due in September 1992. At least a year in advance, the Unicef country office familiarized the Government with their reporting obligations and the procedures. An official government body, the Viet Nam Committee for Protection and Care of Children (CPCC), was designated to produce the report. To assist the CPCC, Unicef conducted a workshop on data-gathering and analysis, and the functions of the international Committee on the Rights of the Child. Between the time that work began on the report and the preparation of the final version several months later, an important consciousness-raising process had occurred. The first draft of the report was essentially superficial, but it gradually took on an entirely different character. CEDC topics—previously taboo—were included, and the authorities adopted a new tone of openness concerning social issues[63]. This experience showed that the Convention had a surprising capacity to transform policy even in environments where extensive dialogue with external partners was not a normal part of the political culture.

Of all the implications of the Convention for Unicef's work, the most profound was that it provided a new framework for its country programmes of cooperation. In the 1960s and 1970s, welfarism as the predominant motif of Unicef's mission had been displaced by the campaign for development and the provision of 'basic services'. Now, in its turn, this idea was being subsumed within a different vision: support for childhood in all its contexts and dimensions, and from age 0 to 18. The most fundamental implication of the new vision was that the social indicators normally accepted as those of classic poverty and underdevelopment should no longer be taken as the only signposts to the mission. Damaged childhood needed also to be analysed from the perspective of the 'new poverty' in the industrialized world, and from the perspective of the protection of children from armed violence, abandonment, economic exploitation and abuse. Although these were conditions extra to poverty itself, they were also conditions closely associated—even intertwined—with poverty.

Addressing the Unicef Executive Board in May 1991, Jan Martenson, UN Under-Secretary-General for Human Rights, stated: 'The most revolutionary element of Unicef's approach to the implementation of the Convention is the integration of [its] principles into country programmes and analyses. For the first time, the United Nations brings fully to bear on its practical activities, international standards of human dignity.'[64] For the majority of Unicef country offices, Martenson's congratulations were still premature. But in a pioneering few, new trends were being set, and increasingly, others were following their example.

For more than a decade Jim Grant had done his best to revitalize the development cause by claiming for children, especially for their survival and health, a position at its leading edge. At the World Conference on Human Rights in Vienna in June 1993, Grant's address was entitled: 'Children's rights: the cutting edge of human rights'. Here was a signal that Unicef was at last beginning to regard the doctrine of children's rights as central to its own policy and mission.

During 1994, the final year of Jim Grant's leadership of Unicef as well as of his life, the child health agenda moved significantly forward. In every region except sub-Saharan Africa, child nutrition levels were improving; measles deaths had dropped; polio was on its way towards eradication, with reported cases down by 36 per cent over the year[65]; IDD was on the run; vitamin A deficiency was in retreat; and guinea worm disease was down to 10 per cent of its former toll[66]. In World Breastfeeding Week, 24,000 doctors signed the Physician's Pledge to protect, promote and support breastfeeding[67]. True, not all the health news was positive: AIDS and malaria were far from under control. Nonetheless, those who in Unicef, in WHO, in other international organizations and research centres as well as in national health services throughout the developing world had been inspired by Jim Grant to revitalize the 'Health for All' agenda could justifiably feel that immense progress had been made.

Although the 'Education for All' agenda agreed at Jomtien in 1990 could not be said to be close to achievement, nonetheless significant progress here had also been made. The new emphasis on people's well-being and their capacity to better themselves within the continuing movement for development cast a new light on the importance of education; schooling was also being increasingly placed at the centre of concern for women and girls. Since Jomtien, there had been a shift in donor policies and resource commitments to basic education. In 1993 and 1994, World Bank lending to education totalled around $2 billion a year, half of which was allocated to primary education[68]. Unicef had more than doubled its resources for basic education, from $37 million in 1987 to $87 million in 1994[69]. However, despite new levels of commitment to basic education goals—notably from the 'E-9' countries: Bangladesh, Brazil, China, Egypt, India, Indonesia, Mexico, Nigeria and Pakistan—there was still a long way to go.

The campaign for universal ratification of the Convention on the Rights of the Child had, meanwhile, achieved extraordinary success. By November 1994, five years after its passage in the UN General Assembly, 167 countries had become States Parties. Addressing the UN General Assembly on 11 November 1994, Jim Grant observed that these ratifications were much more meaningful than mere strokes of 167 presidential pens. In many countries ratification had been preceded—or followed during the reporting process—by a national process of soul-searching. This had led to dialogue with civil society, media scrutiny, legislative change and the creation of new bodies to monitor the national well-being of children. Grant renewed his call for universal ratification by the mid-decade: 'I cannot think of any more appropriate way for the world to signal its commitment to human life and social progress in the year of the United Nations' 50th anniversary than by making the Convention the first truly universal law of humankind.'[70]

This speech—the last public speech of his Unicef career, and of his life—marked an important evolution in Grant's presentation of children's issues. He had not in any way abandoned 'the goals' or the post-Summit process—far from it. But in the past, his public statements on children's rights had mainly concentrated on the economic and social rights that underpinned the fulfilment of the human development agenda. Now, he catalogued the growing number of child protection issues related to war and to the ills of rapid economic and social transition that were increasingly dominating national and international consciousness.

Grant had decided that the moment had come to commit Unicef as publicly as possible to the new range of childhood issues that had accumulated on the international agenda. He had concluded that his own criterion of 'doability' should not be allowed to drive out issues that might be less 'doable' than immunization or curriculum reform, but had to be as important. 'The existence of measurable goals, deadlines and proven strategies in the areas of health, nutrition, education, water and family planning paves the way for accelerated action for children. But due to the lack of comparable goals, deadlines and strategies in the areas of child protection and observation, we run the risk that children's rights in these equally vital areas will be neglected or relegated to a lower priority. We must not allow this to happen.'

Grant's capacity for single-mindedness was a hallmark of his leadership style. He had spent his career in pursuit of the development agenda launched in the 1960s and modified down the many 'development decades'. The assault on poverty and underdevelopment in the South remained the overarching moral framework for his commitment to the children's cause. But he had a keen sense of judgement about when to move the agenda on. The pain of child sexual exploitation; the mutilations by land-mines; the disastrous impact of sanctions on the condition of children; the tragedy of AIDS orphanhood in Africa; the horror of children implicit in genocidal crime; all these issues and others were commanding a level of public attention that could not be ignored. The world's leading international organization for children not only had to engage in these issues within its country programmes and local advocacy campaigns; it had to do so, and be seen to do so, more strongly at international level. The volume of noise around childhood in trouble had convinced him that the time had come to elevate the vision of childhood expressed in the Convention—with all its complexities and sensitivities—to the cardinal position in the international struggle on behalf of child well-being.

By this time, Grant was seriously, and terminally, ill. He made this speech only by dint of extraordinary effort. He remained Unicef's Executive Director until 23 January 1995, a few days before his death. Pursuing his vision unto the end, he found a way to deploy even his final moments as an instrument for his wider purpose. The US was the only major country in the world not to have made any progress towards ratifying the Convention, as indeed it had failed to do for other international human rights instruments. This was a matter of great disappointment to Grant, who had used various opportunities of contact with the Clinton White House to promote the role of the US as a world leader on behalf of children and to press for the Convention's ratification. After its own eight-month review, still the US Government held back.

The day before he died, in response to a message of personal sympathy, Grant wrote to President Clinton asking yet again that the US sign the Convention[71]. At his memorial service on 10 February 1995, Hillary Clinton announced that the US would do so. A few days later, it did. No action could have been more fitting to mark the passing of James Pineo Grant and his extraordinary contributions both to the cause of human development and to the cause of children.

During the 15 years of his directorship, Grant had dominated Unicef. He had inherited an organization unique in the UN system and had developed and deployed its strengths to brilliant effect. He had had the time—a necessary commodity in the shaping of an international bureaucracy—to fashion a special course, focus organizational energies and put his own stamp firmly on the organizational culture. Under his leadership, Unicef had undergone enormous expansion in financial and human resources, its income rising from $313 million in 1980 to $1,006 million in 1994. He had personally raised the organization's profile and influence to an unprecedented degree. In the process he had done more than any other single individual in the past half century to put children on the international political, economic and social map. At his death, hundreds of tributes poured in from all over the world to honour his memory and register the profound impact he had made on individuals great and small.

But the aftermath of such a long and powerful leadership was bound to be problematic. Although he was in no sense an autocrat and inspired love as well as loyalty, Grant drove Unicef very hard. He rephrased John F. Kennedy: 'Ask not what shall be given to you, but what you shall give to Unicef', expecting the same tireless hard work, relentless energy and buoyant commitment to the cause that he himself always gave. He created a climate in which countless functionaries performed well above what they or anyone else would have believed possible. But the constant frenzied activity and the heightened sense of organizational mission had other impacts from a managerial point of view. As the agenda—and organizational size—expanded, from GOBI to child survival, from UCI to Summit Goals, and as one set of achievements led on without pause to multiplying sets of challenges, the experience was exhilarating, but it was also stressful, and the fabric of Unicef came under strain.

In 1993, the Unicef Executive Board requested a comprehensive management study into all aspects of the organization's work. Grant himself gave this management study his fullest cooperation and support. When its findings were delivered in late 1994, even though his health was failing, Grant devoted time to seeing that a suitable structure was set in place to implement its recommendations. The management consultants Booz, Allen and Hamilton described 'magnificent results', but they raised some questions about efficiency[72]. One matter of concern was the identification by the study team of a sense of malaise among Unicef staff. To what extent this reflected the general sense of insecurity currently being experienced throughout the UN system in the uncertain climate of post–cold war internationalism, and to what extent it was particular to the specific pressures within Unicef, the authors of the report were unable to say; their survey data was too limited. But this and other recommendations—on information systems, planning, emergencies, the streamlining of procedures—required careful attention[73].

Also in late 1994, an internal audit revealed that the rapid expansion of activity in one country office—Kenya—had led to managerial laxity and financial irregularity on a considerable scale. Unicef was at pains to explore all the parameters of this episode fully, be completely open about it, bring the culprits to book and introduce procedures to minimize any similar occurrence in future. However, it was a profound organizational shock to discover that what appeared to have been overambition on the part of certain individuals to reach mid-decade and decade goals could have led to such an outcome. These indications of organizational stress, coupled with wider issues related to demands for reform of the UN system, suggested a need for internal change.

On Grant's resignation, UN Secretary-General Boutros Boutros-Ghali appointed Richard Jolly as Acting Executive Director. The question of the post-Grant succession had long been exercising members of the Executive Board. Once again, as in 1979, the US 'possession' of Unicef's directorship was being challenged from Europe. Once again, the key movers were the Scandinavian countries, all of which were major Unicef donors: their combined governmental contributions in 1994 came to $215 million, nearly one fifth of Unicef's entire income[74].

Boutros-Ghali, like Kurt Waldheim before him, found it difficult to reach a decision between the European and US claims. But after Grant's death the question could no longer be postponed. Boutros-Ghali became open to a US candidature as long as another stipulation was met: that the UN Children's Fund should, for the first time, have a woman at its head. In May 1995, he appointed Carol Bellamy, previously an investment banker, then Director of the US Peace Corps, and well known as an ex-New York politician. In her first talk to the Unicef staff in New York headquarters, Bellamy spoke of her own experience as a Peace Corps volunteer in Guatemala and described it as one of the most enriching and influential passages in her life.

The immediate task facing Bellamy was managerial. While continuing along the track already set by the 1990s experience to date, Unicef would at the same time undergo a process of tidying and reinvigoration. There was also a need to maintain continuity and build on the accomplishments of the Grant regime. In her first speech to the Unicef Executive Board, she stated: 'I am fortunate to join an organization that already has clear goals, solid strategies and an overall agenda that will take us through the rest of the decade and into the next century. I want you to know that it is not my intention to steer Unicef in a new direction; I think that Unicef is headed in the right direction. What I see as my initial task is to keep the momentum going—accelerating it wherever possible—and helping to ensure that we get better mileage along the way.'

In the closing years of the 20th century, many forces are at work that will permanently affect the set of institutions that came together in the postwar world and have since constituted the United Nations system. Whatever Unicef's own mandate and idiosyncrasies, this is the international system of which it is a part. The mainspring of these forces is the end of the cold war and of the long ideological confrontation that divided the world and threatened another war of immense destruction affecting everyone on the globe. Because this threat is over, the face of internationalism has fundamentally altered, not only in the political and strategic sphere but in the social and economic. The full implications of what has happened will take many years to manifest themselves and to work their way through institutions, policies and attitudes.

Unexpectedly, a world in which there is no longer an incipient threat of a 'world war' is also one in which the concept of 'world' problems and the prospects of their solution by action taken at the international level have lost credibility. This is the opposite of what was first assumed when the Berlin Wall came down and the 'end of history'—the triumph of liberal democracy—was first declared. As a force for solving today's nationalist and ethnic conflicts, let alone the problems of poverty and social injustice, the new role of intergovernmental talking-shops and organizational bodies is far from clear. Every day, more is expected of international mechanisms invented in a different era for a different generation's tasks. Their failure to solve the problems laid at their door is usually ascribed to the lack of resources made available to them and an absence of 'international political will'. It is as much to do with their questionable suitability for the resolution of problems whose origin does not reside in the existence of powerful empires and overweening nation States and the need to broker relationships between them.

This does not mean that there is no role for internationalism: far from it. Certain issues—notably those associated with the environment and the 'global commons'—cannot be resolved in other fora. And in the context of many others, international networking and exchange—assisted by modern technology—have become a vital part of their debate and of the problem-solving process surrounding them. New methodologies for working at the international level that do not assume the existence of definitive power or political will at the international centre need to be developed. It is not overstating the case to suggest that the methodology invented by Jim Grant for Unicef's work in the period of his leadership—extensive mobilization around 'doable' goals for which the key actions take place at regional, national, local and community levels—provides one model. Whether it will be replicable, or replicated, in appropriate contexts has yet to be seen. Other models for different kinds of initiatives and campaigns will also be needed in an increasingly menu- and options-dominated international culture.

At one level, the world is becoming increasingly globalized; at another, increasingly fragmented. Because or in spite of both of these tendencies, in many countries government's role in the ordering of social and economic affairs is on the retreat. In some settings—in Africa and Eastern Europe, for example—it is the result of economic crisis and transition, and attendant cutbacks in government services. In others—the US and the UK, for example—it is a product of the elevation of market forces and contemporary ideological distaste for state intervention and bureaucracy. In such an atmosphere, it will be hard to maintain—let alone expand—official support for an international campaign against poverty and social inequity. The task is made harder by the number and scale of emergencies that the decade of the 1990s has so far witnessed, and the diversion of resources for international assistance into relief and peace-keeping measures. Without the pressure of public opinion as expressed through NGOs and other citizens' channels, there would probably be even less governmental willingness to invest public money in international programmes devoted to the resolution of other people's intractable internecine problems, let alone to their broader social and economic progress.

In the new climate governing international affairs, certain realities present new and exciting prospects. One of these is that the end of the post-colonial era is bound to be accompanied by the gradual demise of that whole set of values and assumptions that shaped a world-view of 'industrialized' versus 'developing', 'North' versus 'South'. In a world whose geopolitical components have fared so differently in the economic and strategic lottery of national wealth, commodity prices, superpower friendship and investment prospects, the notion of 'global progress' can no longer be viewed holistically. Global analyses of social and economic phenomena seem simplistic and out of date. The product of increasingly refined methods of data collection, situation analysis, programme planning and evaluation echoes the experience of four development decades: there is no such thing as a formulaic 'development' prescription any more than there is a formulaic predicament. In today's world, such ideas seem almost quixotic. Effective responses to problems of poverty both 'new' and old, and of other forms of disadvantage, have to derive from local, national and regional realities, as does their analysis. Diversity between regions and countries and within them; adaptability of strategies to circumstances on the ground; decentralization of decision-making to include the views of participants in the change process: these are the keynotes for the future.

The child-centred development agenda that preoccupied the energies of Unicef over much of the past 15 years—at least during the 1980s—was largely a reversion to the child health agenda. This was the preoccupation with the small child's physical well-being identified in Unicef's founding resolution and which dominated the work of its first 15 years. What Jim Grant realized, 20 years on, was that simple, low-cost technological means existed to tackle major problems of public health, and that no one had bothered to extend these techniques to reach the majority of the human race—to take them to the 'end of the road'. With the eagerness of an earlier generation of international health enthusiasts—a generation to which his father had belonged—he rediscovered and popularized the mass disease control agenda. This idea was willingly embraced by partners throughout the developing world and by the international apparatus of public health. With the aid of modern communications and social mobilization, it had a fantastic success. It was Grant's intention that this would provide a springboard for wider action across the whole human development agenda to which he was deeply committed.

However, certain attributes of the child survival and health agenda worked in its favour. Health problems are relatively uniform. And the medical breakthroughs of the 20th century have equipped public health practitioners with the technological means of transforming human well-being, given a relatively modest degree of human cooperation. Technological advance is far less potent in other areas of the human development agenda. With all the progress in communications, there is no way in which education, or the behavioural and attitudinal change it helps to bring about, can be injected from a syringe or ingested in a sugar and salt solution. To state that the eradication of such symptoms of poverty as illiteracy, environmental squalor, lack of food security and the presence of children in the workplace will be far more complex than the eradication of polio or iodine deficiency is to state the obvious. Whether the success with the child survival and health agenda can pave the way for fulfilling much of the rest remains an open question. Until the millennium, it will not be possible to tell whether such goals as 'universal access to water and sanitation' or 'universal access to basic education' were truly 'doable' in a similar way.

However, if the health agenda is seen as a health agenda and not as the vanguard for something else, the accomplishments of the past 15 years are more than remarkable. There is a very strong chance that before the end of the century, those goals established at the World Summit for Children that encapsulate that agenda will—outside such places as the poorest countries in sub-Saharan Africa and South Asia—have been virtually fulfilled. This will continue to require major effort on all sides. But by the year 2000, it is conceivable that—in so far as it is technologically practicable, a qualifier that excludes such prospects as the conquest of AIDS—the promise of 'Health for All' will have been delivered. If that happens, the achievement will owe much to the mobilizing power of the children's cause and to the joint contribution of Unicef and WHO.

It is important to realize, however, that even if the health goals are reached, there will still be a significant residue of work left undone. All mass public health campaigns, however smart their technology and effective their social mobilization, reach only a proportion of their target. That proportion may be high: 80, 90, even 95 per cent. In the case of some infectious agents, this may be enough to reduce their presence in a population to the point where the disease spontaneously dies out. In other cases it may not. And the remaining proportion of households still unreached by measles vaccine, or ORS packages, or sanitary latrines may take as long, cost as much and be as difficult to reach as the earlier 80 or 90 per cent. In a highly populated country, the unmet group can represent a subpopulation of many millions, and it will be unevenly distributed within the population as a whole. Inevitably, the extremely poor, ethnic minorities, fragmented families, girls, migrants and the dispossessed—all those who routinely suffer discrimination—will be overrepresented within it.

It is at this point that an approach based on human needs converges with that based on human rights. A universalist approach—'Health for All', 'Education for All'—assumes that by extending services ever outward, they will eventually embrace all those in need. In fact, they rarely do so. When an intervention has reached the majority of its target group, therefore, it is logical to abandon it in favour of an approach that specifically targets the unreached. 'Health for All'—and 'Education for All' and 'Water and Sanitation for All' following behind—cannot be allowed to stop short at the majority, even if that majority is a relatively large one.

Under the terms of the Convention on the Rights of the Child, affirmative programmes to reach those disadvantaged by exclusion from care and nurture, whether they bring services or redeem rights, target the same group of children. Those children today categorized as CEDC or children in need of protection—child victims of violence, exploitation, armed conflict, parental loss; children of ethnic minorities, refugees, the landless and lone parents; and girl children within every group—are the children with most need of, and least access to, health, education and social services. Children disadvantaged by unmet needs and children disadvantaged by unmet rights are, at the end of the day, the same disadvantaged children. Children whose rights to protection and participation are least fulfilled are—in the majority of cases—children whose vulnerability could equally well be described in the language of social and economic distress.

In this fusion of these twin strands of the 20th-century children's movement, the future of Unicef surely lies. Whatever have been the dichotomies of the past, the framework of needs and the framework of rights now seem destined to mesh. The idea of 'children as a lever for global progress'[75] is likely to make way for a greater emphasis on children in their own right, on children as subjects and objects rather than as the instruments of a wider social purpose embraced by a concept—global development—whose star is in eclipse.

Many new twists and turns await the story of international cooperation in the new millennium. Unicef will continue to be a small player in the ongoing drama of international affairs. But it can feel some pride, as well as renewed inspiration, that there has never been a time during the past 50 years when the children's cause has enjoyed a greater visibility or when there has been a clearer sense of the need to protect childhood. This applies wherever childhood is threatened, by whatever forces, in societies North, South, East, West, rich, poor and in between. Over the past 15 years, great gains have been made on behalf of child survival. Now, in the words of Carol Bellamy, Unicef is asking the question: 'Survival for what?'[76] As it faces its 51st year, that is the challenge in all its dimensions and its settings that Unicef is gathering its strength to meet.

Notes

Chapter 1. Children: A Cause Comes of Age

[1] Last, Murray, 'Putting children first', in *Disasters*, Vol. 18, No. 3, September 1994.

[2] Miles, Rosalind, *The Children We Deserve*, HarperCollins, London, 1994.

[3] Halsey, A.H., *Change in British Society*, Oxford University Press, Oxford, 1986.

[4] Boyden, Jo, *Families: Celebration and hope in a world of change*, Gaia/UNESCO, London, 1993.

[5] Halsey, op. cit.

[6] See Black, Maggie, *The Children and the Nations: The Story of Unicef*, UNICEF, New York, 1986; this earlier volume by the same author covers the period 1946-86 in much greater detail. See also Part II of *The State of the World's Children 1996*, UNICEF and Oxford University Press, New York, 1995.

[7] Black, op. cit.

[8] UNICEF, *Children of the Developing Countries: A Report by UNICEF*, The World Publishing Company, Cleveland and New York, 1963.

[9] Schneider, Bertrand, *The Barefoot Revolution: A Report to the Club of Rome*, Intermediate Technology Publications, London, 1988.

[10] *UNICEF Annual Reports, 1982, 1983, 1984, 1985*, UNICEF, New York.

[11] Interview by the author with James P. Grant, 8 March 1994.

[12] Grant, James P., 'Health for All by the Year 2000: Sincere Commitment or Empty Rhetoric?' Second Hugh R. Leavell Lecture, published in *Message from Calcutta: Highlights of the WFPHA III International Congress on Primary Health Care*, APHA, Washington, DC, 1981.

[13] This account of Grant's career is informed by biographical material prepared by the Office of the Executive Director at UNICEF before and after his death in January 1995 and research previously undertaken for *The Children and the Nations*, op. cit.

[14] Interview with Grant, op. cit.

[15] Black, op. cit.

[16] Interview by the author with Dr. Nyi Nyi, April 1994.

[17] Black, op. cit.

[18]Note for the record by Dr. Jon Rohde, UNICEF Country Representative, India, 24 July 1995.

[19]Interview by the author with Peter Adamson, February 1994.

[20]*The State of the World's Children 1986*, UNICEF and Oxford University Press, New York, 1985.

[21]Black, op. cit.

[22]Last, op. cit.

[23]Smyke, Patricia, 'The Story of the Convention on the Rights of the Child', unpublished manuscript commissioned by UNICEF, New York, 1993.

[24]*UNICEF Annual Report 1983*, UNICEF, New York, 1983.

[25]Smyke, op. cit.

[26]A number of interviews with UNICEF and non-UNICEF people involved in the Summit were conducted in the months following by Thomas Herwig, one of the UNICEF Summit team members. These interviews, which have not been published, were made available to the author.

[27]*The State of the World's Children 1992*, UNICEF and Oxford University Press, New York, 1991.

[28]'Strategies for Children in the 1990s', UNICEF Executive Board, E/ICEF/1989/L.5, 7 February 1989, and 'Development Goals and Strategies for Children: Priorities for UNICEF Action in the 1990s', UNICEF Executive Board, E/ICEF/1990/L.5, 13 February 1990.

[29]*The State of the World's Children 1989*, UNICEF and Oxford University Press, New York, 1988.

[30]Minutes of the Planning Committee for the World Summit for Children, January-June 1990; *World Summit for Children updates*, 1 March 1990 (et seq.).

[31]Herwig interviews, op. cit.

[32]*The Summit*, a newspaper published by Inter-Press Service to support the World Summit for Children, Nos. 1-4, 25/27/29 September and 1 October 1990.

[33]*World Summit for Children Words and Images*, UNICEF Division of Information, New York, 1991.

Chapter 2. The Global Drive for Immunization

[1] 'Promises to keep: Report of the Executive Director', UNICEF Executive Board, E/ICEF/1991/2 (Part 1), 7 March 1991.

[2] 'Universal Child Immunization, 1990', UNICEF Executive Board, E/ICEF/1991/L.8, 20 March 1991.

[3] Ibid.

[4] Hill, Terrel, Kim-Farley, Robert and Rohde, Jon, 'Expanded Programme on Immunization', in Rohde, Jon, Chatterjee, Meera and Morley, David (eds.), *Reaching Health for All*, Oxford University Press, New Delhi, 1993.

[5] Black, Maggie, *The Children and the Nations*, UNICEF, New York, 1986.

[6] Ibid.

[7] *The State of the World's Children 1986*, UNICEF and Oxford University Press, New York, 1985.

[8] 'Universal Child Immunization, 1990', op. cit.

[9] Goodfield, June, *The Planned Miracle*, Sphere Books, London, 1991.

[10] See *Social Science and Medicine*, Vol. 26, No. 9, 1988; issue dedicated to 'Selective or Comprehensive Primary Health Care'.

[11] Taylor, Carl and Jolly, Richard, 'The Straw Men of Primary Health Care', in *Social Science and Medicine*, ibid.

[12] Wisner, Ben, 'GOBI versus PHC? Some dangers of selective primary health care', in *Social Science and Medicine*, ibid.

[13] Taylor and Jolly, op. cit.

[14] *UNICEF Annual Report 1983*, UNICEF, New York, 1983.

[15] *The State of the World's Children 1982-83*, UNICEF and Oxford University Press, New York, 1982.

[16] *The State of the World's Children 1986*, UNICEF and Oxford University Press, New York, 1985.

[17] Ibid.

[18] Black, op. cit.

[19] *The State of the World's Children 1986*, op. cit.

[20] Black, op. cit.

[21] Goodfield, op. cit.

[22] Interview with Teresa Albañez, Regional Director for UNICEF, the Americas and Caribbean Region, based in Bogota at this time, August 1995.

[23] Black, op. cit.

[24] Goodfield, op. cit.

[25] *The State of the World's Children 1986*, op. cit.

[26] Goodfield, op. cit.

[27] 'The 1985 Turkish Immunization Campaign: Scope and Costs', Note by Richard Reid, Director, Division of Public Affairs, UNICEF, New York, 1994.

[28] Vittachi, Varindra Tarzie, *Between the Guns: Children as a Zone of Peace*, Hodder and Stoughton, London, 1993; and *The State of the World's Children 1986*, op. cit.

[29] Ibid.; see also Chapter 9.

[30] *The State of the World's Children 1986*, op. cit.

[31] Ibid.

[32] 'Universal Child Immunization, 1990', op. cit.

[33] Ibid.

[34] *The State of the World's Children 1986*, op. cit.

[35] *The State of the World's Children 1988*, UNICEF and Oxford University Press, New York, 1987.

[36] 'Universal Child Immunization', 1990, op. cit.

[37]*The State of the World's Children 1986*, op. cit.

[38]*Immunization Programme in India: A brief history 1978-1990*, India Country Office, UNICEF, New Delhi, November 1990.

[39]Ibid.

[40]Black, op. cit.

[41]*Immunization Programme in India: A brief history 1978-1990*, op. cit.

[42]Ibid.

[43]Chatterjee, Meera, 'Health for Too Many: India's Experiments with Truth', in Rohde, Jon, Chatterjee, Meera and Morley, David (eds.), *Reaching Health for All*, op. cit.

[44]*Immunization Programme in India: A brief history 1978-1990*, op. cit.

[45]Interview with L.N. Balaji, Chief of Research, Monitoring and Planning, India Country Office, UNICEF, New Delhi, October 1994.

[46]Ibid.

[47]Information provided by Dr. Jon Rohde, UNICEF Country Representative, India, memo of 12 July 1995.

[48]Chatterjee, op. cit.

[49]Balaji, op. cit.

[50]Ibid.

[51]*Immunization Programme in India: A brief history 1978-1990*, op. cit.

[52]Chaudhuri, Eliana Riggio, 'Universal Immunization in Urban Areas: Calcutta's Success Story', *Indian Journal of Public Health*, Vol. XXXIV, No. 4, Oct.-Dec. 1990.

[53]Chatterjee, op. cit.

[54]Fund-raising kit on immunization, UNICEF, New York, 1994 (update).

[55]'Sustainability of Achievements: Lessons Learned from Universal Child Immunization', Report of an independent steering committee on evaluation, UNICEF Evaluation and Research Office, New York, June 1995.

[56]Stackhouse, John, 'Putting a head count on poverty', *The Globe and Mail* (Toronto), 14 January 1995.

[57]'Universal Child Immunization, 1990', op. cit.

[58]Ibid.

[59]'The Bamako Initiative: Recommendation to the Executive Board for Programme Cooperation, 1989-93', UNICEF Executive Board, E/ICEF/1988/P/L.40, 15 March 1988.

[60]'The Bamako Initiative: An information kit', UNICEF, New York, 1994.

[61]*UNICEF Annual Report 1988*, UNICEF, New York, 1988.

[62]'Revitalizing Primary Health Care/Maternal and Child Health: The Bamako Initiative, Progress Report', UNICEF Executive Board, E/ICEF/1989/L.3, 1 March 1989.

[63]'The Bamako Initiative: An information kit', op. cit; see also 'The Bamako Initiative Progress Report', UNICEF Executive Board, E/ICEF/1992/L.6, 3 February 1992.

[64]*UNICEF Annual Report 1990*, UNICEF, New York, 1990.

[65]'The Bamako Initiative Progress Report', op. cit.

[66]'Revitalizing Primary Health Care/Maternal and Child Health: The Bamako Initiative, Progress Report', UNICEF Executive Board, E/ICEF/1990/L.3, 20 February 1990.

[67]Ibid.

[68]'Experience to Date of Implementing the Bamako Initiative: A Review and Five Country Case Studies', UNICEF Executive Board, E/ICEF/1992/L.20, 13 April 1992.

[69]*UNICEF Annual Report 1993*, UNICEF, New York, 1993.

[70]*The State of the World's Children 1991*, UNICEF and Oxford University Press, New York, 1990.

[71]Ibid.

[72]*UNICEF Annual Report 1992*, UNICEF, New York, 1992.

[73]Safe motherhood and AIDS are covered in Chapter 7, 'The Gender Dimension'.

[74]'Health Strategy for UNICEF', UNICEF Executive Board, E/ICEF/1995/11/Rev. 1, 13 July 1995.

[75]'Progress Report on the Children's Vaccine Intitiative', UNICEF Executive Board, E/ICEF/1993/L.3, 16 February 1993.

[76]'Sustainability of Achievements: Lessons Learned from Universal Child Immunization', op. cit.

[77]*UNICEF Annual Report 1993*, UNICEF, New York, 1993.

[78]'Sustainability of Achievements: Lessons Learned from Universal Child Immunization', op. cit.; data are from 1993, WHO/EPI Information System, 1995.

[79]Ibid., page xiii.

Chapter 3. Unravelling the Nutrition Complex

[1] Black, Maggie, *The Children and the Nations*, UNICEF, New York, 1986.

[2] Ibid.

[3] Carpenter, Kenneth J., *Protein and energy, A study of changing ideas*, Cambridge University Press, Cambridge, 1994.

[4] Brock, J.F. and Autret, Marcel, *Kwashiorkor in Africa*, FAO/WHO, Rome, 1952.

[5] Carpenter, op. cit.

[6] Black, op. cit.

[7] McLaren, Donald S., 'The Great Protein Fiasco', in *The Lancet*, Vol. 2, 13 July 1974, pp. 93-96.

[8] Carpenter, op. cit.

[9] Black, op. cit.

[10]Black, op. cit.

[11]Carpenter, op. cit.

[12]McLaren, op. cit.

[13]Jelliffe, Derrick B. and E.F. Patrice, *Human Milk in the Modern World*, Oxford University Press, Oxford, 1978.

[14]*Food, health and care: the UNICEF strategy and vision for a world free from hunger and malnutrition*, UNICEF, New York, 1992? (n.d.).

[15]See Chapter 5, 'City Streets and Children's Rights', and Chapter 7, 'The Gender Dimension'.

[16]*UNICEF Annual Report 1983*, UNICEF, New York, 1983.

[17]Morley, D., 'Prevention of protein-calorie syndrome', in *Transactions of the Royal Society of Tropical Medicine and Hygiene*, 1968, quoted in *The Lancet*, Vol. 342, 7 August 1993, p. 351.

[18]Morely, David and Woodland, Margaret, *See How They Grow: Monitoring child growth for appropriate health care in developing countries*, Oxford University Press, New York, 1979.

[19]Rohde, Jon, 'Indonesia's *Posyandus*: Accomplishments and Future Challenges', in Rohde, Jon, Chatterjee, Meera and Morley, David (eds.), *Reaching Health for All*, Oxford University Press, New Delhi, 1993.

[20]Ibid.

[21]Ibid.

[22]Rohde, Jon, personal communication, July 1985.

[23]Personal experience of the author, September 1994.

[24]Jonsson, Urban, Ljungqvist, Bjorn and Yambi, Olivia, 'Mobilization for Nutrition in Tanzania', in *Reaching Health for All*, op. cit. See also *"We will never go back": Social Mobilization in the Child Survival and Development Programme in the United Republic of Tanzania*, UNICEF, New York, 1993.

[25]*The Joint WHO/UNICEF Nutrition Support Programme in Iringa, Tanzania; 1983-1988 Evaluation Report*, Government of Tanzania, WHO and UNICEF, Dar es Salaam, 1988.

[26]Jonsson et al, op. cit.

[27]Ibid.

[28]*The State of the World's Children 1985*, UNICEF and Oxford University Press, New York, 1984.

[29]'Growth Monitoring: Intermediate Technology or Expensive Luxury?' Editorial in *The Lancet*, Vol. II, 14 December 1985, pp. 1337-1338.

[30]Ibid.

[31]Gopalan, C. and Chatterjee, M., *Use of growth charts for promoting child nutrition. A review of global experience*, Nutrition Foundation of India, New Delhi, 1985, quoted in *The Lancet*, ibid.

[32]*The State of the World's Children 1985*, op. cit.

[33]Ibid.

[34]*Nutrition into the Nineties*, Report of the UNICEF Workshop on Nutrition Policy and Action, Naivasha, Kenya, April 1987, UNICEF, New York, 1987.

[35]Pearson, Roger, *Thematic Evaluation of UNICEF Support to Growth Monitoring*, UNICEF Evaluation and Research Office, New York, 1993.

[36]Ibid.

[37]Marin, Patricia and de Oliveira, Yedda P., 'The breastfeeding programme in Brazil', in Jelliffe, Derrick B. and E.F. Patrice (eds.), *Programmes to promote breastfeeding*, Oxford Medical Publications, Oxford, 1988.

[38]da Cunha, Gerson, 'Telling the mothers "You can breastfeed!"' in *UNICEF News*, Issue 114/1982/2.

[39]*The State of the World's Children 1988*, UNICEF and Oxford University Press, New York, 1987.

[40]Winikoff, Beverly, 'Modification of hospital practices to remove obstacles to successful breastfeeding', in Jelliffe and Jelliffe (1988), op. cit.

[41]'Tearing down the infant formula posters', in *UNICEF Annual Report 1983*, UNICEF, New York, 1983.

[42]*The State of the World's Children 1992*, UNICEF and Oxford University Press, New York, 1991.

[43]'Report of the Executive Director: Overview of actions for children in 1990', UNICEF Executive Board, E/ICEF/1991/2 (Part II), 22 March 1991.

[44]*UNICEF Annual Report 1992*, UNICEF, New York, 1992.

[45]'Report of the Executive Director', UNICEF Executive Board, E/ICEF/1995/14 (Part II), 10 April 1995.

[46]Murray-Lee, Maggie, 'Baby-friendly hospital initiative takes off', in *First Call for Children*, UNICEF, No. 1992/1, January-March 1992.

[47]*Restoring a breastfeeding culture in Mexico*, Secretario de Salud and UNICEF, Mexico City, 1992.

[48]*UNICEF Annual Report 1994*, UNICEF, New York, 1994, and *UNICEF Annual Report 1995*, UNICEF, New York, 1995.

[49]*Food, health and care*, op. cit.

[50]See Chapter 7, 'The Gender Dimension'.

[51]*Food, health and care*, op. cit.

[52]*The State of the World's Children 1986*, UNICEF and Oxford University Press, New York, 1985.

[53]Sommer, Alfred, 'A Bridge Too Far', in *The Progress of Nations 1995*, UNICEF, New York, 1995.

[54]Ibid.

[55]de Pee, Saskia et al., 'Vitamin A', in *The Lancet*, 1995, Vol. 346, 8 July 1995, p. 76.

[56]*The Progress of Nations 1995*, op. cit.

[57]'Global prevalence of iodine deficiency disorders', WHO Micronutrient Deficiency Information System Working Paper No. 1, WHO/UNICEF/ICCIDD, 1993.

[58]*The State of the World's Children 1991*, UNICEF and Oxford University Press, New York, 1990.

[59]Ibid.

[60]Black, op. cit.

[61]*Small salt producers and universal salt iodisation*, UNICEF Nutrition Section, New York, 16 November 1994.

[62]*Meeting the challenge of iodine deficiency, The Joint WHO/UNICEF Nutrition Support Programme in Bolivia*, UNICEF/PAHO, La Paz, 1990.

[63]'Nutrition for the Mother and Child', Fund-raising documentation prepared by UNICEF La Paz for the 1989-93 Programme of Cooperation, December 1991.

[64]Usher, John, 'Agencies act to bring "hidden hunger" into fuller view', in *First Call for Children*, UNICEF, No. 1992/1, January-March 1992.

[65]Information provided by Dr. David Alnwick, Senior Micronutrient Adviser, UNICEF, December 1995.

[66]'Strategy for improved nutrition of children and women in developing countries', UNICEF Executive Board, E/ICEF/1990/L.6, 9 March 1990.

[67]*Food, Health and Care*, op. cit.

[68]See Chapter 1.

[69]Author's personal observation from firsthand experience of the project in Nigeria, 1989.

[70]'Strategy for improved nutrition of children and women in developing countries', op. cit.

[71]Ibid.

[72]See, for example, *World Declaration and Plan of Action from the World Summit for Children, Appendix: Goals for Children and Development in the 1990s*, II. Supporting/sectoral goals, B. Nutrition (vi).

[73]*UNICEF Annual Reports, 1992, 1993, 1994, 1995*, UNICEF, New York.

[74]Letter from James P. Grant to Mr. Edouard Saouma, Director-General of FAO, and Dr. Hiroshi Nakajima, Director-General of WHO, 18 September 1991, circulated to all Unicef offices under cover of CF/EXD/1992-001 by R. Jolly, Deputy Executive Director, 13 January 1992.

[75]Grant, James P., 'Nutritional Security: An Ethical Imperative of the 1990s', Address at the International Nutrition Conference, Rome, 7 December 1992.

[76]Ibid.

Chapter 4. Water, Environment, Sanitation: The Changing Agenda

[1] Black, Maggie, *The Children and the Nations*, UNICEF, New York, 1986.

[2] Beyer, Martin, 'Water and Sanitation in UNICEF, 1946-1986', UNICEF History Series, Monograph VIII, 1987.

[3] Black, Maggie, *From Handpumps to Health*, UNICEF, New York, 1990.

[4] Ibid.

[5] Beyer, op. cit.

[6] Wahadan, L., Dodge, C.P., Ekvall, T. and Yousif, M.A., 'Cost Effective Water and Sanitation in Sudan', *Water Quality Bulletin*, Vol. 15, No. 1, January 1990.

[7] 'Can Water Mean Health?', editorial, in *UNICEF News*, Issue 116/1983/2.

[8] *The State of the World's Children 1982-83*, UNICEF and Oxford University Press, New York, 1982.

[9] Cairncross, Sandy, 'Water Supply and Sanitation: an Agenda for Research', *Journal of Tropical Medicine and Hygiene*, Vol. 92, 1989, pp. 301-314.

[10]Beyer, op. cit.

[11]Ibid.

[12]'Water and Health: the Facts', *UNICEF News*, op. cit.

[13]Cairncross, Sandy, 'The benefits of water supply', in Pickford, John (ed.) *Developing World Water*, Grosvenor Press International, London, 1987.

[14] *UNICEF Annual Report 1982*, UNICEF, New York, 1982, and *UNICEF Annual Report 1987*, UNICEF, New York, 1987.

[15] *The State of the World's Children 1988*, UNICEF and Oxford University Press, New York, 1987.

[16] 'Report of the Executive Director', UNICEF Executive Board, E/ICEF/1991/2 (Part II), 22 March 1991.

[17] Ibid.

[18] *The State of the World's Children 1991*, UNICEF and Oxford University Press, New York, 1990.

[19] See also Chapter 2, 'The Global Drive for Immunization'.

[20] *The State of the World's Children 1988*, op. cit.

[21] Grant, James P., 'ORT: Celebration and Challenge', Address to the 'Celebrating 25 Years of ORT' Conference, Washington, DC, 2 March 1994.

[22] *The State of the World's Children 1990*, UNICEF and Oxford University Press, New York, 1989.

[23] *UNICEF Annual Report 1983*, UNICEF, New York, 1983.

[24] *The State of the World's Children 1988*, op. cit.

[25] Ibid.

[26] 'Report of the Executive Director: Overview of actions for children in 1987', UNICEF Executive Board, E/ICEF/1988/2 (Part II), 23 February 1988.

[27] 'A Global Review of Diarrhoeal Disease Control' (draft report), UNICEF, New York, 1995.

[28] Grant, James P., op. cit.

[29] Interview with Dr. Felipe Mota, Director of CDD, Mexico, May 1994.

[30] Ibid.

[31] 'Report of the Executive Director', UNICEF Executive Board, E/ICEF/1993/2 (Part II), 19 March 1993.

[32] *The State of the World's Children 1993*, UNICEF and Oxford University Press, New York, 1992.

[33] *Saving 27,000,000 Young Children in this Decade: Goals, Strategies and Activities to Control Diarrhoeal Diseases and Acute Respiratory Infections*, UNICEF, New York, 1993.

[34] Wurzel, Peter, 'Maximizing and Sustaining Health through Water Supplies and Sanitation – The Pakistan Experience', in *Water Quality Bulletin*, op. cit.

[35] Black, *From Handpumps to Health*, op. cit.

[36] de Rooy, C. and Donaldson, L.A., 'Integrated Water and Sanitation Development: The Nigerian Experience', *Water Quality Bulletin*, op. cit.

[37] Akhter, M., 'SWACH: An Integrated Approach to Control Guinea Worm Disease in India', in *Water Quality Bulletin*, op. cit.

[38] Ibid.

[39] Black, *From Handpumps to Health*, op. cit.

[40] Akhter, M., op. cit.

[41] 'SWACH Progress Report', Fifth Progress Report (July 1992-June 1993) for the Government of Sweden, UNICEF, New Delhi, September 1993.

[42]'Rural Water Supply and Environmental Sanitation Programme in India', Second Progress Report (July 1992-June 1993) to the Government of Sweden, UNICEF, New Delhi, October 1993.

[43]Black, *From Handpumps to Health*, op. cit.

[44]'Water, Sanitation and Health for All by the Year 2000: UNICEF Actions for the Years to Come', UNICEF Executive Board, E/ICEF/1988/L.4, 9 February 1988; see also Beyer, Martin, *Review of Water and Sanitation Sector Evaluation Reports*, UNICEF, New York, October 1991.

[45]Esrey, S.A., Feachem, R.G. and Hughes, J.M., 'Interventions for the control of diarrhoeal diseeases among young children: improving water supplies and excretion disposal facilities', in *Bulletin of the World Health Organization*, Vol. 63(4), 1985, pp. 757-772.

[46]Appleton, Brian, 'The Decade Flows On', in *New Internationalist*, May 1990.

[47]'Water, Sanitation and Health for All by the Year 2000: UNICEF Actions for the Years to Come', op. cit.

[48]*UNICEF and the 1990s: The Water and Sanitation Sector*, UNICEF Watsan Section, New York, 17 November 1989.

[49]Saint-Lot, M., personal communication, August 1995.

[50]*UNICEF and the 1990s: The Water and Sanitation Sector*, op. cit.

[51]*Keeping the Promise to Children: Goals for 1995*, UNICEF, New York, 1993.

[52]'Children and Environment: A UNICEF Strategy for Sustainable Development', UNICEF Executive Board, E/ICEF/1989/L.6, 13 February 1989.

[53]*Children and the Environment: The State of the Environment 1990*, UNICEF and UNEP, New York, 1990.

[54]Jolly, Richard, 'A Human-Centred Strategy for Environmental Improvement: The Children's Dimension', Statement to the Preparatory Committee of the United Nations Conference on Environment and Development, Geneva, 28 August 1991.

[55]Grant, James P., 'Saving our Earth by Nurturing our Children', Address to the United Nations Conference on Environment and Development, Rio de Janeiro, 8 June 1992.

[56]'Implementing Agenda 21: A Priority for WES', in *UNICEF Waterfront*, Special Issue, March 1994.

[57]*UNICEF and the 1990s: The Water and Sanitation Sector*, op. cit.

[58]Black, *From Handpumps to Health*, op. cit.

[59]*UNICEF Waterfront*, Issue 6, December 1994.

[60]'Rural Water Supply and Environmental Sanitation Programme in India', op. cit.

[61]'Intensive Sanitation Project Medinipur, Progress Report 1993', Ramakrishna Mission Lokasiksha Parishad, Calcutta, 1993.

[62]'Project Profile: Intensive Sanitation Project, Medinipur District, West Bengal', UNICEF Watsan, New Delhi, 1994.

[63]Reports of the Ramakrishna Mission Lokasiksha Parishad, supplied to the author in September 1994.

[64]'Gerakan Jum'at Bersih (Clean Friday Movement) and Posyandu Kader Jamboree', Briefing Notes, UNICEF, Jakarta, June 1994.

[65]Ibid.

[66]'Indonesian President Launches 'Clean Friday' Movement', in *UNICEF Waterfront*, op. cit.

[67]Briscoe, John, 'When the Cup is Half Full', in *Environment*, Vol. 35, No. 4, May 1993.

[68]Ibid.

[69]Cairncross, Sandy, Hardoy, Jorge E. and Satterthwaite, David, 'The Urban Context', in *The Poor Die Young, Housing and Health in Third World Cities*, Earthscan, London, 1990.

[70]'Safe Water: Lesson from the Barrio', *The State of the World's Children 1994*, UNICEF and Oxford University Press, New York, 1993.

[71]'Planning for Health and Socio-Economic Benefits from Water and Environmental Sanitation Programmes', in *UNICEF Waterfront*, Issue 4, August 1994.

[72]'UNICEF's Strategies in Water and Environmental Sanitation', UNICEF Executive Board, E/ICEF/1995/17, 13 April 1995.

[73]Ibid.

[74]'Water and Environmental Sanitation: A Strategy for Sustainable Development', in *UNICEF Waterfront*, Issue 7, May 1995.

[75]'UNICEF's Strategies in Water and Environmental Sanitation', op. cit.

[76]Black, Maggie, 'Mega-Slums: The coming sanitary crisis', Report for WaterAid (UK), London, March 1993.

Chapter 5. City Streets and Children's Rights

[1] Cousins, William J., 'Urban Basic Services in UNICEF: An Historical Overview', UNICEF History Series, Monograph XIV, 1992.

[2] Brown, Lester and Jacobsen, Jodi L., *The Future of Urbanization: Facing the Ecological and Economic Constraints*, Worldwatch Institute, Washington, DC, 1987.

[3] Ibid.

[4] Donohue, John, 'Some facts and figures on urbanization in the developing world', in *Assignment Children* 57/58, issue on *Social planning with the urban poor*, UNICEF, 1982.

[5] Cousins, op. cit.

[6] Donohue, op. cit.

[7] Ibid.

[8] Cousins, op. cit.

[9] *The Invisible Adjustment: Poor Women and the Economic Crisis*, UNICEF Regional Programme for Women in Development, Americas and the Caribbean, Santiago, 1989.

[10]Cousins, op. cit.

[11]Ibid.

[12]Ibid.

[13]Black, Maggie, *The Children and the Nations*, UNICEF, New York, 1986.

[14]Balcomb, John, 'Building on the people's energy', in *UNICEF News,* Issue 115/1983/1.

[15]Cousins, William J. and de la Soudière, Marie, *Urban Basic Services in India: A Preliminary Review,* UNICEF, New Delhi, October 1992.

[16]*Urban Basic Services Programme for the Poor (UBSP), Approach and Achievements,* National Institute of Urban Affairs, New Delhi, February 1994.

[17]Cousins, op. cit.

[18]Ibid.

[19]Cassim, Jehan K., Peries, Trevor H.R., Jayasinghe, Vinitha and Fonseka, Leo, 'Development Councils for Participatory Urban Planning', in *Assignment Children* 57/58, UNICEF, 1982.

[20]Cousins, op. cit.

[21]*An Evaluation Report of the Baldia Soakpit Pilot Project,* UNICEF, Islamabad, January 1990.

[22]*The Urban Poor in Bangladesh,* UNICEF, Dhaka, 1993.

[23]Cousins, op. cit.

[24]Ibid.

[25]*Mayors As Defenders of Children,* UNICEF, New York, 1992.

[26]'Third International Colloquium of Mayors, Defenders of Children', Information Note, UNICEF, New York, December 1994.

[27]'UNICEF Programmes for the Urban Poor', UNICEF Executive Board, E/ICEF/1993/L.9, 23 February 1993.

[28]Boyden, Jo (with Holden, Pat), *Children of the Cities,* Zed Books, London, 1991.

[29]Ibid.

[30]'Children in Especially Difficult Circumstances', UNICEF Executive Board, E/ICEF/1986/L.3, 27 February 1986.

[31]Black, op. cit.

[32]Swift, Anthony, 'Social Mobilization—The Brazil Experience', unpublished report for UNICEF, 1994.

[33]Ibid.

[34]Bequele, Assefa, 'Emerging Perspectives in the Struggle against Child Labour', in Myers, William E., *Protecting Working Children,* Zed Books and UNICEF, London, 1991.

[35]Zizzamia, Alba, 'NGO/UNICEF Cooperation: A Historical Perspective', UNICEF History Series, Monograph V, 1987.

[36]Cousins, op. cit.

[37]'Children in Especially Difficult Circumstances', op. cit.

[38]Black, Maggie, 'Philippines: Children of the Runaway Cities', Case study in the series *The Urban Child in Difficult Circumstances,* Innocenti Studies, UNICEF/ICDC, Florence, 1991.

[39]Blanc, Christina Szanton (ed.), *Urban Children in Distress: Global Predicaments and Innovative Strategies,* UNICEF/ICDC and Gordon and Breach, Florence, 1994.

[40]Munyakho, Dorothy, 'Kenya: Child newcomers in the urban jungle', Case study in the series *The Urban Child in Difficult Circumstances,* Innocenti Studies, UNICEF/ICDC, Florence, 1992.

[41]Mia, Ahmadullah, *A Promising Path: UCEP Non-Formal Education in Bangladesh*, UCEP, Bangladesh, 1991.

[42]Black, Maggie, 'Street and Working Children', Report of an Innocenti Global Seminar, UNICEF/ICDC, Florence, 1993.

[43]Personal visit in late 1994.

[44]Swift, op. cit.

[45]Allsebrook, Annie and Swift, Anthony, *Broken Promise: The World of Endangered Children*, Hodder and Stoughton, London, 1989.

[46]Smyke, Patricia, 'The Story of the Convention on the Rights of the Child', unpublished manuscript commissioned by UNICEF, New York, 1993; see also Chapter 1.

[47]Ibid.

[48]Schneider, Bertrand, *The Barefoot Revolution: A Report to the Club of Rome*, Intermediate Technology Publications, London, 1988.

[49]Boyden, Jo, *Families: Celebration and hope in a world of change*, Gaia/UNESCO, London, 1993.

[50]Miles, Rosalind, *The Children We Deserve*, HarperCollins, London, 1994.

[51]Smyke, op. cit.

[52]Interview with James P. Grant, March 1994.

[53]Smyke, op. cit.

[54]Ibid.

[55]*The State of the World's Children 1989*, UNICEF and Oxford University Press, New York, 1988.

[56]Smyke, op. cit.

[57]Swift, Anthony, 'Brazil: The Fight for Childhood in the City', Case study in the series *The Urban Child in Difficult Circumstances*, Innocenti Studies, UNICEF/ICDC, Florence, 1991.

[58]See earlier in this chapter.

[59]*The UNICEF Brazil Country Programme Reader*, UNICEF, Brasília, December 1990.

[60]da Costa, Antonio Carlos Gomes and Schmidt-Rahmer, Barbara, 'Brazil: Children Spearhead a Movement for Change', in *The Convention: Child Rights and UNICEF Experience at the Country Level*, Innocenti Studies, UNICEF/ICDC, Florence, 1991.

Chapter 6. Global Shifts

[1] 'The Impact of World Recession on Children', A UNICEF Special Study published as Chapter IV of *The State of the World's Children 1984*, UNICEF and Oxford University Press, New York, 1983.

[2] Arnold, Guy, *The End of the Third World*, St. Martin's Press and Macmillan, London, 1993.

[3] Figures provided by Jan Vandemoortele, UNICEF Office of Social Policy and Economic Analysis, in a memorandum of 28 June 1995.

[4] *World Development Report 1993*, The World Bank, Washington, DC, 1993.

[5] Jespersen, Eva, 'External Shocks, Adjustment Policies and Economic and Social Performance', in Cornia, Giovanni Andrea, van der Hoeven, Rolph and Mkandawire, Thandika (eds.), *Africa's Recovery in the 1990s: from Stagnation and Adjustment to Human Development*, UNICEF and Macmillan, London, 1992.

[6] Sachs, Wolfgang, 'Development: a guide to the ruins', in *New Internationalist*, Issue 232, June 1992; see also Sachs, Wolfgang (ed.), *The Development Dictionary*, Zed Books, London, 1992.

[7] Harris, Nigel, *The End of the Third World: Newly Industrializing Countries and the Decline of an Ideology*, Penguin, London, 1990.

[8] Hobsbawm, Eric, *Age of Extremes: The Short Twentieth Century, 1914-1991*, Michael Joseph, London, 1994.

[9] Ibid.

[10] Ibid., and Harris, op. cit.

[11] Kennedy, Paul, *Preparing for the Twenty-First Century*, HarperCollins, London, 1994.

[12] *The Progress of Nations 1993, 1994, 1995*, UNICEF, New York.

[13] Kennedy, op. cit.

[14] Jespersen, op. cit.

[15] Kennedy, op. cit.

[16] *Report of the North-South Food Roundtable on The Crisis in Africa*, Report of a meeting held in collaboration with UNICEF and WFC, North-South Roundtable, Islamabad, March 1985.

[17] *UNICEF Annual Reports*; UNICEF, New York, see also 'Africa: the permanent crisis', in *The State of the World's Children 1985*, UNICEF and Oxford University Press, New York, 1984.

[18] *The State of the World's Children 1982-83*, UNICEF and Oxford University Press, New York, 1982.

[19] *The State of the World's Children 1991*, UNICEF and Oxford University Press, New York, 1990.

[20] Cornia, Giovanni Andrea, Jolly, Richard and Stewart, Frances, *Adjustment with a Human Face: Protecting the Vulnerable and Promoting Growth*, Volume I, UNICEF and Oxford University Press, New York, 1987.

[21] 'The Impact of World Recession on Children', op. cit.

[22] 'Adjustment with a Human Face', published as Part II of *The State of the World's Children 1987*, UNICEF and Oxford University Press, New York, 1986.

[23] Cornia, Giovanni Andrea, 'Economic Decline and Human Welfare in the First Half of the 1980s', in *Adjustment with a Human Face*, op. cit.

[24] *The State of the World's Children 1987*, UNICEF and Oxford University Press, New York, 1986.

[25] Author's personal experience, Nigeria, 1989.

[26] Cornia, Giovanni Andrea, 'Adjustment Policies 1980-1985', in *Adjustment with a Human Face*, op. cit.

[27] 'Report of the Executive Director', UNICEF Executive Board, E/ICEF/1987/2, 24 February 1987.

[28]'Report of the Executive Director', UNICEF Executive Board, E/ICEF/1986/2, 28 February 1986.

[29]'Report of the Executive Director' (1987), op. cit.

[30]See *Adjustment with a Human Face*; see also *Within Human Reach: A Future for Africa's Children*, UNICEF, New York, 1985.

[31]A study on Adjustment with a Human Face, amounting to a synopsis of the larger study, was published as Part II of *The State of the World's Children 1987*, op. cit.

[32]See 'Reports of the Executive Director', UNICEF Executive Board, throughout the late 1980s. The historical record of 'adjustment with a human face' was set out fully in several articles in *World Development*, 1991, Vol. 19, No. 12, pp. 1801-1864.

[33]'Report of the Executive Director: Overview of actions for children in 1990', UNICEF Executive Board, E/ICEF/1991/2 (Part II), 22 March 1991.

[34]*Famine: A Man-made Disaster? A Report for the Independent Commission on International Humanitarian Issues*, Vintage Books, New York, 1985.

[35]See Chapter 9.

[36]Black, Maggie, *The Children and the Nations*, UNICEF, New York, 1986.

[37]'Report of the Executive Director' (1991), op. cit.

[38]*UNICEF Annual Reports*, 1980s et seq.

[39]*UNICEF Annual Report 1987*, UNICEF, New York, 1987.

[40]*The State of the World's Children 1988*, UNICEF and Oxford University Press, New York, 1987.

[41]'Report of the Executive Director: Overview of actions for children in 1987', UNICEF Executive Board, E/ICEF/1988/2 (Part II), 23 February 1988.

[42]Interview with Djibril Diallo of the Division of Public Affairs by Tom Herwig, carried out in association with the collection of oral history material on the World Summit for Children, March 1991.

[43]Ibid., and interviews by the author with Djibril Diallo and Anthony Hughes in the UNICEF Division of Public Affairs, March 1994.

[44]*The State of the World's Children 1988*, op. cit.

[45]'Report of the Executive Director: Overview of actions for children in 1987', op. cit.

[46]See Chapter 1.

[47]*Economic Decline and Child Survival: Evidence from Africa in the 1980s*, Innocenti Update No. 12, UNICEF/ICDC, August 1992. The material in this newsletter was based on *Africa's Recovery in the 1990s*, op. cit., then forthcoming.

[48]Ibid.

[49]Ibid.

[50]*Human Development Report 1991*, Oxford University Press and UNDP, New York, 1991.

[51]*Children on the Front Line: The impact of apartheid, destabilization and warfare on children in southern and South Africa*, A report for UNICEF, first published in 1987; update published in 1989.

[52]Ibid.

[53]*The State of the World's Children 1990*, UNICEF and Oxford University Press, New York, 1989.

[54]Information provided by Dr. Richard Jolly, December 1995.

[55]'UNICEF Debt-for-Child Development', paper by Eva Jespersen, UNICEF, New York, November 1995.

[56]*Debt Relief for Children: A Pioneering Experience in Sudan*, UNICEF, Khartoum, n.d.

[57]'UNICEF Debt-for-Child Development', op. cit.

[58]Black, Maggie, *AIDS and Children: An Impending Calamity*, UNICEF, New York, 1990.

[59]'Children and AIDS', article in *Africa's Children*, an Information Kit produced by UNICEF for the International Conference on Assistance to African Children, Dakar, Senegal, November 1992.

[60]For a fuller discussion of UNICEF's involvement in programmes to lessen the impact of AIDS on women and children, see Chapter 7.

[61]*AIDS and Orphans in Africa*, Report on a Meeting held by UNICEF at the International Child Development Centre, Florence, June 1991.

[62]Hobsbawm, op. cit.

[63]Kennedy, op. cit.

[64]Cornia, Giovanni Andrea and Sipos, Sandor (eds.), *Children and the Transition to the Market Economy: Safety Nets and Social Policies in Central and Eastern Europe*, UNICEF/ICDC, Florence, 1991.

[65]Black, op. cit.

[66]Allan, Donald, 'The new role for UNICEF National Committees', article in *Children and the challenges of transition: UNICEF in Central and Eastern Europe*, an Information Kit produced by UNICEF, New York, 1992.

[67]'Country File: Romania', in *Children and the challenges of transition*, ibid.

[68]*Romania's Children*, UNICEF, New York, 1992? (n.d.).

[69]'Situation of Children in Romania: an Information Note', UNICEF Executive Board, E/ICEF/1991/CRP.9, 8 April 1991.

[70]'UNICEF Activities in Central and Eastern Europe, the Commonwealth of Independent States and the Baltic States', UNICEF Executive Board, E/ICEF/1992/L.14, 22 May 1992.

[71]Ibid.

[72]*Romania's Children*, op. cit.

[73]'Situation and Needs of Children and Women in Central and Eastern Europe and the New Independent States', UNICEF Executive Board, E/ICEF/1993/L.7, 9 March 1993.

[74]*Central and Eastern Europe: The Heavy Toll of Transition*, Innocenti Update No. 14, UNICEF/ICDC, Florence, December, 1993.

[75]*Public Policy and Social Conditions: Central and Eastern Europe in Transition*, Regional Monitoring Report No. 1, UNICEF/ICDC, Florence, November 1993.

[76]Cornia, Giovanni Andrea, 'Children's welfare: Risks and opportunities in the shift to market economies', article in *Children and the challenges of transition*, op. cit.

[77]*UNICEF Activities in Central and Eastern Europe* (1992), op. cit.

[78]See Chapter 3.

[79]'Overview', article in *Africa's Children*, op. cit.

[80]*Update on the Nutrition Situation, 1994*, United Nations, ACC Sub-Committee on Nutrition, New York, November 1994.

[81]*Africa's Children, Africa's Future: Human investment priorities for the 1990s*, OAU and UNICEF, New York, 1992.

[82]'Ensuring Child Survival, Protection and Development in Africa', UNICEF Executive Board, E/ICEF/1993/L.4, 19 March 1993.

[83]'Debt relief for child development', article in *Africa's Children*, op. cit. Also *Economic Decline and Child Survival*, op. cit.

[84]*Africa's Recovery in the 1990s*, op. cit.; see also a summary version published under the same title, de St. Jorre, John, UNICEF/ICDC, Florence, 1992.

[85]'Progress Report on the Follow-up to the World Summit for Children', UNICEF Executive Board, E/ICEF/1993/12, 9 February 1993.

[86]Ibid.

[87]'Progress Report on the Follow-up to the World Summit for Children', UNICEF Executive Board, E/ICEF/1994/12, 4 April 1994.

Chapter 7. The Gender Dimension

[1] Black, Maggie, *The Children and the Nations*, UNICEF, New York, 1986.

[2] Hazzard, Virginia, 'UNICEF and Women: The Long Voyage', UNICEF History Series, Monograph VII, 1987.

[3] Black, op. cit.

[4] See Chapter 5.

[5] Halsey, A. H., *Change in British Society*, Oxford University Press, Oxford, 1986.

[6] Black, op. cit.

[7] Author's personal experience of policy discussions with senior staff on 'women in development' issues.

[8] Ibid.

[9] Hazzard, op. cit.

[10]Tinker, Irene and Bramsen, Michele Bo (eds.), *Women and World Development*, ODC, Washington, DC, 1976; Boserup, Ester, *Women's Role in Economic Development*, St. Martin's Press, New York, 1970; Newland, Kathleen, *The Sisterhood of Man*, W.W. Norton, New York, 1979.

[11]'Development Begins with Women', in *UNICEF News*, Issue 104/1980/2.

[12]*The State of the World's Women 1979*, Report for the UN Decade for Women; quoted in Morgan, Robin, ed., *Sisterhood is Global: The International Women's Movement Anthology*, Anchor Press/Doubleday, New York 1974.

[13]*The World's Women, Trends and Statistics 1970-1990*, United Nations (with UNICEF, UNFPA, UNIFEM), New York, 1991.

[14]*Girls and women: A UNICEF development priority*, UNICEF, New York, 1993.

[15] *The world's women, trends and statistics 1970-1990*, op. cit.

[16] 'Women, Children and Development', Report prepared for the World Conference of the UN Decade for Women, Copenhagen, Denmark, UNICEF Executive Board, E/ICEF/Misc 343, 8 July 1980.

[17] Hazzard, op. cit.

[18] See, respectively, Chapters 4 and 5.

[19] 'Women, Children and Development', op. cit.

[20] FAO study, quoted in *The World's Women, Trends and Statistics 1970-1990*, op. cit.

[21] Ibid.

[22] Cochrane, Susan, O'Hara, D.J. and Leslie, J., *The Effects of Education, Health, and Social Security on Fertility in Developing Countries*, World Bank, Washington, DC, 1980, quoted in Carnoy, Martin, *The Case for Investing in Basic Education*, UNICEF, New York, 1992.

[23] *UNICEF Annual Report 1988*, UNICEF, New York, 1988.

[24] See, for example, *The State of the World's Children 1985*, UNICEF and Oxford University Press, New York, 1984.

[25] Grant, James P., 'Statement to the World Conference to Review and Appraise the Achievements of the UN Decade for Women', Nairobi, 1985.

[26] Lloyd, C.B. and Ivanov, S., 'The Effects of Improved Child Survival on Family Planning Practice and Fertility', UN Population Division, New York, 1987; paper prepared for the International Conference on Better Health for Women and Children through Family Planning, Nairobi, 1987.

[27] *The State of the World's Children 1992*, UNICEF and Oxford University Press, New York, 1991.

[28] 'UNICEF Policy on Family Planning', UNICEF Executive Board, E/ICEF/1993/L.5, 24 February 1993.

[29] Report of the International Conference on Better Health for Women and Children through Family Planning, co-sponsored by IPPF, the Population Council, UNDP, UNFPA, UNICEF, WHO and the World Bank, Nairobi, 1987; and Lloyd and Ivanov, op. cit.

[30] 'UNICEF Response to Women's Concerns', UNICEF Executive Board, E/ICEF/1985/L.1, 7 February 1985.

[31] Ibid.

[32] See Chapters 4 and 5.

[33] *One Step for Women, a Mile in Development*, UNICEF Regional Programme for Women in Development for Latin America and the Caribbean, Bogota, 1987.

[34] Rocha, Lola, Gomes, M.C. and Acosta, A., *Consolidating Income-generation Projects for Women in Colombia*, Staff Working Paper No. 6, UNICEF Programme Division, New York, 1990.

[35] Mirero, Stephen, *Women, credit and savings*, Women's Development Programme, Eastern and Southern Africa Regional Office, UNICEF, Nairobi, 1990.

[36] *The Invisible Adjustment: Poor Women and the Economic Crisis*, UNICEF Regional Programme for Women in Development, Americas and the Caribbean, Santiago, 1989.

[37]Ibid.

[38]Rocha et al., op. cit.

[39]Ibid.

[40]*One Step for Women*, op. cit.

[41]'UNICEF Response to Women's Concerns', op. cit.

[42]*The State of the World's Children 1987*, UNICEF and Oxford University Press, New York, 1986.

[43]*Women, credit and savings*, op. cit.

[44]'Implementation strategy for UNICEF policy on women in development', UNICEF Executive Board, E/ICEF/1987/L.1, 1987.

[45]Lopez, A.D. and Ruzicka, L.T. (eds.), *Sex Differences in Mortality*, University of Australia, Canberra, 1983; quoted in Sen, Amartya, 'More than 100 Million Women Are Missing', *New York Review of Books*, December 20, 1990.

[46]*The Lesser Child: The Girl in India*, Government of India with UNICEF, New Delhi, 1990.

[47]*Health Implications of Sex Discrimination in Childhood*, A review paper and annotated bibliography, WHO, Geneva, 1986.

[48]*Sex Differences in Child Survival and Development*, UNICEF Regional Office for the Middle East and North Africa, Amman, 1990.

[49]*Indian Women from Birth to Twenty: A Report*, Women's Division, National Institute of Public Co-operation and Child Development, New Delhi, 1990.

[50]Ibid.

[51]*The Lesser Child*, op. cit.

[52]'Progress Report on Achievements Made in the Implementation of UNICEF Policy on Women in Development', UNICEF Executive Board, E/ICEF/1991/L.5, 4 February 1991.

[53]*The girl child in Bangladesh: A situation analysis*, UNICEF, Dhaka, 1990.

[54]*Work Burden of a Girl Child in Nepal*, Ministry of Labour and Social Welfare, Women Development Division and UNICEF, Kathmandu, 1990.

[55]E/ICEF/1991/L.5., op. cit.

[56]'Progress report on Achievements Made in the Implementation of UNICEF Policy on Women in Development', E/ICEF/1990/L.1, 3 January 1990.

[57]'Girls and girlhood: Time we were noticed', in *New Internationalist*, No. 240, February 1993.

[58]*Human Development Report 1991*, UNDP, New York; quoted in *Educating Girls and Women: A Moral Imperative*, UNICEF Education Section, New York, 1992.

[59]*Bangladesh Decade Action Plan for the Girl Child 1991-2000*, Ministry of Social Welfare, Government of Bangladesh, Dhaka (n.d.).

[60]Norwegian Government report to the Council of Europe, and to the UN Working Group on Slavery, reported in *First Call*, UNICEF, April-June 1992.

[61]See the Innocenti series *The urban child in difficult circumstances*; publications on case studies in the Philippines, Kenya, India, Brazil, ICDC/UNICEF, Florence, 1991 and 1992.

[62] *Thailand's children: A Situation Analysis of Children and Women in Thailand*, UNICEF, Bangkok, 1993.

[63] Ibid.

[64] Muecke, Marjorie A., 'Mother sold food, daughter sells her body: The cultural continuity of prostitution', *Social Science and Medicine*, Vol. 35, No. 7, 1992, pp. 891-901.

[65] Srisang, S., 'Tourism and child prostitution in Thailand', in *Caught in Modern Slavery*, Report and Proceedings of the Chiang Mai Consultation, May 1990, ECPAT, Bangkok, 1990.

[66] 'UNICEF Country Programme Recommendation, Thailand', UNICEF Executive Board, E/ICEF/1994/P/L.13, February 1994.

[67] 'Safe Motherhood', UNICEF Executive Board, E/ICEF/1990/L.13, 16 February 1990.

[68] *The Girl Child: An Investment in the Future*, UNICEF, New York, 1991.

[69] 'Safe Motherhood', op. cit.

[70] 'Family Planning: An Essential Ingredient of Family Health', paper by Black, M., for the International Conference on Better Health for Women and Children through Family Planning, Nairobi, October 1987.

[71] 'Safe Motherhood', op. cit.

[72] *Girls and Women*, op. cit.

[73] See Chapter 3.

[74] 'Safe Motherhood', op. cit.

[75] See Chapter 3.

[76] Black, Maggie, *Children and AIDS: An Impending Calamity*, UNICEF, New York, 1990.

[77] Mann, Jonathan, Tarantola, Daniel J.M. and Netter, Thomas W., *AIDS in the World*, Harvard University Press, Cambridge, MA, 1992.

[78] *Children and AIDS*, op. cit.

[79] 'Review of the Impact of AIDS on Women and Children and the UNICEF Response', UNICEF Executive Board, E/ICEF/1988/L.7, 22 February 1988.

[80] 'UNICEF Programme Approach to the Prevention of HIV/AIDS', UNICEF Executive Board, E/ICEF/1992/L.11, 26 February 1992.

[81] Ibid.

[82] Ibid.

[83] Ibid.

[84] *Young Women: silence, susceptibility and the HIV epidemic*, UNDP, New York, 1992.

[85] *Patterns of First Marriage: Timing and Prevalence*, United Nations, New York, 1990.

[86] *The health of youth*, WHO, Geneva, 1989.

[87] *Girls and Women*, op. cit.

[88] *AIDS: The Second Decade: A Focus on Youth and Women*, UNICEF, New York, 1993.

[89] *AIDS and Children*, op. cit.

[90] 'UNICEF Policy on Family Planning', UNICEF Executive Board, E/ICEF/1993/L.5, 24 February 1993.

[91] Ibid.

[92]'UNICEF Programme Approach to the Prevention of HIV/AIDS', op. cit.

[93]'Health Promotion: The Power of Partnership', Working draft, Programming Notebook for Youth and Women's Health, UNICEF Health Section, New York, 1995.

[94]King, Elizabeth M., *Educating Girls and Women: Investing in Development*, The World Bank, Washington, DC, 1990.

[95]'UNICEF Medium-Term plan, 1992-1995', UNICEF Executive Board, E/ICEF/1992/14, Decision 1992/12, 13 May 1992.

[96]*Women in Development and Community Participation*, Multi-Donor Evaluation of UNICEF, Sector Report, Working Paper, December 1992.

[97]*Girls and Women*, op. cit.

[98]Sham Poo, Karin, 'The "Apartheid of Gender" Must End', Statement at the ECE High-Level Regional Preparatory Meeting for the Fourth World Conference on Women, Vienna, 17 October 1994.

[99]Sham Poo, Karin, 'Gender Balance Matters Because People Matter', Address to the Conference on Women and the United Nations, New York, 14 March 1995.

[100] See Chapter 10.

[101] *ASHA, Situation Analysis of Children and Women in Bangladesh*, UNICEF, Dhaka, 1992.

[102] *Women and Girls Advance*, UNICEF quarterly newsletter, Vol. 1, No. 3, March 1994.

[103] 'Gender equality and empowerment of women and girls, a policy review', UNICEF Executive Board, E/ICEF/1994/L.5, 22 February 1994.

[104] Statement of Ms. Carol Bellamy, Executive Director, UNICEF, at the Fourth World Conference on Women, Beijing, 5 September 1995.

Chapter 8. Learning for All

[1] Black, Maggie, *The Children and the Nations*, UNICEF, New York, 1986.

[2] Phillips, H.M., 'UNICEF in Education: A Historical Perspective', UNICEF History Series, Monograph IX, 1987.

[3] *Children of the Developing Countries*, A Report by UNICEF, The World Publishing Company, Cleveland, 1963.

[4] 'Report of the UNICEF Executive Board', UNICEF Executive Board, E/ICEF/431, June 1961.

[5] Phillips, op. cit.

[6] Ibid.

[7] Colclough, Christopher with Lewin, K., *Educating all the Children: Strategies for Primary Schooling in the South*, Clarendon Press, Oxford, 1993.

[8] Ibid.

[9] Phillips, op. cit.

[10]Ibid.

[11]Black, op. cit.

[12]Phillips, op. cit.

[13]Illich, Ivan D., *De-schooling Society*, Harper & Row, New York, 1971; Freire, Paulo, *Pedagogy of the Oppressed*, Penguin, London, 1973.

[14]Colclough, op. cit.

[15]UNESCO, 1989 figures, quoted in Colclough, op. cit.

[16]Ibid.

[17]Ahmed, Manzoor and Carron, Gabriel, 'The challenge of basic education for all', in *Prospects*, Vol. XIX, No. 4, 1989.

[18]*World Conference on Education for All*, an Information Kit produced by UNICEF on behalf of the Inter-Agency Commission of the WCEFA, New York, March 1990.

[19]Colclough, op. cit.

[20]*UNICEF Annual Report 1985*, et seq.

[21]*World Conference on Education for All*, op. cit.

[22]*Facts for Life: A Progress Report*, UNICEF, New York, 1991.

[23]*The State of the World's Children 1992*, UNICEF and Oxford University Press, New York, 1991.

[24]*UNICEF in Viet Nam: Opportunities for Social Investment to the Year 2000*, UNICEF, Hanoi, 1993.

[25]*Children and Women: A Situation Analysis 1994*, UNICEF, Hanoi, 1994.

[26]Personal visit by the author.

[27]*The State of the World's Children 1994*, UNICEF and Oxford University Press, New York, 1993.

[28]'Facts for Life: Lessons from Experience', Draft report, UNICEF, New York, 15 May 1995.

[29]Personal communication from Richard Jolly, August 1995.

[30]'Report of the Executive Director', UNICEF Executive Board, E/ICEF/1987/2, 24 February 1987.

[31]'UNICEF Strategies in Basic Education', UNICEF Executive Board, E/ICEF/1995/16, 7 April 1995.

[32]Ahmed, Manzoor, 'A personal recollection of Jim Grant', in *Education News* (UNICEF Education Cluster), Issue No, 12, April 1995.

[33]Mayor, Federico, Address to the 1989 UNICEF Executive Board, New York, 17 April 1989.

[34]UNESCO, quoted in *The State of the World's Children 1990*, UNICEF and Oxford University Press, New York, 1989.

[35]*A Brief Overview of Literacy and Primary Education: Current Status, Issues and Broadening the Approach*, UNICEF Consultation on Education, UNICEF, New York, 1988; quoted in *The State of the World's Children 1990*, UNICEF and Oxford University Press, New York, 1989.

[36]*World Development Report 1980*, World Bank, Washington, DC, 1981.

[37]King, Elizabeth M., *Educating Girls and Women: Investing in Development*, The World Bank, Washington, DC, 1990.

[38] *World Conference on Education for All*, op. cit.

[39] *Children and Development in the 1990s, a UNICEF sourcebook*, UNICEF, New York, 1990.

[40] Lovell, Catherine H. and Fatema, K., 'The BRAC non-formal primary education programme in Bangladesh', *Assignment Children*, UNICEF, New York, 1989.

[41] Ahmed, Manzoor, Chabbott, Colette, Joshi, Arun and Pande, Rohini, *Primary Education for All: Learning from the BRAC Experience*, Academy for Educational Development, Washington, DC, 1993.

[42] *Reaching the unreached: non-formal approaches and universal primary education*, UNICEF Education Cluster, New York, 1993.

[43] Ibid.

[44] Colclough, op. cit.

[45] Torres, Rosa Maria, *Alternatives in Formal Education: Colombia's Escuela Nueva Programme*, UNICEF, New York, 1993.

[46] Colclough, op. cit.

[47] 'World Conference on Education for All: Meeting Basic Learning Needs', UNICEF Executive Board, E/ICEF/1990/L.14, 9 April 1990.

[48] *Towards a comprehensive strategy for the development of the young child*, UNICEF Education Cluster, New York, 1993.

[49] Myers, Robert, 'Going from basic services to integrated strategy', in *UNICEF Intercom*, No. 51, January 1989.

[50] *UNICEF Annual Report 1982*, UNICEF, New York, 1982.

[51] Chatterjee, Meera, 'Health for Too Many: India's Experiments with Truth', in Rohde, Jon, Chatterjee, Meera and Morley, David (eds.), *Reaching Health for All*, Oxford University Press, New Delhi, 1993.

[52] 'Early Childhood Development', UNICEF Executive Board, E/ICEF/1984/L.1, March 1984.

[53] *The World's Women: Trends and Statistics, 1970-1990*, United Nations with UNICEF, UNFPA and UNIFEM, New York, 1991.

[54] *Towards a comprehensive strategy*, op. cit.

[55] Ibid.

[56] *Meeting Basic Learning Needs*, Consultative Group on ECCD, UNICEF, New York, 1993.

[57] Information note, Child-to-Child Trust, London, 1995.

[58] *UNICEF's Response to the Jomtien Challenge*, UNICEF Education Section, New York, 1992.

[59] *Education News* (UNICEF Education Cluster), Vol. II, No. 3, October 1992.

[60] 'UNICEF Strategies in Basic Education', op. cit.

[61] See Chapter 8.

[62] *Strategies to Promote Girls' Education: Policies and Programmes that Work*, UNICEF Education Section, New York, 1992.

[63] *Girls and Women: a Unicef Development Priority*, UNICEF, New York, 1993.

[64]Personal conversation with Lucia d'Emilio, UNICEF Education Officer, La Paz, Bolivia, May 1994.

[65]Note on Teacher Empowerment Project, Madhya Pradesh, from Jim Irvine, Senior Education Adviser, UNICEF ROSA, October 1994.

[66]Article by Manzoor Ahmed in *Education News* (UNICEF Education Cluster), Issue 10, Vol. 4, No. 3, November 1994.

[67]*Education News* (UNICEF Education Cluster), Special Summit Issue, Vol. 4, No. 1, April 1994.

[68]*The African Education For All Initiative* (draft), Fay Chung, UNICEF Education Cluster, New York, March 1994.

[69]Colclough, op. cit.

[70]'UNICEF Strategies in Basic Education', op. cit.

[71]*Children First!*, Issue One, 1995, UK Committee for UNICEF.

Chapter 9. Children at the Front Line

[1] Black, Maggie, *The Children and the Nations*, UNICEF, New York, 1986.

[2] Richardson, John, *Assessment of UNICEF's Emergency Response, Part Two—Phase One, The Headquarters Perspective: Issues and Concerns of UNICEF Staff*, UNICEF, New York, July 1991.

[3] Memorandum from Charles LaMuniere, Director of UNICEF Emergency Operations, to John Richardson on his *Assessment of UNICEF's Emergency Response*, UNICEF, New York, 1 October 1991.

[4] Black, op. cit., and Richardson, op. cit.

[5] Black, op. cit.

[6] See Chapter 1.

[7] Black, op. cit.

[8] Ibid.

[9] Shawcross, William, *The Quality of Mercy*, Simon and Schuster, New York, 1984.

[10]Ibid. and Black, op. cit.

[11]Black, op. cit.

[12]Richardson, op. cit.

[13]Studies undertaken for the International Symposium on Children and War, Finland, 1983, quoted in 'Children in Situations of Armed Conflict', UNICEF Executive Board, E/ICEF/1986/CRP.2, March 1986.

[14]Black, op. cit.

[15]See Chapter 5.

[16]Vittachi, Tarzie V., *Between the Guns, Children as a Zone of Peace*, Hodder and Stoughton, London, 1993.

[17]*The State of the World's Children 1986*, UNICEF and Oxford University Press, New York, 1985.

[18]Vittachi, op. cit.

[19]'Emergency Operations in 1989', UNICEF Executive Board, E/ICEF/1990/11, January 1990.

[20]Dodge, Cole P. and Raundalen, Magne, *Reaching Children in War*, Sigma Forlag, Bergen, 1991.

[21]Ibid.

[22]Dodge and Raundalen, op. cit.

[23]Minear, Larry, *Humanitarianism under Siege: A Critical Review of Operation Lifeline Sudan*, The Red Sea Press, Trenton, 1991.

[24]Ibid.

[25]Ibid.

[26]Woollacott, Martin, 'The West can save the Kurds—and a little self-respect', in *The Guardian* (London), 18 January 1995.

[27]'Emergency Operations in 1989', op. cit.

[28]'Children in Situations of Armed Conflict', UNICEF Executive Board, E/ICEF/CRP.2, 10 March 1986.

[29]'Disasters: Devastation and opportunity', in *UNICEF News*, Issue 109/1981/3.

[30]'Children in Situations of Armed Conflict', op. cit.

[31]*Children on the Front Line: The impact of apartheid, destabilization and warfare on children in southern and South Africa*, UNICEF, New York, 1989.

[32]*UNICEF Annual Report 1989*, UNICEF, New York, 1989.

[33]Ressler, Everett M., *Children in War: A Guide to the Provision of Services*, UNICEF, New York, 1993; see also *The State of the World's Children 1996*, UNICEF and Oxford University Press, New York, 1995.

[34]*UNICEF Annual Report 1991*, UNICEF, New York, 1991.

[35]*Children Working for Peace*, an Educational Pack prepared by UNICEF for use in Education for Development work in schools, UK Committee for UNICEF and Oxford Development Education Committee, 1995.

[36]Ressler, op. cit.

[37]Dodge, op. cit.

[38]Ressler, op. cit.

[39]*Anti-personnel Land-mines: A Scourge on Children*, UNICEF, New York, 1994.

[40]Ibid.

[41]Ibid.

[42]Ibid.

[43]*The State of the World's Children 1996*, op. cit.

[44]Report in *The Guardian* (London), 14 October 1995.

[45]Report in *The Guardian* (London), quoting a recent report in *The Lancet* on a study undertaken by the Harvard School of Public Health, 4 December 1995.

[46]*The State of the World's Children 1996*, op. cit.

[47]'UNICEF Response to Emergencies', UNICEF Executive Board, E/ICEF/1994/11, 22 February 1994.

[48]'What It Means to be Human: The Challenge of Respecting Children's Rights in the 1990s', Statement by UNICEF Executive Director delivered on his behalf by Stephen Lewis at the 50th session of the UN Commission on Human Rights, Geneva, 8 March 1994.

[49]*States of Disarray: The social effects of globalization*, UNRISD, Geneva, 1995.

[50]Memorandum from Peter McDermott, UNICEF Emergencies Officer, 27 November 1995.

[51]Presentations on Somalia by SCF personnel and others at the Development Studies Association seminar on *The United Nations and Humanitarian Assistance*, held at QEH, University of Oxford, 16-17 January 1993; Report of Proceedings.

[52]'UNICEF Emergency Operations in 1992', UNICEF Executive Board, E/ICEF/1993/11, 24 February 1993.

[53]Memorandum from Peter McDermott, op. cit.; and Richardson, John, *Review of UNICEF's Emergency Relief Operation in Somalia, December 1990-August 1994*, UNICEF, New York, June 1995.

[54]Proceedings of DSA Seminar, op. cit.

[55]Richardson (1995), op. cit.

[56]Ibid.

[57]Proceedings of DSA Seminar, op. cit.

[58]Conversation with Peter McDermott, November 1995.

[59]*Children: Innocent Victims of War*, a UNICEF fund-raising kit, UNICEF Programme Funding Office, February 1993.

[60]Penrose, Angela, 'UN Humanitarian Machinery', in Childers, Erskine (ed.), *Challenges to the United Nations, Building a Safer World*, CIIR and St. Martin's Press, London, 1994.

[61]Richardson (1995), op. cit.

[62]*The United Nations in Development, Reform Issues in the Economic and Social Fields: A Nordic Perspective*, Final Report by The Nordic UN Project, distributed by Almqvist and Wiksell International, Stockholm, 1991.

[63]Penrose, op. cit.

[64]*UNICEF Annual Reports 1991-94*, UNICEF, New York.

[65]Ibid.

[66]Richardson (1995), op. cit.

[67]'UNICEF Emergency Operations in 1992', op. cit.

[68]Richardson (1995), op. cit.

[69]*Evaluation of UNICEF: Sector Report on Emergency Response*, working report by AIDAB, CIDA, DANIDA, SDC, New York, October 1992.

[70]'UNICEF Emergency Operations in 1993', UNICEF Executive Board, E/ICEF/1993/11, 24 February 1993; 'UNICEF Response to Emergencies 1994', UNICEF Executive Board, E/ICEF/1994/11, 22 February 1994.

[71]Duffield, Mark, 'Complex Political Emergencies: an Exploratory Report for UNICEF' (unpublished paper), Birmingham, 1994.

[72]Jolly, Richard, 'International Approaches to Emergencies: Key Issues for Policy and Research on Support, Prevention and Recovery' (unpublished paper), January 1993.

[73]Duffield, Mark, 'The Political Economy of Internal War' in *War and Hunger: Rethinking International Responses to Complex Emergencies*, Zed Books and SCF, London, 1994.

[74]Ibid.

[75]Duffield, op. cit.

[76]Richardson (1995), op. cit.

[77]*UNICEF Emergency Operations in Former Yugoslavia*, an Information Kit, Zagreb, April 1994.

[78]*Hadlock: Filipino children caught in the crossfire*, UNICEF, Manila, 1992.

[79]*Angola: Fundraising documentation kit*, UNICEF, New York, 1993.

[80]*Emergency Country Profile—Sudan*, UNICEF, New York, May 1995.

[81]'UNICEF Reponses to Emergencies', UNICEF Executive Board, E/ICEF/1994/11, 22 February 1994.

[82]Minear, op. cit.

[83]*Emergency Country Profile—Sudan*, op. cit.

[84]*UNICEF Rwanda Emergency Fundraising Kit* (Update #5), UNICEF Programme Funding Office, New York, April 1995.

[85]Slim, Hugo, 'Military Humanitarianism and the New Peacekeeping: An Agenda for Peace?' Paper written in 1995 for *IDS Bulletin on War in Africa* (forthcoming).

[86]Richardson, John, *UNICEF's Emergency Response*, an update of the 1991 Global Evaluation of Emergencies, UNICEF Office of Evaluation and Research, New York, April 1995.

[87]'UNICEF Emergency Operations', UNICEF Executive Board, E/ICEF/1995/5, 28 December 1994.

[88]Black, op. cit.

[89]Presentation by Thomas Hammarburg at UNICEF Global Innocenti Seminar, ICDC, Florence, May 1994.

Chapter 10. Towards 2000 and Beyond

[1] Author's personal experience.

[2] Article in *Tequio*, a quarterly publication of the UNICEF Office for Mexico and Cuba, Vol. 5, No. 20, October 1994.

[3] *The State of the World's Children 1995*, UNICEF and Oxford University Press, New York, 1994.

[4] Ibid.

[5] *Local Action – Global Goals: Decentralization of the National Programmes of Action for Children*, Innocenti Update No. 16, UNICEF/ICDC, Florence, December 1994.

[6] 'Progress Report on the Follow-up to the World Summit for Children', UNICEF Executive Board, E/ICEF/1994/12, 4 April 1994.

[7] Stackhouse, John, 'Putting a head count on poverty', in *The Globe and Mail* (Toronto), 14 January 1995; also Katz, Ian, 'Malaise behind the missionary fervour', in *The Guardian* (London), May 15 1995.

[8] 'Overall Progress in the Implementation of Evaluation Activities in UNICEF', UNICEF Executive Board, E/ICEF/1992/L.9, 14 April 1992.

[9] *Evaluation for Action: Report on UNICEF Evaluation Focal Points,* UNICEF/ICDC, Florence, June 1989.

[10] *The Progress of Nations 1993*, UNICEF, New York, 1993.

[11] *The State of the World's Children 1995*, op. cit.

[12] 'Some good news from the developing world', press summary from the SOWC Report Press Kit, UNICEF, New York, 1995.

[13] OECD figures, quoted in *The State of the World's Children 1996*, UNICEF and Oxford University Press, New York, 1995.

[14] Ibid.

[15] 'World Summit for Social Development', in *First Call for Children* (special supplement), UNICEF, January-March 1995.

[16] Black, Ian, 'Diplomats sink hopes for aid plan at UN summit', in *The Guardian* (London), 10 March 1995.

[17] *Profiles in Success: People's Progress in Africa, Asia and Latin America*, UNICEF, New York, 1995.

[18] 'Role of UNICEF in the Implementation of the Convention on the Rights of the Child', UNICEF Executive Board, E/ICEF/1991/L.7, 6 February 1991.

[19] Himes, James R., *Reflections on the Relationship between Implementation of the Convention on the Rights of the Child and the National Plans of Action*, UNICEF/ICDC, Florence, 26 May 1992.

[20] Newman-Black, Marjorie, 'Introduction', in Newman-Black, Marjorie (ed.), *The Convention: Child Rights and UNICEF Experience at the Country Level,* Innocenti Studies, UNICEF/ICDC, Florence, 1991.

[21] Ledogar, Robert J., 'Implementing the Convention on the Rights of the Child through national programmes of action for children', in *The International Journal of Children's Rights,* Vol. 1, Nos. 3-4, 1993, pp. 377-391.

[22] 'Progress Report on the Follow-up to the World Summit for Children', UNICEF Executive Board, E/ICEF/1994/12, 4 April 1994.

[23] See also Chapter 6.

[24] *The State of the World's Children 1991*, UNICEF and Oxford University Press, New York, 1990.

[25] Hewlett, Sylvia Ann, *Child neglect in rich nations,* UNICEF, New York, 1993.

[26] *The State of the World's Children 1991*, op. cit.

[27] Miles, Rosalind, *The Children We Deserve,* HarperCollins, London, 1994.

[28] Ibid.

[29] *AIDS, The second decade*, UNICEF, New York, 1993.

[30]Interview with Robert Smith, Director of the UK Committee for UNICEF, March 1995.

[31] *UNICEF Annual Report 1991*, UNICEF, New York, 1991, and *UNICEF Annual Report 1993*, UNICEF, New York, 1993.

[32] *UNICEF Annual Report 1995*, UNICEF, New York, 1995.

[33]'UNICEF External Relations Policies and Function', E/ICEF/1989/L.4, 7 February 1989.

[34]Black, Maggie, *The Children and the Nations*, UNICEF, New York, 1986.

[35] *The State of the World's Children 1996*, UNICEF and Oxford University Press, New York, 1995.

[36] *UNICEF Annual Report 1988*, UNICEF, New York, 1988, and *UNICEF Annual Report 1993*, op. cit.

[37]'UNICEF External Relations Policies and Function', op. cit.

[38]Hetzer, William, 'Introduction', in *Animation for Development*, UNICEF RTFS, New York (forthcoming).

[39]McBean, George and McKee, Neill, 'The animated film in development communication', in ibid.

[40]*Partnership in Action, UNICEF and NGOs working together for children*, UNICEF, New York, 1991.

[41]Miles, Rosalind, op. cit.

[42]*The State of the World's Children 1996*, op. cit.; and *Children at War*, Save the Children Fund UK, London, 1994.

[43]ILO statistics, quoted by Moore, Molly, in 'Poverty weaves the figure in the carpet', in *The Guardian* (London), 27 May 1995.

[44]Bruce, Florence, 'Reviewing strategies' in *Children worldwide*, ICCB, Geneva, Vol. 19, No. 2, 1992.

[45]Hanif, Mohammed, 'Camel kids are still riding', in *Anti-Slavery Reporter* 1994, ASI, London, 1994.

[46]Ekachai, Sanitsuda, 'Slaves of the modern world', in *Bangkok Post*, 8 May 1990; reprinted in *Voices of Thai Women*, Issue 4, December 1990.

[47]Rialp, Victoria, *Children and hazardous work in the Philippines*, ILO, Geneva, 1993.

[48]Black, Maggie, *In the twilight zone: Child workers in the hotel, tourism and catering industry*, ILO, Geneva, 1995.

[49]Ibid.

[50]'Rights of the Child: Sale of Children, a Report submitted by Mr. Vitit Muntarbhorn', UN Commission on Human Rights, E/CN.4/1992/55, 22 January 1992.

[51]See Narvesen, O., *The Sexual Exploitation of Children in Developing Countries*, Redd Barna, Oslo, 1989; *The Sexual Exploitation of Children: Field Responses*, ICCB, Geneva, 1991; and O'Grady, Ron, *The Child and the Tourist*, ECPAT, Bangkok, 1992.

[52]'Rights of the Child: Sale of Children', op. cit.

[53]Boyden, Jo and Myers, William, *Exploring Alternative Approaches to Combating Child Labour*, Innocenti Occasional Papers, UNICEF/ICDC, Florence, 1995.

[54]Ibid.

[55]Ibid.

[56]'Procurement policy—child labour', UNICEF Executive Directive, CF/EXD/1995-007, 23 May 1995.

[57]*Children in Bondage: Slaves of the Subcontinent*, ASI, London, 1991.

[58]*UNICEF India Policy on Child Labour*, UNICEF, New Delhi, 3 February 1994.

[59]'World trade and working children', draft paper from Anti-slavery International and personal discussion, August 1995.

[60]Boyden, Jo and Myers, William, op. cit.

[61]Blanc, Cristin Szanton (ed.), *Children in Distress: Global Predicaments and Innovative Strategies*, Gordon and Breach and UNICEF, Florence, 1994.

[62]Hammarberg, Thomas, quoted in Black, Maggie, *Monitoring the Rights of Children*, UNICEF/ICDC, Florence, 1994.

[63]Lindblad, Bertil, *Vietnam: The Process of Reporting on the Implementation of the Convention on the Rights of the Child*, UNICEF, New York, May 1994.

[64]Quoted in Newman-Black, Marjorie (ed.), *The Convention: Child Rights and UNICEF Experience at the Country Level*, op. cit.

[65]*Child survival—World Development Newsletter*, Vol. II, No. 1, January-February 1995.

[66]*The State of the World's Children 1995*, op. cit.

[67]*BFHI News*, The Baby-Friendly Hospital Initiative Newsletter, January/February 1995.

[68]'UNICEF Strategies in Basic Education', UNICEF Executive Board, E/ICEF/1995/16, 7 April 1995.

[69]Ibid.

[70]Grant, James P., 'Child Rights: A Central Moral Imperative of Our Time', Statement to the Third Committee of the 49th General Assembly of the United Nations, New York, 11 November 1994.

[71]Confidential memorandum from Robert Cohen to Richard Jolly and Guido Bertolaso, UNICEF, New York, 17 February 1995.

[72]Statement by James P. Grant, Executive Director, UNICEF, at the UNICEF Executive Board, New York, 5 October 1994.

[73]Ibid.

[74]*UNICEF Annual Report 1980*, UNICEF, New York, 1980, and *UNICEF Annual Report 1995*, op. cit.

[75]'What It Means to be Human: The Challenge of Respecting Children's Rights in the 1990s', Statement by James P. Grant delivered on his behalf by Stephen Lewis, UN Commission on Human Rights, New York, March 1994; see also Grant, James P., *Child Rights*, op. cit.

[76]Bellamy, Carol, Statement to the Third Committee of the 50th General Assembly of the United Nations, New York, 20 November 1995.

Index